The Plundering Generation

THE PLUNDERING GENERATION

Corruption and the Crisis of the Union, 1849–1861

MARK W. SUMMERS

New York Oxford
OXFORD UNIVERSITY PRESS
1987

Oxford University Press

Oxford New York Toronto
Delhi Bombay Calcutta Madras Karachi
Petaling Jaya Singapore Hong Kong Tokyo
Nairobi Dar es Salaam Cape Town
Melbourne Auckland

and associated companies in
Beirut Berlin Ibadan Nicosia

Published by Oxford University Press, Inc.,
200 Madison Avenue, New York, New York 10016

Library of Congress Cataloging-in-Publication Data
Summers, Mark W. (Mark Wahlgren), 1951–
The plundering generation.
Bibliography: p. Includes index.
1. Corruption (in politics)—United States—History—19th century.
2. United States—Politics and government—1849–1861. I. Title.
E415.7.S96 1987 973.6 86-32422
ISBN 0-19-505057-6

1 3 5 7 9 8 6 4 2

Printed in the United States of America

This book is dedicated to my mother and father,
Evelyn and Clyde Summers,
whose lifelong love of justice has proven them
incorruptible by temptation or time.

Acknowledgments

This book owes a weighty debt to the crooked dealings of Americans in a past generation and the honest advice and help of friends in a present one. Every archives that I visited gave me help, but two places stand out. The staff of the Library of Congress's manuscripts division helped eagerly and beyond the normal bounds of patience and duty. At the New Hampshire State Archives, the curators kept the doors open a bit past closing time because I had not quite finished some appalling letters to John H. George.

To Ludwell Johnson, who independently came to the same idea for a title—though for a different time and subject-matter—I am grateful for permission to use it as well: it's too clever to pass up. I also owe thanks to *Civil War History* for permitting me here to use portions of my article, "'A Band of Brigands': Albany Lawmakers and Republican National Politics, 1860," from their June 1984 issue.

Two friends glimpsed the project at its dawning, Larry Schwartz and Jonathan Hoff. As I wielded my muckrake before their eyes, they asked the one question that all history must face: "So what?" If I make clear why the corruption of the 1850s amounted to more than a series of lurid tales, I owe the credit to them and to Richard McCormick, who asked the same questions of the final manuscript.

Many others saw this work in its rougher stages, and their advice was good: Peter Hoffer, James Oakes, David Bailey, William R. Childs, and

Thomas Cogswell. Bill tried to deflate its windiness, Dave scourged its silly generalizations, and Tom demanded more proof, adding suggestions with a wit and zest that this manuscript could use itself. Best of all readers was my father, Clyde W. Summers. I could tell that the style and argument had gone badly amiss when he kept falling asleep trying to read it. But there was nothing slumbering in his criticisms. There he was vigilant and energetic in picking logical lapses out and in exposing the weaknesses in the structure. Not a page stands now as it did before he took it to task.

Lexington
May 1987

M.W.S.

CONTENTS

III Prognosis—The Corruption of the Parties

IV Corruption and the Death of the Union

INTRODUCTION

"Never were such efforts made to secure a political object of this description," D. D. Barnard wrote a friend about the Senate race in New York. "The State creeps over like an old cheese, & swarms of maggots are out hopping & skipping about all the avenues to the Legislature."[1] An unwary reader might imagine that he was reading of the "Great Barbecue" after the Civil War. In the 1870s, as any schoolboy could tell him, nearly every law and man seemed to be for sale; and though scholars strain to correct this view, it is hard not to connect the postbellum period with the nadir of public ethics. Barnard's Republic, however, had already reached a state of squalor six years before the Civil War began.

Historians need to pay closer attention to the deeds Barnard witnessed, if only for the reflected light they cast on events twenty years after. As a student of the Reconstruction era, I wondered what made it so much more corrupt than what had gone before. Some historians have blamed it on the postwar emancipation and enfranchisement of the slaves. The freedmen, they argue, were unfit for the political responsibilities that Reconstruction imposed on them and became the tools of demagogues. Other scholars have blamed the growth of large corporations that the war and Republican ascendancy had so encouraged. Still others have pointed to the breakdown in public ethics that a war always seems to produce, or to the unusual growth in government services that war made possible.[2]

I can hardly dismiss any of these explanations for the *kind* of corruption that flourished after the war. But as I scanned newspapers of the 1850s, something puzzled me: there, too, lamentations about corruption abounded. Indeed, the cries seemed more strident than the postwar ones, for those who lamented were not only appalled by the graft and fraud of their day, but frightened of it. To them, corruption seemed to menace free institutions, as would-be tyrants used public depravity to achieve their ends. Corruption after the war was always blamed on one effect or another of the great sectional conflict—but how to blame debauched morals on a war that had not yet been fought or even contemplated by most Americans?

The further I examined the 1850s, the more puzzled I became. In all ages, some Americans have persuaded themselves that the glory has departed from our Israel, and those versed in the history of classical republics spent a century anticipating freedom's fall. Always before their eyes they glimpsed the decay on which they blamed the last days of republican Rome and Florence. Was such rhetoric really much more than a random thread from a fabric of political belief long since worn away, the ideology of the American Revolution? Might it not be simply a polemical conceit? At least one recent historian has argued so, and certainly classical republican ideas seem archaic in the world of Lincoln and the locomotive.[3] Was the talk worth taking seriously? After all, antebellum editors were usually political shills, and where party interests were concerned, they treated truth as too precious a thing to subject to the wear and tear of everyday use. They were gossips, blacklegs, and hypocrites, who painted others' indiscretions as robberies and their own enormities as fiscal irregularities. All these doubts I held, all these objections I kept in mind. Yet the more I read, the more the rhetoric convinced me. The more I weighed the defenses that accused officials made against charges, the more dissatisfied I grew with their justifications. All too often, solid facts lay behind the verbal abuse, and in private correspondence appeared corrupt acts that the professional slanderers failed to find. Here was an old ideology taking on new life because so many incidents nurtured it. Something important, something alarming had taken place in the 1850s.

There *was* corruption, a good deal of it, and though it was more present in cities than in the countryside and in the North far more than in the South, it could be found virtually everywhere. Were a mapmaker interested in coloring the United States to fit different levels of depravity, he might well leave a handful of states along the South's Atlantic coast and in New England untinted, while the Great Lakes states would be shaded from the pink of Indiana to the deep scarlet of Wisconsin, and Rhode Island, New York, and Louisiana would appear jet-black. Where an area had dramatic economic development or bitter party contests, where canals and railroads ran, the cartographer might daub in varying degrees of intensity, though he might find his paint-pots inadequate to suggest the moral atmosphere of Washington, Albany, and Chicago. Officeholders sold their places, voters their suffrage, legislators their good will. Treasurers ran off to Canada or Arizona with public funds, Congressional committees uncovered bribe-takers and blackmailers in the House, Cabinet officers shared in private claims, party committees made vote fraud almost an efficient system. A few historians have seen this dark side to antebellum politics, and my work is no substitute for theirs, but I have fit what they found into larger patterns and gone in directions that they neither had the time nor any reason to go.

More important, I have tried to show why the issue of corruption is more than a sideshow during the boisterous 1850s. This book may make stimulating reading, but it is meant as more than an exposé. Just how corrupt the 1850s were is worth noting, and how deeply corruption permeated the fabric of the political system is important to anyone interested in the dynamics of policy-making. Perhaps ages of corruption are not so much aberrations in American history as we would like to believe; perhaps corruption is an inevitable result of a political sytem in which rival interests and parties strive to gain advantages. Still, I hope to show more: that corruption's existence in the 1850s disturbed Americans, that its use as an issue revealed their fears for the Republic and their doubts about the trustworthiness of government by the people, and that both the Jacksonian party system and the Union itself were shaken by the way in which political ethics aggravated the problem of sectional differences. Corruption helped destroy the Whig party and discredit the Democratic leadership. Antislavery men made the ethical debauch a standard charge against the Slave Power, and their use of the issue helped wreck the Buchanan Administration, elect Abraham Lincoln President, and make any sectional compromise more difficult. Southerners alarmed by the direction in which the Union was heading had one more cause for distress, one more charge to level at the Northern promoters and politicos, one more reason to dread the rise of antislavery men with their new sense of the potential of government power.

At the same time, I hope no one will mistake my intentions. There are several things I am *not* trying to prove. First, I do not suggest that all politicians in the 1850s were corrupt. Most of them were not. A few had unusually high scruples where the misuse of money was concerned. Even a few corruptionists had ideals that they would never sell, especially principles about slavery.

Second, I am no peculative-determinist. Corruption does not fully explain why Congress did as it did. Corruption could buy members only when they already had open minds on the issue for which bribes were proffered—as well as open palms. Pay-offs could swing the unpledged men and turn a narrow defeat into a narrow victory, but usually a measure needed solid arguments in its favor besides the chink of coin. If Texas bondholders, Illinois railroad promoters, and high-tariff lobbyists all found reasons to exert themselves for the Compromise of 1850, so did many Americans who saw the issues as the extension of slavery and the preservation of the Union. Most representatives voted just as their party's rank and file at home would have wanted.

Third, I am not blaming the sectional crisis on the corruptionists. Issues of slavery and sectional rights were enough to cause the disaster of the secession winter. Had every statesman on either side been chaste as snow, every compromise an entente among high-minded men, the disputes between slave and free states could still have been contested bitterly. Northerners would still have cherished the myth of the Slave Power plot and Southerners the vision of a Consolidationist conspiracy. Republicans would most likely have won the Presidency, and the cotton South would probably have seceded. The corruption issue was simply one more irritant, and perhaps an inevitable irritant, since whatever the proof, either side might well have branded the other with the epithets of thief and swindler. To explain behavior by crying corruption is far more convenient than to credit it to principles that one finds distasteful.

But what an irritant the corruption issue was, and how it affected the precise terms of political discourse! And it says much about the moral flavor of political ideology in the years before the Civil War. The Slave Power myth could have been expressed without any mention of corrupt motives. Southerners' dread of Lincoln and the North could have existed free of distrust of the ethics of both the man and his section. Still, the fact remains that neither Northern nor Southern visions *were* so created. Corruption *did* exist. It *did* become an issue in the quarrel between North and South, it *did* affect government policy, it *did* undermine Americans' faith in the Jacksonian party system and lead them to seek alternatives, it *did* encourage intellectuals to lose faith in democracy and Southerners to lose faith in their allies' good intentions. It was *not* just a rhetorical device by men who had studied classical republican thought for too long.

Finally, I trust that no one will consider this the exhaustive account of every political misdeed in the antebellum years. Others might with profit look into matters briefly touched on here: the plundering of state institutions in Illinois and Wisconsin, the frauds at the Minnesota polls in 1857, the "revolution of 1856" in San Francisco, the disbursal of Internal Improvement fund lands in Florida, the Senate races in Pennsylvania, Rhode Island, and New Jersey, and the impeachment of judges in Wisconsin and Texas. There are too many scandals for any one book to do justice to them all.

The story set forth in the following pages may seem a depressingly sordid one. Certainly the 1850s had those "swarms of maggots" that Barnard saw. But I hope the reader will see that the nation was crept over with tokens not only of moral decay but of moral health—indeed, perhaps, a more robust moral health than we enjoy today. An age of sinister doings and corrupt men was also an age in which other people, aghast at the wrongdoing, chose to smash the parties and perhaps the Union itself to revive the principles they associated with the founders of the nation. The years before the war are years not only of peculation but of men rising above petty issues and chasing after the high ideals that they glimpsed in times past. Without the idealism of so many Americans, political corruption would not have been news. It would have stirred no response from press or people. Instead, the response was deep and powerful, and in its own way more dangerous to the maintenance of the Union than the corrupt practices that elicited it, for it was not the thieves and spoilsmen but their enemies, Republican and Southern Rights man alike, who dreamed of a nation purged of slavery or purged of Yankeedom.

The Plundering Generation

PROLOGUE

The Republic Degenerate

Thrust into the 1850s, a modern American might be amused or astonished at how seriously people took the most general charges of political depravity. Wickedness, it seemed, loomed everywhere. The Republic trembled on destruction's brink. In our day, talk of dishonesty in government sounds familiar, but the stridency with which the accusation was uttered then rings strangely. As one newspaper paraphrased its rival, "Darkness follows. Chaos comes again. Corruption stalks abroad. Nobody is honest but ourselves. We alone can save our fellow-citizens from forty thousand horrors."[1]

Was there in fact anything all that dreadful to save them from? This is really not one question, but two, one factual and the other interpretive. First, were the 1850s as corrupt as contemporaries claimed? Second, was corruption so serious a problem as to threaten the Republic?

Certainly the fear was nothing new to Americans. Some of them liked to see their past not simply as a struggle against English tyranny but against English decadence. To maintain stability at home and in the colonies, the eighteenth-century British leaders relied on what one historian has called "the informal constitution," that web of family connection, preferment, privilege, and patronage—as well as outright bribery—that turned potential enemies into real friends. In the 1700s, certainly, the "informal constitution" meant a bridge between the separate powers of the lawmakers and the law-enforcers, a sort of executive influence that the laws of that day did not contemplate and the laws of today would have punished with prison terms. It was not a very cheap system, certainly not a very virtuous one, but it worked for the Crown, decreased party discord, and permitted British society a stability welcome after the century of upheaval that the Stuarts had stirred.[2]

However broad the jurisdiction of the formal British constitution, its informal counterpart all but stopped in Ireland's western strand. In the American colonies, Crown officials found buying the voters nowhere near as easy a task as did Whig patrons in the rotten boroughs of England. There were too many to buy, and colonists had a nasty habit of turning every minor issue into a matter of high principle—which made them unpurchasable at any price. Royal governors had patronage, but never enough, and as the years passed they lost some of the spoils at their command. Corruption needs indifference, acquiescence, or a consensus about major issues as its breeding-ground; but from the Carolinas, where Regulators rose in arms against those rulers in the Tidewater who plundered or neglected them, all the way to Massachusetts and New York, where mobs, ministers, and barristers hectored the established authority, the "informal constitution" betrayed its limitations.[3]

What made it more unpopular was Americans' association of its every invocation with tyrannical plots. The colonists knew just what a corrupt ministry could do to overthrow liberty. Writers on the outskirts of political thought in Great Britain—often no more than disappointed office-seekers—became popular spokesmen for American suspicions: Henry St. John Bolingbroke, John Trenchard and Thomas Gordon, James Burgh, and "Junius." Americans read them all, but they needed no outlanders to tell them what their own editors insisted during the 1760s, that corruptionists ran Westminster—enemies of the hard-won liberties of Englishmen, officials who now stretched their influence across the Atlantic to subvert freedom in the New World.[4]

To protect their liberties from British attack, Americans stumbled into revolution, but for some theirs was also a crusade against polluted ethics. By 1775 no activist needed be told that American liberty could only be secured by cutting it off from the contagion of British parliamentary politics. What if America was afforded a legislature of its own within the system, Patrick Henry cried. The mother country which boasted "that Bribery is a part of her system of government" would buy an American house of commons as easily as the King had bought the British one. "When I consider the extreme corruption prevalent among all orders of men in this old rotten state," Benjamin Franklin confided from London, "and the glorious public virtue so predominant in our rising country, I cannot but apprehend . . . to unite us intimately will only be to corrupt and poison us also."[5] So the Revolution had come about and a more perfect union of the states was made, one in which no centralizing ministry would be able to crush the lesser governments, which, it was hoped, would defend the people's interests.

Such had been America's promise: liberty and virtue, though some stressed one and some the other, just as some would hail the central government as a promoter of order and others would praise it as a protector of liberty. Nor was the original promise forgotten. Succeeding generations looked back and saw their history as proof that the promise had been kept. Virtuous the fathers of the Republic seemed, and in every generation a new political movement rose on the promise that it would realize the original dreams of the Revolution. The "Revolution of 1800" invoked the spirit of 1776 to give itself the air of a restoration.[6] When the Jeffersonian polity began to fall apart, supporters of Andrew Jackson sent to the White House a man they associated with Revolutionary patriotism and Revolutionary self-denial. In some ways the heralds of the common man, the Jacksonian Democrats also harkened back to an older, purer political order. Their enemies responded by donning the party label "Whig," which recalled the first battle for liberty and virtue, and if some sought for moral standards unheard of in their ancestors' day, all of them decried the growing executive power of Jackson's regime as if he were George III come in new attire.[7]

But by 1850, the founders of the Republic had long since died, and their political heirs were passing away rapidly. To many Americans, the virtue that the Revolutionary generation had bequeathed to politics had gone into the grave with them. Returning to the capital after a few years' absence, former Secretary of War William Marcy sensed alarming changes. "In social life there is great extravagance," he wrote a friend, ". . . The treasury doors have been so often opened that they appear to yield to the slightest pressure, & turn easily & smoothly on their hinges." As an acquaintance from upstate New York reminded him, the ailment had spread beyond Washington. So much power had the canal contractors in the Empire State and so adept were they at "bare-faced corruption" that Democratic local nominations were infected with bribery and sharp practice. In Pennsylvania, "railroad jobbers and bank officers" descended on the legislature for favors and boasted that they could buy a working majority. Political quarrels in the Keystone State were "little else than debauchery and open, undisguised profligacy," wrote one antislavery Democrat in early 1851:[8]

> The same demoralization is rapidly spreading over the whole country, and threatens to engulf the land in a sea of black and stagnant corruption. You look in vain, now, for that purity, high devotion to principle, and moral elevation, which characterized the democratic party in the days of Gen. Jackson.

To this, one of the writer's fiercest antagonists among the conservative Democrats agreed. No blushing purist in politics, James Buchanan larded his letters with laments at the "contractors, speculators, stock jobbers, & lobby members which haunt the halls of Congress," and predicted that unless their schemes were foiled, America would soon sink to the standards of public disservice set by Great Britain.[9]

Admittedly, quite a few complainers were old Jacksonian Democrats, no longer at ease in a party that had replaced some of its idealism with pragmatism and had grown increasingly agitated by the Whigs' hold on the White House and the Treasury. Second-generation Jacksonians, who revered the doctrines of limited government, hard money, and special privileges to none, bewailed the party as it had become. Government had become a mere speculators' machine, wrote Francis P. Blair, whose Washington *Globe* had defended the Jackson Administration against every slur. From Old Hickory's champion, former Senator Thomas Hart Benton, came the same cry, and among the younger generation, David Wilmot and Gideon Welles deplored the decline of political virtue since their boyhood.[10]

Still, it was not just a Jacksonian lament nor a jeremiad by men who had seen political honors pass them by. By 1852, Whigs were echoing their enemies—about the debaucheries of fellow-Whigs. So far had their party lost its moral justification, former Congressman Horace Binney thought, that the best thing it could do was disband. New York's governor denounced the senior senator as a trading politician; as head of the party organization on which both men relied for success, Thurlow Weed blamed the Whig national leadership for the moral decay he saw all around him.[11] Nor was the outcry purely an eastern affectation. From New Orleans editors to the Ohio and Michigan constitutional conventions came alarmed references to the "broad stream of corruption" flowing "through the length and breadth of the land."[12]

Governments changed, but the uproar only grew louder. The Whigs left Washington in 1853, never to return. Political issues shifted. New leaders arose to make use of them, but the recriminations went on. One lobbyist would testify that the special interests knew how needful money was to pass any measure. "I suppose there is nobody who knows the organization of Congress who expects to carry anything through it merely from love of justice," he confessed. Was that the general reputation of the members, one congressman asked. "That is the general reputation of Congress," said the lobbyist.[13]

By 1858, condemnation of the special interests grew stronger, and the election frauds more brazen. "We speak of the corruptions of Mexico, of Spain, of France," Georgia Senator Robert Toombs told his colleagues, ". . . but from my experience and observation . . . I do not believe to-day there is as corrupt a Government under the heavens as these United States." "Nor I either," chimed in John P. Hale of New Hampshire, and other senators muttered their agreement. Had England been held up as a shocking example before? By 1860, Earl Grey was able to bolster his attack on Parliamentary reform with examples of what democracy had done to debauch America. With embarrassment, the New York *Evening Post* reprinted his catalogue of vices: honest men excluded from office, purchased state legislatures, government contracts awarded to incompetent in-laws of Cabinet members, a corrupted people embracing larcenous leaders. What made the editors' embarrassment acute was that the charges could not be denied. America had cut itself off from Old World corruption, but now it had fostered a domestic brand even more flagrant.[14]

So loud a rending of garments must excite our suspicion. After all, since the Puritan days, the jeremiad and its insistence that the children could never match the virtues of the parents had been a staple of national oratory. In fat times, speakers had reminded Americans of how little they deserved their good fortune. In times of adversity preachers had forced listeners to realize what their enormities had brought down upon them. Every age was treated as an age of decline by somebody. We should ask: did the complainers believe their own words? How could they?

The closer we look, the more skeptical we might feel. That such men as Benton, Van Buren, and Weed should express concern at this new era of corruption seems fabulous. Weed, after all, was "King of the Lobby" at Albany even then, and since the 1820s he had hired his services out to supplicant banks and railroads. Surely he could not have forgotten how during the 1830s he had organized city roughnecks to bludgeon and brass-knuckle the Whigs to victory at the polls. Benton had entered the Senate in the 1820s as a shill for John Jacob Astor's for company and had earned his pay by exposing and wrecking the factory system by which the War Department had supplied the Indians' wants. As for Van Buren, "the little Magician" had a reputation for shady alliance and shifty practice. Even if his own hands had remained clean, the former President had risen with the aid of Tammany Hall's peculators, and had not scrupled to enrich faithful newspapers (such as the now-righteous Blair's) with spoils. Could it be that these men had embraced virtue as they approached the status of elder statesmen?[15]

In fact, all these men broached fears for the Republic, and their private letters attest to the sincerity of their concern. "Was ever such corruption in high places, more open and shameless, or more villainous?" Weed mused. In a letter to Gideon Welles, Van Buren outdid Jeremiah:[16]

> In the midst of scenes of this description, when developments of the most flagrant abuses of public trust, abuses, which in the better days of the Republic would have lighted a flame of honest indignation through the length and breadth of the land, and caused instant & severe scrutiny in Congress, are we? . . . when respectable . . . Representatives . . . witness such offenses in silence . . . it should not surprise you that the pure & self denying doctrines of the old Republican creed are disregarded, not to say contemned.

But even if the onlookers believed what they said, were they right? Certainly the grim picture of the 1850s could be modified in three ways. There *had* been corruption before; many specific charges were groundless or unproven; and what was defined as corrupt included behavior that some people might consider perfectly proper.

Though it may have been worse than any other era in their lifetime, Americans made too stark a contrast between present and past. Even before the American Revolution, colonists had been deeply mired in more political depravities than they chose to admit. Landlords along the Hudson knew how to bring out a dutiful vote through bribes and threats. Virginia politicians knew that the way to a voter's suffrage was through his stomach and plied voters with rum punch and barbecued hogs, or as one contemporary put it, swilled the planters with bumbo. During the War for Independence, patriots enriched themselves with profiteering, smuggling, and favoritism in the bestowal of war contracts. The nation's financial system was founded on the assumption of state debts and the founding of a national bank, and in both cases statesmen in Congress voted themselves a profit. The Secretary of Treasury himself acted as an agent for his brother-in-law in picking up depreciated securities to be funded at full value. With reason critics jeered at the speculation fever:[17]

> To specs both *in* and *out* of Cong.
> The four and six per cents belong.

Each later generation contrasted its own depravity with the founders' selflessness, and each was half right. One historian has dubbed the Era of Good Feelings the first great Age of Corruption—perhaps it *was* the second—and has assembled a mass of damaging material to prove his case: malfeasance in the War Department, favoritism and shifty accounting practices in the Treasury, defaulting clerks, and venal state legislatures. Pledged to cleanse the putrefaction from public office, the Jacksonian leaders presided over an age of land grabs from the Indians, bank-bribed senators, and "pet banks" that let political cronies manipulate public funds. It was also the acknowledged start of the federal spoils system. Would those who cherished the memory of Jacksonian purity have recognized the truth in John C. Calhoun's attacks on Jacksonian decadence? Perhaps they would not have agreed that the President had built a coalition of powerful, selfish interests "held together by the cohesive power of the vast surplus in the banks," but his phrase—remembered as "the cohesive power of public plunder"—was a commonplace of the 1850s.[18]

The truth was that there had always been a difference between idealists' professions and politicians' acts. The former placed faith in laws and liberties; the latter trusted the informal constitution to make many interests act as one. That was just one more reason for Hamilton's financial program; it underlay Henry Clay's "American system" and was at the heart of the spoils system of Jackson's day. Prate though statesmen might of the virtue of the founders, men like Weed and Van Buren knew that it took more than virtue to make the system work. It took political organization and newspapers fed from the public trough to defend incumbents. It took rewards. Tammany Hall might give street-cleaning contracts to its friends at lavish prices. Customs collectors might be chosen for their loyalty rather than for their honesty and even, like Samuel Swartwout in 1838, flee after having filched nearly $1.25 million. All such practices made men who disagreed about principles stifle their differences for mutual gain.[19]

In this system, government and the financial interests found ways to overcome their differences and to ease the restrictions that some republicans would have placed on special privilege. From the start of the nineteenth century, the banks found that they could obtain any charter from New York that they wanted—if they salved the lawmakers' consciences with money and gifts. The truth was not lost on the Bank of the United States, which nursed legislators in Harriburg and congressmen in Washington with loans. In some cases, government directors in state banks advanced themselves large sums from the coffers, after having filled those coffers with state bond issues. Land speculators in high office used the government to protect their investments. Georgia officials endowed a land company with millions of acres in return for a nominal payment to the state treasury and a generous payment to each individual state legislator.[20] The tradition of corruption did not mean that the 1850s were no worse than other ages, but it did suggest that Americans had never quite attained their ideals of political purity.

It is also true that press and politicians in the 1850s filled the political atmosphere with smoke from corruption charges, but could not always produce a fire behind the haze; and from this it might seem easy to conclude that because some accusations were false, none of the others could be true. No election would pass without charges that "every fraud & artifice was resorted to" by the opposition. No revelation of a state government's financial recklessness could pass without foes thundering that, wicked as they deemed the incumbents, never had they imagined such unparalleled corruption in the public accounts. With clocklike regularity, the party press would brand this scandal or that the worst in all history. When a party was left out of a coalition, it always became "a most infamous and corrupt coalition" or "a coalition so corrupt as to shock even those who have profited." Such talk was only natural: most newspapers were strident partisan organs, quick to define their enemies in the ugliest moral terms and to print those facts most convenient to their case. In an age of overblown rhetoric, an editor's words could easily paint the contrast between his friends and his foes in extreme terms.[21]

Making charges was easy, proving them more difficult, and many editors never tried. Asked to supply proof, they protested that the facts were "common knowledge" or impossible to procure. Perhaps so. Bribetakers are not in the habit of leaving signed confessions of their doings, though some did so in the 1850s. Lobbyists might chat with reporters in an informal way, but few would risk their places by itemizing the funds at their disposal to fill up an evening edition. But congressmen had a right to feel exasperated when, denounced as grafters, they haled their accusers before them and came out with gossip. As editor of the New York *Times*, Henry Raymond had published and commented on charges of corruption supplied by his Washington correspondent, James Simonton, but on the stand, Raymond could not back up his words. No, he told his questioners, he could give no specific names of corruptionists. Bribes were given, but he could not say how much or to whom. He could not mention any specific acts that had passed by dishonest means. Simonton knew that a House clique had stalled bills until it was paid off, but only by common report. After all, he protested, in his articles he had cautioned, "[W]e did not think these things could be proved." For all their evasions, Raymond and Simonton were well justified in their suspicions. Other witnesses had more damaging testimony. But Simonton's reluctance to testify at all was typical of the hit-and-run behavior of the press. In his case, the House was so incensed that it locked him up for contempt and later stripped him of a reporter's privileges.[22] Many other editors made charges with far less ground than did he or Raymond.

Some charges were not simply unproven. They were claptrap. The Philadelphia *Daily News* promised to unveil a Democratic enormity so brazen that it would cast all past swindles in the shade, but added that they would need a few days to produce the proof. They never produced a scrap. Eager to probe Republican election fraud in 1858, a North Carolina congressman called for investigation into one Pennsylvania district. The first four witnesses were all too cooperative. All of them blamed the Democrats' defeat on internal divisions, insisted that the Republican had won fairly, or took back their own original insinuations. In disgust, the North Carolinian ended the investigation right there. But for untruth, the New York *Tribune* outdid all rivals. At the end of July 1852, it reported a city primary in such lurid detail that even Democrats were shocked. The spectacle on July 29 was just as one might have expected in the poorer wards: voting held in rumshops and gambling dens, prostitutes and thieves herding their leprous dependents to the polls, violence and ballot-box stuffing the order of the day. But what shocked Democrats most was something that the *Tribune* reporter had overlooked in his eagerness to excite readers: there had been no city primary on that day. It had been scheduled for *August* 29 instead. (Perhaps it would be fairer to accuse the reporter of premature truth, since the primary when it did occur was universally admitted a disgrace.)[23]

Accusers did not usually lie outright, but at times they drew conclusions about public officials' intentions that went beyond what known facts would bear. That the opposition spent lavishly in Westchester County *could* mean, as the Bridgeport *Republican Farmer* thought, that they were using money to buy votes. That the Chicago comptroller had failed to draw up an annual statement as the law required *could* be read as proof that he had thefts to conceal. That the Massachusetts legislature's expenses had risen that session *could* mean that someone had plunged his hand into the till, if one passed over the fact that the number of towns sending representatives had also risen by a third. Where the facts were against them, partisan editors employed innuendo as well as inference. The New Orleans *True Delta*, for example, so phrased accusations against a state senator that it *seemed* to accuse him of having taken a bribe rather than having voted for a bill that, among its other provisions, provided him a lawyer's fee. A little creative writing could turn a former Maine treasurer's financial embarrassment into an incident that seemed to show him a looter of the public funds and a bilker of his own brother.[24]

Not all false conjectures were such cynical manipulators of the facts. Every action can be seen in several ways. If one view was to see it as one step in some broad, sinister plot, party rivalries made that explanation a popular one. After all, corruption, like conspiracy, was a convenient explanation for the inexplicable. Any argument might win a partisan but among the best was the rationale that the opposition had none but selfish motives and that on this issue or that, no good men could differ. Voters might fail to understand the intricacies of hard-money doctrine; they might even wonder what was wrong with a centralized banking system or think the whole topic a crashing bore, but no one had to think twice once persuaded that the issue was one between the patriot Jackson and the bribe-giving "Monster Bank." Why explain the balance of trade to win over a man to high tariffs, when you could make him feel a firmer commitment by convincing him that the tariff reductions passed Congress only after applications of British gold? From the start of the colonies, Americans had inherited a British penchant for seeing everything in terms of corrupt conspiracies, from the Scarlet Whore of Babylon's conspiracy to subvert the Church of England to the Essex Junto's plot to set up an independent New England with Josiah Quincy reigning as King of the Codfish.[25] Minds that saw conspiracy all over were just as ready to see corruption everywhere, and not always correctly.

The false charges of corruption thrived, however, because so many corruption charges had proven to be true. When so much legislative testimony and court evidence showed fraud and robbery in high places, it was easy to assume that every act about which there was some ambiguity must be motivated by equally base desires. In some cases, the accusers drew the right inferences—there really had been corruption. They could not produce the proof, but historians with access to personal papers vindicated them. Yet we must admit that often the best any scholar can give is the Scotch verdict, "not proven."

Finally, Americans differed so much in defining corruption that it is easy to assume that, because the term was elastic, it was also meaningless. Certainly it stretched wide enough to cover virtually anything that the opposition did, but shrank to so restricted a meaning that it was wholly unfit for one's own allies. You rewarded your friends for their efforts; your enemies divided the plunder. You brought major interests to contribute money for campaign expenses; your foes raised a corruption fund to buy voters and in return opened the treasury to freebooters. Even the most elementary standards did not get universal sanction. Partisans here and there could insist that importing illegal voters was legitimate if the other side started it, or that treasury embezzlement for speculation was all right if the money was replaced eventually, or that it was proper for a lawmaker to take a bribe as long as he waited to collect his money until the session had ended.

Such rationalizations should not blind us. Most Americans agreed that certain acts were corrupt: supporting a measure or setting free a defendant in return for a "consideration," embezzlement, rigging election returns, importing voters or manufacturing voters out of ineligible classes, using public office for private gain, and (except, perhaps, in Rhode Island, where it was fashionable) buying the "floating" vote.

Admittedly, there were grayer areas. Was the spoils system corrupt? Not always, but most Americans thought it was when the rewards clashed with public interest or violated the separation of powers. What about awarding government printing to party faithful or canal contracts to any but the lowest responsible bidder? This provoked even more dispute, though most observers knew malfeasance when they saw it. What about lobbying? Here, too, everything depended on circumstances—though most contemporaries treated lobbying as one of the worst kinds of corruption, even when no money changed hands. There were even more shadowy categories of wrongdoing: extravagance, increasing one's own perquisites in public office, manufacturing public opinion. The "outs" always treated these as corruption, while the "ins" always implicitly admitted such actions as wrong but saw them as laxity rather than depravity. What all this meant was that many actions that today might not be deemed corruption were seen differently then. Although not everyone could agree on the outer bounds of corrupt behavior, on certain essentials Whig and Democrat were in perfect agreement.

From all these cautions it might seem that the Bentons and Van Burens had let their imaginations run away with them; after all, corruption was not wholly new. Some charges were false or impossible to prove. Some contemporaries used the term "corruption" loosely. All this must be conceded, but it does not change one essential fact any more than every unproven charge discredits those for which the evidence was irrefutable: Americans talked about corruption more than ever in the 1850s, they proved the crimes of fellow citizens or confessed their own, and they convinced themselves that public ethics were worse than before and still degenerating. And they were right.

If by corruption we mean "the use of public position for private advantage or exceptional party profit, and the subversion of the political process for personal ends"—a definition that covers all the wrongs that most Americans would have listed as corrupt in 1850—then the evidence is overwhelming. In every way the decade before the Civil War was corrupt. The 1850s were as depraved as any other age and, at least from the evidence available to historians, far more debauched than the 1840s. Steamer magnates bribed through lavish mail subsidies, promoters and bankers bought legislative approval for railroad aid, street gangs dominated the polls for one party machine or another. Dead men voted in New Orleans, purchased "floaters" voted in Providence. State treasurers fled to Canada to escape prosecution, while a Wisconsin governor escaped to Arizona for his health. Political depravity spawned its own vocabulary: "pipe laying," "Galphinism," "suckers and strikers," "grinding committee," "smelling committee," "wire pullers," "shoulder-hitters," "Plaquemining," and, as we shall see, "Buchaneers" and "dough-faces."

If many charges were wind, many investigations uncovered less than they might have. Legislatures would stack their committees or restrict them to one aspect of a broad accusation. Thus, New York lawmakers chose a committee to look into canal swindles, but before it could report, the assembly dropped both Democratic members and added on two friends of the officers being investigated. Whether the resulting report was less damning than one a balanced committee might have given we can only surmise, for the moment the document reached the legislature it vanished along with the testimony taken. When Attorney-General Levi Chatfield declared that friends of the canal had offered him $10,000 to support them, the legislature packed a committee with his enemies. One member had already announced that he thought the state officer a liar, because if any bribe had been offered, Chatfield certainly would have taken it. When a state treasurer ran off with the funds, most administrations chose investigating committees stacked with their own friends. Out of these came cursory examinations and incomplete explanations of who had benefited. If the treasurer remained in power, the majority party blocked efforts to investigate at all, or, if a joint resolution of inquest passed, as it did in Iowa, stole it before it could be enrolled and replaced it with another measure that could do the incumbents far less damage.[26]

Even so handicapped, the press and legislative hearings afforded convincing evidence that something had gone askew with the ethical sense of many public servants. Partisan newspapers made true charges as well as false, and always their foes made detailed replies. When the accusation was groundless or vague, the battle between party organs served the public official well; but often it was the defender that proved the truth in the original charge, by admitting the truth, quibbling over particulars, issuing preposterous explanations, or simply arguing that the offenders' enemies had no right to talk: they were doing the same thing. Testimony showed men almost eager for bribes and unable to tell right from wrong. In New Jersey's legislature, for example, one Tompkins of Essex rose to protest the assembly's passage of a bank charter. A fellow-member, he claimed, had confessed to him that the charter's friends had offered $1000 for his support of their bill. "A great sensation followed," a correspondent added, but not the kind of sensation that Tompkins had hoped for. Up rose the accused member with injured dignity. Yes, he had been offered $1000—and he could not curb his indignation at Tompkins for breaking a confidence. Had the member from Essex not promised to keep their conversation a secret? Was there no honest dealing left in the world?[27]

A very few were proud of their cleverness, though they never distinguished between smartness and corruption. One member of Nebraska's territorial legislature, who owed his election to false means, actually boasted to the press that he, Mr. Purple, had been informed that the majority wanted a member from Burt County. Burt County was virtually uninhabited, so the election was easily arranged:[28]

> I harnessed up and took nine fellows with me, and we started for the woods, and when we thought we had got about far enough for Burt County, we unpacked our ballot box and held an election, canvassed the vote, and it was astonishing to observe how great was the unanimity at the first election ever held in Burt County. *Purple* had every vote! So Purple was duly elected, and here I am!

Even the most righteous men could excuse bad methods in the name of political success. One election in Exeter, Rhode Island, showed that. Whig and Temperance party votes turned out a town council tolerant of the saloons. Their majority, Democrats cried, had come when four voters were bought with two quarts of gin. An outrageous slander! the Providence *Journal* protested. There had been five voters, already drunk and leaning toward the Democrats, and Whigs had traded their votes not for two quarts but a full gallon of Holland gin. In the cause of abstinence, such a method was justified by its results.[29]

Indeed, the most surprising part of the decade's corruption is how feeble the excuses of the accused were; perhaps it shows how strongly Americans reacted against the wrongdoers, that any man accused felt obliged to find an explanation for himself, no matter how dubious it sounded. Thus, Louisiana Democrats replied to charges of fraud and violence at the polls with simple declarations that Whigs were just as bad a set of election-stealers. "No doubt the democrats used money in Pennsylvania in 1856," said the Detroit *Free Press* in response to charges of vote-buying, "but if the black republicans did not use more, it was because they could not get it." Confronted with proof that he had pocketed money due the Michigan Treasury from the railroads, State Treasurer John McKinney pleaded that he had not committed embezzlement. To embezzle, he argued, an official had to take money out of the state's coffers, and he had seen to it that this money never went in. When others failed, the oldest excuse was trotted out. A Vermont sheriff accused of having sold deputyships pleaded that he was simply following the common practice of his day.[30]

The lamest excuse probably was that the bribe-money given had been an inexplicable gift. Yet witnesses were desperate enough to insist on it. One was the lobbyist F. W. Walker, who admitted that he had taken a $2500 fee from the winner of a bindery contract for the Thirty-fifth Congress. He could not imagine what the money had been given to him for. No, the payment did not strike him as queer. "I do occasionally receive windfalls without a word being said as to what they are for. I have . . . had a gentleman put $200 in my hand without saying anything about any measure whatever; and I do not know that a gentleman, who has done a similar thing on three or four occasions, ever had a measure before Congress in his life."[31]

What made the 1850s so degenerate? No one reason will explain the change. Presumably the return of prosperity in the mid-1840s and the great boom that gold discoveries ushered in made the search for wealth almost natural and released the restraint on how it was to be attained. "There is too much wealth in the State," a Whig leader wrote as he looked on the New York legislature of 1854, "and since three dollars a day don't pay very great profits, there is danger that too many members will be in the market."[32] Certainly it had much to do with the decline of the Jacksonian party system and the slackened commitment to the issues on which it was formed. It was easier to pass internal improvements and subsidy legislation at that time than at any time since the flush 1830s. In the scramble for special charters and financial favors, a measure's smooth passage almost cried out for logrolling, even bribery. The growth of the spoils system opened new opportunities for personal profit. So did claims growing out of the Mexican War and the settlement of Indian land cessions. As this book will show, the land boom, railroad mania, and professionalization of party politics all spurred on corruption in the 1850s.

There is another explanation for the sharp contrast between the publicity that corruption got in the 1850s and its relative neglect in the 1840s. Political depravity may have been all the more visible because of the growth of the independent big-city press and its ability to gather news from state and national capitals. In 1846, for example, only Baltimore and Washington newspapers thought Congress worth covering with a special correspondent. By the 1850s, at least fifty newspapers had representatives in Washington, all of them eager to pick up enough gossip and sensation to fill their columns. The same revolution in reporting occurred at state capitals. Relatively independent of party subsidies, the New York *Herald*, New York *Tribune*, New York *Evening Post*, Cincinnati *Commercial*, Springfield *Republican*, and Chicago *Tribune* could afford to strike in every direction and unmask wrongdoing even in the party to which they professed allegiance. Their financial success allowed them to go beyond the printed debates of Congress and the stump speeches of aspiring statesmen to do real investigative reporting. With several times the column space of the average newspaper and six times the frequency of publication, the urban daily could publish more than snippets of news. It could and did print entire legislative debates, the reports of investigating committees, proceedings from local courts, affidavits from vote-sellers—in sum, a broad array of evidence to show the pervasiveness of corruption.[33] No earlier age had such effective means for a thorough exposure of political depravity.

Was it possible, then, that the difference between decades was not one of ethics but of reporting? An absolute answer eludes us. It is easy to prove that specific charges took up less space and attention before 1850, both in newspapers and private writings. After 1850 the partisan press increasingly found corruption the best explanation for what their foes did and an issue worth using to win voters. None of this is conclusive proof that earlier times were less corrupt than the 1850s, for no proof can be conclusive. All we can be sure of is that less corruption was *exposed.* Still, to judge from the number of Congressional elections challenged for fraud, congressmen expelled for corruption, legislative investigations into official wrongdoing, or state treasurers who fled with the funds, the evidence is strongly suggestive. Corruption was news, but not because the press made it so. It was news because there was so much of it, and it was everywhere, from Maine elections to California lawmakers on the take. By any reasonable standard of proof, contemporaries were right to think that public ethics had fallen badly, even precipitously.

Nor should the comparison of decades matter much. The real question is, why was corruption of greater concern in the 1850s than ever before? Either there was more corruption than there had been, or else both parties chose to see more of it because it seemed a winning issue. If the latter is the case, we may hazard a guess that they did so because they feared for the Republic and were looking with special scrutiny to find those age spots that would prove their fears, just as a hypochondriac examines himself for symptoms of every disease; and like every hypochondriac, they found what they were seeking.

We can understand Americans' disgust. What is more difficult to understand is their fear, for fearful they were. In the 1850s, corruption was given an apocalyptic importance, and orators used the most extreme terms to explain it. Should the system of patronage be extended to cover the bestowal of contracts and land on party favorites, Henry Dawes of Massachusetts told the House, "one might well despair of the Republic." Let the people themselves be corrupted, the Charleston *Mercury* warned, and as with Rome, so with America, public virtue's loss would lead to "the final catastrophe of chaos and night." One might expect this from Republican congressmen under a Democratic Administration or from a strong exponent of Southern Rights in a South not yet ready to abandon the party system's conveniences and compromises. But one could hear the same words from judges, who took every opportunity to pontificate on the threat corruption posed to the Republic. "When official corruption can go unwhipt of Justice," wrote an Illinois jurist, ". . . then organized society is ready to dissolve, and governments cease to exist." By the end of the antebellum era, when the government did seem to be dissolving before the secessionists, Reverend Henry Ward Beecher blamed the crisis on the corrupting avarice that permitted slavery in the South and larceny in the North. "Our foundations are crumbling," he told parishioners. "The sills on which we are building are ready to break. We need reformation in the very beginnings and elements of society. If in other parts of our land they are in danger of going down by avarice in one form, we are in danger of going down by avarice in another form."[34]

So one mystery leads to another. If there was corruption, why was it taken so seriously? How was it related to the disintegration of the Union and to the ideal of republican government? Few editors would have agreed with Raymond of the *Times* when he pronounced corruption a greater threat to America than was slavery,[35] but many Americans would have said that the peril not only made democratic government less responsive to the public interest, but endangered the Republic itself.

I

Pathology — The Corruption of Democracy's Rewards

1

Spoilsmanship

"There never were before so many pure and disinterested patriots who were willing to serve their country in any capacity or station," the Hartford *Courant* joked in early 1853, as Democrats replaced Whigs in the nation's capital. "Like the frogs of Egypt, they not only fill the streets of Washington, but come even into the houses of those who have patronage, and into their bed chambers, and upon their beds, and into their ovens, and into their kneading troughs."[1] The editor was referring to the spoils system, which with each change of administration unleashed limitless desires on a limited government.

Rewarding office to political friends and dismissing all foes were not generally viewed as corrupt practices in themselves. They were the natural effect of victory: who would be fool enough to propose policies and leave enemies to implement them? The political scramble might be venal, but it was only a venial sin. Yet the spoils system is the proper place to begin the study of the corruptions of democratic politics, for although not corrupt itself, it was corrupting in its effects. By the 1850s this was clearer than ever before. Patronage politics set the ethical tone at every level of the government. It let incompetents and rogues turn public office to private profit. It induced conscientious partisans to apologize for grafters. As an instrument of party discipline, it became a weapon for one faction to use on another and sometimes a safecracker's tool, but it was perilous to its users. In an age of sectional conflict, it would do grave injury to the Jacksonian party system and the Union itself.

By modern standards, there was not all that much to fight for. The national government remained small. If land agents and postmasters are included, some 20,000 people worked on the federal payroll. State governments were not much more extensive, and most cities had hardly enough officeholders to cope with the most basic problems. Even important posts could only offer meager salaries.

The spoils system also had many arguments in its favor. For government to be effective, it should be run by those sympathetic with the dominant party's program. To fulfill their plans, the parties needed internal unity, and bestowal of offices seemed the most effective way to still discontent. Rotation in office could be seen as an advance for democracy, as more Americans, especially those without the advantages of education and long experience in public life, were allowed to share in the rewards of party victory. Yet with these things said, the offices *were* fought over and savagely. "I have now on file at least 1000 applications," an officeholder lamented, ". . . I am applied to almost hourly to intercede for some one for some office. . . . I never saw the like before, and hope never to see it again!"[2]

Every office was part of the patronage system, both elective and appointive. Among the elective offices, rewards were parceled out in the form of nominations, as when Edwin Morgan was nominated for governor of New York to reward his long record of Whig money-raising. Judgeships became the coin to recompense political service. When state railroads went to court, party loyalists became state attorneys, when the state built a canal or railroad every place from brakeman to commissioner was fair game. No party could afford to leave such a paying proposition as the state works in any hands but its own. Thus Democrats discovered in the canal counties of New York in 1851, as the votes were counted. In 1853, Western & Atlantic operatives entered Georgia politics to frustrate Governor Howell Cobb's bid for the Senate, a fate that he could have prevented had he fired more of them.[3]

Any enumeration of government jobs renders an incomplete account of the spoils system. Profits were another part of the spoils. Banks vied with one another to serve the dominant party well enough to be entrusted with tax and canal revenues. Politicians used their influence on private corporations to supply jobs for the party rank and file there, and this was an important supplement to the patronage system. Even when a party left office, it could still hold members' loyalty by finding them rewards to sustain them until the next election. A timely word from the governor could get a deserving Democrat the route agency on the Pennsylvania Railroad; a letter from Thurlow Weed could get a good Whig a spot on the Democratic New York Central. Railroads had to oblige both parties: giving offense might bring on reprisals. "If the Road wants their tonnage tax repealed," a Republican warned a friend of one supplicant, "they must behave better towards our party."[4] That behavior was defined largely in terms of jobs provided.

So the patronage system was broader than it might first appear. It also paid better. Many offices paid the most scanty salaries, but made up for it in fees charged. The sheriff of San Francisco County thus made four times the President's income, while the collector of the port of New York might do better still. Other positions were less famously profitable. "The office of Marshal is worth from ten or fifteen thousand dollars per annum," an insider confided. "This is not generally known, *but I know it*, and mean to get it if I can." How precisely the consulate in London could pay its holder $15,000 a year was unclear, but that was the value one applicant placed on it.[5] Every place had other perquisites. The fees and salary for the Commissionership of Public Buildings might make it seem unprofitable, Benjamin French admitted, but there were compensations. "Splendid bouquets come here daily . . . and a *bath house* is coming that, in all probability, never would have come had not 'the Commissioner' . . . owned these premises! Such things will happen . . . in spite of all he can do," and certainly if he did as little to prevent them as inertia allowed.[6] None of these "drippings" of office could be calculated in the expenses of a government's budget, though they were part of the costs of a patronage system and widely accepted.

Patronage jobs were not just profitable. They could also become the center of political fiefdoms, for many offices had appointive powers of their own. The astute beneficiary could create a following that would raise him to higher office or protect him against dislodgment. By his power to do others favors, a placeman could create alliances where most helpful. That was why everyone wanted to be Philadelphia county attorney. He granted every license, approved of all bail, and was in contact "with all that class who make & unmake public men."[7] Rightly, Pennsylvania politicians concluded that no other state office had half as much influence as his.

When an officer fattened his income in ways that the law did not allow, he could turn this power to grant favors into a shield of adamant. Investigation became nearly impossible when investigators could be bought off. Inspecting new York penitentiaries, independent agents discovered "constant rascalities" and shady deals with contractors, but because the head of Sing Sing had chosen the keepers, clerk, and inspectors, he was so able to cook the accounts that no evidence could pinpoint his malfeasance, and his allies kept the account-books out of investigators' hands. The chief engineer of the Philadelphia water-works was accused of having condemned and sold copper and cast iron to contractors to fill his purse. As soon as the engineer found jobs on the payroll for relatives of city councilmen, all investigation was suppressed.[8]

With offices such valuable rewards, all parties tried to increase their number at their foes' expense. Thus, legislative quarrels with the governor centered around who should bestow the places. Did Philadelphia city officials need to reward a few more faithful followers than they had offices for? They had the Pennsylvania General Assembly add six trustees to the city gas-works. Did Republicans yearn to fill water-commissioner jobs already chosen by Brooklyn's city fathers? The New York legislature created a new water-works district covering Brooklyn and chose their own partisans to run it.[9]

Patronage also was one way to keep the Jacksonian party system together. Factionalism always threatened the Whigs and Democrats. In theory at least, a wise distribution of spoils could ensure harmony. A President could try to bring peace in two ways: he could favor one faction and starve the other to death, or he could award prizes all around and hope that all would be satisfied. Each option had problems. An Administration always found that in choosing between factions, it was not trying to decide between two groups, easily discernible everywhere, but between more than seventy. Each state and territory had its own factional quarrel, and in each the Administration was asked to take sides. But how was a chief executive to know which were his true friends? Factional names—Woolly Heads, Silver Greys, Wildcats, Barnburners, Hunkers, Softshells, Hardshells, Forty Thieves, Tammany and Mozart Hall men—may have meant as little to harried executives as they did to later generations.

Not surprisingly, then, the national spoils system was federal at its heart. It looked to local political leadership for recommendations, advice, and dissent. So tightly did state parties link into the national system that no application for office could succeed without more prestigious support. Even when they had no official powers, prominent party figures were asked for letters of endorsement. Congressmen were importuned to wait on Cabinet secretaries to strengthen applicants' cases, and one senator had his colleagues adjourn over the weekend so that he could gratify his constituents, "even if he had to take a maul and beat down" Cabinet officers' doors.[10]

So important were state and local rivalries that the spoils system became a means of soothing these differences as well. Each state took its federal allotment seriously. New York's governor thought it only just that one federal job in seven go to his state, and Virginia was still more overweening. Under the Fillmore Administration, it was said that one young resident of the Old Dominion called on the Secretary of the Treasury to demand a post. The official was staggered. "From *Virginia*, sir?" he shouted, "from Virginia, sir, and six weeks in Washington without an appointment! You have indeed been badly treated!"[11] Within the states, different sections had the same jealousies that only patronage could allay.

As the Union waxed and as the ideology that had held together the Jacksonian parties waned, the pressures behind the spoils system intensified. In the 1830s, many politicians had deplored the spoils system. By the 1850s, almost all of them shrugged it off as a necessary evil. Offered alternatives, statesmen would find reasons to resist them all, even as they deplored the place-hunters as scavengers and resented the charge that political preferment explained party loyalty.

Whigs in particular had made a career of denouncing the spoils system; it fitted well with their fear that through his control of the offices a President would be able to usurp the powers of the legislative branch. But by the end of the 1840s it was hard to take a Whig seriously when he put on moral garments. In office, his party made the spoils system its own, all the while proclaiming that it acted against its better nature and purely from necessity, that unlike the Democrats, Whigs got no enjoyment out of dismissals. Earnestly they insisted that they had removed as few people as possible, and when they left office in 1853 urged their foes to show equal charity to incumbents. But of five thousand postmasters, the Taylor Administration had forced 2800 to resign within a year and fired almost all the others. This was all the more embarrassing, since Zachary Taylor had come in as a "no-party" man, which in effect meant every party sharing the places. Yet this stand became untenable almost at once. Party allies warned that without a strong show of gratitude, Whigs would fail to stand by their President. East of the Blue Ridge Mountains, clerkships were worth $80,000 to whoever had them, wrote Thomas Ewing, and this money would subsidize Democratic newspapers. As Secretary of Interior, Ewing was eagerly partisan and utterly proscriptive. Under a past President, he had gained the sobriquet, "the Butcher," and he was back plying his cleaver under Taylor.[12]

Nor did the patronage system grow less frenzied when one party succeeded itself. By 1857, the concept of "rotation in office" had become so immutable a rule that Democrats chosen by Pierce feared for their heads under James Buchanan. And rightly—the new President set down the rule that no appointee could expect reappointment unless there were exceptional circumstances. Not even William Marcy could appreciate that rule. "Well, they have it that I am the author of the office-seeker's doctrine, that 'to the victors belong the spoils,'" he commented, "but I certainly should never recommend the policy of pillaging my own camp."[13]

It was not the worst of systems. Many appointees were both skilled and honest. Marcy came into Pierce's Cabinet to appease New York factions and Jefferson Davis took the War Department as Pierce's sop to the Southern Rights faction. Yet both did their jobs well and ruined their health in pursuing their duties. The trouble was, the spoils system did nothing to reward the Marcys and Davises for their integrity, only for their partisanship, and there were all too few such men, all too many men like the consul to Turin who had his post confirmed even after his usefulness was blasted by the publication of his letter scorning "counts who stink of garlic, as does the whole country" and diplomats with "heads as empty as their hearts."[14] There were also too many offices, for even a sinecure was one more berth for party friends—say, consulates without duties and collectorships without any customs to collect.[15]

Inefficiency was bad enough, but the spoils system encouraged more serious abuses. The partisanship that made the patronage process necessary also made improper behavior relatively safe from scrutiny, until another party came in. That offered a strong incentive to turn offices to personal or family gain. Nepotism, for example, was hardly more respectable than today, but much more flagrant. In Arkansas, the two Democratic factions looked more like Scots clans, rival coalitions of closely intertwined families, each of which was intent on absorbing a larger number of offices. On one side were the Johnsons and Seviers, on the other the Rectors, Hindmans, and Conways. Scarcely a member of "the Johnson dynasty" had been overlooked than the Democrats allotted places. Euclid became attorney for the state bank and circuit judge, Benjamin rose to district judge, Richard H. became public printer, the governor's private secretary, and then nominee for governor. Senator Johnson's uncle Ambrose Sevier became minister to Mexico, while his son-in-law took on the Little Rock post office. The Rectors made a damning case about the family connections, but with Elias as federal marshal, Jock as clerk in the surveyor-general's office, Henry Rector's father-in-law a clerk in the federal court, his brothers-in-law secret mail agents and federal clerks, it might well be wondered which family was the more overweening. Arkansas was extreme, but not unique. In other states, particularly Georgia under Howell Cobb, governors thought nothing of giving jobs to relatives. Federal officeholders were just as unscrupulous. The Chicago postmaster found clerkships for two relatives, both of whom were caught robbing the mails. Even statesmen of high reputation could plead for their kin, and different departments practiced reciprocity by choosing the relatives of one another's heads. A trivial form of gain, perhaps—yet Americans treated it as a more serious abuse to choose a man because of his family ties than because of his party ties, and even a hardened political boss was appalled when the President gave a secretaryship to his son-in-law.[16]

The more valuable an office was, the greater the temptation became to sell it. Visiting Washington in 1858, a Democratic editor was aghast at how openly his party's leaders bartered offices. He saw the brokers in the Senate antechamber, in the departments, even in the White House, "and the actual sum of money to be paid for an office is as publicly named . . . as the prices of dry goods are named between a dealer . . . and his customers." In Whig New York and Democratic Nebraska alike, enemies accused the governor's friends of charging handsome prices for all the posts they could not find family enough to fill. Buying office was most pernicious in law enforcement and administration, but lobby agents at the police headquarters in New York City demanded a fee to arrange for patrolmen's jobs, and not all applicants saw anything wrong with this, though they did protest the price.[17] Because of the possibilities from fees, any job involving collection of money became a prime object of bidding. One deputy collector of revenue complained that he had not received his full pay because it was spent buying the place from the collector, though he, too, demurred at the price rather than the practice.[18]

Only slightly less open to censure was the payment of an agent to arrange for appointment to office. Yet the office-brokers did a thriving business, and Thurlow Weed was among the best in that line. So unreasonable were the city agents that one would-be policeman turned to Weed for less expensive help in getting on New York's force. Neither he nor any other applicant was ashamed to offer money for such services. For higher offices, the price was simply higher.[19]

These were not just anomalies; they were abuses inseparable from the whole principle that office was a reward rather than a sacred trust, a political plum rather than a public service. Offices were paid for because they could be made to pay, and the spoils system made it more likely that officeholders would make them pay in any imaginable way, for no matter what the placeman's talent or conduct, he could expect no more than four years of power. All through the 1850s the press reported the rascalities of officeholders. Collectors of the revenue would indeed collect and then dash for Canada. The federal collector at Sandusky, Ohio, vanished with $20,000 of public money and his deputy's wife. Postmasters occasionally added to their salaries by pilfering money traveling through the mails or forging their own names on promissory notes.[20]

Perhaps the greatest tragedy of spoils politics came in 1860 when Isaac Fowler, Democratic postmaster for New York City, suddenly revealed a $160,000 deficiency in his accounts. Likable, with friends in either party, Fowler held his place for seven years by satisfying all factions, though as head of Tammany Hall, he satisfied them more materially than the other factions. But behind the affable style and winning smile, Fowler was too weak to stand up to party pressures. At election time, post office money could always help Democratic challengers. At other times, the party knew that Fowler would find postal revenues to sustain individual politicians' needs. For five years the postmaster stole revenues and trusted to Democratic promises of repayment. The promises were broken. After October 1858, the books did not pretend to balance, but Fowler stayed on until he could hide his shortfall from the public no longer. Then he wrote a full confession to his superiors, was removed, and within days the authorities had sworn out a warrant for his arrest.

That was only part of the story; the other half was the way in which patronage politics saved Fowler from prison. The federal marshal, a loyal Tammany man, went to Fowler's hotel. Instead of calling on his victim, he stood on the downstairs lobby until midnight, drank heavily, and roared about his intention to hale Fowler into court. To no one's surprise, by the time the marshal reached Fowler's rooms, they had been stripped bare and he was on his way to Havana. Privately, other Democrats were relieved to see Fowler dismissed. "We have long ago observed that *reform* was needed in that office," a Bostonian wrote; but men like him had kept still until Fowler's guilt reached the press. Democrats simply would not turn one another in.[21]

A broader, more acceptable side effect of the spoils system—but no less pernicious and corrupting—was its effect on voting. As parties outside power always complained, incumbents had a tremendous advantage because they could muster the money and legal force of their appointees to wage a campaign. Officeholders paid assessments or they were fired, voted as directed or looked for other jobs. For the best speakers, an Administration could find jobs as special post office agents. Since the agents had unlimited free travel on the railroads to investigate abuses of the mail service, an orator so endowed could do his party good service everywhere. It was also custom that government workers take off time from their duties to campaign for officials who put them in.[22]

The patronage influence also distorted the choices that the voter had, as dissidents inside the party were quick to point out. By the use of spoils, the incumbents could often master the machinery of the parties and keep out a challenge by reformers. No matter what the economic conditions might be for most Americans, the officeholders had a ready source of cash in the assessments they imposed on their subordinates. They also could organize more easily than could party members without control of the offices. When party conventions met, they included more than a fair share of appointees. In a sense, this was only natural; an official position made a partisan more visible and more likely to win a contest for convention delegate. At the same time, his official powers made it possible to win friends where most needed. When the Democratic state convention met in 1859 in New York, the delegates Tammany Hall sent read like a page in the Federal Register. The Philadelphia Democratic convention included officeholders all the way from policemen and Mint employees to post office clerks.[23]

Thus, it was easy to argue that the party powers did not represent the rank and file, but only themselves. If this was so in Philadelphia or New York, it was even more true in states where the federal officers came from one party and the state government belonged to the other. There, with only the national Administration to hand out the awards, an opposition faction had no posts of its own from which to use influence. In states where the national Administration had no chance of mustering a majority at the polls, the conventions became a gathering of the officeholders, for the officeholders, by the officeholders. It was a common joke that New England Democrats had chosen policies unpopular enough with the people to assure that there would only be Democrats enough to fill the federal offices Down East—and send pliant tools as delegates to the national conventions. At the 1860 Democratic convention, if one Republican paper is to be believed, a western Massachusetts delegate pleaded that he had supported Stephen A. Douglas for President to appease his constitutents. "D--n you," another delegate stormed; "you haven't any constituents but the Springfield postmaster and me; we called the convention; there were 40 delegates, all postmasters, and they elected you because we told 'em to—so don't talk to us about your constituents."[24] The story was surely apocryphal, but it was only an exaggeration of a trend that everyone recognized.

That truth helps explain why many Americans—Whigs in particular, but also dissident Democrats, spokesmen for states' rights, and independent editors—reacted to the spoils system with fear and not just indignation. There was, to be sure, not one patronage system, but several, and at times they worked at odds with one another; the state party backing one faction and the national organization marshaling Administration support to endow another. Indeed, this dissonance was one reason for the strong position of state parties inside the national system. Deprived of favors from the top, a loyalist could always look for preferment from the state or local machine. His faithfulness to the state party allowed him greater freedom in taking a stand that the national party opposed. In addition, the state parties cherished their right to dictate whom the national parties should appoint within their borders. Thus, a New York Whig could detest the Compromise of 1850 while his party's President made it the test of political orthodoxy; the Albany Whig managers would see to it that there were berths enough for such dissidents.

This situation was good not just for promoting free debate inside the parties. It also protected republican government from centralization. As long as the balance was maintained, the faction running the national bureaucracy could never impose its will on the state parties, and without their cooperation no national program could invade the states' rights. As long as one party controlled the state patronage and another the federal patronage, local leaders could check the most nefarious designs of a corrupter and dictator.

Now, in the 1850s, contemporaries sensed a disturbing change in the relationship between national and state patronage, and that change boded ill for the relationship between the central power and local leaders. Apparently the central government was getting strong; the state parties had become more beholden to it for patronage, more inclined to do its bidding. Two trends—democratization and centralization—had combined to menace the state machines. Letting the people rule was all very well, but that meant reforms that made more state offices elective; the fewer appointive ones there were, the fewer the rewards that the states could give. Between 1848 and 1854, nine states refashioned their constitutions, while others made substantial alterations. The new documents increased the number of elective offices. Elsewhere, states liquidated the public works and deprived state administrations of their best spoils. What this meant was that the state party found it harder to keep the peace at home without support from Washington. That support would have to be reciprocal: do as the Administration bade to obtain the favors only the Administration could give. In the meantime, the number of offices at the President's command increased, as did the boldness with which patronage was used to whip dissident state organizations into line and to advance a specific point of view on certain issues.[25]

Within the central government itself, observers also sensed the balance shifting, in this case away from Congress and toward the President.

Whigs had long insisted that spoils would do precisely that, but by 1850 Democrats were saying the same, and they continued to make the charge even after their own party returned to the White House. Indeed, their cries grew louder and more specific. Congressmen might inveigh at how costly government had grown, but their voices rose to a scream when any reformer tried to trim patronage posts in their districts, and it was this greed that Presidents counted on. Southerners liked to insist that in such scrambles, Northerners alone participated. "I wish to God they had," Senator Robert Toombs of Georgia responded: "but I cannot in truth and honesty say that they have, because I believe that $100,000 put in almost any State I know, from here to the Rio Grande, will have a very mollifying effect in the Senate of the United States." Such a greed *could* be used to undercut Presidential power—and in the case Toombs raised, it had been—but other Democrats saw in the President the greatest and most dangerous mollifier.[26]

Reformers were right, as far as they went, but they missed the other side of patronage. Far from sweetening all tempers to suit the executive, it may even have added to the rage that dissidents felt. As President Franklin Pierce discovered, to reward everyone was to satisfy no one, and those he appointed were not as willing to show the same broad-mindedness in their choice of subordinates. Presidents Taylor and Millard Fillmore tried proscription of factions they disliked, only to find that some partisans thrive on martyrdom. An office was good for tempting almost anyone, but the temptation was not always strong enough to make him do anything to get it, and an office given made one friend and a dozen disappointed enemies. For all the dark fears of the Whigs, the Democratic Administrations of the 1850s could neither bring the dissidents in the party to heel nor swing the voters of the North behind the so-called "dough-faces."

Instead, the squabble over offices made each faction more indignant at the slights it had suffered. Hunker rose to battle with Barnburner, section accused section of special advantage. Federal patronage did not settle most fights; when a dispute broke out, it became easier for both sides to conclude that spoils alone explained the "soreheads" on the other side. Any reconciliation between factions raised the suspicion that the hunger for spoils had brought the rivals together and that the moment offices were given, the fighting would be renewed. How natural that politicians should so assume, when they believed that patronage could do so much to make the rank and file think alike.[27]

So what people thought they saw clashed with the reality, in part because so many Democrats and Whigs were less corrupt than they seemed, and less likely to settle their quarrels for a sinecure. If the Jacksonian party system had any marked tendency, it was not toward the orthodoxy that patronage from Washington could enforce, but toward the disintegration that federal rewards only seemed to further. If national party leaders were gaining power, they were destroying the parties in the process—a preposterous situation.

And what did patronage politics do to the tone of American public life? Certainly the spoils system mingled legitimate rewards, necessary compromises, and freebooting. No two people could agree on where the compromises ended and the plundering began, but many Americans—especially Whigs and Southerners of either party—thought the whole system destructive of the virtue without which no republic could last. Spoils might be necessary, but they made organizations based on issues more unstable. Too many of the rank and file would endorse whatever principle the dispenser of favors afforded, said the reformers. What kind of Whig triumph would it be, when, as in Brooklyn in 1848, the party's backers marched under the banner, "One dash more and the Navy Yard is ours?"[28] When the navy yard was lost to them, how many would work to further the Whig program?

So the spoils system piled irony on irony, as the process that should have soothed tensions promoted them and fostered inner contradictions in the Republic. Patronage was necessary to the two-party system's functioning, and the two-party system was admitted to be essential to the protection of republican values, but the spoils system also demoralized the people and put the Republic of the Fathers in jeopardy—thus said the reformers. Too much patronage, a legislative committee warned, "vitiates the public taste and enervates society. Can our people . . . hope to escape the vices which naturally flow from this patronage, and avoid the uniform fate of other nations?" At the same time, politicians found their public professions and private practice impossible to reconcile. The worthy steward, everyone agreed, should let the office seek him out rather than seeking the office; but offices proved notoriously shy with those too diffident to press their own case. Every placeman had to do just what no good American must be seen doing. He must barter ideals and compromise issues to share in the loaves and fishes. No party could put through its programs without putting in its friends, but moralists insisted that to proscribe any man for his views was tyranny. Acceptable behavior for a republic clashed regularly with normal practice in politics. As a loyal Whig, Simeon Draper could moan, "It is hard to see scamps . . . get honest men's places," and to welcome bandits into one's household to protect oneself from "rapine and murder," but he added, "we are *obliged* to have such tools thrust upon us. . . ." Corrupt men were the curse of any party, Elias W. Leavenworth grieved, and "it is most unfortunate for us that we have so many of them. . . ."[29]

So it was, but what is "hard" or "unfortunate" is already something the observer finds bearable. It was this that made many Americans inveigh at the whole concept of professional politics and, indeed, at the idea of party organization in general. "Politics!" sneered a hero of one drama, "fie! . . . the spasmodic exertions of an insect over the frothy surface of a bucket of dirty water." Spoils blighted, spoils corrupted—that was the message reports of the quadrennial scramble in Washington gave the public. Rather than let the navy yards and custom houses continue to blight his country's politics, a Maine congressman vowed, "I would rather see them sunk in the middle of the Atlantic ocean."[30] Had the men who chose the placemen been sunk, too, no doubt many Americans would have breathed an amen, for by 1854 the spoils system had discredited the Jacksonian party system irretrievably. If its most salient purpose was to provide jobs for the hungry, then a political contest became a sham. If politicians were out for office, they could not be out for the public good—it was impossible. It was for this reason that Americans increasingly distinguished between the Republic and "the politicians," "the officeholders," the "Court-house clique" that kept power for its own profit.[31]

The suspicion of spoils corruption was more than the party system could bear. As early as 1850, voters were endorsing new parties whose main virtue was that they stood no chance of winning office. In every Northern state, the two major organizations had to flirt with third parties and make coalitions; regularly the newspapers grumbled at placeholders' "corruption," when they meant no more than patronage-dispensing, and added to the sense of public uneasiness. When a new party arose in the mid-1850s, it would be proudest of the claim that its candidates had never held office before and never sought for place under the spoils system. "He has never fed at the *Federal Crib*," boasted one editor of his candidate for Congress, "and has not been contaminated by the pap." That qualification was vital, for only men inexperienced in office-seeking could usher in "the long desired era of reform," said another newspaper. It was not only their money that made members of this new American party approach Cornelius Vanderbilt and George Law with invitations to run for President, but the fact that both were professional businessmen, and neither a professional politician.[32]

We should not overestimate the impact of this disaffection. Many thousands of partisans kept their loyalty to the party system, and no one mounted an effective challenge to the spoils system in the 1850s. Indeed, the American party did not last, among other reasons because for many disaffected voters it served as a catharsis, a release of frustrations before they returned to the spoils-hungry organizations from which they came. "Men rush into it like schoolboys," one reporter noted, "bursting out of school, rejoicing to get out of the sight of the master with his irksome platform of discipline."[33] Undoubtedly, that was true, and explained why where the Americans might do well in one election was where they were weakest in the next. But there were other legacies of the belief that spoils was corrupting, that the corruption was strengthening the central power and the President, and that the party system itself needed a thorough purging, and those legacies, as we shall see, had a more long-range impact. However much a catharsis it was, the American party movement was a symptom of that deep malaise with spoils politics as usual and the impact of its corruptings. Not only the unity but the legitimacy of the two established parties had been thrown into jeopardy by 1854.

2

The Hireling Press

In April 1852 the New York *Evening Post* reported one of the most welcome funerals in many years. The corpse was the New York *Express for the Union*, a champion of the Compromise of 1850 and its business backers. It had been well paid for its convictions, said the *Post*, as an autopsy would show. "In its insatiable stomach was found a coach worth \$1,000, 200 boluses of coin, each containing \$40, . . . supposed to have been the complimentary token received by it for undertaking the support of the Castle Garden movement, ten thousand dollars more in one lump, awarded to it . . . for widening Wall Street; and a roll of bills from the Dry Dock Bank, presumed to have been part of the money furnished by the steamboat interest to carry democratic votes. . . ."[1] If by this the *Post* meant that the Brooks brothers who ran the *Express* had supported conservative Whig convictions because they were paid to do so, it was mistaken, but its charges that the editors welcomed outside funding was all too true. So did most newspapers, for the 1850s were the halcyon years of the hireling press.

Running a newspaper was a costly business and had grown more so during the past decade. To start up in New York City would have cost \$10,000 in 1840, Charles A. Dana calculated, but \$100,000 ten years later. Far-fetched though Dana's figures sound, they fit the facts. When Henry Raymond set up the *Times* in 1851, he had to raise \$69,000 to start with and in the first year spent another \$78,000 on newsprint, labor, and editorial staff. By permitting the newspapers free delivery in their home counties, Congress eased the publishers' money worries, but other innovations added to their costs. With the spread of telegraph lines, fresh news became easier to get and more essential to a major press, but it was expensive. For the latest overseas events, the New York Associated Press would sell their services at $100 for each 3000 words. The new rotary press allowed the production of tens of thousands of copies of each issue, but such machinery was particularly costly. As larger newspapers experimented with local correspondence, Washington reporting, and interviews, they hired larger, more professional staffs. A publisher could ignore all these changes, and many did so, but in doing so they risked losing their audiences to a rival that could provide the improved services.[2] For all their changes the money must come from somewhere.

Even without adjusting to innovations, publishers found it difficult to keep from going broke. Big-city newspapers might pay their own way, and their news-gathering abilities assured them a wide audience. Iowa farmers read the weekly edition of the New York *Tribune* and learned more from it than from any paper in the state. A *Tribune* or a Boston *Daily Advertiser* needed no subsidy from the public till. Small-town newspapers did. Without the means to become impressive sources of information, they appealed to a more select audience—Democrats, Whigs, merchants—and found even that not enough. With a modest market to split up, two or more papers in a village could just barely make ends meet. Their proprietors tried every expedient to cut costs. Many presses were little more than compilations of clippings from other newspapers or republications of Congressional debates. Local talent might write the weekly editorial and nothing more. Even then, the business proved discouragingly meager. One publisher sold out his interest in an Illinois paper with relief. "If God will help me in my resolution," he vowed, "I will never have to do again with a one horse paper in a one horse town, particularly if that paper depends for its support upon a horde of d--n unlicked Irish whelps and Dutch ignoramuses."[3]

Some editors persisted in publishing party newspapers and tried not to worry about the cost. They found theirs a chastening experience. "Since Cooper has conducted it," a backer of the Philadelphia *Pennsylvanian* complained, "we have sunk $6500. . . . [I]f we don't do something with it, the sheriff will take the trouble off our hands, very soon." Other editors had to pay hundreds of dollars from their own savings to keep the presses rolling.[4]

Why, then, did they do it? If their own letters to public officials can be trusted, editors stuck to a losing concern out of missionary zeal. Without them, the opposition would give the news with its own slant and sway the people to its side; theirs was an essential party function. "The prospects for a young Democrat in this little hole of Whiggery are decidedly gloomy," wrote a Kentucky newspaperman. "Yet notwithstanding, here's at them!"[5] In fact, a good partisan also hoped to make the press pay handsomely and he expected the party organization to help him do so. If it controlled the government, then the editor demanded public revenues as his right. When offices would augment the paper's income, proprietors asked for them. "I want an office worth $500 or more, not less," wrote a North Carolina editor. If he could hold it for two years, he believed that he could amass enough to return home and sustain a Whig sheet. Did Democrats wish to keep the Highland *Eagle* publishing? Its owner could do so only if he got a place in the Peekskill customs house.[6] What was at stake was not just party funding but party recognition, all the more because the organization included so many different voices, each clamoring to be acknowledged as the orthodox one. According to the editor of the Boston *Post*, even a nominal token of the Administration's favor—say, the right to print the laws—would confer "a sort of *quasi* official rank" that would inspire the rank and file to subscribe to that paper over all others.[7]

If most newspapers could not do without a party subsidy, politicians could not do without a supportive press. The need was greater then than today because the editors so trimmed all news to fit their preconceptions and because the rank and file so relied on the designated press for guidance on what a good party loyalist should stand for. Party organs could brazen out any scandal once they had collected a steady clientele. In upstate New York, many Democrats would vote however the Albany *Argus* directed, because they had never read anything else, an antagonist wrote, "and with the obstinacy rather characteristic of age, will not believe any other to be orthodox." Organs in New Hampshire and Ohio boasted the same influence. As a result, the politicians needed a supportive press everywhere and could only crack the opposition's hold in a community by setting up a rival paper there.[8]

Party leaders never doubted the impact of a hireling press with at least some of their followers. When they lost an election, candidates insisted that a good organ would have made the difference. When Democrats did poorly in New York City, they railed at the lack of a reliable voice and opened negotiations to fill the need—negotiations that collapsed because no faction would permit a press that another might control. As soon as the party had a press anywhere, the cry shifted to the need for the *right kind* of press, and officeholders' correspondence was choked with fulminations at the endowed editors as traitors. When Senator Andrew Johnson of Tennessee differed with the editor of the Knoxville organ, he was advised to create a new paper. "This must be either done," a friend wrote him, "or the present editor must be *killed off*, or else his *constant harping* . . . must sooner or later . . . poison the public mind against you." Nor would it do for an editor to try to appease all factions by an inoffensive partisanship. Mild support was worse than none. Let their nominees pledge public advertising only to those organs that stood foursquare for the ticket, the Philadelphia People's convention resolved. No wonder they had lost Lehigh County, Pennsylvania partisans raged. Their press was a sniveling, mealy-mouthed concern.[9] All this bickering testified to the vital importance of the party press, as well as to its role in provoking quarrels inside the ranks. But a friendly paper could not survive without cost. The parties must sustain the papers if they wanted the papers to sustain the parties, and that meant contributions from the rank and file, often assessments on government employees, public jobs, and public contracts.

Both at the state and national level, administrations handed out government positions to deserving editors. Printers especially prized postmasterships; every postmaster could send material through the mails free by signing his frank to it. Editors could use such mailing privileges, and since most newspaper owners turned their presses to churning out campaign literature at election time, a postmastership allowed the party to spread its message without cost. Other jobs were equally welcome and equally available. When the Democrats wanted to choose federal land office receivers in Wisconsin or customs collectors in Connecticut, they turned to the leading newspapermen there. These positions entailed the right to hand out official advertising; no editor had to ponder long which press to endow. How lavishly the patronage system treated a paper the Boston *Times* showed. Under the Pierce Administration, it published government advertising, its publisher put two brothers in the customs house, its editor lodged his brother there as well, and an assistant editor became dispatch-agent.[10]

Jobs were only the first installment of a government's largesse. In New York, Whigs saw that at least six editors became dummy partners in canal repair contracts in late 1851. Wisconsin lawmakers rewarded loyal Democratic papers by taking 459 subscriptions to the Kenosha *Democrat*, or four copies per member. At the rates they paid, representatives assured each member the equivalent of ten newspapers a day, and senators provided twenty-six. There were far more lucrative privileges: printing of election returns at the state level, publication of legislative journals and executive documents, laws of the United States, and federal advertisements for naval supplies, land sales, and post office routes. In Washington, newspapers fought for the special privilege of reporting Congressional debates and printing them as news at $7.50 per column. Every document that the government used, from blank forms and envelopes to departmental stationary, was let out by contract, and again favoritism played a crucial role in allotment.[11]

Was there anything wrong with this? Was it not, in fact, one more extension of the spoils system? There were similarities, to be sure, but two distinctions made the problem more serious: first, the printing, unlike most political offices, was a swindle on the taxpayers, and second, it was used to buy or silence published opinion and to reshape public perceptions of what the officeholders were doing.

As to the first point: the profits from patronage could be immense, since the cost for which the work was done and the payment given had little relation to each other. To the Democratic machine of David C. Broderick in California, state printing contracts meant $270,000 of revenue for the party coffers each year. When the New York *Express* printed a private advertisement, it charged six cents a line, but for public ones it demanded ten cents and as much for reporting the Common Council's proceedings. The $17,021.45 it received from the city government in 1860 was among the reasons that it had nothing to say about the corruption that its fellow-editors saw about them. Even had every penny of Congressional printing expenses been applied to costs of publication, critics still wondered whether all the printing was necessary. No one listened to the drivel on the floor, a South Carolina senator argued; why, then, should Americans be taxed to read it? "Who ever examines the advertisements in a State paper?" the New York *Tribune* asked. Why was it necessary for the surrogate to send notices affecting New York City to Albany for publication? As far as the usefulness of the practice went, why not send them to Syracuse or Nova Scotia?[12]

The printing was not just a needless expense. Printing contracts were a scandal because nothing impelled the lawmakers to give them to the lowest bidder. Where no law forced such a reform, publishing costs soared. In Ohio, for example, Democrats had elected Samuel Medary to do their work at $18,900 a year. Whigs pushed through the lowest bidder system and halved expenses. Then the Democrats returned. So did Medary, and costs rose to $26,220. To appeals for reform, the majority party would always find reasons for the old system of rewarding party friends. Men would bid impossibly low and demand repayment, they explained. To force applicants to bid against each other would "degrade a highly honorable profession." It would only replace old corrupt practices with novel ones. Spurious arguments, but they served their purpose. As in Ohio, Pennsylvania Whigs ordered printing bestowed on those who asked the least, and as in Ohio, Democrats undid the rule as soon as they returned to power. The real reason for resistance was obvious: the newspapers siphoned a portion of their exorbitant profits into the party treasuries. Where the law did enact the lowest-bidder principle, matters were only slightly better. Bidders would offer to do the work for a pittance and then return to ask additional compensation or extras for stitching and binding. Printers joined to submit identical bids, all exorbitant; the winner would divide the profits with the losers. Beneficiaries might get a contract and then sell it; even then the ultimate contractor did far better than breaking even.[13]

Because the most money was at stake in Washington, the worst scandals broke there. Until 1819, the government had assigned its printing to the lowest bidder. Then the Congress authorized each house to select its own printer and established rates which stayed in effect over the next thirty years. As the cost of setting type and purchasing paper plummeted, the profits soared. By the mid-1840s, a net profit of 60 percent was not thought unusual. The Twenty-Seventh Congress cut the 1819 rates by a fifth, but then restored the old schedule and gave the printers a $40,000 bonus. Under pressure from the Whigs, the 1846 Congress decreed that both houses must award work to the lowest bidder. The winning contractor charged 59 percent less than he could have under the 1819 rates, and still turned a profit.[14]

He could do so because the law had so many loopholes. Congressmen knew little about typesetting and nothing about the comparative costs of different forms of type. A cunning contractor could promise good paper and use a flimsy variety instead, produce samples of his work on the heavy brand stipulated in government contracts and then make the final copies on a lighter one, which cost $1.45 a ream less. To make paper weigh more, the publisher added mineral substances that added one-fourth to its bulk. Again, the contractor who applied for binding work could show the Committee on Printing samples bound with linen head-bands, but delivered work with head-bands of paper.[15] Every such cheat was possible because a Congress, once it had ordered some work, hesitated to annul any contract, no matter how slovenly the fulfillment, especially when the contractor was a loyal party man.

Thomas Ritchie's printing misadventures showed the problem with the contracting system—and how closely it was connected to spoils politics. From the first, his contract with the Thirty-first Congress sparked controversy, in part because his Washington *Union* had replaced the *Globe* as the Democratic organ in the mid-1840s. Though his defenders explained away his miscalculations as the poor judgment of a veteran printer with no head for figures, an investigating committee intimated that Ritchie had conspired to kill the contract system through deliberate underbidding and poor craftsmanship. As printer in the last Congress before the reforms passed, Ritchie worried lest future contractors use their printing profits to set up a rival Democratic newspaper in the capital. That could be prevented by rigging the bids to keep out challengers. The 1846 law had forced each bidder to produce two sureties. Ritchie evaded the measure's intent by having his press foreman and journeyman printer put in bids for which he and his son-in-law would act as surety. In effect, he had made himself his own security. Nor had he ever meant to fulfill his bid. As Ritchie's foreman declared, the firm meant to so disgust Congress with the contract system that Democrats would end it and pay whatever Ritchie asked.[16]

The conspirators did this by delaying the work and asking added compensation. They pleaded that they had not been able to proceed because the Congress had not given them money when it was needed; but the Senate secretary and House pay clerk testified that even when the money was available in the contingent fund, Ritchie had not applied for it. Even Ritchie's defenders agreed that he had bid impossibly low to begin with. Yet even as he complained that his contract was profitless, Ritchie was applying for still more work from the executive departments on the same impossible terms. His firm failed to meet the contract deadlines, because he had taken on too much outside work after his agreement with Congress—hardly an unavoidable mischance. Ritchie claimed great losses, but in spite of requests by members of either house, refused to itemize where he had lost money or how much. Requests for his accounts were ignored. In his defense, Democrats argued that no "paper calculations" would show the loss. Enemies replied that the reason they would not do so was because Ritchie's printing losses were inextricably bound in with his expenses as editor of the *Union* and that the money was meant as a subsidy to the Democratic press.[17]

Ritchie's need may have come from his association with the *Union*, but that association ruined his chances, for there were many Democrats who did not like the party organ nor its support for the Compromise of 1850, nor did they like the idea that he would be subsidized to continue his support for conservative policies. The claim for additional compensation looked like a steal, and freesoil Democrats and Southern Rights men branded it so at once. Under the relief bill, the New York *Evening Post* estimated, Ritchie could expect a $400,000 profit. A Washington printer put the gain far lower, though $150,000 was still enormous. Ritchie employed some of the best lobbyists in town to plead his cause. W. W. Corcoran, the banker, had invested in the *Union*, Senator Henry Foote acted as agent before the upper house, and Benjamin French hoped for $2000 for his efforts (though he was pleasantly surprised to get $250 in the end). None of their exertions worked. Too many Democrats wanted someone else to edit the *Union*, someone of a different viewpoint, and they joined with enough Whigs to kill the extra allowance first in one house and then in the other. The price for considering Ritchie's claims was his resignation from the paper, which he gave. The Thirty-second Congress eventually put through an appropriation for extra compensation, though far less than Ritchie had sought.[18]

Nor was this the only time that sustaining a party organ led to scandal. The *Union* was never free of it. Whoever the fortunate printer was, he was expected to use some of his profits to keep the majority party's press going in Washington, for the press could not pay for itself. Nor did the problems depart with Ritchie. Democrats patronized the *Union* and expected it to speak true party doctrine, which usually but not always meant the party's Administration. Thus, funding became embroiled with the issue of what kind of Democrat was most suited to set the tone for state organs. As soon as Robert J. Armstrong became the new owner and A. J. Donelson the new editor, fighting broke out afresh. Described by one acquaintance as "wholly destitute of literary culture,—incapable of writing a sentence," Armstrong was able to drink fifty-six bottles of wine in twenty-four hours, a feat that helped kill him. He was less objectionable than Donelson, who offended the Southern Rights wing at once. Both men appalled the strict constructionists by their sympathy with steamship mail-subsidies. Since Armstrong's son-in-law happened to be an investor and lobbyist for the foremost beneficiary, this sympathy was not surprising. "Donelson is already out for the steamboat monopolies," wrote a former editor. "He will secretly be in for all the log rolling claims & schemes in Congress & we shall have a thorough betrayal of every honest principle of the Democracy. . . ."[19]

Again, enemies found their chance to attack the new management by uncovering another "steal." As one incentive to induce Armstrong to take over the organ, Senate Democrats had promised to take the publication of the census out of the Interior Department's control and allot it to the *Union* at whatever price the paper demanded. The partisan aim was obvious: to take lucrative contracts from the Whig executive branch and give it to the Democrats and to annul the lowest-bidder principle. "This bill was the bellows," an antislavery senator snorted, "which gave wind to the organ and filled its pipes." So it was, but the price of passage was Donelson's retirement—until incoming President Franklin Pierce restored him as editor. Under new leaders in subsequent years the *Union* still relied on Congressional printing to fill its pipes.[20] Year on year the quarrel persisted over which true Democrat should have the opportunity to sustain his paper by robbing the government. In 1853 disgruntled Democrats joined Southern Rights men to give Senate printing to the pro-Southern Washington *Sentinel*, while Administration men kept the House printing for the *Union*. Two years later Senate Democrats swung behind the *Union* only after its new editor sold out his financial stake to someone else less associated with the Administration.[21]

The cream of the jest was that all this jockeying made no difference as far as who did the actual printing. No matter who was nominated, he assigned his work to Cornelius Wendell, a practical printer who bought a half-share in the *Union* in the mid-1850s. Wendell's success in robbing the government made Ritchie's efforts seem modest, and again he was able to profit because of his political connections, but there was a difference. Until Wendell's arrival on the scene, incumbents had used public revenues to support their newspaper allies; under Wendell's management, the newspapers became an important funder of incumbents' campaigns.

No matter whom Congress chose, the former Whig made a large profit from the printing, binding, and delivery. "He is a whole souled fellow and deserves success," a colleague wrote. Wendell was so successful, indeed, that even party enemies scrambled to take shares in his firm. Between 1853 and 1859, he guessed, he collected $3,838,000 for public printing, and $2 million of it was clear profit. Experts insisted that they could have done the legislative work for less than half the price, and Wendell confirmed their estimates. Senator Simon Cameron had once been a printer, and he guessed that the government was paying five times the fair rate. (For some items he was certainly right. In 1860, New York postmaster John A. Dix discovered that his predecessor had spent $4000 a year on labels and blanks that could be bought for $1500, and $480 a year for letterheads that local printers offered to supply for $92. "I cannot designate the practice of the office by any other terms than a system of atrocious swindling," the choleric Dix wrote.)[22] Democrats could have prevented this pillage, but they shared in the proceeds. This was why printing costs soared in the 1850s.

Indeed, the breakdown of morality coincided with one effort by Congress to bring reform. In 1852, it created a Superintendent of Public Printing with a $3000 salary. Such a man might have given the contractors trouble or held Wendell in line, but the man chosen, A. G. Seaman, let the suppliers of paper and print do as they pleased for some of the stealings. As investigators would reveal in 1859, Seaman's management was slipshod, his accounts incomprehensible. Entries were made to conceal the actual diversion of funds. Congress had ordered books that had been paid for but never printed. Engravers and lithographers gave Seaman a rebate on each contract. For Seaman to be inattentive to discrepancies in paper samples cost one firm $12,000. In all, the contractors admitted to $30,000 in kickbacks. As for Wendell, he, too, might have caviled at the shoddy paper quality, had the contractors not hired him as a special agent with a 3.5 percent share in each contract.[23]

So the printing system was closely linked to the party organs, spoils politics, and plundering appropriations. But a worse consequence was the way in which the funding affected what newspapers said and how worthy of trust their politics were. The spoils system almost encouraged a shakedown in the party organ's interest, as postmasters and clerks were forced to contribute to the Administration press. In Cleveland, the collector of the port had to give $500, as did the federal marshal. Still, perhaps prominent officeholders thought the price worth it, for they got discretion in return. A newspaper subsidized by the party would not hang the Administration's linen in plain view. Though leading Ohio Democrats knew their allies were mulcting the public works, no party newspaper gave the warning. Less cooperative presses lost their patronage.[24]

Party officers by no means were alone in buying newspapers' opinions. Businessmen, too, needed reliable organs and at times raised money for it. When the Milwaukee *News* endorsed the LaCrosse & Milwaukee Railroad land grant, it seemed to be expressing an independent judgment; only later would an investigation show that the firm had bought it for $12,000. That the Milwaukee *Daily American* disapproved of the same grant was no more surprising, for a rival railroad company had added the editor to its payroll to do just that. When the Camden & Amboy had a fatal accident, the Albany *Evening Journal* spared the directors no abuse for their recklessness. When the New York Central had a similar catastrophe, the *Journal* pardoned it as one of the inescapable consequences of railroad travel. That the editor was an investor and hired lobbyist for the Central made all the difference.[25] A very few newspapers in the mid-1850s had put their principles up for sale. Unwilling to barter editorial policies, some publishers opened their columns to "special correspondents" for a fee.[26]

That party newspapers would subordinate the editor's personal opinions to the party line was something readers came to expect. They were less prepared to deal with partisans' purchase of the opinions of the independent press; indeed they never knew that it occurred. In fact, the parties used money to sweeten the independents at every Presidential election. To square New York City's penny press in 1852, Democrats estimated that $3000 was needed, while Pennsylvania Republicans some years later knew that they could insert helpful political material as news in the Philadelphia *Public Ledger* for $100. Buying up uncommitted presses was a good investment because the party tie so discredited a newspaper among any but fierce partisans; when an independent endorsed one party's candidate or policies, readers paid more attention. This was why one Democrat advised his superior that only the nonpartisan press's support could sway New York City to Franklin Pierce. "Recollect," he wrote, "that the party press has no perceptible weight with the masses, for eight or nine years this city has gone with the cent press and it cannot be counted upon without it." So, too, Democratic Governor Horatio Seymour found that his party could better use the mildly Whig New York *Times* than any other organ. The editor assured Seymour that the paper would stay neutral, but give the Administration the benefit of the doubt. This was far better than outright support, Seymour wrote, because the public would trust the *Times* more. He urged the Administration to give it some favors and leak it all the news it found fit to print.[27]

We must not take the indictment too far. Patronage stopped the mouths of many editors, but not all. The more a newspaper enjoyed financial independence, the more its publishers could afford to be the custodians of their own consciences. Other men found spoils just one argument among many against breaking with the party. Still other editors might weigh the advantages of government contracts against the loss in subscriptions that an unpopular stand would bring, and would decide that the former could never make up for the latter. Until the party line had been laid down, newspapermen also could use their discretion in deciding whether to give a measure their endorsement, cautious acquiescence, or dismissal as unworthy of mention. Chicago had several Democratic journals in 1854, but none of them supported the Kansas-Nebraska Act with much more than a mumble that there might be grounds on which some Democrats might find it worth all the trouble it would stir. The Administration had to set up a new press to sustain its cause. Ohio Democratic editors gave up their preferments to join the opposition and sold their shops to regulars who could endorse the act in good conscience. Four years later, when the Buchanan Administration made support for the pro-slavery Kansas constitution a test of loyalty, some presses temporized. Others sought some way to back the principle of popular sovereignty and the constitution that was its antithesis, and other organs damned the bill and took the consequences.[28]

Yet no one doubted that many party presses took the line that spoils dictated. At their worst, the organs struck many Americans as an appalling spectacle, and the hireling reporters looked even more alarming. Able reporter and loyal Democrat though Francis J. Grund of the Baltimore *Sun* and Philadelphia *Public Ledger* was, his work as a paid lobbyist for steamship managers and Texas bond speculators affected both his reputation and his reliability. Disappointed in his hopes for a consulship, he turned on the Pierce Administration and shifted from fawning apologetics to brutal diatribes. "Now I like Grund," Congressman Thaddeus Stevens sneered. "You can always *buy* him."[29]

That was the last thing a degenerating political sytem needed. "In this age of corruption we need honest, independent men for Editors and Publishers," a New Yorker wrote. Others agreed. Corrupt times demanded a press clean enough to expose wrongdoing in both parties. But so closely had the "intrigues of public men" allied themselves to the "suppleness" of the purchased press, thought North Carolina Justice Thomas Ruffin, that the people were lulled into the peace of political slavery.[30] The umbilical cord between the intriguers and their apologists was the public treasury. It was therefore necessary to cut the connection, not just to end a source of corruption in government but to restore the purity of the press and to return it to its role of social guardian.

Men out of power and those who, because of their views on slavery had the least chance of ever coming into it, denounced the party-paid press most loudly. Perhaps they raised their voices in part because the spoils lay beyond their grasp, but a commitment to principle drove them on still more. The complaints came strongest from the Horace Greeleys and William Cullen Bryants, unhappy that their parties showed the South too much devotion, and from the Southern Rights men, fearful that slavery's enemies were having all politics their own way. Why did so few Americans share their concern, they asked. It must be that a hireling press was upholding the established party structure because the status quo meant two organizations divided by no real issue but plunder. Thus, the falsity of American politics depended on the corrupted press. "The press must be free to be pure," Congressman A. W. Venable of North Carolina insisted, "independent in order to be respectable—honest in order to be useful." When Ritchie's claim came up, Venable's reply echoed the antislavery men's views for once: "the press . . . which cannot live without being fed from the public Treasury, ought to die, and the party which cannot live without the aid of such an organ ought also to die."[31] Implicit in such claims was the faith that such a party *would* die. By ending the parties' subsidizing of newspapers, idealists could break the time-servers' power and elect men more interested in the public good.

The view had merit. Patronage did skew party opinion to fit the will of the national Administration. It did still editors whose inclinations might have been more outspoken. The Kansas-Nebraska Act showed how much the spoils could do as well as their limitations. So much of the Democratic press fell into line at once, a compliance that antislavery men tied to the patronage dispensed to editors. New England papers, a reporter fumed, "have been pensioned on government money and their servile echo is thus secured." No Democratic paper in Washington protested the act, but then, all three together took $300,000 in government advertising and funding. Was not the link obvious between the public advertisements on page four and the slurs against anti-Nebraska men on page two? In his district, a Pennsylvania congressman told the caucus, the people utterly repudiated the Kansas-Nebraska Act, but the press backed it. How could it be otherwise, when the presses "had been plied with *douceurs* in the shape of advertisements and the like"?[32]

Yet, how convenient the cry of corruption was for free-soilers and Southern Rights men! Rather than having to argue the rights and wrongs of the issues, they could proclaim their foes bought, their arguments insincere. The cry of "hireling press" did away with the need to see how closely moderates and major party men fitted the American political tradition. To explain how Californians voted on lying proslavery newsmen was an evasion. To claim that editors acted so because they "looked well to their bread and butter" was, however true, an escape from troublesome musings about whether orthodox Democratic belief and the proslavery argument might not share certain crucial assumptions. By declaring that Massachusetts backed tariff protection solely because the mill-owners were subsidizing the Whig press and had bullied Democratic organs into silence, the New York *Evening Post* changed the issue from one of ideas to one of ethics. Free trade thus attained moral legitimacy by what its enemies did. The claim that manufacturers had to buy press opinion suggested that Bay State voters were naturally inclined against protection, whether in fact they were or not.[33]

The issue of prostitution in the press, therefore, also solved the problem that those outside the party mainstream had in explaining why so many Americans failed to see sectional tensions in the same way that fire-eaters and free-soilers did. All political groups declared a faith in representative democracy, but representative democracy seemed to put the people squarely on the side of the centrists. How could one still put one's faith in the people, when they seemed almost wilfully blind to the real facts about the sectional crisis?

Corrupted editors made ideal scapegoats. *They* were to blame, and not the people, for what the masses did. Politicians and their paid journalists had deluded the people, stopped them from hearing the truth, and fed them lies. The people *were* virtuous. Once they knew the truth, they *could* be brought round. But the truth could never be known until the press lost its tie to the political machinery and the spoils system. "Sir," Venable cried, "we shall never be able to clean the Augean stable of our Government . . . until we have delivered the party press from the Treasury. As long as the press is fed by the party who controls the Administration, there will be skillful apologists for any and every abuse."[34] Till then the people would slumber while wrongs multiplied around them.

Much might be done to fight the corruption. Led by Whigs in the North and by the New York *Tribune*, reformers tried to restrict printing to the lowest bidder. By 1860 investigations of Wendell and Seaman's plunderings had so discredited the idea of party organs that the Washington *Union* had closed its doors. Michigan's new constitution added limitations on who could partake in printing contracts and on what terms they would be awarded, while other fundamental laws specified fees for printing the laws.[35] Still, these were only a beginning. In 1860 most states still let the majority party sustain its newspapers from the public revenue. In the South, press subsidies would grow after the Civil War, while in New York City the Democratic machine would bribe most of the press into complacency with robbery for a decade.

In 1860 no less than in 1850, Martin Van Buren's words held true about the "scenes . . . in regard to the public printing." They were "sickening to every patriotic mind."[36] That sickness had spread far. It had infected the party system itself, limited the willingness of subsidized papers to speak out, and in the process limited the possibility of the dominant party adapting to satisfy the will of the rank and file. It distorted party regulars' ability to understand the issues. It had enhanced dissidents' conviction that the arguments of their enemies were unworthy of notice; it had discredited the party presses seriously as expressions of the rank and file's opinion and robbed them of the power to be an intermediary between government and people. It had furthered the sense that in the 1850s for the professional politicians and pundits, belief was a matter of barter. Well might Van Buren find the scenes sickening. They were not just one of the symptoms but one of the causes for the ill health of the Republic in the generation leading to the Civil War.

3

"My God, We Have Voted Like Hell!"

Days before Maine's 1858 elections, James Shepherd Pike was desperate for contributions to the Republican war-chest, for money would beat the Democrats as nothing else would. "In Aroostook they have rather more, but they have more votes to pay for," he wrote. That second *more* was no gaffe. Pike really meant that his party and its foe alike would buy voters wherever they could find them. "We have got in between [$]700 and $800 into the Aroostook," he commented soon after, "mostly for those French cattle, & I have already placed [$]1000 in this county & [$]200 in Hancock. . . . Unless the rascals pour more money at the close than I believe they are able to, we will smash them both in the District & in this county." But when the votes were counted, the Democrats did surprisingly well in the unincorporated French plantations of the hinterlands. Pike knew how. "We have been swindled damnably," he stormed. There must be an "instant census" to see how many bona fide voters actually lived there. When Republicans chose a commissioner to scrutinize election frauds, they named Pike. The next winter he reported to a legislative committee with all the righteous indignation he could muster.[1]

There were frauds worthy of his indignation. The French plantations had grown surprisingly on Election Day. One such polling place reported 176 votes in 1857 and 360 in 1858, all but twelve of them Democratic and nearly all of them vanished by the time Pike reached there. On Hancock

Plantation, 115 people cited as having voted could be found nowhere, and 51 more were unfit for the suffrage. Only 153 voters stood on the official list, and even that was suspect, since the winning candidate had not compiled it until the day *after* the election. The local clerk recalled that many who voted had not appeared on his own list, but pleaded that he could do nothing about their lawbreaking, for they voted so fast that checking off names was impossible. "They piled over one another like a flock of sheep. The new names were kept on a separate paper in a book by a Frenchman. It was all hubbub, and the Devil to pay."[2]

In fact, it was not the Devil but William H. Dickey who did the paying. A lawyer, doctor, and "almost anything," one supporter praised him for knowing "more law and gospel than anyone here." As inspector of customs and postmaster, he certainly put neither into practice—not as long as he was running for state senator. It was he who operated the ballot-box that day and forced every man to show his vote. All Republicans but a few were turned away. When one voter protested at the fifteen-year-olds that the Democrats were parading to the polls, he got a drubbing. "My God, we have voted like hell," Dickey shouted. "I have not worked so long for nothing."

Neither had the voters! The election was as disorderly as it was fraudulent. Most participants were Frenchmen from areas without schools or roads. Interviewed later, not one of them could tell who was President or governor. Pike claimed that none could read and write. "They act more like wild beasts election-day than like men," said the assessor. "There could be no more pulling and hauling among a parcel of wolves just out of the woods, than there is among them the day of election." Those who visited Dickey's general store left it intensely drunk. A few stripped themselves naked and leaped around. "I never saw people act as bad as they do," a witness commented; "they don't act like human beings at all." Not that Dickey paid them in drink alone. He passed at least $1000 over his counter to buy their votes. At other plantations the going rate was $1 to $1.50, which a member of the federal revenue service passed out next to the polling-window.[3]

Vote-buying, vote-importing, violence, and intimidation—what could happen in Maine could happen anywhere, and in the 1850s it did with increasing frequency. What election did not have a few fraudulent votes cast, one newspaper asked. Many polling-places had more than a few, and many Americans would notice three other themes that ran through Maine's experience: first, that the Democratic party seemed to have a particular fondness for a pollution of the ballot-box, second, that there was a link between the corrupted suffrage and federal officials' actions, and third, that the corruptionists found foreigners an especially easy tool for overturning the real majority's will.

Not every irregularity was a case of corruption. So informally was voting done in places that the law could be construed different ways. It was curious, but hardly criminal, as was done in Massachusetts, to cast all the votes into a hat. Two states kept *viva voce* voting, and in others the voters wrote out their slips themselves. The latter system was sure to cause trouble, when only one particular form of a candidate's name was permitted on the ballot. Take the case of Thomas B. Atkinson, candidate for the New Jersey House. When the polls closed, his friends had voted for Thomas B. Alkinson, Thomas B. Atchinson, T. B. Atkinson, Thomas B. Askison, Joseph B. Atkinson, and just plain Atkinson. Some of the voters may even have been voting for the Atkinson running in an adjoining district. By applying the rules rigorously and accepting only one form of his name, the board of canvassers would have been legally right, and in defiance of the popular will, since Atkinson would have lost by six votes.[4] In most states, the parties avoided such mischances by passing out printed ballots to their friends, with a formal list of one slate alone; not only could most voters escape the rigors of spelling, but the parties could escape the perils of ticket-splitting, the one irregularity they dreaded the most.

A very few Americans insisted that there was no significant amount of fraud at all in the 1850s elections, but their claims tax all credulity. Improper voting in Baltimore County? It never happened, said one resident: "that county preserved within her borders purifying influences enough to save the whole state." "Not one vote in five thousand was illegal in the townships," the Detroit *Free Press* protested.[5] Naturally, each party admitted that its foes might corrupt the election—but never itself. In fact, both parties did it, though Democrats seem to have had an edge. Baltimore corruption was too clear to conceal, and the *Free Press* itself would air charges of debauched elections in the backwoods.

Not all charges could be proven. Indeed, to cry "fraud" was the regular pastime of whichever party lost an election, and the historian must treat the clamor with caution. Still, at times the number of voters itself was enough to excite suspicion. Until 1853, for example, New Orleans's vote had never risen beyond 11,000. Before the election, yellow fever took 20,000 lives. Yet the returns showed 13,000 voters citywide. Whig parishes turned out no more men than in 1851, but Democratic precincts outdid themselves. In 1851, the Fourteenth Precinct had cast 778 votes; now it cast 1,139. Rather lamely, the Democrats insisted that the returns were honest, that the yellow-fever epidemic had simply spared the voters.

Splendid was Divine providence, jeered the New Orleans *Bee*, to show such selectivity! Strangers should learn from this to register the moment they entered New Orleans.[6] That Democrats had swollen their ranks with outsiders seemed a more plausible explanation than immortality through registration.*

Backwoods spokesmen blamed ballot-box corruption on city life. What else could one expect from the close contact of merchant nabobs with money to spend and landless drifters with principles to sell, they asked. Certainly *one* kind of election fraud came easiest in the metropolis: the colonization of outsiders to vote a specific ticket. When village registrars knew each elector by sight, strangers might be spotted at once and turned away. But that did not mean that city elections were more corrupt—only that small towns had to buy residents' votes rather than import outsiders. The fewer the voters, too, the less money it took to buy a winning margin. Baltimore, by contrast, took larger resources than any party could supply—except in a Presidential year. The truth is that by the 1850s, colonization, like vote-buying, appeared everywhere, even in the most modest hamlets. In the 1840s, wholesale naturalization of foreigners had been Baltimore's special problem, said a Marylander, but no longer. By 1851, party organizers in outlying counties would stand at the polls waiting for newly arrived inhabitants to appear and clutching sheafs of blank naturalization forms. Foreigners would receive their party ballot

*How significant *was* fraud in actual numbers? Historians disagree. Insisting that illegal voting would explain the remarkably high turnouts during the late nineteenth century, Philip Converse has seen corruption as affecting at least 5 percent of the vote; to this, William Gienapp has pointed out that voter turnouts were just as high in areas where no vote fraud was ever suggested, that more people seem to have voted because more people actually did vote. Howard W. Allen and Kay Warren Allen, examining the Gilded Age, claimed that vote fraud was actually rare. Like many other historians, they noted that the critics were genteel reformers, with no love of a full vote, fair or otherwise. My suspicions incline closer to those of Peter Argersinger, another student of the Gilded Age political system: he notes that the number of contested election cases seriously underestimates fraud, since no candidate from the party that held the minority of legislative seats would trust to the majority's disinterested judgment: such cases were notoriously settled on pure partisan grounds. Nor would vote fraud necessarily inflate vote totals: buying voters would not change the number voting, nor would creative counting by partisan boards, where opposition electors are undercounted even as friends are overcounted.

What can be said with certainty is that in many elections, there was *enough* manipulation of the voters *or* their ballots to affect the result; that in private all parties acknowledged its existence and most of them abetted it in one way or another; that it was worse in primaries than elections, worse in state than Presidential elections.

and certificate of election at the same time, the second as a reward for casting the first.[7]

In fact, as the decade would show, the places most susceptible to vote fraud were those most like the frontier area that Pike investigated, where population was expanding quickly and the new voters might be inhabitants or purchased invaders. Newly settled lands proved new frontiers for corruption. Thanks to them, the Democrats nearly stole the Wisconsin governorship in 1855; both sides tried to tailor-make a majority in Minnesota in 1857; no one paid attention to Nebraska frauds because so many people were so upset at the Democratic swindles in Kansas; and San Francisco vote frauds grew even faster than the city's population.[8]

More to blame than the city was the party system itself and the fierce loyalties that competition inspired. As the party organizations grew more sophisticated and as the patronage available to the winner grew, so did the determination to win at any cost. Partisans would rarely admit in public that they had interfered with a fair count, and when they did they pleaded self-defense. Yes, the Detroit *Free Press* admitted, Rhode Island Democrats bribed the voters—but their enemies had started it, and affluent citizens simply would not attend the polls without pay. In private letters, loyalists were more frank: the nation's good depended on winning this election or that, and if it took some money, a good organizer should not scruple about using it. Some internal disputes could not be settled by reason. Then partisans justified solutions less fit for front-page publicity. Troubled by backers of a rival candidate for Congress, an ally of Orsamus Matteson advised him to silence them. "What is surest and quietest will be the handsomest way," he added.[9] Presumably it was not the cheapest.

Partisans tried many nefarious tactics to beat their foes, and not all qualify as corrupting. For example, a disgruntled faction might pass out a ballot that at first glance seemed a perfectly ordinary Whig or Democratic vote. Only the most careful elector would read to discover that the malcontents had switched the names of candidates around to run the wrong man for each office, had omitted certain offices entirely, or had placed a new man in the running for some position. Such trickery broke no law; nor, necessarily, did the plying of voters with drink on Election Day, even when the treat was aimed at swinging their votes. Some states forbade the candidate to set repasts for the electorate, but his friends could do as they pleased, and in any case, custom was stronger than law. In many places, no candidate could expect to win without such a show of generosity, and a Georgia Democrat thought that the key to victory would be to set up groggeries in all doubtful counties.[10] The results often looked like those on the French plantation. Since even enemies of the saloon bought votes with libations, Election Day could turn into a drunken carnival and often did.

Gulling voters lay beyond the law's reach. Swilling them was honored custom, but threatening them was another matter. Courts prosecuted those who intimidated voters, when they could. Yet this practice, too, flourished. Certainly throughout most of the South it was more than a man's life was worth to cast a ballot for the antislavery party—or to distribute them. Massachusetts businessmen bullied their workers to vote Whig, government officers coerced their underlings, and one New York canal superintendent mustered his workers and marched them to the local justice to swear that they would vote Whig. Those refusing the oath were dismissed.[11] When the government used force to drive off the opposition's voters—and this happened only rarely—it was still more alarming. Yet in New York and Chicago, the police became the strong-arm men for the reigning administration. "Forward, policemen bold!" the Chicago *Times* jeered:

> Nick, let it not be told
> Democrat votes were polled
> Because ye blundered!
> Drive them with blows and knocks,
> Treat them to bolts and locks,
> Seize ye the ballot-box,
> Carry it off with you, noble six hundred![12]

Funds worried Americans more than force. Worse than the threats, rum, forgeries, was the buying and selling of votes, and of this contemporaries saw a great deal. They knew it as corruption, and in all forms it was reprehensible, but some forms were more reprehensible than others.

The most traditional form of corruption, perhaps the least objectionable, was the purchase of legitimate voters' suffrage, since the purchased man would have voted anyhow. Yet many observers thought that this old evil took on new proportions during the 1850s, became more public, and shifted from small rewards—"a glass or a breakfast"—to cash payments, given from vast corruption funds. How much did the briber pay? That depended on how close an election was thought to be and how important the parties thought its outcome. In most cases, a voter would settle for a dollar or two, though ten dollars became the customary rate in New Jersey, and in Michigan Democrats paid off in flour and provisions. At a crucial election, managers might pay as high as $50 for a vote, though that was rare outside of Rhode Island, where bribery had become the accepted custom. At every election were the "floaters," uncommitted votes waiting the bids of either party. They were not disappointed.

Because of the lack of voting machines and the party-made ballots, buying individual voters had less risk than today; the briber could be sure that the floater would vote as directed. Indeed, practical politicians preferred to buy votes in bulk by negotiating with a "striker," a man who could deliver a large supply of electors. Some strikers were too young to vote, but as the head of street gangs, they knew comrades more fortunate, others were pimps who could turn out a red-light district's eligible males for whichever party paid the most handsomely. Woe to the nominee for city ward office who did not appease the denizens of the rum-holes! One New York candidate visited the polls, and the strikers and floaters closed in, demanding payment. The politician was nearly torn to pieces before he could be rescued, and as he fled the pack cursed him for "a mean cuss" and emptied out the ballot-boxes, tearing up every ticket bearing his name.[13]

The will of the people, even when purchased, was still the people's will. It was a worse corruption when outlanders were colonized to outweigh the votes of local residents. "Pipe-laying," as the practice was known, had been around at least since 1838, when New York Whigs brought Pennsylvanians in to vote the ticket, on the pretense that they had come to lay pipe for the city aqueduct. By the 1850s, government control of the public works had become an essential part of the colonization process. Any state-run canal or railroad could shunt workers into districts where incumbent candidates needed them most. Not all partisans were as brazen as Louisiana Democrats in 1855, when they shipped Irish workers into Plaquemines to work on the public works—when no such works used white labor anywhere in the parish. But subtlety did not bespeak moral restraint. If anything, the problem had grown worse by the 1850s, because the parties had discovered how useful railroad could be for carrying floaters where they were most needed. "We saw this at the last election," an Iowan cried. "We see it in every election." Neither party needed public works to produce colonists, but it did give incumbents a special advantage.[14]

In fact, corruptionists could obtain newly made residents from anywhere: sailors along the Great Lakes and in New Orleans proved floaters in more ways than one, at harvest season a doubtful district swarmed with strangers who had come to pick the corn and had been hired just before the election, and Philadelphia witnessed a host of "organ-grinders" who appeared in record numbers just as the city canvass came to a close.[15]

Repeating voters were still more improper and reprehensible than the pipe-layers. Politicians recommended using the latter in their letters, but never the former. A good party man could explain away vote-importation as no more than a redistribution of resources to where they would do the most good. To gain votes here, the party had to yield them there (of course, if the colonists came from another state with an election on a different day, this rationale broke down). Nor did colonization require public officials to act as accomplices in the fraud. Repeating did. Only with the authorities turning a blind eye could the same men vote several times at the same polling-places. Colonization *could* fall within the law—registration laws were lax or nonexistent—but repeating always fell outside it.

Yet repeating occurred, especially in large cities and along the frontier. Seven lumbermen in one precinct in St. Anthony, Minnesota, seized the polling-place, drove off the opposition and cast sixty-three votes. Repeaters could better avoid detection by voting only once in each precinct and then moving to the one next door. Scrupulous San Francisco Democrats changed the clothes on the Sacramento men they voted, before bringing them back a second time. Again, it must be noted that repeating was not an individual's transgression, but one that demanded management from above. Party lieutenants paid off repeaters and kept lists of those electors least likely to show up, so that no repeater would claim the same name as the man just ahead of him in line. Of course, if the state lacked a registration law, such a precaution was needless, but in New York City Democrats found it indispensable as they assembled their "Caravan," a hundred-man group with a thousand names and addresses between them, each worth a vote in some district.[16]

Election officials helped out. Where voter lists were compiled from assessment rolls, city officers added fictitious names to the roster weeks before the election to give newcomers and repeaters aliases enough under which to vote. Philadelphia's list included corpses and long-time nonresidents, and such tactics helped John Slidell's followers in New Orleans earn the nickname "resurrectionist." If the Whig party did not keep an open eye, the New Orleans *Bee* predicted, Democrats would turn all the alligators and oysters upstate into legal voters.[17]

The last form of corruption was the most controversial and excited the most bitter partisan response, for it was the method most associated with the Democrats north and south: the wholesale naturalization of foreigners, long before their time of legal residency had been completed, to swell the vote. Each state set its own restrictions on how long a foreigner must wait before voting, but forgery, false swearing and friendly city judges could make mock of all statutes. Across southern New England, foreigners with papers forged in New York City approached the bench for voting certificates. Elsewhere, the courts became voter-mills just before election, and ground naturalization papers out to all comers. Cincinnati Democrats had their criminal court swear in new citizens in job-lots of a hundred. Within the judge's chambers, the floor was packed, the ground around the courthouse almost inaccessible. New Orleans and New York City provided thousands of naturalization certificates in a day—the day just before the election.[18]

Not everyone objected to such methods. The sudden desire for citizenship at the end of a canvass, defenders claimed, only showed how much foreigners had come to cherish the republican ideals of America; if one party supported rapid naturalization, surely that showed only its compassion for newcomers. But surely there was more fantasy than logic in arguing that foreigners showed their patriotism and parties their selflessness in a deal by which the latter paid for naturalization costs and encouraged perjured oaths of long residence in return for the former pledging his vote, and that was often what happened. Democrats were on stronger ground when they declared that their foes would not have objected to the voter-mills half so loudly had the new electors voted differently.

It was not just naturalization that linked the foreigner with corruption of the ballot. To hear Whigs tell it, foreigners were more easily bought, more conveniently colonized than natives. And why not? They had the least stake in American society and understood republican principles least clearly. They were also so often unskilled: forced to work as day laborers on the railroads, docks, and canals, the very places where the vote was most mobile and labor most transitory, they became prime subjects for colonization. In fact, the honors may have been more even. Many Americans understood party necessity better than they did "republican principles." Even so, that was not the way the Democrats' enemies saw things, and they gave the Irish a special place of dishonor. When Kentuckians crossed the river to vote in Indiana, they were damned as Irishmen; when Lafayette, Indiana, went Democratic, the opposition paper blamed it on "Irish aliens," imported in such numbers that "the very hills adjacent to the city were vocal with 'Erin go Bragh.' . . ." Perhaps they were right. Kentucky Democrats privately explained their own defeat one year on their failure to buy sufficient Irishmen and to import all the foreigners they needed.[19]

The law had an imperfect cure for all these excesses of democracy. Strong residency laws, well enforced, could have done much. No such laws existed. Some states required state but not local residence, which made it easier to shift votes into districts where they would do one party the most good. Iowa demanded a twenty-day residence in the county, other states had no requirements at all. Maine owed its disaster in 1858 to the "Wildcat Law," which let any three persons declare themselves a plantation and set up a voting place. Nor was any residence requirement better than the means for enforcement. Some states with registry laws never let them go farther than the printed page. Thus, Maryland's 1851 constitution mandated a twelve-month residence for any state voter, but the legislature did not pass a registration law to make the provisions effective for another fourteen years, Michigan took ten years to pass a law to implement its constitutional mandate. Where the law existed, officials lagged in making it work.[20]

Even the legal barriers to voting invited fraud. Certainly they did so in Rhode Island, where voters had to pay a dollar registry tax. Poor citizens could not afford it, and, perhaps on the assumption that poor men would vote Democratic, the Whig authorities insisted on keeping the requirement. By the 1850s, however, the law had simply pressed both parties into wholesale purchases of the right to vote. Whichever organization could raise the largest sum to pay off registry taxes with could bring in the heaviest vote. Between buying the right of a poor man to vote and buying the suffrage of a voter already on the books by paying him money, ostensibly to reimburse him for his registry tax, was the smallest of steps. Democrats insisted that Rhode Island had the most corrupt suffrage in the nation.[21] If the number of votes paid for in proportion to the total number cast is any measurement, the Democrats were right.

Pliable election officials did what less supple laws forbade. Election fraud enjoyed official protection at times. By the proper location of polling-places, Chicago officials cut down on the opposition's turnout, and by keeping polls open only briefly in Democratic wards, they made sure that many partisans would be left, ballot in hand, with no place to cast them. The law might demand that any would-be voter not on the assessment list produce a witness to swear his residency, but election judges often ignored the requirement. Where an election inspector was known to be reliable, as in Hillsboro, North Carolina, the party sent all voters rejected in other districts to him. Many honest election officials let transgressions pass out of natural timidity. After all, a voter deprived of his suffrage on suspicions of fraud could sue, and some did. Then the court might fine the officer for misconduct. Physical threats appeared only rarely, but there was one Philadelphia election where an inspector signed certificates declaring both candidates for one office the legal victors. This anomaly was possible, as a later affidavit showed, because one contestant's bullies informed the inspector that if he refused to sign the certificate, they would blow out his brains. Finally, some election officers may have given up strict enforcement from a sense of frustration: what good did it do to refuse a suspect voter, when he could go to the next precinct and cast his vote there instead, when his friends could so easily pay his fine, and when, as in one state, the governor could order prosecutors not to continue with cases of vote fraud?[22]

Corrupt officials were most useful when the votes were counted. It was a common saying that when San Francisco's polls closed "the election had just commenced," and the same could be said for neighborhoods in New York, Chicago, and New Orleans. In a rural Illinois county, officials assured their ally a one-vote majority by altering a precinct's total from a one to a nine, and a notorious San Francisco county supervisor, acting as election inspector, counted the votes to put himself into power—an act of remarkable audacity, since he had not even run for the job.[23]

Thus, the pollution of the ballot-box owed much to the partisan spirit of the early 1850s, but the corruption was worst and most uncontrollable inside the party organizations themselves. City primaries were worse than general elections because no laws governed them at all, nor would they until after the Civil War. No law could assure that each of the rival factions have the right to an inspector at the polls: factions merged and disappeared too quickly for that. Parties found it more difficult than government authorities to keep up-to-date lists of their own members. Consequently, the primaries came in for torrents of abuse, mostly deserved. One Whig faction might bring in Democrats to help it against a rival faction; Lancaster Whigs disagreed only about whether the Democrats had behaved rowdily or with decorum while perverting the selection of convention delegates. So customary did vote-buying become in the primaries that even men who have passed through history with clean reputations thought little of raising a majority that way. Editor Henry Raymond, founder of the New York *Times*, for example, denounced corruption with sincerity. Yet he went to Senator Hamilton Fish to ask $1000 to buy the party's nomination. "[T]ruly a pretty suggestion," Fish jotted in his diary, "but corruption in connection with these primary elections has become so prevalent that one loses astonishment at its evidence in any quarter."[24]

Corrupt and disputed returns begat violence in the party conventions, as contesting delegations battled it out. Each faction did well to bring along bodyguards and strong-arm men to protect its interests. At least twice in the 1850s, New York Democratic conventions turned into riots between competing armies of thugs. City primaries also could turn violent. When New York City Whigs quarreled in 1852, a grand fight followed in the Fifth Ward, in which one man was hurled from a second-story window and the ballot-box was heaved into a back room to forestall the counting of ballots. Smart politicians learned to hire bruisers to assure protection at the polls for at least some of the voters, though bullies could be expensive, especially when they were gang leaders responsible for a coterie of brawlers.[25] Such disorder had a chilling effect on any fair count. "In some wards it has become as much as a man's life is worth to vote at all," the New York Municipal Committee complained in 1854, "unless he votes as he is ordered. In other wards, the respectable citizens of both parties have retired from all primaries in disgust or affright, and abandoned them entirely to bullies or blacklegs, who now have there the especial control."[26]

Blacklegs, colonizing, and naturalization cost money. So the corruption of the ballot-box forced both parties to raise substantial sums to carry the day. A county in Maine, Pike predicted, would cost at least $5000 by the decade's end; New York City battles cost far more—$5000 for a single state senate seat in 1851. Statewide offices cost more still. Charles Gayarre put the Louisiana governorship at $25,000: all of it to manufacture votes in New Orleans, buy up the primaries, and square the press. But from where was the money to come?[27]

Illegitimate and legitimate expenses all came out of the pockets of the party rank and file. In particular, candidates were expected to contribute heavily. Indeed, that was why the parties chose some of them. Not all candidates paid willingly. When Samuel Dickson was told that a Whig nomination for Congress would cost him $1000, he was thunderstruck, but only at the amount. Another nominee had been taxed only half as much, he pleaded. Quite properly, he wondered if the principle of giving nominations to the highest bidder might not end in making "money be the thing & merit or service be thrown entirely out of the question." He had a right to wonder, and he was not alone, though so widespread was the practice that most nominees gave without complaint and in the amount the party directed.[28]

Where the candidate could not provide the sums sufficient to carry the election, the parties used their officeholders and assessed them without mercy. Thus election corruption was not only linked to the party system and to the elected officials enforcing the laws, but to the spoils system itself. Everywhere the collector of customs or postmaster served as party manager. He would provide temporary jobs for loyal voters, he might even dun his employees to pay for the privilege of having colonists brought in. To see that a good turnout was arranged, California Democrats set up new positions across the state: flour inspectors along the coast, census-takers inland, at least one per county. When state and federal spoils systems backed rival candidates, each mustered its officeholders to serve the cause.[29]

Assessments, colonization, vote-buying, violence, rum, rowdyism, creative counting, repeating, striking—it made for gripping drama but an imperfect expression of the people's will. Was it the inevitable price of free government? Some thought so, not the least the Democrats, who used their pessimism to block all efforts at reform. "Corruption will exist," one Iowan argued. "Provide your laws as you will, you cannot entirely prevent it," and therefore, it would seem, should not try to prevent it at all. Laws to compel a longer residence of voters would never work: parties would simply raise more money and bring in outsiders earlier, a Marylander declared. Indeed, by making each vote more expensive, any such change would bring on "a flood of corruption." Whigs and later Republicans took a less pessimistic line. In part, they flattered themselves that their foes did most of the corrupting; in part, they blamed the pollution of the ballot-box on the ease with which any adult male could qualify for the vote regardless of ability. They clamored for reform, and if their desires were sincere, they also were confident that the changes might alter the returns to Democrats' disadvantage. A registry law would leave Democrats in the minority, they agreed, for no fair turnout of people could vote for men so wrong in every way. "If we can once get the State, and pass a good Registry law to protect us from fraud," a Minnesotan wrote, "we are safe for all time to come."[30]

It was not so simple. Reformers did pass laws forbidding bribery of the voters, and a few party caucuses vowed to strike any candidate from the lists who treated electors to win their support. A few states even wrote the ban on bribery into their constitutions. Maryland went farthest in 1851, when it forbade the governor to pardon anyone convicted of the offense. When residency requirements were proposed, however, all consensus vanished. Democrats fought any restriction at all. Outside of New England most states had neither a registry law, naturalization period, nor a demand for a residence longer than a few months. That was just how Democrats preferred it. Forty days' residency before voting in any county? Indiana Democrats pronounced the idea abhorrent and unconstitutional. Let the would-be voter decide for himself at any time he pleased whether he was a resident—even if he came to the community an hour before the polls opened! County residence at all? "What are these county lines?" scoffed an Iowa partisan. Counties were simply "organizations for carrying on the business of the state at large." Should the voter be bound to one place by a legal fiction? In Iowa, Indiana, and elsewhere, reformers tried to pass a registry law and were beaten.[31] Nor could they ban assessment of officeholders.

That left only the parties to keep their foes to a fair count. Only by keeping a close watch could they protect the ballot's purity. But this, like corruption, cost money and added to the need for assessment on government employees. Poll-watchers had to be paid, and the party funded the inspectors that state laws might demand for every precinct. Every party regular became a special deputy of sorts, with duty to keep enemies under scrutiny.[32] No better recipe for violence at the polls could have been proposed: men without legal sanction trying to protect an honest count, against another party aided and financed in its corruptions by funds taken from public employees. And violence there was.

For if one thing is clear, it is that the pollution of the ballot-box had serious effects on American politics, and added to the tensions between different groups. First, it added to the chaos at election time and in the conventions. The knowledge that the two parties were capable of fraud and the intoxication that the practice of treating voters had made a necessary part of Election Day were an explosive combination; add to it the sense that foreigners were being used by Democrats to swindle the American people out of their right to choose officials fairly, and rioting seemed near inevitable. Bullies on either side brandished revolvers and knives at the polls, and what could be brandished could just as easily be used. In 1851, Democratic "short-boys" drove election inspectors out of one ward and chose their own, while in a nearby precinct, Whig rowdies beat every Irishman who came to vote. When the police arrived, the nativists pitched into them for interfering with their amusement. In St. Louis, Whig rioting trimmed the German Democratic vote considerably and ended with two houses aflame and one immigrant dead.[33]

The violence and corruption also undermined the moral sanction on which the parties depended. When delegates to party conventions were chosen in so cavalier a fashion as the city primaries chose them, they lacked the legitimacy that they might have possessed. That made it all the more difficult for a minority to bow to the majority's decisions and made factional fights all the fiercer. A dissident could persuade himself that he and not the majority spoke more nearly the will of the unbought rank and file. Consequently, gatherings exploded with charges that cliques had packed the membership. In most cases, of course, "packing" simply meant that the other side had done a better job of getting its friends to the primary and that they would have a stronger influence in party councils than their faction deserved, but it was also true, as one Whig said in defense of the charge that his side had packed the convention, that for years neither party had held a gathering free of rigged delegate selection. Other assemblies were sundered with charges that one side had voted forged proxies.[34] Whatever the reason, it was argument enough for the losing faction to leave the party and run on its own, and it was just such bolting that weakened the habits of loyalty on which the second party system so relied.

For Whigs, then, the issue of corruption was a serious one, the more so because Democratic managers and immigrant voters seemed most to blame and had most to gain from a polluted franchise; for dissident partisans, corruption inspired desertion from the ranks, but for men already disenchanted with the party system from other causes, the corrupted elections reinforced their sense that the second party system was a fraud. Indeed, for many Americans the corruption must have had a sobering effect. It forced them to question the success of the political structure and of the decisions that elected authorities made. Could men elected by such dubious practices really speak for the people in their districts? Could parties ready to sacrifice all ethics to win office be trusted to uphold the cause of the North or of the South—or would they deal those away, too, for advantage? If the political system itself bore responsibility for the corruption around the elections, then how could any real reform be expected from existing parties? And if no such reforms were begun, could the Republic long survive? Disenchanted with his Whig allies, John Whipple of Rhode Island voiced the most frightening vision. Men paid to vote for one party or the other would find it natural to demand payments in the jury-box, on the city council, or as witnesses in criminal cases. Such a demoralization must spread through society.[35]

What was to be done? Some old Whigs knew what to do, and as the parties began to break up in 1854, they moved to create a new party that, by restricting voting and officeholding to the native-born, would deprive the Democrats of their capacity to commit fraud. Nativists founded secret organizations, commonly called Know-Nothing lodges, and under the more respectable title of the American party they elected mayors, city councilors, legislators, and congressmen who took their point of view.

The Know-Nothing movement was many things. In most places, it rallied those fearful of Catholics or immigrants. As the Whig party collapsed in the mid-1850s, conservative members sought in the new organization a refuge from parties dedicated to slavery's expansion and restriction; other Americans joined to take political advantage of a movement that seemed on its way to majority party status. Whatever its aims, the American party lived only briefly, faded as the slavery issue assumed a new prominence, and died disgraced.

Know-Nothings could storm at the Pope or at ignorant Irish hod-carriers, but they owed their rise to the way in which Whig and Democrat had manipulated the political process as well; and because the Democrats were more famous for illegally voting the foreign-born, Whigs were more likely to join the nativist organization. In upstate Louisiana, they assailed "the court-house clique," in Ohio they decried "a packed, bribed, and drilled convention," and in California and New York City they raged at the citizenship mills that the courts became just before Election Day. Yet the Know-Nothing party was not just Whiggery in a new mask. Democrats disgusted with their own leaders joined too and orators in their speeches attacked "the intrigues of *two* corrupt parties." "When I joined this organization," a Louisianian remarked, "it was with the full reliance that I was joining a 'reform party,' whose aim was to do away with the abuses of the old political parties and to infuse everywhere political honesty." It was in a sense a revolt against the Politician, and most of all in his role as manipulator of the voters; and Know-Nothings often took pains to stress that they had no hostility to the foreigner and no desire to keep him from America's shores—only to end his use as the corrupt tool of designing politicians, by making the voting requirements more strict. Finally, the rise of the Know-Nothings can often be traced to one particularly corrupt election in the cities. New Orleans Whigs, for example, may have allowed the Democrats to stuff the ballot-boxes in late 1853, but they did not suffer the same trick twice. The following spring in the city elections, when 932 registered voters cast 1400 votes in the Seventh Ward, a mob broke into the polling-places, destroyed the ballots, killed several Irishmen, and injured scores more. From then to the end of the decade, the Know-Nothing movement ran New Orleans.[36]

The nativists would not succeed. By 1856, the party formed to punish the politicians looked too much like a party for politicians' benefit. Democrats scourged it as a coalition of plunderers, "broken-down hacks," "office-seeking leeches," and fanatics. In Pennsylvania, Know-Nothing legislators betrayed their reform vows by supporting for senator the recently converted Democrat, Simon Cameron. Cameron had the worst reputation as a corruptionist in the state. In the cities, American political machines showed that they could use fraud, violence, and bribery at the polls as easily as had the Whigs and Democrats. No party based on the purification of politics could afford such a reputation, but in another way the issue of election reform broke down the new party. Formed in 1854, the Republican organization also had a hostility to Democratic vote fraud: who suffered more from it than they in Kansas, Wisconsin, and Pennsylvania? For Republicans' own protection they had to support registry laws, but they also knew that endorsement of such laws was just the bait to draw most Know-Nothings: so seriously did the nativists take the issue of vote fraud that no measure could please them half so much. In New England and New York, Republicans would win the Know-Nothing vote by championing the Know-Nothing cause.[37]

That desire to reform, even restrict the suffrage stayed with the Grand Old Party long after the Know-Nothings had become a mere memory. Though Republicans gave blacks the vote after the Civil War and made sporadic attempts to protect it, they prided themselves on being the upholders of a fair count; it was left to Democrats to emphasize the need for a full one. Across the North, Republicans enacted registry laws, across the South and in major cities they arranged for federal election inspectors. The more reform-minded Liberal Republicans carried still further the loss of faith in the wide-open election process. They had good reasons for skepticism. Elections still were stolen, sometimes by buying floaters (as they may have been in Indiana in 1880 and 1888), and other times by unscrupulous election officials. New laws were passed to limit the voters' power to abuse their suffrage: state supervision of party primaries, literacy tests, the Australian ballot system, and measures to keep minor parties from sharing candidates with each other. All such reforms did not just purify the voting process. They stultified it, actively discouraged the poorer sort from voting at all, strengthened the dominance over office that the two major parties held, and weakened the democratic basis for government generally. Yet the blame cannot rest on the Liberals. The abuses they saw were real and severe restrictions on government by the people in themselves. Excesses in the election process were to blame for the retreat of democratic politics, and those excesses had already reached noticeable and alarming proportions in the years before the sundering of the Union.

4

Offices of Profit and Broken Trust

Straining to defend Governor Hamilton Fish's name, one of his New York friends found all efforts thwarted by one unanswerable reply. "I spoke of your purity," he reported, but the governor's accuser only answered, 'ah he has been in *Albany* a few weeks.' This gave me great pain."[1] The pain was no worse than the pain of many Americans as they viewed their officials in the 1850s. It was the paradox of the age that citizens defended democratic government as the best, their own government as the most democratic, and their officeholders as among the worst in the world. Lobbyists might bribe a lawmaker, appellants might buy a judge, but they did not corrupt them. Politicians, it would seem, could no more be made worse by outside stimuli than prostitutes could be debauched by their clientele.

Newspapers were quick to see the legislative branch at its worst, even when the editor and the lawmakers came from the same party. Indecorous and quarrelsome, state representatives met for two months of indolence followed by two or three days of bustle, during which hundreds of bills passed or failed without a reading. New Yorkers celebrated their Thanksgiving in April each year when the General Assembly adjourned, even though they grudgingly conceded that Pennsylvania's legislature was more purchasable still—and Pennsylvanians agreed. Reportedly, anyone who wanted a price list of members on the market could get one at Harrisburg. Elsewhere lawmakers closed their session in a quarrel over which party had filched more books and knives by padded expense accounts. Never ones to waste words, Indianans ended deliberations by throwing books at each other.[2]

Most of the pilfering that reporters mentioned was petty enough, the sort of profiteering that contemporary Americans see in Congressional junkets and increased perquisites. In the 1850s, more critics would have called it corruption. How much members took, they would have argued, mattered less than that anything had been taken. Officials were not meant to grow rich from their positions nor to take more than the expenses of mileage and supplies necessary for their duties. Instead, it seemed that electees would bend every law to add to their share, and this, said critics, betrayed their public trust.

Congress seemed to afford the best pickings, if only because it met longer than did any other assemblage. In collecting for mileage, members would overestimate distances, sometimes with a better sense of fantasy than geography. If payments indicated distance, Ohio stood twice as far west of Capitol Hill as Kentucky. Sometimes, mileage computations broke the law outright. Taking away the Treasury's power to audit members' accounts in 1850, the Senate declared that each member should be the sole judge of his own case. "Constructive mileage" excited more public controversy: paying senators as if they had journeyed home and back between the close of one session and the opening of the next later the same day. In 1849 and 1851 most senators took it without apologies. Indeed, by 1851 some members showed a constructive memory to match their mileage, and protested that the six-year-old practice had gone on without interruption since 1789. But the press outcry became so loud that most aspiring Presidential candidates and nearly all Whigs refused to touch the windfall. In 1852 they did away with it entirely.[3]

Congressmen supplemented their salaries in other ways. Every session the clerks provided them with free documents and books, as well as twenty-four copies of the *Congressional Globe*. These the lawmakers sold back to the clerks, who would then give them to members of the next House and pay to take them back again. In 1857, House officers saved themselves exertion by giving freshmen a choice between sets of the *Globe* and their money equivalent. All 131 new House members preferred the cash. "I may say that a more wasteful, more prodigal, more wicked system of disbursing the public money never existed on earth," one senator raged. Perhaps he was the more upset because of the example public officials were setting for their appointed officers. In 1858, a Congressional investigation showed that while the government printed costly books for free distribution among the people, the House doorkeepers got to them first. As soon as volumes left the press, the functionaries spirited them out of the supply room and sold them below cost to city booksellers. In return for their aid in this traffic, congressmen received a large supply of books to pass on to public libraries back home. These too ended up on the shelves of Washington bookshops, and the profits ended in congressmen's wallets.[4]

State legislators too collected for fraudulent mileage, per diem paid for days not in session, newspapers bought by the dozens, books sold and the profits pocketed. None of the scandals excited more than a few days of controversy, though the speaker of the Arkansas house was so displeased at one attempt to collect pay for a recess that he resigned in protest. One Massachusetts assemblyman outdid all rivals in sharpness. Noting that his colleagues had been paid for one hundred days and had met for only sixty-five, he offered a deal: since he had not attended at all, he would ask payment only for the thirty-five days during which he and his fellow-members had been at home![5]

Scandals in the executive branch threw those of pilfering legislators into perspective. True, much of the "stealing" was of the same trivial sort. Michigan's State Treasurer took travel money to visit Vermont and as a member of the Board of State Auditors ruled on his own account. The trip, he explained, was to examine the capitol in Montpelier, to compare it with Michigan's planned construction—a poor argument, since the Vermont statehouse had burned down just before he made the trip. But other thievery was of a more serious nature. To spend too much on pens or papers only added slightly to taxpayers' costs, but by pilfering from the departments they ran, members of the executive branch took advantage of citizens helpless to protect themselves. In New York, Ohio, Wisconsin, and California, investigations showed a systematic plundering of public services for the poor, the imprisoned, and handicapped. The resident physician at the California lunatic asylum drew pay for employees long since discharged. He also put inmates to work assembling a personal collection of over one hundred stuffed birds, animals, and reptiles. New York's prison investigation revealed padded accounts, vouchers passed in for work never done, supplies that never got to the convicts for which they were intended, and work at embroidery and shirtmaking that prisoners did for one inspector's family. At Sing Sing, the prison agent owned a cemetery nearby and used the convicts to keep it in repair and to cut and dress the marble.[6]

The worst stealing took place in the state treasury itself, because financial juggling was possible there without too much publicity. California's State Treasurer mislaid nearly $50,000 through incompetence in executing bonds. The comptroller's clerk extracted $100,000 in cash and replaced it with $100,000 in warrants worth sixty cents on the dollar. Then he vanished. Indiana uncovered defalcations by both treasurer and auditor.[7]

How could such scandals have happened? To stress the depravity of the men guarding the coffers provides too easy an explanation. Instead, more respectable men in politics and business must share the blame. Behind the defaulting officials stood promoters who profited from an illicit partnership of private enterprise with public revenue. Behind the embezzlers, too, stood the party leaders who brought them into the treasury, protected them while they were there, extracted a share of the proceeds for the party, and apologized for or concealed their crimes after the scandal broke. In at least four cases, the guilt touched many prominent figures, as the treasurer did what partisan ethics and business practice had so encouraged.

Vermont State Treasurer Henry M. Bates came closest to working alone. Until his exposure, he had kept a good reputation. His home town could always depend on the former bank cashier for heavy contributions to the Republican ticket at each state election. Such generosity assured him a regular renomination, but the money was not all his own. Over six years, Bates had borrowed heavily from the banks in the state's name and failed to jot down the transaction in the books. He speculated badly in marble and soapstone firms and in buying farmland that had "verd antique marble" on it. Late in 1860 he confessed himself short $48,000 in public funds. At once the governor ordered the attachment of Bates's property to secure Vermont against loss. At once was not soon enough. Already warned, the treasurer had deeded his lands to one of his bondsmen and fled. Democrats screamed that some of their members had known about the defalcation for two years and had warned Republican officials in vain, though if so, the former's silence over the interval showed a charity toward their foes unparalleled in public life.[8]

Party considerations ran more strongly through Maine's scandal that year. There, Republicans had placed former clergyman Benjamin D. Peck in charge of the treasury. A former editor of the *Temperance Journal*, "Elder" Peck had as high a reputation as Bates. Republicans prized his attacks on the ungodly, vice-ridden Democracy. Once in office, however, temptations overwhelmed the Elder. "I had not got warm in my seat," he later confessed, ". . . before I was urgently importuned by some of my bondsmen and others, to loan the money of the State, and for this reason—that I could in this way add to my income from office." It seemed so easy. Republican bankers would take state money as deposits,

Republican leaders would draw low-interest loans from the treasury for timber speculation, and Peck would be taken in on the ground floor on some larger deals. Ignore the fact that the law forbade the treasurer to involve himself in trade or commerce as a factor or broker agent or to find any way of profiting by state money, either by placing it in banks or lending it out for personal benefit—the temptation was overwhelming.

Peck gave in at once. Not only did he borrow or misuse $94,023.99 in public money, but he managed to borrow or extort $36,000 more from the banks, which no doubt presumed that indulging the treasurer would show good business sense. Some revenues went for "expenses" outside the Elder's official salary: living costs, home repairs, a horse and carriage, contributions to churches and party nominees. Some $82,673.60 was lost in Canadian timber speculations. In partnership with "gentlemen in high social and political standing," as Peck called them, and with their rubber checks and government funds, the Canada firm bought 266 square miles of woodland, plus a sawmill and booms. Peck still thought himself barely within the law. He would rifle the treasury, but replace the funds with money borrowed as a private individual. Then expenses mounted. The speculation grew beyond control. Beginning as a mere $35,000 venture, it doubled in cost. Setting up a sawmill took longer than expected, selling the timber proved impossible. As costs mounted, Peck took more from the till and failed to replace it with private loans. Exposure was inevitable.[9]

We might sympathize with Peck, but not with Silas Holmes and John McKinney, Michigan State Treasurers in the late 1850s. They were rascals to the marrow, and McKinney would end up in prison. When Holmes took the job, he was quick to use it to oblige C. T. Anthony, his former partner in the Detroit dry-goods trade, with a $16,000 loan. That was a modest prologue to Holmes's transaction with Hazleton & Co. of New York. Having agreed to buy $263,000 in Michigan bonds, the firm guaranteed to provide a $4000 premium to the state. It never did so. Nor did it produce the purchase price for the securities. Before the bonds were handed over to Hazleton & Co., the law demanded that it offer security for their payment. None was given or sought. In return for such a free use of state funds, the treasurer obtained $3800 in "loans" which he was assured need never be repaid. Silence was golden, indeed! Holmes never mentioned the company's irresponsibility during his term. Auditor-General Whitney Jones knew about the treasurer's malfeasance; he had seen the accounts. But the two men were inextricably intertwined in their business dealings, so he too kept silent.[10]

Out went Holmes, in came McKinney, but the arrangement only worsened. To repair the Sault Ste. Marie Canal, Michigan floated a loan and issued $100,000 in bonds. Again Hazleton & Co. won the bidding, by promising a $3000 premium on them. In July 1859 the treasurer traveled to New York to collect the purchase price. Holmes and Jones went along. Already bankers were murmuring that the canal loan was unconstitutional and the bonds an unsafe investment. McKinney may have expected trouble, but Hazleton & Co. had made a contract, and there was no reason to doubt the company's good faith; Jones and Holmes assured McKinney that the firm had an unblemished record for square dealing. Then, to McKinney's amazement, Hazleton & Co. told him that they would pay only $53,000 in cash. The other $50,000 they wanted to keep for up to a month to help, as they claimed, to negotiate the sale of the bonds. McKinney must take a promissory note for it. The firm would credit him for the whole $103,000 at the Artisans' Bank, as long as he would not collect it all just yet. For security on that loan, Michigan was offered the bonds of a land-grant railroad between Flint and Saginaw that had not yet been built.

McKinney consulted Jones and Holmes and was given complete reassurance. Later, Democrats would charge that Jones had been slated to be president of a Lansing bank that the Hazletons meant to set up, and that Holmes and McKinney numbered among the foremost stockholders without advancing a penny of their own, but the accusations cannot be proven. All that was certain was that McKinney came home with half the sum he should have brought, that he lied to the governor about his dealings, and that the governor did not choose to probe the details of the trip too far. A less discreet Board of State Auditors did examine McKinney's accounts and revealed the shortfall that autumn. The governor hastened to New York to obtain new guarantees for the public funds. These guarantees proved worthless. The Artisans' Bank, never lustrous for its integrity, but sure to give the treasurer a bonus for letting state funds be deposited there, overextended its operations and closed down. The scandal that broke in January 1860 rocked the state and deprived the governor, auditor-general, and treasurer of renomination.[11]

"A more high-minded, incorruptible man than Silas M. Holmes never held office in this State," a Republican paper boasted. That was the official cry of every organ about the whole state administration. Insiders knew better. With the fall elections behind them, Republicans ordered an investigation. McKinney was summoned, but refused to testify. The senate locked him in the city jail for contempt. His Deputy Treasurer

Hunter gave so incredible an account of affairs that the investigating committee concluded that he was concealing every transaction he could not deny outright and lied in his every explanation. Holmes contradicted Hunter, but the investigators branded him a liar as well. How much had been stolen could not be proven, because between the day that the investigation began and the day on which he was summoned to testify, Hunter systematically destroyed all the books and papers in the treasury that might concern the financial tangle. The treasury account-books could be produced, but they did not mention public monies lent to private parties or deposited in banks. These accounts, it turned out, had been kept in side-books since Holmes's time, and these books had disappeared. The main account-books mentioned gross sums received by officials for payment of interest by railroads still in debt to the state. Nowhere did they say from whom the money came or whether this was all that they paid or on what account. Such practice was worse than slipshod. It was done purposely to conceal embezzlement.

Uncertain though it was about the actual numbers, the investigating committee had no doubt that Holmes, Hunter, and McKinney had profited shamelessly from their offices. A firm owed money to the state as well as a personal debt to Holmes, who took his money from that paid by the company to the commonwealth. McKinney drew money from the treasury for personal use without vouchers and without the warrant from the Attorney-General that the law demanded. Railroads paid their debts to McKinney in person, and the money went no farther. Just before leaving office, the treasurer stole $2100 from the vaults in cash and cashed checks in the commonwealth's name at a bank.[12] The scandal was even worse than Democrats had said, and they had never failed of imagination in describing Republicans' misconduct.

There was no room for Democratic gratification in Ohio when a similar scandal broke out there, for two of the three guilty parties were of their own party. For months, rumors had circulated that something was very wrong in the Republican-run treasury. A legislative investigation had shown serious mismanagement by William H. Gibson's predecessors, but just how far the scandal went became clear only in June 1857, when the news broke that the state was missing over $650,000. The vaults were virtually empty. The first reports hinted that Gibson had embezzled money for land speculation in Minnesota, and even though Governor Salmon Chase forced him to deliver up the keys at once, Democrats demanded a full investigation of these Republican frauds.[13]

The story that came out made spicy reading for both parties. For ten years, custodians of the public funds had convinced themselves that those who helped themselves could never do wrong by their party. In 1847, Democrats had installed Albert A. Bliss as treasurer. A practicing attorney who did well and wanted to do better, he found a way at once. Leading Columbus bankers rushed to become his bondsmen. In return, they wanted to hold state funds for their reserves and promised Bliss a share in the profits from investing state money. One institution alone gave him a $4000 profit each year. So well did Bliss fare that he was soon able to acquire $30,000 in stock in the City Bank of Cincinnati, though he did it with public funds and under two dummy names. On a salary of $1200 a year, Bliss bought $25,000 in stock in the Summit County Bank, $4800 in Columbus City Bank stock, $4000 in Lorain Bank stock, extensive tracts of real estate—all of it, he later insisted, by tapping his own private income. Investigators were unimpressed by his plea that when he wrote checks on the Ohio treasury to pay for these purchases, he did so "as a mere convenience."[14] Certainly Bliss's reign was a convenience for the banks with state deposits; they prospered more than any others. So did railroad companies, assured of easy loans because Bliss had dipped into the sinking fund for Ohio's canal system to grant them aid.

As talk of misconduct spread, Democrats resolved to try a different treasurer. In 1851, they nominated John G. Breslin, a man of great abilities, fine manners, and intense ambition. In the campaign that followed, he all but pledged that he would end Bliss's wrongdoing. By the time he assumed office, his resolution had faltered. The outgoing officer was $65,000 short in his accounts, though he repaid some of it later (how much is unclear: Bliss kept the books so badly that he himself could give no sound explanation of where the money went). Some $85,000 that the accounts overlooked also had vanished, but Breslin did not harry his predecessor about it. Instead, he made friends with Bliss's clients, took over the loans that Bliss had extended the railroads, and renewed the arrangement with the banks. Bankers tumbled over one another in offering Breslin the greatest inducements to patronize them. As owner of the Marion Bank, State Supreme Court Justice Ozias Bowen outbid the rest by promising a 5 percent return on all public funds. Using Bowen's cashier as a front, Breslin became a major stockholder in the Marion concern.

Halcyon days followed. Important Democrats obtained loans on easy terms from the treasury, Democratic newspapers had money advanced them. Breslin became a railroad promoter and incorporator on Ohio funds. In 1855, when Democrats renominated him, it was genius on Breslin's part to have the Republicans nominate his brother-in-law Gibson as his opponent. Already, Gibson had become Breslin's partner in major investments. In 1854, Breslin had advanced enough public money to establish the Seneca County Bank, and Gibson had become its president. Within two years, the impecunious lawyer had turned into an investor in banks in Indiana and Maryland and president of a railroad company. Gibson thus had every reason to keep the accounts secret when Republicans came to power, and so he did. Leading Republicans asked for loans and got them. Republicans investigated and took Gibson's word that the books balanced or soon would. By the time the treasury was emptied, Breslin was in Canada, beyond the law's clutches.[15] Nobly, he took all the responsibility for the shortfall, but he did not return to stand trial.

All four stories had one or two themes in common, and they revealed much about the countless lesser defalcations as well. First, they showed that to many public servants the proceeds of their offices seemed theirs almost by right, to use as they would—as long as nothing was missing when time came for an accounting. If old copper from outmoded vessels was discarded, navy yard employees saw no wrong in taking it to sell at a profit. Nor did D. S. French, an Indiana county treasurer, see how he had transgressed in lending out public funds to political friends. When the courts cut his term short, he denied moral responsibility for the missing $4,781.90. After all, he argued, if he had served his full term, the debts would have been repaid and no one out a penny.[16]

At the same time, many officeholders insisted that they had the right to add to their own compensation or define it; that the legal rates were not an established salary, but a minimum from which to begin. Just such a faith made Navy Agent Prosper Wetmore insist that he had the right to $200,000 more than his salary. The federal government paid agents for doing certain specific duties, he argued. Any extra business that he did for the public should be repaid with fees that he could set as he chose. The Grand Rapids county treasurer agreed to return three-quarters of the tax revenue he had purloined, but demanded the rest as due him for having done official work in the twenty days beyond the expiration of his term. Federal district attorneys, marshals, district court clerks—all, like legislators, construed the law to get the highest payment possible, and the step from collecting fees not belonging to them to embezzling funds already gathered was a short one.[17]

In some cases, indeed, the defalcations came from ignorance of what the law said or how much had been borrowed. Those who juggled the public funds needed accounting skills to tell how much was left or to find ways of replacing it, but the spoils principle assured that many public servants would barely know how to add and subtract. During his first year in office, Gibson rarely visited the capital, never counted the treasury funds, and never let his subordinates into the vaults to find out. "I attempted to keep my private funds distinct from the public funds," he explained, "but found it difficult to do so." So tangled were Ohio transactions, the investigating committee concluded, that if all three peculating treasurers and their business friends sat down with the account-books before them, they could not have come up with a credible explanation of where the money had gone. Philadelphia's county treasurer defaulted on $175,000, but where it went was unclear. Running an ice-cream parlor on the side, the officer had poured public money into it, but was not sure how much. As a witness testified, he could not tell the debit from the credit side in the books.[18]

If ignorance about the details, major defaulters knew what they were doing well enough. To claim that they had simply misinterpreted the discretionary powers of office persuaded no one, for they used every means to keep their actions secret. They filed false vouchers for expenses, dispensed money to imaginary people, bought stock under false names, forged other officials' names on government warrants, destroyed the incriminating evidence, and when investigation began, fled the country for places where they could protest their innocence without having to prove it.[19]

But it was not the cupidity of mere individuals that brought about the shortfalls: that was the second important point. The real blame should have been accorded to the way the economic and political system worked—a system of profit for banks panting to become depositories, for railroads and lumber companies accustomed to a financial partnership with officeholders and ready to convince them that it was standard practice. It was the fault of a party system that saw every office as a reward and a position in which the appointee had the right to make all the profit for himself that he legitimately could, as long as the party shared in his good fortune. Lastly, it was the fault of a partisan age, in which, for the sake of unity, law-abiding men closed their eyes to malfeasance and protected the defaulters in their ranks.

Men inveighed against the rascally treasurers and indicted them. But in every state, it was the bankers and businessmen who expected loans or rights of deposit and encouraged the treasurers' greed by becoming their sureties and using the privilege they bestowed to make public officers forget their duties. That there was a relationship between agreeing to act as bondsmen and seeking influence may not have been as clear to officeholders as it seems in retrospect. Benjamin B. French, for example, needed securities before he could act as Commissioner of Public Buildings in Washington, D.C., in 1853. He feared trouble in raising backers. Instead, he was deluged with offers. "This shows the confidence of the people here in me," he boasted.[20] He may have been right, but it is tempting to imagine that his recent service as the President's campaign manager, assistant private secretary, and confidante may have entered the bondsmen's minds.

Both state and county treasurers took it as established custom to make alliances with the bankers, deposit the money in preferred establishments, and collect interest on it as their personal perquisite. County treasurers unwilling to lend out funds to speculators could please them by letting them "assort" the currency, which usually meant the replacement of valuable bank notes paid into the treasury for taxes with depreciated warrants. "So intimately blended were the transactions of County Treasurers and small bankers," said Ohio's investigators,

> that in some parts of the State . . . upon court houses were bankers' signs, and from the very doors of the Treasurer's office protruded 'Bank,' while within, occupying the same office, and owning the safe in partnership with the county, was the banker who loaned the people's money at three per cent. per month and perhaps 'assorted' for the Treasurer.

It had become standard practice. "Other treasurers had done it," Elder Peck pleaded, "and it was generally known that all treasurers would do it."[21]

Indeed they would, when the political system allowed them an apology, a long concealment, and a friendly climate. As Senator, Salmon Chase wrote a letter hailing the City Bank of Cincinnati as "no doubt a safe institution . . . managed by excellent and liberal men," and the Mechanic's and Trader's Bank as one "with which I do all my own business." He had set pen to paper to persuade his old ally Breslin to deposit state funds there, and there the money stayed until both firms went bankrupt. Chase made no profit from his letter and in both cases also stressed that he knew about the institution only from common fame, but under the party system of the 1850s, no treasurer could ignore the senator his party had elected. It was no accident that Ohio treasurers gave easy loans to their own parties' organs, or that Gibson should lend money to Kimball & Co. of Cleveland, a company headed by Republican Attorney-General Francis I. Kimball. Nor was it too surprising that those "gentlemen in high social and political standing" that Peck indulged with loans included prominent Republicans like Neal Dow and Democrats Ezra Carter, Jr., former Portland customs collector, and Dudley F. Leavitt—nor that all three had posted bonds for his good performance in office.[22]

Not that other public officials knew about the defalcations long before they occurred. Usually they knew nothing for sure. They did their best not to know. Government scrutiny was deplorably remiss. In Ohio, for example, the state made regular inspections of the treasurer's books until Bliss came in. Then the examinations ceased, but no one complained about it. Only in 1856 did the legislature compel periodic inspections, though neither the law that year nor the statute passed the next caught the mutual malfeasance of Bliss, Breslin, and Gibson. At times the treasurer could put on a good enough show to gull well-intentioned investigators. To conceal his deficit, Gibson borrowed $200,000 to brandish when the inquisitors arrived. He showed promissory notes from banks for money they owed the state, to show where much of the money had gone, and never added that the notes had already been redeemed and were no better than waste paper any longer. Yet one must conclude that the examiners in most states were deceived because they wanted to be. Maine's legislature chose a committee that hurtled through its inspection and came to rosy, entirely false conclusions about Peck's administration. Neal Dow himself sat on the whitewashing committee. Similar investigations hoodwinked the public in Vermont, Indiana, and elsewhere.[23]

Other state officers were not just ignorant of what their colleagues were doing. They fell over themselves trying to stay ignorant.* For months, Ohio's Board of Public Works had known about Breslin's dealings. It did not even try to block his renomination. Michigan's governor failed to question Gibson about his transactions in New York because he thought such an action "impertinent." Maine's governor claimed that he had long had reason to suspect Peck. Even so, he retained him in office for months longer.[24]

The result was that righteous partisans would claim that they knew how badly matters had been handled all along—after the scandal broke. Vermont Republicans admitted that they had known about Bates's irreg-

*The same wilful blindness struck the Maine treasurer's business partners. Neal Dow swore that he had warned Peck never to lend to any man unable to repay the sum at once—which Dow could not do, either. Peck's timber-speculating cronies all claimed that they had never thought the treasurer a man of private means, but denied all suspicion that he might have used public funds for his capital; how he could have produced such large sums they did not know. "The Committee have no desire to bandy contradictions with Mr. Leavitt," the committee report added, ". . . but they could hardly help feeling that his declarations and some others with which they were favored on this topic, were little less than an insult to their intelligence."

ularities for some time and said nothing. Peck's defalcation surprised Republican James S. Pike, but that treasury affairs had been mismanaged did not. From doing business with the treasurer, he confided to a friend, he had seen that Peck was utterly unfit. So Ohio Republican James Ashley had felt about Gibson from the first, and his suspicions intensified when Gibson had refused to let the legislature see his account-books. But only after the treasurers were dismissed did Ashley or Pike voice his suspicions and then only in private. No partisan blew the whistle on men in his own party.[25]

When a postmortem investigation had to be made, the same partisanship colored the final report. Maine Republicans chose a committee headed by young James G. Blaine. He gave a cursory report, skirted over Peck's connections with the banks, and rebuked the Republican accomplices discreetly. Usually the report left the treasurer as whipping-boy for the multitudes abetting him. The same spirit also let some defaulters escape with their gains. Though Gibson was forced to surrender the keys in June 1857, Ohio took another year before it tried to force restitution of those public funds he still held. In June 1858 the former officer still wandered free in New York with $132,000 of public funds in his keeping. No legal efforts were made to force Breslin to settle until more than twelve months had passed. By then, he had transferred his property into other states' jurisdiction. Indeed, Gibson's hand reached into the treasury for long after his dismissal. Within a week of leaving office, he received $22,000 that two institutions owed Ohio; he did not rush to pass it on to the new treasurer. A year later, he arranged for the state to lend him $14,000 more through an intermediary firm.[26]

The party system thus made official peculation easier. It also shifted the terms of debate into the narrow channel of individual impropriety. In the 1830s it might have been different, for Democratic hostility to the banks was at its strongest. Then the party of Jackson would have pointed out that such swindles were natural when financial institutions treated tax revenues as deposits and made partnerships with the custodians of the people's money. Then the scandals in Maine, Ohio, and Michigan would have been used to indict the tie between bankers and bureaucrats. But times had changed, and so had the men at the head of the Democratic party. Two decades after Andrew Jackson's attack on the "Monster Bank" the parties preferred three alternative explanations for wrongdoing.

First, they might blame *bad men* for all that went wrong and turn the evil into one that new leaders would cure. Second, they could make the debauchery a lesson in partisan loyalties. The stealing was all the fault of

Republicans, the blame lay on all Democrats. If the people would only turn to the party of All Honest Men, no such scandals would happen. Third, and most convenient for escaping their own sins, the party in power could blame that vague, general atmosphere of ethical laxity that the 1850s spawned. For that, the only true cure was a broad popular reawakening. The system itself needed no change. Everyone was to blame, and so no one was specifically at fault.

This tergiversation showed up worst in the party to which the embezzlers belonged. No one could question Governor Chase's integrity. He had fired Gibson and sought Democrats to lead an independent investigation of the state treasury. Yet Chase did little to harry the fallen officer and much to belittle Republicans' guilt. "Breslin took every dollar of the money," he told an audience. "There was not one dollar of the people's money taken by any officer of the Republican administration. There was not a dollar of it in the treasury when the Republican party assumed the Government." If there was any crime by Gibson, the Republican press chimed in, it was only his heartfelt loyalty to a greedy brother-in-law. By raising the issue of the empty treasury, Democrats were but trying to hide their own robberies of the treasury, lunatic asylum, state house construction funds, and canal system (the voters were not impressed, as Republicans found when the votes were counted that October). With considerable—if wasted—imagination, Vermont Republicans blamed Democrats for Bates, because the opposition had known about the thieving for two years and not brought it to public attention.[27]

Many reforms could be tried, and some were. A few states, notably Ohio, put through an independent treasury that held public funds and kept them from being deposited in banks. New constitutions forbade any collector of public money to sit in the legislature until he had settled his accounts, set specific rates for lawmakers' mileage and per diem and restricted their expenses on supplies, and did away with the extra compensation and special fees that officers took for doing work for the state. Maryland's constitution abolished the attorney-generalship entirely because his post had such notorious fees and spoils.[28] But if anything, public morals worsened over the decade.

Amerians could not shrug off the embezzlements and despoliation as the price of democratic politics. The consequences of a venal government were as alarming as that venality was newly visible. Public officials might represent the commonwealth. They might represent their constituents and the local interests. Either was acceptable to republican political economy. What was not acceptable was a leadership that represented itself. Then its decisions became tainted: neither the will of the people nor of the nation were served, only that of the profit-takers. Those decisions deserved no respect, nor did the men who made them.

When the issue was minor, this lack of respect was not so serious a matter. When it was an issue of broad sectional or ideological importance, the lack of trust in the placemen's good intentions became catastrophic, and here it was that the partisan argument that everyone was on the take, that corruption was not one party's fault but was the spirit of the age, proved itself most dangerous. If one was predisposed to believe that lawmakers could be bought and sold, that state officers acted for the money they could gain and that their more circumspect brethren would shield them from attack, how could one trust a sectional compromise that gave either North or South special advantage? How could one trust that Democrats who broke the official party line to support a canal-repair bill or a steamship subsidy had been swayed by reason? Each treasury-robber stole a little from the trust on which the Union itself was based.

II

Pathology — The Corruption of Government Favors

5

Suckers, Strikers, Borers, and Bribes

"Congress is a humbug!" Benjamin B. French raged in a letter to his brother Henry, "—and Washington is—no place for an honest man." But Washington *was* a place for French, for he was what Americans in his day described as a "borer," the era's most disreputable profession. French was a lobbyist and a gifted one.

Political theory provided no place in a republic for lobbyists, corrupt or not. Disinterested legislators were supposed to enact the measures required by public interest or at least the people's will; Presidents and judges were supposed to put that legislation into effect. But by the 1850s, not all the real policy-makers sat on Capitol Hill or around the Cabinet table. Observers spotted them in the hotel lobbies as well. In 1853 a Washington corespondent could pick out borers in abundance: mail contractors, Texas bond speculators, claims agents, steamship subsidy men, New York dry-dock promoters, and the lobbies' purchased reporters—an all-too-imposing crew.[1]

For all the prating of the press, lobbies did not exist simply because of the depravity of special interests. Nor were they so new a phenomenon, though Americans found them more visible and common than in past years. In the complex world of public legislation, private parties had always had to make the case for themselves. Any old ideals of how public business should be conducted had never been well followed. By the 1850s, they were more dated than ever. To restrict lawmakers' authority, state constitutions had cut legislative sessions short. With so little time for handling business, the last days of a session resembled bad days in a madhouse. Measures passed without discussion or were buried without a hearing. Editors boasted that elected officials came "fresh from the people," which meant that no one was given much chance to master political rseponsibilities. Many general assemblies were elected for one-year terms, and most legislators could not expect renomination: under the second party system, each community in a district demanded a term for its favorite son. Members assumed power without legislative experience to guide them and left office before they quite knew what they were doing. Committee chairmen could hardly give guidance on legislation when they had not even mastered the rules of order, and even committees in Congress were lucky if the majority would permit them the services of a single clerk.[2] Perhaps the chance to turn legislative position into a career would have made incumbents more responsible, though this is mere conjecture; and many an experienced politician became experienced in stealing. What is clear is that such a democratic turnover and such a lack of professional help assured that the legislative branch would lack talent and would compound petty localism with inexperience. What the short lease on power did to legislatures, the spoils system and doctrine of "rotation in office" did to members of the executive branch. They were not hired for their skills but for their party services, and if they lasted four years they counted themselves lucky.

Thus while the need for legislation had grown, the skill of officers to deal with lawmaking had declined. What business could afford to leave its interests in the hands of a body full of parochial interests, especially when most other businesses had sent agents ready to give certain measures priority? "The mass of the members are a thoughtless, careless, light-hearted body of men, who come here for the 'per diem' and to spend the 'per diem,'" one lobbyist explained to his employers. Quickly officials' sense of responsibility vanished. Then "they become as wax to be moulded by the most pressing influences."[3] A lobby was vital, to assure that the legislative wax took the proper imprint, and some lawmakers welcomed the intruders as sources of professional guidance and expertise about the matter on which they were most concerned. With some justice, the Albany *Atlas* complained that the lobby had virtually superseded the legislature, for in some respects it had. Agents might write the laws that members proposed or produce written arguments that members could invoke as their own, and they carried the decision-making process into hotel rooms and dining halls.[4]

By 1850, there were lobbies for almost everything: New York businessmen who hoped to preserve the Trinity Church's property rights, promoters who wanted a special charter for an East River ferryboat line or the defeat of someone else's special charter, entrepreneurs who just wanted to be let alone. Whatever their needs, they looked to the "third house" for comfort. New York City officials hired agents to check the caprices of upstate legislators. In a telling testimonial to the importance of such outside pressure, a Louisiana senator informed his constituents that no lawmaker could assure them of its fair share of river and harbor improvement money, but that a lobby of "men of influence and ability" could. So ubiquitous was the lobbyist that he even invaded legislative chambers and rested his feet on members' desks (though when one intruder dared to try it in the Speaker's chair he was thrown out and his claim with him). Newspapermen had to swear that they represented no special interest before Congress let them prowl the floor, but no one took the oath seriously. In Hartford and Trenton, interested parties sat next to state senators, suggested amendments to bills, called them off the floor to persuade them, and disrupted business by conversing too loudly.[5]

How did the lobby work? How well did it work? Since agents were more frank about their efforts than their successes, the first question is more easily answered than the second, but the good wire-puller wanted as little publicity about methods and results as possible, even when those methods were above reproach. When a court case threatened to publicize their names, Massachusetts's most influential persuaders were thrown into a panic. The best borers covered their tracks well. To plead the claimant's case in public, they hired thoroughly respectable front men with close connections to party leaders. An agent might, as Congressman Orsamus Matteson did, denounce schemes openly that he took pay to sustain privately, and insist that he was making the case only for wicked, nameless third parties. Other lobbyists feigned distinterested motives for support for a measure, or claimed that they were lobbyists for an entirely different matter than the one that brought them to the Capitol.[6]

Companies welcome the secrecy, and not only because any law passed by bribery would be annulled the moment reformers tied the beneficiaries to corrupt tactics. If directors were kept in the dark about what methods their emissaries used, they could profess a naïve outrage at any wrongs committed and lay all blame on the lobbyist. They might even withhold payment of a lobbyist's fee on that account after practicing a deliberate and selective ignorance, as the Baltimore & Ohio did in the case of Alexander J. Marshall. Marshall's maxim was one that others practiced: "the company should have or know but one agent . . . and let that agent select the sub-agents from such quarters and classes, and in such numbers as his discreet observation may dictate."[7] Such a policy encouraged shady dealings and the abdication of moral responsibility. It also meant that when an investigation took place, the final report almost never linked the wrongdoers with company officials or with government figures. Always it was wicked lobbyists who were involved, acting beyond corporate authority and leading public officials astray. Thus the lobby became a protective buffer between businessmen and congressmen on one side and a wrathful public on the other.

Under the circumstances, lobbyists had a right to expect high pay for the risks they ran. On paper at least, they were well sated. At its best, influence-peddling assured easy money for minimal work. Businesses preferred to pay lavishly, since they were paying not only for services but for discretion, but usually they arranged the payment as a proportion of the sum they expected the lobbyists' influences to raise from government action. That way, as Marshall pointed out, agents would work their hardest.[8] It may also have made them less scrupulous, for success was a chancy thing at best, even for a zealous borer.

No agent could have outworked Benjamin French, but half his work came in collecting what his clients owed him after their claims were won. Always he began the legislative session blinded with visions of opulence. The most promising, least savory schemes found him a ready defender: the Ebony steamship line, French spoliation claims, Thomas Ritchie's printing contract, the Mexican War indemnity, Indian claims, and those of guano prospectors on Pacific islands. To his chagrin, things always would go wrong. Just at the hour of victory, his clients would revoke his power of attorney and vest it elsewhere. Indian claims would pass Congress, only to vanish into the courts. Employers failed to pay or passed on rubber checks. At session's end, French would bewail his modest profits and announce, "If ever a fellow was sick of [claims and subsidy bills] and all that sort of thing, I am that fellow." Yet he never sickened enough to stop trying, and year after year made the same doleful complaint. French's frustration is worth seeing; but it is just as important to see his readiness to enter the fray again. The rewards promised were too great to pass by. "A gentleman gave me $50 yesterday just to go talk with a member of Congress 10 minutes," he boasted, "and if a favorable report is made on the case . . . I am to have $200 more—and if it gets through Congress, probably a thousand."[9]

However the fee was arranged—and some companies put it in bonds or stock that would exist only after legislative dispensation—lobbyists expected rich rewards and some got them. Just for dropping his backroom opposition to a patent extension, one borer boasted that he got $10,000. Lobbying could indeed make a man rich. One Washington clerk's $3000 job gave him enough for room and board, but his efforts for steamship interests brought him wealth enough to keep an open house, attend fashionable levees and match them with lavish dinners of his own, and to ride in a private carriage. Who, then, would *not* be a lobbyist, given the opportunity?[10]

Anyone could be, of course, and sometimes firms would send an employee to plead their case, but more often supplicants left the job to professionals, men who had made lobbying their career. They were not precisely a guild, and many of them had another job on the side, but professional agents resented amateurs interfering with their business.

Some were quite ready to wreck any bill that did not come to them for support first. The "strikers" were the most dreaded group of lobbyists. They were in the capital not to provide services but to exact tribute. A striker would use his connections to endanger outsiders' interests at the legislature. He might even introduce nuisance legislation that threatened some interest with taxation or regulation; the interest then would have to rush to the capital to stifle the bill by judicious payments. Insurance and railroad companies were prime targets for attack. Among the most notorious practitioners was George W. Bull, the New York State legislature's sergeant-at-arms. Combining his talents with those of a few state senators, he could bring injured parties running and did so until 1851, when he framed a bill regulating gambling houses. Bull approached the gamblers and informed them that for a price he could bury the bill in committee. Morally outraged, the gamesters ran to their assemblyman, who revealed the shakedown and forced Bull's dismissal. (Bull was out but not down. He continued to "strike" and in 1857 even tried to extort money from fellow lobbyist Thurlow Weed.)[11]

The best lobbyists had more scruples, for it must be stressed that most lobbyists were honest, much lobbying was no more than providing facts to the lawmakers, and corruption was applied as a last resort. There was a general unwritten code of conduct among agents. To bring in a new agent after the case had been entrusted to a lobbyist was considered unethical, and when this was done, employers did so surreptitiously and after much rationalizing. Weed was offered $17,500 to support a bill lowering Brooklyn ferry fares, but he returned it because he had already pledged another promoter that the cheap-ferry bill would not pass. When their interests did not clash, there was nothing against an agent taking on many clients at once. Indeed, the best agents had portfolios bulging with interests that they were serving simultaneously.[12]

Naturally, those who lobbied most effectively had good contacts in the government from the first, though they may have felt guilty, as French did, about holding a public office and serving as agent at the same time.

Newspapermen could trade in their press experience for an agency and do well at it, though many of them combined both occupations. When they reported favorably on a project, it was hard to tell whether they were reporting the news or "puffing" a client. Francis J. Grund, Uriah Painter, James S. Simonton—the most important Washington corespondents—were also among the most effective agents. Former government officials also profited from their connections, as French did when he made a partnership with a former patent office clerk. Their firm never hid its skill in opening doors at either end of Pennsylvania Avenue; indeed its advertisement stressed the "long and general acquaintance with the manner of doing business in Congress and the Departments" that permitted the two men "various facilities so necessary for . . . business." Having still better contacts, political managers could bring party allies to an appreciation of corporate interests. Albany politicians might demur at a bribe, but told that "the old man [Weed] has got an interest in the bill" they became as friendly to it as the bill's sponsors could ask: everyone knew that Weed could reward party faithful from spoils and campaign funds. Democrats could feel the same pressure from party chairmen who doubled as railroad presidents.[13]

Lawmakers in retirement had the most influence. Many incumbents left office to become attorneys and agents. When Congress next assembled, they mingled on the floor with former colleagues and pressed for any number of interests; a few sitting members merged their official duties with lobbying. Albany assemblymen specialized in "practicing law in the legislature," as the New York *Evening Post* styled it.[14]

What kind of work did a lobbyist do? Mostly, it was entirely legitimate: an agent's main aim was to persuade. Department officials must see the merits of a claim, congressmen must not act without understanding the implications of their action. Lobbyists collected witnesses to testify before Congressional hearings, circulated petitions throughout the country, and spent hours visiting offices or congressional boarding-houses to sway members. To make their arguments best, lobbyists had to make public opinion and bring it to bear on public officials by buying the goodwill of the press. Newspapers had close links to party organizations, and a party's imprimatur could sway uncommitted partisans. Editorial opinion was one of the few ways available to guess what the public was thinking. Most editors were open to persuasion, a very few to purchase, and several took pay to act as agents of the special interests themselves. Reporters cost less, but their support could be equally important. With no Associated Press, the individual writer often gave a newspaper its only glimpse of affairs at the capital. To acquire correspondents' friendship, railroad and steamboat companies gave them shares of stock, claims agents gave them a percentage of the claims. But here too even the corrupt agent could turn honest reporters to his purposes without bribery. Always eager for news to send home, reporters took leaked information gladly; often the publicity served a special interest's ends.[15]

Hospitality in its best sense was also part of the agent's stock-in-trade. A skilled lobbyist would rent a mansion and invite officials in for a banquet of sumptuous food and delightful company. At its best, such a dinner became one of the year's great social events. Everyone came, from Free-Soil Yankees to fire-eating Southerners. Idealists could reconcile their differences over bottles of champagne and oyster suppers. Conversation never flagged. The only subject that never arose was the host's ulterior motive. Perhaps as the gathering was breaking up, he might take a few guests aside for a confidential chat about his pet proposal, though even then it was considered in bad taste to discuss the matter with feeling. Such entertainments might turn more rowdy, and might even break up a legislative session if held while debate was going on, and in some cases pretty women—often highly paid and effective persuaders—were hired to apply their charms at social gatherings. Perhaps such techniques translated into votes—disgruntled antislavery men claimed that one "snug little public dinner" in 1850 cost them nineteen New York representatives—but usually the lobbyist was simply buying good will.[16]

Agents provided other favors, more overt but just as indirect. Any borer with long-range plans made friends without bringing up a quid pro quo. Among the best providers of such favors was W. W. Corcoran, partner in Washington's prestigious banking firm of Corcoran and Riggs. "I know there is no man in Washington who can so well serve you in a thousand ways as Corcoran," an editor confided to one senator. That was quite true. Corcoran offered loans to political allies at low interest and was slow to ask repayment. Did they want an extension? That too could be arranged. Congressmen wanted to speculate in lands, and Corcoran helped them do so or brought them into schemes of his own. House members needed an advance on their per diem, and Corcoran provided it. Politicians had friends to take care of, and Corcoran obliged them with loans, letters of recommendation and jobs. In the banker's letter-books appear the names of almost every important man in Washington. Corcoran did not buy their votes (though he kept several high officials on his payroll), but he made connections through his business transactions, and when he wanted favors done in return he knew just whom to ask.[17]

Just where did doing favors end and corruption begin? It is hard to tell, precisely because agents did favors and asked nothing in return. Was it pure good will that impelled the manager of the People's Line ships to supply Weed with bay rum, boxes of lemons, raisins, and assorted Havana preserves? Or did he consider that the People's Line could use Weed's protection in Albany? When Weed offered a legislator money and made clear that it was not a loan, there need have been nothing sinister in his doing so; but was Weed nonplussed when the lawmaker wrote back, "entirely unmanned and overwhelmed with surprise and gratitude," to offer his services at any time Weed might request them? It was equally obvious that when the New Jersey Railroad bought supplies from lawmakers at inflated prices, it had the pending bridge bill on its mind more than the need for lumber. But no one on either side mentioned an exchange of favors, and the company denied so intending.[18] Was it possible—just possible—that no corrupt transaction had taken place?

In Washington, gambling-houses thrived on this uncertainty, for it was around the card tables that some of the most expert lobbying was consummated. In some cases, agents could exercise unsuspected influence by losing hand after hand and then taking advantage of their prey's good humor. At other times, a gambling debt masked a bribe. An attorney showed how this was done: the agent would approach an elected official and assure him that voting right would put $500 into his pocket. "I don't take bribes," the legislator might reply. "Oh no, of course not," the lobbyist would protest. "I don't talk about bribes. But . . . suppose you come around to my room tonight and take a little brandy and water, and have a little game of whist." That night, against a very accomplished player, the legislator would win $500.[19] That way the borers would make thousands of dollars by taking loss after loss.

Other gamblers specialized in blackmailing. Everyone knew about Washington's "gambling hells," where congressmen came out losers and faro-dealers came out winners. One of the most fashionable houses belonged to one Pendleton, and if he dubbed it "the Palace of fortune," others christened it "the Hall of the Bleeding Heart." A lobbyist of genteel breeding (he could trace his ancestry back to Virginia's first families), praised for his lavish table and well-stocked wine cellar, Pendleton opened his doors to newspapermen, politicians, and other lobbyists. Did influential men lose at poker? Pendleton tided them over. "A few weeks' faro, and a Congressman is cleaned out," *Harper's Weekly* complained. "Where does he then dine?—at Pendleton's. . . . Where does he drink?—at Pendleton's. When he needs money . . . where does he mortage his mileage?—at Pendleton's. He belongs to Pendleton's." And so he did, as the member found clear when Pendleton wanted a measure passed. Reluctant statesmen risked exposure as gamblers and welchers, unless they voted right. Small wonder that leading financiers entrusted their cause to the gamester.[20] Nor was Pendleton the sole practitioner.

Even when the promise of a quid pro quo was clearer, agents kept their intentions ambiguous and made the transaction difficult to trace. When French sought an official's help in a claims case, he never mentioned the word *bribe.* "Now, Johnson," he said, "you can do us a good turn . . . and if you will we shall feel *under great obligations to you.*" A mere pledge of affection? Hardly! "If we succeed handsomely," he confided to his brother, "his wife will get another ring, certain, and perhaps more!"[21]

In truth, the experienced borer used bribery only as a last resort, and not just for the obvious ethical and legal reasons. First, pay-offs raised the cost of putting through a claim. What firm would pay $3000 for a piece of local legislation? Poorly financed railroad projects could hardly empty their treasuries to win a charter—expiring even as they triumphed. Second, bribery worked only with honorable men who, once bought, would stay so. Not all of them did. Senators took payments and then absented themselves from the chamber on the day of a vote until their retainers had been refreshed. John Egerton of the New Orleans & Mobile Railroad thought he had bought an explicit promise of support by his thousand-dollar contribution to one city councilor, and was furious when the officeholder ranged himself with the company's enemies and even accused a leading editor of being another Egerton purchase. "Surely the declaration's bold," the editor gibed,

> That we can e'er be bought or sold;
> And by the man who's proved himself
> Recipient of the fruits of pelf!
>
> . . .
>
> When we are bought, we always show
> For every cent a *quid pro quo*!
> But *some* are bought who ever fail
> In the conditions of the sale.[22]

In such a case, what could the injured party do?

Third, agents and their employers trusted each other so little that neither could aford to trust the other with a corruption fund. An official who carried out his part of a bargain before seeking his pay would find it hard to collect; so would lobbyists who used bribery, as Marshall discovered when he went to court to force the Baltimore & Ohio to pay his fee. Lobbyists might bilk both the lawmakers and his own employers, as the Pennsylvania agent did when he lined up the votes and then ran off with the entire fund before legislators could collect their due. "Such is the corruption of the times that bribery does not pay expenses," the Providence *Journal* summed up. "There is a lack of honor among the class of people to whom it is proverbially necessary."[23] Before bribery could work efficiently, businessmen would have to find a more upright class of corruptionists.

Fourth, bribery worked less well than argument. Lobbyists were no irresistible force, any more than they were one well-organized gang. On a measure in which constituents had an interest, even venal politicians would decline a bribe or demand too high a fee. Certainly a California lawmaker might absent himself on a crucial vote for $4000, a witness admitted, but only when the former lacked strong opinions on the bill under consideration. Only waverers could "perhaps be influenced" by a bribe, though to be sure, the promise of payment made a waverer of many a public servant. Too strongly pressing a case could mar all the agent hoped to accomplish as members, harassed beyond endurance, voted otherwise from spite. Paradoxically, while many measures needed good lobbying to pass, the least publicity of the lobby's presence would be fatal. At once the press would denounce the agents. Then potential converts would hold back; legislators in the market would demand a higher price. Fearing public outcry, honest men would draw back from even a worthy proposal the moment it was labeled a lobbyist's scheme. Should the firm get its way, the publicity would bring on financial damage, possibly ruin, as it did to the LaCrosse & Milwaukee Railroad.[24]

Thus, the lobbyist took a terrible risk when he approached an official with a bribe, for a misjudgment of the man's character could mean an embarrassing, too-public scene. So it was when Byron Kilbourn's agent approached a Wisconsin senator and asked his price for supporting a railroad aid bill. "I told him to say to Byron Kilbourn," the senator later boasted, "that if he would multiply the capital stock of the company by the number of leaves in the Capitol Park, and give me that amount in money, and then have himself, Kilbourn, Moses Strong, and Mitchell *blacked*, and give me clear title to them as servants for life, I would take the matter under consideration." Some legislators were simply unbuyable, and this was doubly vexing: first, because they would not bargain, and second, because they might turn against a measure out of revulsion for the methods used on its behalf. A few suspected bribes even when none was offered; others understood the lobbyists perfectly and rejected them outright. New Jersey State Senator Ralph Stults knew that backers of one charter were buying him and not his wood and corn when they offered him $8500 for both, and he would not sell out so cheaply. "For

God's sake, if anything can be done for you, let us know what it is," the borer pleaded. Could he underwrite a $500 loan? "No," said Stults. "Or more?" the lobbyist persisted. He pled in vain.[25]

But for every Stults, there were officials who actually courted bribery. Sometimes they threatened to block all action until paid off, and it was as common in Congress as in California's senate. "It was a d--d outrage," protested a company counsel to requests for $100,000. "A set of d--d scoundrels," the go-between with the extortioners agreed, "but there they were, and nobody could get anything . . . through without them. . . ." There they were indeed, and promoters, persuading themselves that their goals served the public interest, usually convinced themselves that any means were justified for so good an end. As one businessman explained, it was better "to be robbed of hundreds of dollars than to be robbed of thousands, by losing his property."[26]

So, for all the ambiguous phrasing of lobbyists and the reservations that borers had about using bribes, there is no doubt that when money was called for, lobbyists dispensed it. How much they spent cannot be known. Every bill was different, and the amount paid out depended on the return the legislation would yield or the department ruling that the lobbyist expected. Observers made wild estimates of the amount spent: $250,000 to $500,000 by city railroad promoters in the 1860 New York legislature, for example. No such statistics could be proven, as neither companies nor lobbyists offered to open their account-books and make an itemized list. From testimony before investigating committees, however, it would seem that a state senator could command as much as $1000 in cash for his vote on a major piece of legislation, and an assemblyman could expect $100 or $200. For moving a measure up on the calendar, clerks got $50. When the lobbyist paid in stock or bonds, the face value might be higher. Wisconsin State Senators received $10,000 in LaCrosse & Milwaukee Railroad bonds for their support—or would have, had the securities they received sold at par and the railroad not gone bankrupt within a year.[27]

Lobbying, then, stripped of all myth, covered many practices, only a few of which we would deem corrupt. It had its uses to the legislative process. That was, however, not how contemporaries saw matters. Unwilling to draw the line between private consultations with lawmakers and corruption, between personal appeals and bribery, they saw lobbying in any form as a frightening perversion of the public will and a threat to the Republic. Democrats were especially fearful; but then, they had long seen the connection between moneyed interests and corrupted lawmakers, and they defined undue influence all too broadly. For example, those friendly dinners that lobbyists gave excited their ire. No one denied that the dinners had some influence in making lawmakers listen more favorably to lobbyists' pleas, and *some* influence, said Democrats, was too much. To sway the public officials' judgment through food and drink was corruption, for all its subtlety.[28]

Hatred of lobbyists only fed fears of their influence the more. It was that hatred that made agents so secretive. Admitting that $15 to $20 a day might be a generous wage in most professions, Nahum Bryant asked $3000 for his services because of the damage to his reputation that services as a lobbyist must entail. It was the same, his lawyers rather infelicitously explained, as the difference in pay between that of a foot soldier and a spy. Accused of lobbying for steamship magnates, former Senator John P. Hale quickly replied that he had really been a mere errand-boy carrying documents to other congressmen. The argument was absurd. House doorkeepers could have done the job much more cheaply, but Hale's plea showed how embarrassing to anyone with future political ambitions the label could be. Even Weed, "King of the Lobby," felt compelled to issue a public defense and to insist that he had never lobbied for any bill of which he had disapproved. But if the ill favor with which the public greeted the lobbyist compelled secrecy, that secrecy added to the uneasiness that people felt. If lobbyists worked behind the scenes, was it not a sure sign that they were up to no good and that they owed their strength to bribery first and foremost?[29]

But judges, editors, orators did not respond to the lobbyist with just hatred, but with fear. The lobbyist, it would seem, endangered American freedom. So the state courts made clear. To hire an agent to plead a client's case before a legislative committee was legitimate; to provide documents pertinent to a special hearing was proper, too; but beyond that, the judges declared, lobbying interfered with the due process of lawmaking. Perhaps the agent had used no illegal means. Possibly he simply arranged for private chats with individual legislators, the better to put his case. To the courts, no such distinctions could be drawn. The agent was undermining the integrity of a government based on the people's will. If he was unable to collect his fee, the courts would not help him. If a lobbyist shared in the claim for which he pressed or accepted a fee contingent on a bill's passage, the court could decree the arrangement "champerty" and void the whole contract.

So strict a judgment stemmed from the assumption that legislators must exercise their judgment strictly on the merits of each case, where their constituents had not given them specific instructions. Thus the representative was responsible to the people at home but not to any specific interest group among them; to the higher good of the commonwealth but not to the many competing interests that vied for attention in it. Personal friendship, gratitude, even too great a familiarity with those pleading for one side would bias lawmakers' judgment and corrupt the results as much as would an open bribe. Without public faith in their disinterestedness, legislators would not do their job, said the courts, and without that respect, faith in republican institutions must perish.

So eager were judges to express revulsion for the lobbyist that they left the interpretation of precedent and fact behind and embraced the broader issues of republican virtue. The New York Supreme Court was like others:

> Our government is founded theoretically upon the most pure and exalted public virtue. . . . It is against the genius and policy of our government that her legislature and executive officers shall be surrounded by swarms of hired retainers of the claimants upon public bounty or justice. The nuisance has become almost intolerable; and all that is required to make it quite so, is for courts to tolerate contracts in respect to the services of these retainers, and by action, enforce claims for their services.[30]

Ironically, the heightened awareness of corruption and lobbying made the atmosphere worse: reports of Congressional venality further encouraged businessmen that only bribery could achieve their ends. But there really *was* corruption, and there really *was* something to be worried about. Public figures could cite the lobbyist as one sign of the moral decay that the 1850s was showing, but it was not just a symptom. It was a cause of broader depravity. Just as the spoils system had, lobbying set the tone for public life. With speculators and lobbyists feeling at home in Washington, as a Supreme Court justice warned, it was only a matter of time before corruption would become the natural condition of politics. Then would it be said of us as of Rome—"*omne Romae venale.*"[31] Could Rome's imitator escape Rome's fate?

6

Public Self-Improvements, Steam Beggars, and Railroad Robbers

What made legislatures so prone to corruption during the 1850s? For prone they were, as their members admitted. Contemporaries offered many reasons, not all of them plausible. The least satisfactory argument and the most common was that the party in power was by nature made up of thieves (a point invariably made by the party out of power). Nearly as unpersuasive—and certainly as elitist in its assumption about what kind of people were worthy to govern—was the claim that venality grew because "politics had sunk into a trade." Wistful pundits spoke of that fabulous time when legislators were chosen "like Cincinnatus, for their eminent public virtues." In fact, politics had always been a trade for many men, and eminence had never carried along higher ethics.[1]

A better explanation blamed the short lease on power that most public servants had. Because in most states the turnover in legislators was almost total every two years, inexperienced men dominated committees and appreciated expert advice from lobbyists on framing bills. Officials unable to expect a long political career, aware that for good or ill their constituents would not return them, may have felt all the freer from moral responsibility. Who would call them to account? It made the temptation to profit by the bills they passed overwhelming.[2]

For a generation, Jacksonian Democrats had offered another explanation: any government that dispensed special privileges to moneyed interests invited its own corruption. A government that enacted revenue laws lavish enough to bring in a treasury surplus all but beckoned the greedy private groups to share in it and to bribe the government to give them special access to the funds. That, said Democrats, was just what lobbies did.

Whigs felt few misgivings about government power in the economy. To them, the legislature was a force for good. By using the revenues collected from all, it could induce economic growth that spread prosperity wide. Friendly legislation could expand credit to areas unable to set up sound banks on their own, protect manufacturers from cheap foreign competition, open the roads and waterways that would expand the market of Boston merchant and backwoods farmer alike. Old-style Democrats saw matters differently. Government favors meant not just prosperity—that would come by giving everyone a fair chance in any case—but special privileges to those whose organizations already gave them more advantage than they deserved in dealing with weaker rivals. In the Gilded Age, businessmen would apply the shibboleth of laissez-faire to deprecate action on behalf of the poor, disadvantaged, and unskilled. In the 1850s, government action had different implications. The most prominent evils, Democrats insisted, came from government using its wealth to help the rich and powerful: railroads seeking a monopoly or a slice of Western lands, bankers craving special charters on terms ruinous to their competitors, manufacturers asking a tax on incoming goods that would deprive consumers of a choice on prices. "Special privileges to none!" Democrats thundered. "Government is based upon equal rights."[3]

The increased use of the corporation as a legal device made it impossible to stand by this credo, and from that system corruption became a near-necessity. In 1800, most incorporations were for public services, from towns to turnpikes. Then other business ventures discovered the potential of the corporation as a means of organizing a firm and raising large sums of money. In particular, those wanting to set up banks, railroads, and insurance firms wanted to incorporate. Yet each applicant had to ask the legislature for a special charter. The process was time-consuming, troublesome, and sure to encourage corruption. Lawmakers complained that the charters left them little time to deliberate on other subjects. Incorporators found delays in getting started and shakedowns by legislators unwilling to give special consideration without a special financial dispensation.

At first, Democrats had tried to ban certain kinds of charters. Failing that, they proposed general laws that would permit the businessman to win a charter without meddling with the general assembly: on meeting certain conditions, anyone could get a charter. By 1850, many states had taken a fancy to the innovation that, said reformers, would prevent corruption and break the power of those monopolies that used their money to forestall any rival sharing in state privileges. And yet the evil of special charters remained, for every company could accept the general law or seek a special charter with additional privileges written into it: not until the 1870s would policy-makers in a majority of states make general incorporation mandatory. So, during the 1850s, special charters remained the rule, incorporation under the general law the exception. Why settle for the basic privileges of the latter, when you might attain far better ones under the former? As long as this was so, the applicants needed a loud enough voice to be heard above the babel of other favor-seekers: that took a lobby and sometimes bribery. Certainly the crush for special charters was not aimed at seizing outrageous advantages. Most charters resembled one another in their general features. But to get them, businessmen had to pay, either in cash or in support of larger, logrolling schemes that would include other beneficiaries.[4]

Take railroads, for example: every state wanted them, many governments were ready to pay public funds to build them. Across the South, strict-constructionist Democrats found themselves steadily outvoted by friends of internal improvements. Only public aid would make the cotton states as prosperous as New England, cried Alabama assemblymen. Railroads meant fresh lands opened to development and worn-out lands revived by outsiders' immigration. So legislators introduced a crowd of charters in what one Texas editor called "a general mania."[5]

Yet translating this enthusiasm into actual charters came less easily, for local ambitions canceled each other out. Some diehard Jacksonian Democrats disliked railroad aid of any kind. Others warned that if one city got its desires, the government would have to give every other community its wishes as well. No town would brook new advantages for its rivals. Ohio farmers roared that charters came from a conspiracy of Cincinnati financiers determined to monopolize all trade, while Sussex County men would rather break up the Delaware legislature than subsidize a line through New Castle and Kent.[6]

To remove all these complications, only an active lobby could bring relief. The less it scrupled in its methods, the more it might wean members from their parochial prejudices. Thus, during the 1850s, nearly every legislature was crammed with lobbyists for every special privilege imaginable. Often they worked against one another, sometimes they made shaky alliances to permit a host of well-endowed interests. Their methods varied from the officious to the illegal, from the drunken orgy to the free pass and the cash in hand.

As with definitions of lobbyist corruption, railroads' inducements often were ambiguous enough to be read as corruption or public relations. The free passes that railroads granted, for example—how are we to judge them? Most railroads provided free passes to officeholders whose favor they sought. Not every free pass was political, and not every political award was a bribe. Courtesies were extended to every officeholder and leading editor in some states. Yet cases arose when the passes appeared on members' desks just as an important railroad measure reached the floor. Insuring a friendly atmosphere might not be corruption; overbearing the members' judgment was. The gifts, said one Ohioan, helped explain why his state's laws looked as though a body of railway directors had enacted them. So common had the dispensation become that the railroad was at times not so much actively corrupting as gratifying a customary desire. Legislators enjoyed the privilege so regularly that to have taken it away would have biased their judgments against railroad bills.[7] When the New York legislature learned that one company meant to do away with free passes, it introduced a bill rescinding charter privileges. Only by producing 350 season tickets for the solons did the company stifle the measure. Demanding an investigation of the same line, New York's City Council sent a committee to Albany. Back the members came with many kind words for the directors and ninety free passes for the councilmen.[8]

A legislature that could bestow privileges could withdraw them as easily, and the privileged always needed to protect themselves from challengers, especially where the charter granted monopoly rights, as it did with the "Joint Companies" in New Jersey. The Camden & Amboy Railroad and the Delaware & Raritan Canal had clung to exclusive rights of transport between New York City and Philadelphia since 1831 and would permit no rival to be chartered. Smaller companies worked with the C & A or stopped working at all, paid extortion money or saw laws passed to put them out of business. Everyone knew what made the legislature so pliable. Railroad president Robert F. Stockton boasted that "he carried the State in his breeches' pocket." He certainly bore the legislature there, and his money sent him to the Senate in 1851. But how did he carry the lawmakers? "Free tickets on railroads, free lunches at hotels, and seducing influences of even worse character," a legislator recalled. "Both of the political parties courted [his] favors, and became [his] servitors." Democrats served more faithfully than Whigs, for Stockton channeled federal patronage to the party faithful in the state. While the legislature sat in session, the Joint Companies kept open house at the Trenton House, though in one effort to divert school funds to the railway, they opened festivities at three hotels simultaneously.[9]

In 1854, when the Camden & Amboy sought an extension of its charter until 1889 and a fifteen-year renewal on its monopoly, it got both. Members devoured terrapin and gulped red wine, drank toasts to the Joint Companies, and roared with delight when a railroad executive boasted, "*I glory in a monopoly.*" The Senate rushed the extension bill through before members could read the printed copy, and only one Democrat voted against it. It was, said the New York *Tribune*, "one of the most corrupt and unjustifiable laws . . . that ever marked the putridity of politics and the decay of a State." That fall, the Joint Companies poured money into the campaign to prevent a Whig victory and repeal of their privileges.[10] So it turned out, every time that foes challenged the monopoly or sought a charter for some rival.

If a company would do so much for legal rights, what would it not do for a share of public revenues? The scramble for subsidies alarmed Jacksonian Democrats more than did the special charters, for if the latter oppressed the consumer, the former would make Americans pay for their own exploitation. Unlike the movement for special charters, the efforts for subsidies looked to Congress. By the 1850s, the Treasury held more than ever before, but the supplicants were more numerous than ever before as well. And—just as in New Jersey—they were also more successful in persuading Democrats to give them a chance at public funds. In the process, they showed that whatever Democratic doctrine *said*, the party's *acts* showed it no more than a lure to catch voters.

Least important among the influences on Congress in the 1850s was the tariff lobby. Though the tariff was at its lowest in thirty years, supporters of a protective schedule fought a lonely campaign. High-tariff men tried to work out a logrolling arrangement with backers of railroad land grants in 1850; they got nowhere. Every session, supporters of high iron duties descended on the Capitol and had to fight the railroad promoters who were pressing for lower rates still. When it did become visible, however, the lobby showed itself as unscrupulous as any other. In 1857, Congress reduced duties on raw wool. A victory of the consumer over the privileged interests? Hardly. That autumn, the Massachusetts woollen factory of Lawrence, Stone & Co. went bankrupt. When the stockholders wondered where the money had gone, they learned that $87,000 had been spent to buy the tariff reduction the winter before. Congress investigated, and while they found no sitting members who received pay, they found many practices that did the House no credit.

W. W. Stone had gone to Washington to persuade congressmen, found the task beyond his means, and hired a lobbyist, John W. Wolcott instead. On his advice, Stone paid the Democratic free-trade newspaper, the New York *Journal of Commerce.* On the advice of Congressman Orsamus Matteson, Republican manager Thurlow Weed got $5000 for his political influence. Matteson also advised that $30,000 go to buy thirty votes he knew to be on the market. One congressman received $4000. Two others including the Speaker got what Stone called loans, though he asked the Speaker to stack the Ways and Means Committee in his favor in return and listed the loans on the so-called "tariff account." The firm gave A. R. Corbin, clerk to the House Committee on Claims, $1000 for his influence, though he double-crossed them as soon as the cash was in hand. At the session's end, Wolcott wired his employers for $74,000 to pay off congressmen. What and whom he paid he would not say. On this point, as on so many others, the committee majority felt the witness less than candid.[11]

Other groups sought a more direct government support. The most controversial subsidy went to steamship firms seeking special compensation for carrying the mail to California and overseas. During the early 1840s, their agents had appealed to the federal government for such an arrangement. In 1845, Congress obliged by authorizing the Postmaster-General to let mail contracts to American firms. By the end of 1852, taxpayers were underwriting six steamship lines with $1.4 million a year, including the ones to Bremen and Le Havre. The Sloo line, which shared the mail route to San Francisco with William H. Aspinwall's Pacific Mail line, had pledged to build first-class war steamers to carry the mail, though only Aspinwall's company built a single boat to standard and on time. Even without a subsidy, the mails could have been carried profitably; with it, the companies had a bonus to use against competitors. The promoter George Law, for example, might lose money on his run to Panama by charging steerage passengers $5 and cabin occupants $25, but the mail subsidy made up for it all.[12]

Naturally the arrangement satisfied no one but the beneficiaries. Every port wanted a route of its own, and during the first half of 1852, seventeen new firms applied for an estimated $80 million in benefits. In the early 1850s, no session met without what one observer called "the steam beggars" invading the Capitol and trying to wrest new privileges with the lobby's help. Not every scheme passed, of course. Law's proposed line to Liberia, the so-called Ebony line, had earnest entreaties from the Virginia legislature and American Colonization Society, and as in everything he turned his hand to, Law mounted a very professional lobbying campaign. But neither champagne, cigars, aid for the Illinois Central's land grant, nor Law's own personal buttonholing of members on the House floor in 1850 could put the measure through.[13] What he and lobbyists like him did manage to do was to make the political atmosphere that much more sordid with charges of corrupted members.

No scheme had the publicity of the Collins line from New York to Liverpool. Hoping to control the North Atlantic passenger traffic, Edward K. Collins got a handsome ten-year subsidy of his mail delivery in 1847 and promised to build five warships in return. In 1851, he was allowed another six trips a year at the same rate. "A great deal is said about the excellence of these steamers," one congressman gibed. "They are certainly the deepest-draught steamers I have ever yet heard of—drawing thirty-three feet in the National Treasury." Not surprisingly, bankers W. W. Corcoran, Elisha Riggs, and James and Stewart Brown found them excellent investments and assembled a lobby for their protection.[14]

But were they as good an investment for the government? Collins's defenders pronounced his ships priceless as an upholder of American prestige against perfidious Albion. Surely no patriot would want British ships to command the Atlantic trade, they pleaded. Yet only by matching the Cunards' subsidy could Congress prevent that fate. And what other vessels could shift into serviceable warships at a moment's notice? Properly juggled, figures showed that the Collins line ran at a loss and that no other mail-carrier could do the task more cheaply. Old-line Democrats knew better. This was the very kind of special privilege that their party had long since gone on record against—and it was doing just what Democrats had always said monopoly rights would do. In the name of patriotism, the grant let one particular firm undercharge its domestic rivals. Obligated to make five vessels, the firm never made more than four, and borrowed the money from the government to do it. It never repaid the loan, and what "warships" the money built! The final product might tickle a landsman's taste, but Navy Yard workers knew them "not worth a sixpence for war purposes." Their whole design was wrong. A single broadside would immobilize the sidewheels; the decks were too light to bear a gun-battery. As for using the ships to haul war supplies, Congressman James Orr remarked scornfully, "it would be a novel spectacle to see superb state-rooms . . . filled with barrels of pickled pork and the *salons* with rusty bacon sides." The Collins line hid its 40 percent profit each year, but any observer could see how well it did by a glance at the Brussels tapestries, chandeliers, silver tea-services, and rosewood furniture on board. But did the post office really need to bear its letters in such luxury? Finally, the Collins ships were inefficient. They used twice the coal of other ships and cost more in repairs after six years than the original outlay for construction. Other companies could do the job quicker and cheaper.[15]

To Jacksonians, then, the Collins subsidy amounted to a "war declared against the Treasury" in the name of monopoly rights. They fumed the more in 1851 and a year later when the owners returned to the capital to rewrite their original contract for additional compensation. After a stiff fight, Collins won his case. By 27 to 19, a Democratic Senate gave a three-year supplement, while the Democratic House with only two votes to spare followed suit.[16]

Collins overbore all common sense in just the way Democrats had always said that special interests would gain their way, once government agreed in principle that public money should go for private enhancement: bribery and lobby fuglemen. With the Democratic party organ paid to publish fervent editorials for an increased subsidy, the promoters sent some of the best reporters and merchants in the land to Washington: Benjamin French, Francis J. Grund, and J. Knox Walker all plied their trade effectively. French himself boasted that his work swayed the waverers in the House, and this made him all the angrier when he received only $300 for his day's work, while other lobbyists made thousands. Collins appeared in person to talk with representatives. On the pretext of heaving into port for repairs, the *Baltic* sailed up the Potomac and opened its salons to wild Congressional entertainments. The company sent petitions to allies across the nation so that public opinion made to order could flood the capital. Favorable news coverage in Northeastern cities was bought. So were congressmen. "Any bill can be carried by those who have millions at their command, with hampers of champagne annexed," Congressman Thaddeus Stevens told his colleagues.[17]

Perhaps it could, but Presidential approval would be less easily gained. Three years later, the Collins lobby came back to renew its special payments. Again a powerful lobby worked the House. So persistent were rumors of corruption around the measure that the New York *Tribune*, till then a hearty friend of the Collins line, turned against it on those grounds alone. Only bribery saved the bill from defeat, said the New York *Evening Post*. Bribery was not enough. President Franklin Pierce vetoed the measure, and the House could not override him. Instead, both chambers attached a rider to the naval appropriations bill that permitted extra compensation until the Administration decreed a stop to it. The Administration did so within a few months. Disgusted, the Collins lobbyists would later charge that their employer paid them in promises alone. The most that the French brothers got was a rubber check. "Fine chaps, these Collin liners," Benjamin wrote brother Henry. "I'll pay them yet, with compound interest." "When you see the new doorkeeper," Henry wrote back, "tell him that I am coming there in season to help *defeat* Collins this year. . . . [L]et him know that I have not forgotten their behavior."[18]

Of course the Collins line did not succeed purely or even primarily because of bribery. Nor did any of the "steam beggars." Collins, Law, and their friends had many favors to give, and they gave some of them well in advance of their appeals for aid. Lawmakers and newspapermen were offered the chance to buy company stock cheaply. Collins lent some presses money, and the Sloo line put influential editors on his payroll. Their words may well have persuaded many undecided men that the subsidies were right—even good Democratic party doctrine.[19]

But all such favors took money, and that fact underlay the real corruption in the steamship subsidy wars. Corporations used the government money to buy friends, to protect their special relationship with the government. "A million dollars a year is a power that will be felt," Senator Robert Toombs thundered, ". . . and I know it *is* felt. I know it perverts legislation. I have seen its influence; I have seen the public treasury plundered by it."[20]

By the time Toombs spoke, the mail-steamers had lost their ascendancy and Collins had gone bankrupt, but another more persistent pressure had replaced them in the lobbies. For many years, railroads had relied on loans from the states to cover construction costs. Then in 1850 came the break—one of those that helped make the decade more corrupt than those that had gone before. Southern and Western interests combined that year to put the first major land grant through Congress. Over 3.7 million acres went to the Mobile & Ohio and the Illinois Central to help them build a trunk line from Chicago to the Gulf. The grant assured both lines of success. Other companies hurried to Washington to ask for the same consideration; and again, with the same hopes of an effective monopoly on commerce, since the firm with a land grant could drive into bankruptcy all rival schemes not so well endowed. So corrupt was the passion for public lands on the House, one congressman argued, that the best reform would be to give the beggars all they wanted at once and be rid of them.[21]

Over the next four years, the hunger for land grants sharpened. To logroll their schemes through, rivals would make peace and ally with one another. Then the moment the subsidy failed to pass, its backers would turn and rend every other project. Railroad schemes merged and sundered. "I may want them *all* killed," Alvah Hunt of the Iowa Central wrote Thurlow Weed about other land-grant bills. ". . . If the Iowa Senators & members *remain* selfish and 'piggish' I shall certainly 'kill round' if I have the power to do so." Just such parochialism destroyed his own road's chances: Ohio congressmen were interested in a road out of Fort Wayne that wanted its own land grant through Iowa and annihilated all its rivals.[22]

By the summer of 1854, the scramble had lost all propriety. A Wisconsin railroad grant was said to have offered a $2000 fee to one man to bring his congressman round. "C. C. Clarke says you told him that Etheridge, Hunt, Jones, &c. were provided for, &c.," the Iowa Central's agent wrote Weed, referring to leading congressmen. "How?—am I to do anything more? Let me know tomorrow, as Harrington asks me . . . if his dfts for $5,000 on certain gentlemen will be honored, now that [the Minnesota land grant] has been consummated."[23]

A scandal very nearly undid the whole session's work. Minnesota territory was underdeveloped, which meant great opportunities for land speculators; and those opportunities could increase with construction of a feeder from Lake Superior to a trunk line between Chicago and the Pacific. Such a road could make many men's fortune, especially the fortunes of the politicians dabbling in lands at the town site of Superior, which hoped to be the railroad's eastern terminus. The speculators included the Rice brothers, Democratic leaders in Minnesota, Senators Jesse Bright of Indiana, R. M. T. Hunter of Virginia, and Stephen A. Douglas of Illinois, as well as a cluster of congressmen. To create the railroad link, however, would take a federal grant, and on these terms many companies ran to Congress to receive exclusive rights to Minnesota's public lands. The Minnesota & Northwestern, a subsidiary of the Illinois Central, already had a territorial charter that guaranteed a generous land grant. If the road won the federal allotment too, it would be the most important line in Minnesota. Calling on its allies, the Michigan Central and New York Central, the Illinois Central sent its best agents to sway the House and allied itself with lobbyists for the extension of Colt's revolver patent and the Collins subsidy. Former Congressman George Ashmun was hired to sway New England representatives (even as he worked to raise a corruption-fund among the railroad men, to use to lower duties on railroad iron). Congressmen Elihu Washburne and John Wentworth of Illinois rarely agreed on anything, but together they rousted out friends from both parties to put through this particular subsidy. Wentworth was a shill for the Illinois Central, Washburne its foe, but Washburne had been promised that an independent company would get the land grant. The subsidy, he announced, was "the greatest thing in the U.S. if properly managed."[24]

But was it properly managed? With lobbyists behind it like Congressman Matteson and professional agents George Harrington, Thurlow Weed, and George W. Billings, it had trusty backing. Harrington himself dispensed some $5000 in bribes, and if reports were true, Congressman Thomas Clingman of North Carolina may have passed out $10,000 more in stock. One Tennessee congressman accepted a bribe to stay away on the day of the vote. Other members demanded lands around Superior for their support.[25] All these efforts passed the land grant early that summer.

It did not stay passed. Late in July, Washburne rose in a rage: the House had been duped! Between the time the bill passed and the moment it went to the Senate, someone had changed the wording to give the Minnesota & Northwestern the grant. The changes were no "mere verbal alteration," as the chairman of the House Public Lands Committee claimed, nor were they an afterthought. Lobbyist Billings had planned them in advance and had brought together the chairmen of both chambers' Public Lands Committees and House Clerk John Forney to arrange the alterations in secret. A landholder at Superior, Forney pocketed $2500 for his services. A House committee, chaired by another property-holder at Superior, investigated briefly and whitewashed the whole affair. By then the damage was done. On August 3, Congress repealed the land grant.[26]

It would seem, however, that congressmen acted only from embarrassment about the publicity and not from second thoughts about the subsidy policy, for by 1856 the scramble had resumed. Lobbyists had improved their logrolling techniques and learned discretion about airing their grievances in public. That spring, most major lines joined efforts and shared the fifteen million acres that Congress gave. Again, the agents proved energetic. Again, Weed, Harrington, and French labored. Two years later the president of the Iowa Central would explain that to get 900,000 acres, he had had to spend $700,000 in Congress, mostly on what he called "pecuniary compliments." For its land grant through Wisconsin, the LaCrosse & Milwaukee paid out $105,000, though reportedly some congressmen were paid for but not bought. Other members voted to enhance the value of their Minnesota lands. The Minnesota & Northwestern got no renewal of its land grant, but another Minnesota line did, one in which several congressmen from New York were financially interested. When the lands were parceled out to stockholders they at least had the grace to send their friend Weed in their place.[27]

Corruption begat corruption, and this too fit what the Democrats had long foreseen. They had insisted that depravity at the nation's capital would infect the states, as local officials strove to take advantage of the favors rained down upon them from above. Wisconsin proved them right, for no sooner had the struggle ended at Washington than it began in Madison. Behind every intrigue stood Moses Strong and Byron Kilbourn, prominent Milwaukee Democrats and members of the so-called "Forty Thieves" faction. While a paid lobbyist for Kilbourn's Milwaukee & Mississippi Railroad, Strong served as speaker of the Wisconsin House and pushed through bills to its benefit. When the other directors drove Kilbourn from the firm's presidency for embezzlement, he and Strong set up a new company, the LaCrosse & Milwaukee, and turned their efforts to obtaining a federal land grant. When Congress endowed a road to the western tip of Lake Superior, but neglected to specify which road, Strong and Kilbourn had to fight off rivals in Chicago as well as in Milwaukee.

Fight them off they did. Though the Chicagoans were *said* to have bought fifteen Wisconsin lawmakers, testimony shows that Kilbourn bought nearly all the rest. Though a joint legislative committee unanimously agreed to give the federal grant to no existing firm, three of the seven members reversed themselves: Kilbourn saw to that. Had the public had the chance to vote on Kilbourn's land-grant measure, one senator predicted, the LaCrosse & Milwaukee would not have won one vote in three. Outside the cities the giveaway excited "a general hostility," and among his constituents, nine-tenths were opposed to it. All arguments proved in vain. In the streets, Kilbourn's lobbyists bragged that they had bought a majority of legislators. For days, a forlorn hope of foes tried every parliamentary delay they could think of and every amelioration of the bill giving Kilbourn's company two million acres of land. No amendment could withstand the majority. At last one legislator rose in disgust. Let his friends stop trying the impossible, he cried. Everyone knew that the majority sat there with bribes in their pockets. Let them earn their pay without delay.[28]

When the land grant was finally signed into law, it proved a dear purchase. Milwaukee postmaster Josiah Noonan had long opposed Kilbourn's wing of the party. Now he saw the means of driving it from public life, if he could find Republicans ready to lead the battle. Using his official patronage, he printed and circulated thousands of petitions demanding an investigation. At the head of the examiners was Horace A. Tenney, a lawmaker who promised to give the scoundrels a run for their money. And so he did. Early in 1857, Tenney's brother wrote to congratulate him on such a "successful time in the legislature." He added, "It proves that the Tenneys are equal to any emergency. I am glad also to hear that you now have no need in money matters. I *reckon* that your services are appreciated in a more solid way than formerly." They were—$25,000 worth. That was what Strong paid Tenney for silence, and in February 1857 the chairman reported that any investigation would cost too much to be worth opening.[29]

The reckoning was only delayed, for by fall the public was in an uproar over the frauds. Republicans campaigned on the charge that the La-Crosse & Milwaukee had bought the Democracy bag and baggage, and challenged scrutiny into their own uprightness. As the railroad tumbled into bankruptcy and its creditors called for an accounting, the president revealed the heavy spending—well over $800,000—used to make the Wisconsin government see reason. After that, investigation could no longer be blocked. The governor demanded it, the legislature called a joint committee, and at its head put a supporter of the Chicago promoters.

The committee did a relentless and thorough job. When Kilbourn and Strong declined to testify, they were locked up until they reconsidered. The evidence they imparted then was more shocking than anyone had dreamed. Fifty-nine assemblymen, nineteen senators, and a host of influential politicians had taken bribes. Only four legislators voted for the land grant without taking money for doing so. For their friendship, public officials had collected somewhat more than a million dollars in corporate bonds. For $17,000, state house clerks expedited business. To speak well of the line and suppress rumors of corruption, the editor of the Milwaukee *Sentinel* got ten thousand dollars, while larger sums silenced the *Wisconsin Banner* and *Patriot*. Governor Coles Bashford, a Republican, had shown astute business sense in forcing the company to change his $50,000 bribe in bonds to the same amount in cash as soon as the land grant passed. When the bill first came to him, he vetoed it, because he wanted his brother placed on the board of a subsidiary road. His demands satisfied, he had signed the second land grant.

It is hard to say which was more depressing, the lack of ethics or the lack of finesse on both sides. To be sure, bribes were not handed out in the main street of Madison, and the money was wrapped in plain paper, but one week after the bill's passage, the claimants shoved their way into Strong's law office to receive their pay in person. The only wonder is that the revelations had taken so long to become public, long enough for Bashford to move to Arizona.[30]

What made the scandal all the more alarming was that the corruptionists lost none of their sauciness once they were found out. Usually, a public figure would deny all accusations and continue to do so even after all the damning proof had piled up; his excuses might be weak, but the charge of corruption was one he never accepted. But now the thieves had come to see stealing as one of the privileges of office, a unique response for that age; perhaps their own forced retirement from office had left them with a feeling that they had nothing to lose. A few officials accepted their bribes as though they were fees for services rendered and felt no remorse. When the new managers of the LaCrosse & Milwaukee tried to recall the bonds given as bribes, they were rebuked for their bad taste. Instead of protesting that they had misunderstood the pay-offs as something else and returning them, the legislators wrote indignant replies. Buying lawmakers was a hallowed tradition, S. W. Barnes complained. "But it is of recent occurrence that after having obtained the benefits . . . they should repudiate the very means by which they succeeded, and I presume that the time is far in the future when any other . . . will undertake it." Isaac Woodle thought the request a capital joke. Even with his spectacles, he sneered, he could not "*see* the importance of returning the said bonds . . . although [he had] looked." Possibly when he obtained a telescope, he said, "for which I have sent a special messenger this morning," his moral vision would improve.[31]

Asked to explain the payments, only two men denied the charge outright. The rest admitted that they had received railroad bonds—but these were merely a gift. True, they had been promised compensation for their votes and had gone to Milwaukee to collect it—but surely no committee would confuse this with a bribe. He had received no "corruption bonds," Barnes said: only "construction bonds," and these "for services honestly rendered." If there was any breach of ethics, it was in the company offering its securities, not in his accepting their offer. Indeed, Barnes went on, he had been unable to dispose of the bonds for more than half their face value. If anything, the railroad had a moral duty to give him more, to keep its end of the bargain. To be sure, Assemblyman George W. Parker conceded, he had taken the company's promise of payment into account when he backed the land grant; undeniably, he had collected and still kept his reward—what of it? After all, there was always the chance that the company might have broken its promises. Only members paid in advance were truly bribed. Besides, he and other legislators agreed, the payment was given once the session had closed. Having adjourned, they "were no longer a Legislature" and, he said, "our acceptance could in no way be considered or regarded as a bribe, . . . it could not by any possibility have any corrupt influence or effect upon us . . . it could in no way affect our honor or integrity as men . . . and further, that coming at the time it did, *and especially when we remembered that the Company had just received at our hands 3 to $10,000,000 worth of lands as a gratuity*, WE COULD NOT FIND IT IN OUR HEARTS TO REFUSE."[32]

The same ethical collapse affected the railroad men who offered the bribes. What crime was there in spending money to pass a land grant, one defender asked. The public approved of the bill, and only money could have pushed it through. If bribery was necessary, bribery was proper. Conceding that he had bought legislators, Kilbourn stood by his view that "there was *nothing* in the *whole proceeding* repugnant to the *strictest principles of morality*." So railroad men spoke elsewhere when their interests were at stake, though they were wise enough to save their words for private, and in public to couple their defense of bribery as an ugly necessity with reminiscences of "strikers" they had kicked out the door. Defeated in committee, one foe of a bridge charter refused to accept his setback. As "a matter of self preservation I must strike hard in defence of what I deem my rights," he wrote, "and shall therefore feel at liberty to use every & any method to defeat their operations."[33]

We would be foolish to dismiss these words as mere rationalization. In many cases, it was not they who corrupted the politicians, but the politicians who demanded payment for their votes. Far from being the tool of business interests that Democratic rhetoric imagined, the legislators were equal parties to the deal, and within limits the businessmen's masters. The Mattesons made the first overtures; the Bashfords took what was offered and then demanded second helpings. New York legislator was the same kind of menace. He helped pass the bill forming the New York Central Railroad, but afterwards he demanded an exorbitant payment. This was robbery, Matteson agreed, but the directors had best settle with him, "*for he knows too much to be quarreled with. . . .*"[34]

This relationship helps explain why Thurlow Weed became an indispensable orchestrator of lobbyists for railroad aid. The Whig manager was too influential in politics to leave as an enemy. When the Democratic financiers of the New York Central wanted extra compensation for a construction company, it was Weed they employed. When an honest broker was needed to end strife between the Pacific Mail Company and Commodore Cornelius Vanderbilt's interests, Weed was the logical choice. It was Weed and his cronies Harrington and Matteson who descended on the Capitol in 1854 to push Wisconsin land grants, Minnesota giveaways, Illinois Central favors. For his aid in furthering the Minnesota land grant, the sinister Robert Lowber "sold" Weed $750,000 of shares for a dollar.[35]

The fact was, by 1855, business and politics had become an interlocking directorate, and not only because both sides wanted such a relationship but because company positions became the coin with which politicians' favors were paid, and directors knew that there were times when they must put a good Democrat on the board to appease the powers in Congress or the state government. In other cases, politicians wrote in the names of their friends as railroad officers as the price of passing a charter.[36] Such an alliance made the role of government as a bestower of privileges all the more difficult to eradicate, and it had certain nasty effects on the parties, the election returns, and the ways in which government functioned.

First, the intertwining of railroad policy and politics meant that railroads became a political weapon. When New Jersey Democrats chose an electoral ticket in 1860, they included an officer, the secretary, and the chief superintendent of the Camden & Amboy. Through the 1850s, one might have mistaken the New York Central's board for a meeting of the Democratic state central committee. In 1860, for Congress Democrats ran its president and general superintendent, ran two other officers for assembly, and let its vice president chair the state committee. Railroad workers were bullied to vote as their employers directed. Those with wood and supplies to sell the line were informed that the ones whom the Central contracted with depended on who voted Democratic. Did the Central managers wish to run the company or the government, the New York *Tribune* asked. Both were good businesses, but it seemed a shame to ask the same promoters to manage both at once.[37]

Second, and more ominous, the corrupting effect of favors to the special interests undermined the whole party system. Jacksonian Democrats could hardly keep up the cry of special privileges to none when their leading spokesmen championed subsidies. What kept the Democratic party of New Jersey from being a mockery, when its editors varied their fulminations at monopoly with sweet words for the state's own exclusive corporation? Yet the same hypocrisy seemed to infect the Whig party. What did the words for the high tariff mean, when the long-time champion of Protection, Thurlow Weed, would hire himself out to lobby for reduction of the tariff on wool?[38]

Indeed, the problem of corruption did not just make the parties look like frauds in general, but set party regulars against one another. In the Democratic ranks, the true believers in the doctrine of special privilege to none, radicals and Barnburners as they were known, took a new, bitter dislike to the conservative Hunker wing, because the latter had sold out the old faith. Far more likely to conciliate the South where slavery was concerned, the Hunker was also readier to take a positively Whiggish interest in subsidies to steamships, land grants for railroads, special charters for banks, and other schemes of "plunder." It was easy for the radical Democrats to see the party as sold out in the fullest sense of the word, and they had reason to feel so. They could point to Edwin Croswell, editor of the Albany *Argus*, or to his political comrade, Senator Daniel Dickinson of New York, and their alliance to the Southern Rights men like Elwood Fisher, publisher of the *Southern Press*. But it was well known that the shipowners had Croswell on the payroll and had sent him to Washington to kill any investigation of the Sloo line subsidy, that Dickinson had done the dirty work on the Senate floor, that the *Argus* was solvent because of the steamship lines' funding, and that Fisher's paper survived only on a similar grant. Less well known was that Fisher owned $500,000 of stock in the Sloo concern, but the radical Democrats would not have been surprised.[39] How easy it became, then, for the radical Democrats to see party divisions in terms that permitted no reconciliation, no compromise: between true Jacksonians and thieves.

So strong became the stench of corruption around the grants that some Whigs too were beginning to reconsider. Again, the most vociferous were those outside of the mainstream of the party, antislavery men like Horace Greeley and Thaddeus Stevens, disaffected Southerners like Senator Robert Toombs of Georgia. Perhaps that uneasiness about the subsidy policy on which Whiggery had so long based itself made easier their transfer to a new party in the mid-1850s, but their concern was sincere, for all that.

They were afraid, these keepers of the Jacksonian flame and these disenchanted Whigs, for they saw with the piercing vision that only outsiders have when they look on a political system that others run. To them, the subsidy policy was not just bad for ethics. By spreading revenues among the organized interests, government skewed the economic system. By inviting businesses to compete for favors, aid programs tainted the political system. Last of all, it may well have been imperiling American freedom. As the central government collected more revenue and dispensed more favors, federal power grew more important. Like the spoils system, which made job-seekers turn to the national Administration and do its will, the subsidy system made contractors see federal support as their first resort and state aid as their last. Then the autonomy on which the Union was based was in jeopardy. "All parts of the nation look up to the Federal Government for contracts," Senator Andrew Johnson complained, "they look up here for jobs; they look up here for cases of speculation and fraud; and the Government furnishes the means for them; while your States . . . are sinking into mere petty Corporations, . . . mere satellites of an inferior character, revolving around the great central power here at Washington." This was corruption in a different sense, but no less dangerous for all that: the unofficial government of large corporations and central authority could undo the formal order of states' rights and checks and balances.

Once begun on that road, the plunderers and usurpers would have built up a constituency that allowed them to continue to advance. That Democrats seemed ready to support such Whiggish notions as subsidies struck the old Jacksonians as proof of how deeply the corruption had already changed the old-fashioned sense of right and wrong. "What will it cost?" Andrew Johnson asked. "How much corruption, how much speculation, how much fraud, will ensue? Can any one tell?"[40]

7

How Public Works Worked the Public

For a developing country like the United States, economic growth was too important to leave to businessmen. While the Manchester School in England spun out its theories of laissez-faire and tried to bring Parliament to impress them into law, American states were funding and managing banks, railroads, and canals. Only with a network of roads and artificial waterways could the country develop a broad market economy, and in the short run commerce and manufacturing interests relied on government to do the developing. Often, tax revenues subsidized private firms, but until the 1850s, most states dabbled in some form of public ownership. New York's Erie Canal had been a tremendous success. From it, Pennsylvania, Ohio, Michigan, and Virginia had taken the model for their state works. South Carolina and Georgia built railroads that the government operated, while Florida and Louisiana cities held controlling interests in the stock of private railway companies. Such a sublime faith appealed more to Whigs than to Democrats, though both parties had their advocates of public works. State-run lines would last well into the 1870s. Indeed, in North Carolina they would expand after the Civil War. But by the 1850s the craze for public works had begun to diminish. New constitutions forbade the state's involvement in moneyed corporations. Laissez-faire's advocates were increasing. They had no need to turn to David Ricardo or Adam Smith for argument. The corruption on public works was argument enough.

Some canals never turned a profit; others only made money in their first years. By mid-century most of them ran at a loss. Was this the fault of their managers, the canal boards and boards of public works? So critics thought. They suggested that the public works were being run in wasteful ways that no private owners would tolerate, because the people's business was nobody's business and because the spoils system made sure that the public works would be run to subsidize the party rather than to turn a profit.

Since Whigs attacked Democratic administration of canals and Democrats attacked Whig officeholders, each side was more interested in damning numbers than in accurate ones. By excluding the indirect financial benefits that the public works brought to their clientele and by counting only the gross receipts on each canal, critics of the state works could show that the public had lost a vast sum. At the same time, the figures lied in *both* directions. The canals' administrators proved their accounts in the black—once they left out the "extraordinary expenses," and every year had its "extraordinary expenses." Where the numbers proved more damning, the public officials cooked the accounts. When the New York State Engineer filed an official estimate of repair costs, his superiors suppressed it, lest critics of the canal have the numbers they needed.[1]

Where did the truth lie? Were the canals mismanaged, even criminally? Certainly some of the administrators handled their jobs honestly; but others could marshal only political skills enough to put them into office, but none of the financial skills required for keeping the books. Officers in Pennsylvania and Ohio could not say how much they spent, in one state because the board kept no books, and in the other because certain books vanished at an opportune moment. Such laxity made misapplication of funds likely. Officers' contempt for legal niceties made it certain. Ohio law forbade the canal fund commissioners to lend to private firms, but the commissioners did so anyway, disguising it as a mere deposit of money with the Columbus Insurance Company, and endowing four railroad projects without a pretense of legality.[2]

The worst abuses occurred when the state contracted for labor or materials for the public works. Then the taxpayers *were* robbed, and the canal officers connived in that robbery. The boards overpaid contractors for repair work and accepted construction materials below the quality stipulated. Contractors soon found that a public works project paid easily, because no officer looked into the work closely. Foremen issued wages in depreciated scrip and pocketed the state's coin. Along the Pennsylvania State Line, contractors agreed to provide 90,000 white oak crossties at seventy cents each—quite a bargain, when the going rate was forty cents, but they outdid themselves and bought the much less durable Spanish oak instead, which grew on one canal commissioner's property. Suppliers padded their records by charging for goods never delivered or in excess of the amount needed.[3]

Obviously, the state did not get good work for the price it paid. The contractors did a shoddy job; the legislature would raise another appropriation to repair what was ill done. It was a proud day for the Ohio Board of Public Works, for example, when it completed the Flatrock Aqueduct, but before a single boat could pass through it, the structure gave way. As an investigation showed, the builders had ignored the most rudimentary precautions. Crevices had been filled not with cement but with sand. Headers to link the face stone to the masonry in the aqueduct walls were never placed. This was not mere negligence. Engineers and commissioners colluded with the contractors and split the profits.[4] So, too, a contractor on the Erie Canal used shoddier materials than his contract allowed. Presto—the terms were changed and a division engineer was $500 richer.[5]

Between dereliction of duties and outright corruption lies the finest of lines, as Canal Commissioner John C. Mather showed. In 1853, the New York legislature looked into the repair bills along his section of the Erie Canal; they seemed unusually high. In one year, Mather had paid as much for repairs as one-seventh the original cost of building the whole canal. Where had the money gone?

Investigators were not sure. Mather had failed to have the check-rolls signed or sworn to, as the law compelled. Some receipts were signed in names different from those which the account books listed as having received payment. Superintendents paid for materials that vanished the moment they were bought. Mather had done construction without legal authorization and had spent ten times as much in mileage as the law permitted. On eighteen separate occasions, he had hired his own team of horses to work on the canal—which the law expressly forbade officials to do. Investigators were especially intrigued with his purchases for timber-docking at nearly twice the market price. Had Mather been guilty of sloppy bookkeeping? of wastefulness? or theft? His inquisitors were unsure, though they unanimously recommended impeachment.[6] Very possibly most of the charges of malfeasance along the canals in Pennsylvania were no worse than misfeasance.

It took no overly active imagination to assume that some leading officials along the public works were thieves; some *were.* Ohio Public Works Commissioner James B. Steedman bought stone from himself at

$500, though it turned out that the stone never belonged to him and that the state government had already bought it for canal construction. Buying a farm alongside the canal for $2800, he collected $2700 in damages to its riverbank from the authorities (all good Democrats like himself). Still more brazenly, Eric Canal Commissioner Charles Cook used his influence to extend a tributary canal northward across his own property from his home town to Seneca Lake, and all without legislative permission.[7]

Avaricious men deserve some of the blame, but the real corrupters of the public works policy were the spoils system and the process by which contracts were let to private parties. Because public works commissioners could choose their own work force, the parties turned the canals into engines of patronage. On the other hand, if they left repairs to private firms, partisan officials could award firms that had done the party good service. In effect, to repair the canals the government might hand out jobs as spoils or contracts as spoils. In either case it wanted a good partisan rather than a man of business principles.

As long as officials let the terms enforce themselves, letting out contracts was risky enough, but when they gave it to favorites regardless of what was bid, the state was sure to be plundered by men with political pull. Some states put the lowest-bidder principle on their books, commissioners elsewhere declared it their guiding principle. In practice, the rule was rarely enforced. A glance at the winning bids showed that the Ohio and Pennsylvania boards allotted work to whom they liked. While Ohio law forbade any firm to offer more than one bid for the same work, companies took on bogus names to do so. Inevitably, the boards rewarded leading politicians with the repair and supply contracts. Not that all politicians really did the work they took on: a contract was a commodity to sell to real businessmen for a slice of the profits. When a Democratic nominee for the Ohio Board got a canal contract and sold it for $1000, he protested that he had done nothing illegal. True, he was the state engineer and thus responsible for the estimates and for supervision of the work done, but, said his apologists, Mr. Backus was also a private citizen and in that capacity had the right to speculate in anything he chose. But could the two roles be so easily separated from one another, particularly when Backus in his official capacity had had the connections that allowed him a special deal in his private capacity?[8]

No party held a monopoly on such maneuverings. In New York, Whigs ran the public works for most of the 1850s and bestowed contracts as they chose, but Pennsylvania and Ohio Democrats saw to it that division engineers gave party friends repair contracts or stepped aside themselves. Nor, indeed, would Republicans prove much better. Taking time off from their imprecations at Democratic pillage, Michigan Republicans left canal repair work to Holmes & Clark. Clark was the governor's close friend, and Silas Holmes until recently state treasurer, and the company also included Michigan's senior senator. All men of "known wealth and responsibility" they may have been, but their politics were known far better. Politicians simply could not be ignored in so partisan an age.[9]

What was true at the top held true all the way down the line. Contracts went to good party men and work to those who would vote the ticket as instructed. Because of all the jobs dependent on his whim, ambitious politicians took special pains with the choice of canal commissioner. At election time, local superintendents drove their underlings to the polls and ordered them to vote the straight ticket or face dismissal. Canal revenues must be deposited in local banks, but which firms became the beneficiaries depended on their political allegiance. In New York, the state asked for 4 percent interest on what it deposited, when the going lending rate was 6 percent. Whig bankers took the funds, though they had to pay tribute for "election expenses" on top of what was due the state, had to select deserving Whigs as directors, and give the canal auditor and his friends "loans" that need never be repaid. Party newspapers took a profit from the advertisements that commissioners placed to promote contract-lettings.[10]

So political necessities skewed the public works system, but control of the public works also skewed political power. The faction dominating the state canals and railroads held impressive advantages over all rivals. From Lancaster to Lycoming came the cry that Democratic canal officers, "from defaulting collectors to thieving mud bosses," had dictated the party ticket nearly a year in advance. From their base on the Ohio Public Works Board, politicians feared no challenge, not as long as they could dispense favors enough to satisfy nosy legislators. Just before the 1855 elections, Commissioner Steedman boasted that "no matter which party beat which at the election, he would have control of the Public Works for the next five years." Just after the returns were in, the Board arranged five-year contracts with private firms to maintain and repair the canals. The allotments proved a disaster. So much fraud did a legislative investigation find that a majority of the committee called for the contracts' annulment.[11]

Alas, Steedman had bult his allegiances too solidly into the political system to be dislodged so easily. When resolutions were offered to repudiate the contracts, the bill faltered. Former congressmen and judges as well as present contractors hastened to the capitol to plead with their party fellows for lenient treatment. Among the state officers, only the governor spoke out for repudiation. In the end, the legislature arranged a compromise; it was the more independent judicial branch that dared disallow the contracts as a fraud.[12]

Enemies of state partnerships with business need not have concentrated their attention on the public works. In the 1850s every such partnership had shown signs of a corrupting influence both on the political system and on the businesses themselves. So it was with banks the states had endowed with a public bond issue and state-appointed directors. Most such institutions had collapsed a decade before, though they still could excite controversy, but where some vestige of the banks remained, receiverships became partisan jobs, and the political leadership got special favors.

In Arkansas, planters and farmers had hoped for an easy form of credit. In 1837, they persuaded the legislature to set up a privately run, publicly funded bank. The firm quickly lent all it had to those who could offer land as collateral, suspended, and left taxpayers to pay the bond issue that capitalized the firm. Arkansas was no richer than before, but a few of her solons were: the planter-politicians who ran the bank. Those borrowing money could appraise the value of the lands they offered as security, and they overvalued their properties ten times over. Those gaining the most belonged to the "Family," the interconnected Democratic clans dominating politics. They sat on the board, chose relatives for bank appraisers, managers, and trustees, and gave themselves the most generous loans. The trustees in bankruptcy compromised old debts on terms especially favorable to the Democratic leadership. As the official agents of the Real Estate Bank, the trustees liquidated the firm's assets so effectively that by 1856 the creditors found nothing but a bare vault. The trustees had seen to that: they had collected cash due the bank and had pocketed it. When debtors settled accounts by giving their slaves or lands to the trustees, both were leased out, but little or no revenue from either source reached the bank.[13]

The same political profiteering helped set up the second Indiana State Bank in 1855. Most of the original stock subscribers were politicians who wanted bank stock for the same reason their chums wanted canal contracts: to sell them at a large profit to practical businessmen who could do the work. Only twenty-eight men held the stock in seventeen branch offices. They could do so because insiders opened the subscription books in such obscure places that only their friends knew where to go. Some towns opened the books for only a few minutes. In another community a state senator opened the subscription lists (for a $5000 fee) on the third floor of a hotel, and no one but his cronies knew of it.[14]

So dubious a concern took special attention before the legislature would give its approval. When first proposed, indeed, the bank charter seemed doomed to fail. When it won a majority in the senate, the governor, who had not expected it to get six votes, was thunderstruck. He was not long at a loss for an explanation. Nor was the investigating committee two years later. The promoters had bought their privileges. The bank handed out jobs, stock, and promises of branch offices for lawmakers' home towns. Long before legislators declared the bank bill "conceived in sin and brought forth in iniquity," the bank had darkened its sinister reputation by selling out to men outside the state.[15]

From such unfortunate tangles of public and private enterprise, it might seem that the relationship of state and business was uniquely susceptible to abuse. That was not the case at all. Indeed, any agency that the government ran, even a nonprofit one, was open to corruption, as long as it needed to purchase supplies or deal with contractors. Most states could show the same payroll-padding and overcharges that the public works endured in many other public services. Ohio Democrats ran the lunatic asylums even more appallingly than the way they let Steedman run the canals. Partisans did all construction work, and though they had awarded low bidders, the officials had permitted the contractors to collect two or three times their original estimates. So badly built were the newly completed asylums that major repairs were needed before inmates could be allowed within. Contractors had installed defective water-closets, shoddy furniture, useless cooking ranges, and broken pumps in the institutions, always at exorbitant prices. D. Richmond & Co. demanded $2,681.60 for grading, an excessive sum since all the companies together had done no more than $200 of grading and D. Richmond & Co. had done none at all! Investigators found the same kind of frauds in contracts to erect a new state house and prison, and what Ohioans found matched the findings in New York, Wisconsin, and California.[16] Certainly no one suggested that the problems of the asylums and prisons could be solved by leaving them to private enterprise. No one suggested that the corruption came from the debilitating involvement of government in the management of the criminal and insane.

That was, however, the way that critics responded to the public works systems in the 1850s. They insisted rightly that the corruption would go on as long as the public works were left in politicians' hands. But instead of urging that the canals and railroads be taken out of politics by some form of professional bureaucracy just as Congress was doing with printing contracts, they declared that only the divorce of business and state could end abuse. Why did they do so? In part, it came out of the tradition of the two major parties. Democrats had always feared the partnership of public and private agencies, lest the moneyed men pervert government to their own uses. Surely the way in which contractors bilked the state proved their case. Whigs had always held special reservations about the spoils system. It left important matters to bunglers and thieves, and surely management of the public works showed this at its worst. Political manipulation of vital arteries of commerce hurt every businessman that used them, and this made conservatives cry for a public works system based on business principles.

But there was another part of the argument against the public works that became louder during the 1850s. Not theory, but the issue of corruption and mismanagement impelled Americans to divest their governments of the state canals and railroads. The economists did not need to tell citizens that private enterprise would be more efficient. Disgruntled partisans were making the point clearly enough in their exposures. Voters needed only look at how political hacks had let out contracts and privileges to see that public ownership as it was constituted was not working. From there, they reasoned that any alternative would be an improvement.

Even had divestiture not been more efficient, then, the reformers' purpose would not have faltered. They wanted to rid the government of the public works not simply to promote a more efficient transportation system, but to rid public life of one of its leading corrupters. It was an ethical matter. In stead of bandying terms like "laissez-faire" and "invisible hand" about, supporters of private ownership used other words: "annual robberies," "this source of corruption," "that rotten and corrupt body, known as the Canal Board," "a fountain of debauchery and profligacy for many years."[17] Thus Whigs who favored the positive involvement of government in the economy could support divestiture to end the spoils system's corrupting impact, while Democratic incumbents who had attacked intrusive government would defend the status quo. How could government be restored "to its original purity"? Only by destroying that great engine of patronage upon which parties in power relied.[18]

The fight was far from selfless. For one thing, private railroad lines resented state competition and sent their lobbyists to the state capitals to seek divestiture. Year after year, the Pennsylvania Railroad worked to have the state sell its works on terms that only the Pennsylvania Railroad could meet, and its efforts paid off in 1857. It is also undeniable that much of the pressure for private ownership came from the spite of parties unable to share in the spoils. But the charges were bipartisan and in the Northeast universally conceded, at least in a general sense. One reason was that factionalism, not just partisanship, had corrupted the canals, and factionalism made sure that the abuses would ever appear before the voters' eyes and explain one group's victory over another. Because there were never offices enough to sustain all factions, those left out of the profits or beaten in the state conventions cried out loudly at the frauds and rigged politics that had frozen them out.[19] Spoils politics thus corrupted the canals and assured that the corruption would be exposed, but we must not assume that the charges were false because they served one party or clique inside the party. In private, partisans gave the same response that they gave in public; testimony before legislative committees showed that the charges were true, and far from being a ruse to overcome the enemy, the accusers seem to have come to believe that divestiture alone could save the political system from utter debauchery.

The efforts that state employees made to protect their privileges only reaffirmed the reformers' belief that the canals had perverted public policy. In 1860, for example, the Ohio government nearly leased its public works for a ten-year period. As the leasing bill came to a vote, the capital swarmed with what Democrats labeled "hungry muskrats," the canal placemen and those who hoped for jobs in the future. They would not allow their livelihood to vanish without a fight. So influential were they that the Speaker of the Ohio House, who had spoken in the lease's favor, cast the deciding vote against it.[20]

Yet the reformers had their victories. Scandals in New York tightened the restrictions on canal management during the 1850s. Pennsylvania and Ohio by 1861 were out of the public works business almost entirely, and other states had not simply liquidated their state banks, but in a few cases, convinced that they had been robbed blind, had repudiated the state bonds underwriting those institutions. New states entered with guarantees against the mistakes of the older ones, as their state constitutions forbade public ownership in any form. It was true that the halcyon days of public railroad construction would not open in the South until the close of the Civil War, and New York would control its canal system until late in the century. But the same lessons could be applied there that Ohio and Arkansas had learned in the antebellum decade: a mixed enterprise invited mismanagement and theft. Divestiture would come from the very same arguments about corruption and the link to spoils politics. Both before and after the war, private enterprise would win its victories in the name of public virtue.

8

The Nine-Million-Dollar Steal

Wherever the canals ran, charges flowed. No state works could escape talk of peculation and patronage politics. Yet New York's Erie Canal stood alone. No charges were as sensational as those it elicited, and no scandal could match the one that broke out in the winter of 1852. Before it had run its course, the greed of the contractors had devastated first one party and then the other. To its harshest critics, the story was known as the "$9 Million Steal."[1]

New York's public works were the envy of every other state and an example of how canal-building could draw commerce. New York City owed its rise no less to the Great Lakes trade opened up by the Erie Canal in the 1820s than to its port facilities, and farmers upstate got a high price for their harvest because there were cheap means for shipping it out. For all that, the public works had swirled in controversy since their founding. Both parties agreed that the canals must be kept up, repaired, even enlarged, but disagreed about how to raise the money. Democrats insisted on a pay-as-you-go policy, where every appropriation carried a tax; Whigs thought the commerce of the West too important to leave to such restrictions. If money was ready in the treasury, the state could use that, but if need be, authorities should go into debt to keep the canals in good order.[2]

These policies had not only separated the two parties, but split the Democrats. The radical Barnburner wing was ready to stop the public works entirely rather than let a penny be paid irresponsibly, while the conservative Hunkers were ready to make some compromise on the issue. Long before the slavery issue deepened the rift between the two factions, the canals had grown into so bitter an issue that it pierced their ranks at election time. During the 1840s, the Barnburners had the best of it. In 1846, they managed to write a ban into the new state constitution on any new debt without a tax, and mandated that both must win the voters' approval at a general election.[3] Such a policy did the canals no good. By 1850 they had fallen into disrepair, and each new railroad cut into their trade. This hardly concerned the radical Democrats, many of whom were directors on those railway lines.[4]

Something had to be done, and Whig Governor Washington Hunt leaped into action. Troubled by the divisions in his own party over the Compromise of 1850 and the slavery issue, confident that the canal issue would unite Whigs and splinter their enemies further, committed to helping the canal, which brought life to his home town and supplied the waters to turn his factory wheels, he called on the legislature for money to complete enlargement of the canal system somehow. Hunt favored a constitutional amendment to permit fundraising, but as a fair man he mentioned alternative policies. It was one of the latter that the Whig legislature seized on. The majority prepared a bill to raise $9 million by selling certificates that could be paid from future canal revenues and till then would circulate as legal tender. This, Whigs pleaded, was not in the strictest sense a debt, because there was no express undertaking to pay nor declaration of liability by the state—only by its canals. Canal revenues would be reserved to redeem the certificates.[5]

Such hairsplitting did not convince Barnburners for a minute. With the radicals setting the tone, Democratic leaders branded the bill utterly unconstitutional. It contracted a debt without raising a tax or calling an election. Since the measure gave all contracting power to the Canal Board, where the Whigs held a slight majority, it seemed obvious that the Whigs meant to endow their friends—however unreasonable their bids—and use the funds to build an organization that would push their candidate into the Presidency a year hence. It was, simply, a corruption fund.[6]

The more the bill was pressed, the more Democrats shouted about its backers' methods. Into Albany swarmed the former presidents of broken banks, eager to use the canal certificates as a reserve on which to make loans; canal employees ready to do the state administration's bidding; and stock jobbers and "leeches" of all descriptions. It was charged that Whigs promised contracts in advance to pass the bill through the Assembly. Democratic members, with local canals to care for, were promised aid; other Democrats found their pet projects held hostage. Of the four Democrats in favor of the bill as it passed the Assembly, two were canal contractors.[7] At the same time, railroad lobbyists fearful of the competition a well-ordered canal would raise, helped the opposition. A complementary bill to cripple railroad competition by imposing a toll on their freight added to the companies' hostility: the proceeds would help enlarge the canal.[8]

Neither the motives nor the methods on either side explains why the bill turned into a constitutional crisis, nor why neither side gave way and party presses took on a hysterical tone. Antislavery Democrat William Cullen Bryant thought he knew why. He had long hoped for a political realignment on the slavery issue. Now the canal question made antislavery Whigs and antislavery Democrats into bitter foes. By forcing the issue, Senator William Seward and his manager Thurlow Weed meant to unite all Whigs behind them, Bryant speculated, and the enlargement bill brought most Democrats together, with the radicals reasserting their old devotion to fiscal responsibility. In the process, Bryant's allies had forgotten sectional disputes entirely. Unquestionably, many Democrats welcomed the crisis for just that reason. Barnburners who had walked out of the organization three years before because of the slavery issue wanted to return and in good standing. By turning the canal bill into a test of party orthodoxy, radicals not only showed their own devotion to true Jacksonian doctrine, but proved themselves better Democrats than their most conservative colleagues. By defining the issue as one of corruption and constitutional process, they also made sure that the more moderate Hunkers, even some of those friendly to the canals, would join them in laying down the line to the more conservative members.[9]

So compromise was out of the question. Democrats tried to soften the measure. A strict party vote dismissed all changes. Democrats, too, abjured halfway measures like court challenges and formal protests. Rather than permit the bill's passage, their senators warned, they would resign. Lack of a quorum would give the quietus to hundreds of bills, including those for appropriations and supply. Did the canal's friends want action on these? Let them put enlargement last on the calendar. Assured as they were that the governor would call special elections for every vacant seat, the Whigs stood fast and were ready for the Democrats when all but three resigned. Both houses adjourned, the governor issued his proclamation, and the Democrats welcomed the crisis with near-euphoria. Never was exhilaration more foolish: with special elections in the Democrats' twelve districts alone, it was a contest the party might easily lose.[10]

And lose it they did. Branding the senators "revolutionaries" and obstructionists, Whigs played on Democrats' unsporting way of blocking a vote they were sure to lose, and they courted the so-called Canal Democrats, upstate Hunkers. The senators from the canal districts came home to find their self-immolation tremendously unpopular. Whigs organized rallies all across the upstate, where prominent Democrats excoriated their colleagues as foes of commerce. The Canal Board sent its employees out to canvass for enlargement. Canal boats were draped with banners provided by the Whig state committee. All but one of the six senators from the canal districts were beaten, and the exception won by a margin of five votes. In all, the canal's friends picked up seven seats.[11]

After that, the $9 million bill sailed through both houses. Again Democrats proposed restrictions. Almost all were rejected. To appease the railroads Whigs offered to free them from the tolls that their charters had decreed. Once more Democrats saw corruption and lobbyists' pressure. Attorney-General Levi Chatfield excited the legislature when he declared that a prospective canal contractor had offered him a quarter-share in the pickings with a guaranteed profit of $10,000. Chatfield presumed that the offer was meant to buy off any court challenges to the bill, and said so. Honestly enacted or not, the $9 million bill passed easily, and Whigs went home sure that they had made a record on which they could beat Democrats easily that autumn.[12]

They were mistaken. The canal issue could hold party lines firm only if both sides cooperated, the Whigs by embracing a winning issue and the Democrats by clinging to a losing one. But Democrats would not cooperate. As soon as the bill had passed, they wheeled around to become its most earnest champions. Not that they endorsed it—"if we could repeal it, we would," the Rochester *Daily Advertiser* insisted—but they made a show of bowing to the people's will and claimed that if the law must go into effect, it was better that honest Democrats, not thieving Whigs, administer it. Indeed, the boldest Democrats garbed themselves as the sole friends of the canals. To hear some orators tell it, the only real doubters of the previous spring had been Whigs like Governor Hunt, the only real wreckers of canals since their founding had been Whig spendthrifts.[13] Except for being bogus at every point, the argument was superb, so splendid that Whigs were almost incoherent with exasperation at their opponents' nerve.

The strategy also worked. Downstate, where the canal issue mattered less, Whigs split over the slavery issue. Upstate, Canal Democrats and Barnburners buried their differences over slavery and spent their rage on Whigs who would plunder the $9 million that the canals so richly deserved. When the votes were counted, Democrats had carried most of the state officers and judgeships, an assembly majority, and most ominously of all, a majority on the Canal Board.[14]

What made that ominous was the way in which Whigs had framed the law. One provision *seemed* to oblige the government to award contracts to the lowest responsible bidder, but language specifically compelling it to do so had been voted down. Feasibly, all the lettings might go to the lowest responsible Whig or any Whig at all. That was where a second difficulty arose. Another provision directed the canal *commissioners*, largely Democratic, to give out the contracts, subject to the Canal Board's approval. If work was delayed until 1852, then Democrats could both allot and approve the contracts—a frightful thing for any Whig to contemplate. At best, they might bestow all contracts on their friends. At worst, some of the new Board members might block all contracting until the courts had studied the law's validity. If Whigs wanted anything, they must act quickly and make some deals that the Democrats already on the Board could profit by. Otherwise the minority needed to stall action only until New Year's Day.[15]

At first, the process seemed to be proceeding in an orderly way. Contractors submitted bids for work along the section. To help them, the state engineer presented standard forms to specifications and contracts. By November's close, over 3000 bids on 300 lettings had been collected. Then matters in Albany grew hectic. Board members began to open negotiations with each other about their preparing a slate of preferred contractors that could be forced upon the canal commissioners. Contractors filled the capital to press their claims. One hopeful offered to drop a thousand dollars in Attorney-General Chatfield's path for a suitable share of the lettings (the offer was not accepted, but somehow the bribe-giver ended up with a $360,000 repair job). A contractor promised a rival $2000 for withdrawing his bid. Everyone assumed that "those who had the most money" would win out, that no one could succeed on his merits. Rumor said that Weed had drawn up a list of beneficiaries before the bids were in and before he himself went on a European cruise. His ally, former Congressman David H. Abell, used what he pretended was that list to get a cut of the proceeds. To forestall other bidders and in spite of the law's strictures, some firms placed many bids for the same section and used a different partner's name each time.[16]

Under the pressure, party leaders—both Whig and Democrats of all factions—caved in. If Weed had not been on vacation among the ruins of Rome, he might have prevented the sack of Albany, though his friends held out no such hopes. The speculative fever ran too strong, and the

Whig manager's absence only let it run that much freer. Whigs had hoped for the lion's share of the lettings before the fall elections, and it was said that fifteen partisans had created a company to absorb all the work. If so, the returns stifled their plans. Now an alliance with Democratic contractors was the way to win favors. Pressure increased on Democratic Board members, including Chatfield and Lieutenant-Governor Sanford Church, to break the party line for a share of the spoils.[17]

This strategy was sure to succeed, because Democrats had fallen to fighting over which of their supporters to endow. Among the largest bidders was George Law, generous contributor to party coffers, promoter of steamship lines, experienced canal contractor, a speculator of inexhaustible greed. Behind his bids stood several canal commissioners, including Hunker Democrat John C. Mather, whose brother Calvin had shared in Law's profits. But while some Hunkers liked Law, others did not. Those who backed former Governor William Marcy for President knew Law as the bankroller of a rival. Barnburners for their part detested the promoter as a corruptionist.[18] The only question was, could Law's Democratic friends make a satisfactory alliance with the Whigs? or could the other Democrats bring over a few Whig Board members into an unbeatable combination of their own?

Day by day the alliances shifted. Slates of beneficiaries were made and broken. Thus, Whig State Engineer Hezekiah Seymour proposed to give Law one-third of the work. When two Democrats on the Board cut the apportionment to one-ninth, Seymour threatened to rejoin his fellow-Whigs, vote Law his $3 million, and leave Weed's friends the other two-thirds. Keeping their designs as secret from the other officers as they could, some Whigs arranged a deal for a precise division of the spoils between Democrats and themselves. Law would take his share from the Democratic half; his enemies would have their friends taken care of, too. Indeed, rumors flew through Albany that this slate might better be called "George Law's letting." But no sooner was this deal offered to the Board than members left out of the spoils objected and vowed to stop all action. Even a new set of rewards to Board members' friends could not prevent adjournment until the twenty-second of the month.

Exhausted, in despair, the Board decided to leave all award-making to the commissioners alone and to endorse their handiwork. A resolution directed them to give the work to the lowest bidders, though some officers later insisted that the resolution was meant merely as a suggestion. With barely a week left of their authority, the commissioners set to work. "There has been a scene of the most corrupt brokerage," State

Treasurer Alvah Hunt wrote a Whig ally. He did not add that he had been part of it as Board member and backstairs negotiator, nor that he would see to it that one firm got a contract only after it took in a penniless friend of his as partner.[19]

With only hours left, the Canal Board met on December 31 to look at the finished allotments. Attorney-General Chatfield was enraged anew, and for the usual reason: his Democratic friends got too little. For all that, he advised that the slate be accepted as the fairest to both parties that anyone could work out. Any rejection would mar the value of state securities, and on those securities alone could the contracts be financed. The Board took Chatfield's advice, though his acquiescence looked still stranger because it barely lasted into the new year. Within a week he had risen in the newly constituted Canal Board with a resolution to disallow all the contracts for not having gone to the lowest bidders. The next day, Canal Commissioner Mather submitted a resolution to have the legislature look into the contracts. Within a fortnight, the Democratic Board had asked for the power to test the law in the courts and to rescind all contracts.[20]

By then the whole case had become public knowledge, in one of the most delicious scandals New York had known. Insiders had known about affairs for a month. "There has been a *terrible* time here in regard to the canal contracts," Marcy wrote a supporter. "I have kept entirely out of the matter." He had, in fact, involved himself on behalf of some friends. So had Alvah Hunt, though he lamented that had he foreseen the scramble, he would have resigned and gone home, knowing that "my hands are clean."[21] No one escaped with clean hands—or with empty pockets.

The moment the bids were published, Barnburners charged fraud, and rightly so. In spite of the resolution of December 22, the repairs and construction had not been let out to the lowest bidders. In nearly every case, the commissioners accepted a comparatively high bid. For example, E. Ennis & Co. asked $27,264 for section 241, while D. Kenyon asked $21,119; Ennis won then, and on other sections, as well, over similar challengers. Five had offered lower bids than the gainer of section 333, and so it was from Albany to Buffalo. On section 265, there had been 48 bids lower than the winner's; on section 333, 23, on section 367, 30 bids.[22]

Apologists pointed out that the winners often took the work for less than the estimate the engineers had made for costs. If the award could have been lower, it still asked a reasonable amount. Also, was it not better to give the contractors too much than too little? If they got too little, they would abandon the work when it was half-done and the money ran out, or else would demand extra compensation. To these, the critics had powerful replies. First, State Engineer Seymour's estimates were themselves open to dispute. As an audacious Whig spoilsman, he had hoped to give contracts to his friends and had drawn up his estimates with their profits in mind. George Law himself proved how inflated the figures were. He took section 255 for $46,000 less than the official estimate. Yet he predicted that he could make at the very least a 5 percent profit.[23]

Second, even had the estimates been based on impartial study, they were not meant to show actual costs. Several subordinate engineers explained that their figures included an extra 5 to 25 percent to assure a profit on top of actual expenses, plus another 5 to 10 percent for unforeseen contingencies. The estimates thus exceeded the work's actual outlay by well over 30 percent in some cases. Yet some bidders had asked far more than the engineers' estimates and got preferment.[24]

Third, the argument ignored the fact that contractors could come back to the state for more money anyhow, as compensation for digging into two ill-defined substances, "hardpan" and "quicksand." If this extra sum were included, one division engineer guessed, the canal repairs would cost another three million dollars. Besides one dissenter asked, how much had the state ever lost by underestimating contract costs? Between 1826 and 1851, documents showed that the government had provided a bit under a million dollars for contract overruns, out of $40 million spent. That came to 2.5 percent. But here, between the lowest bidder and the winner lay a difference of 19 percent, over $1.5 million.[25] An expensive way to limit the risk that lower bidders *might* ask for more.

That the contracts had not gone to the highest bidder was the feeblest argument of all. Of 8,312 bids taken on the western division of the Erie Canal, 5,741 were higher than the ones accepted and only 2,571 were lower. Compared to those, the winners might seem moderate; but testimony showed that the moderation was as fraudulent as the grounds on which firms were rewarded. The highest bids were false. To make their own bids look legitimate, contractors had arranged with one another to put in impossibly high offers that the canal commissioners could reject. Contractors were not just told that they could ask for lavish payments. The engineers actually encouraged them to ask for all they could get. That was his recommendation to all firms, said one engineer, as "it is much more agreeable for the engineers to have to do with contractors who are making something in their work."[26]

Nor were the contractors professionals. The winners included men without a day of experience. The son of a former state senator got one section. A stone-mason and six editors suddenly found themselves with new occupations. Contracts fell to two constables, a billiard-saloon keeper, some hotel owners, a hardware merchant, a tailor, some dairymen, farmers, even minors. N. E. Paine's firm beat out 69 lower bids, including some nearly $100,000 lower, but Paine's firm contained not a single contractor. Instead, it included two Rochester editors, a former state senator, an ex-county judge, a one-time county treasurer, and ex-Congressman Abell.[27]

It was clear that the contracts were political pay-offs, meticulously arranged to award both parties equally. Making a fair split took greater skills at mathematics than most politicians had. For one thing, some of the contracts were backed by men in both parties. Yet when the commissioners defended the contracts' fairness, this was what they meant by it: neither party diddled the other. As the allotment proceeded, each party kept memos just to make sure that the balance was kept. Sometimes the commissioners chose a firm with a two-to-one Democratic majority; that forced them to give another section to a group with the same balance in Whigs' favor. There were exceptions to pure numerical advantages. A Democratic state senator whose principles forced him to resign in protest the spring before wanted a contract now. He was judged as deserving as much as "any two whigs, however meritorious," because of "the great wear and tear on his conscience." But in general, the Commissioners had kept the scales even. The whole business proceeded with utter courtesy:[28]

> One man of each side would say of one bid, this must be so, I must have control of such a piece of work; this was called 'making a point'; then another from the opposite side would make another point, and after proceeding this way for some time, the rest of the work was decided to be given to the lowest competent bidder.

That courtesy meant profits for the friends and relations of award-makers. Canal Board member Christopher Morgan got a contract for his brother, as did Commissioner Mather for his, and Commissioner Follett for his son. A second assistant engineer received one award, superintendents along the line got still others. The law forbade members of the government from taking out contracts, but one state senator got a contract and then resigned his seat, and a canal appraiser took his award without compunction. Before the final allotment was made, nearly every important Whig politician upstate had a share. A. B. Dickinson,

Henry J. Raymond, Samuel Allen, Seth White, David Abell—the list reads like the attendance record of a meeting in Thurlow Weed's rooms during the legislative session.[29]

Political "dummies" were expected to sell out to real contracting firms at once and collect a profit for surrendering the rights they never could have exercised. The contractors could still afford to make the repairs: there was money enough for a pay-off, labor costs, and profit. An inexperienced miller sold out for $1000, precisely the difference between his own bid and the purchaser's lower estimate. Such awards verged on extortion plots, and a few cases were more flagrant still. Fisher & Groat had been given a contract to build culverts. Then the commissioners ordered Jacob Groat to share his profits with the state treasurer's friends or lose the contract. A clerk for one of the canal superintendents was told that his bid had been accepted over all lower contenders, but he was shocked to learn that the contract was only in his name. The canal commissioners forced him to sell out to George Law for $75 or get nothing.[30]

With new charges appearing daily and Barnburners crying for a searing investigation, the assembly had no choice. It set up a committee. Not all the witnesses cooperated. Abell found reasons to absent himself in Salt Lake City. Others testified obligingly enough, but could not recall much, and the investigators did not try to whet their memory. A few witnesses had fabulous stories to tell. George Law explained his involvement as purely sentimental. Having worked on so many other projects, he hoped "to connect his name with that great enterprise," the Erie Canal. A legislator who helped push through the $9 million law, Henry J. Campbell, was so deeply interested in the bid of one Hamilton W. Bradshaw that when Campbell won section 208, he handed it over to his rival without asking a penny of compensation, or so Bradshaw claimed. Then there was Andrew B. Dickinson. He could not deny that he had come for a contract and got one. Yes, he conceded, he was quite a close friend of Commissioner Cook, "and I believe he would have awarded me as much work as I was entitled to without my asking his aid." So though the two men shared a room in Albany all through the allotment, Dickinson insisted that not once had he mentioned his own bid in conversation. To that one Whig insider commented, "[P]eople say tell that to the Marines, the sailors will not believe it." As for Cook, he protested that compassion for Dickinson lay at the heart of the award. The poor old farmer had mortgaged his property for a $2500 debt and needed help. That Dickinson owed that debt to Cook's brother went unmentioned.[31]

Calvin Mather was the most curious witness of all. A lawyer without practical contracting experience, he had stayed in Albany during the lettings and taken a two-thirds' interest in a contract sought by N. G. King and Company, after King had asked his help in gaining favorable treatment. As George Law's lawyer, Mather remembered talking to the state engineer about reasons why Law should get a third of the work. Yet he stoutly denied that he had peddled influence. His work for Law was strictly unofficial. King no doubt got the contract because of conservative Whig sentiments: so few of them had bid at all. Mather could not see any connection between King's overtures and Law's retainer, and the fact that Calvin's brother John was a canal commissioner. He denied absolutely that he had ever spoken of the contracts with his brother.[32]

When the investigating committee drew up its findings, majority and minority split along political lines. The majority report was a whitewash, and a slapdash job of it at that. That some contracts were let out for prices above the engineers' estimates, it thought, was made up for by blunders in the opposite direction; for the canal commissioners had bestowed other contracts at so low a rate that the firms endowed would either have to drop the work halfway through or else demand more money. Admittedly, said the majority, some of the winners were higher bidders than the losers, but many other bids had been higher still, and some of these exorbitant bids had been entered by the most prudent, capable contractors in the state. The decisions were foolish, politics had affected the commissioners' judgment, but, said the majority, no successful bribery had been proven, and therefore there was no corruption and fraud.[33] Thus, the majority tried to prove the canal commissioners honest men by demonstrating the extremity of their incompetence.

Chairman A. B. Conger spoke alone for the minority, and he minced no words. Let the majority insist that no fraud had been shown; Conger cited case after case of charges made and proven. To him, the contracting appeared a swindle from its outset. All bids had been made by ignoring the resolution of December 22, by violating the principle of taking only sealed bids and awarding only to bidders, and by rereading the phrase "safe and advantageous to the State" to mean "*terms safe enough for the State and highly advantageous to the successful bidders.*" The contracts had been null and void when made, Conger concluded, and the state need not pay them. Two weeks later he introduced a bill to submit a new $6 million loan to the voters, to be paid for by direct taxation, as a replacement for the $9 million loan.[34]

Such an investigation was heaven-sent to the Barnburners. It bore out their every prediction for what Whig canal policy would do if implemented and, better still, the scandal embarrassed the Hunker Democrats, who had been found cheek by jowl with the Whigs and with their hands in the till. For years the Hunkers had used Barnburner hostility to slavery to brand them unorthodox, even disloyal to the Democracy. This scandal let the radical Democrats turn the tables. Who more closely followed the party line here, they asked. But the revelations also outraged many Hunkers, particularly those more conciliatory to the radical wing, and made them all the more ready to take their antislavery brethren back into the party in good standing. Among the angriest attackers of the frauds were some of the "canal Democrats" of 1851, and they were not appeased when some of their fellows joined with Whigs to instruct the Canal Board to accept the contracts.[35]

If the friends of enlargement hoped that the state would disburse the $9 million before Democrats could force a court test, they hoped in vain. The Canal Board itself supported a disappointed contractor when he asked for a mandamus to award a letting to himself. Then Canal Auditor G. W. Newell declined to hand over money for work completed, and the state court of appeals agreed to hear that case. In May, the justices declared the canal law unconstitutional, the certificates invalid, and all lettings under the law as without force.[36]

The Whigs were ruined, as well they knew. What they had hoped to make into a winning issue in 1851 had now become an utter liability. "I shall never be done rejoicing that Weed and you were out of the state when the Albany troubles occurred," Seth Hawley wrote Senator Seward. "All the leading men of our party who were there were more or less damaged and accused. . . ." By mid-January, Whig insiders were predicting that the whole state ticket must be changed that fall, for every incumbent had been discredited by the contracts. Many disaffected Democrats now had a cause to fight for, and they fought with all the zeal that they had failed to show for compromises on the issue of slavery. The party chose a Hunker hostile to the $9 million swindle for governor, and propped him on a platform rebuking the jobbery of the previous December. At the same time, party strategists kept ties open with "the ultra canal interest" and the "army of contractors" by favoring canal enlargement, albeit on more cautious financial principles.[37]

Democrats found it easy to shift all the blame for corruption to the Whigs. At least three Congressional nominees had been beneficiaries of the contracts, and in one New York City district, Whigs ran James Brooks, behind whom, Barnburners muttered, George Law stood. Democrats carried every state office and both houses of the legislature—apparently the perfect ending.[38]

But the story was not complete. The scandal had one last blow to deal, this time to Democratic ranks. The Whigs would recover. Chastened by defeat, they ran reputable men for the Canal Board in 1853 and promised a canal policy that would meet all legal and ethical challenges. They won that fall, and the following winter passed a liberal appropriation for canal enlargement. This time, however, they also ratified a Democratic-sponsored constitutional amendment to permit a $10 million loan. The Whig legislature set up a Letting Board to hand out contracts, but this time they ringed it round with restrictions. The Board could reject proposals that were the result of collusion or put the state at a disadvantage. Engineers who estimated falsely were liable to five years in jail and a thousand-dollar fine. Instead of sitting in Albany, the Board must travel to where the work would be done to seek bids. Any contractor who failed to do all the work given him must forfeit 15 percent of the construction cost estimates. No state officeholder or canal employee could hold even an indirect stake in any contract.[39]

By 1854, New York Democrats would be at each others' throats. For this they could blame the canals. Barnburners remembered Mather's role in late 1851 and thirsted for retribution, even if it offended Canal Democrats, as indeed it did. Given a new lease on power, the Democratic Assembly of 1853 could not resist reviving the old scores, and pressed resolutions explicitly repudiating the contracts that the Court of Appeals had already voided. It launched a deadly investigation of its own Canal Board members, took the power to make repair contracts away from the Democratic commissioners, and so needled the Hunkers that their most adamant members turned to the Whigs for help. Of course, cried the Barnburners, they had been Whigs in all but name since the lettings, and the Canal Board included the worst of the lot. On issues of "public morality, official integrity, the public interest, & even private & personal honor, there was a cordial & efficient *union.*" Let them all be purged! they cried. In the fall elections, the scandals of the past would be trotted out again and again to belabor enemies within the party. After that, neither side felt like reconciliation. For years to come, Democrats would run two tickets. Not until 1862 would they elect a governor again—and this time he would be sensible enough to leave the canals alone.[40]

9

"Frauds Astounding Even for New York"

Ask an American where corruption flourished best, and he would have pointed to the nearest city. Because most citizens lived in the countryside, they might be explained away as hayseeds fearful of what they had scarcely seen and understood not at all. The trouble was, city-dwellers made the same deduction about depravity's most fertile soil. At times, their complaints almost took on the flavor of boasting, as when "Doesticks" declared that a close study of candidates in his city had told him that urban politics had several rules:[1]

> No one is eligible to the office of Mayor of this city unless he has forged a draft and got the money on it; and on at least two separate occasions, set fire to his house to get the insurance. . . . As to offices of more importance, I should say . . . that no man can ever be elected Governor of the state unless he is guilty of a successful burglary, complicated with a midnight murder.

The fact was that every major city liked to delude itself that its officials were among the lowest of the earth. Had not New York existed, a dozen other communities would have claimed themselves the worst city since Sodom. "No one who has done business in the East can have an idea how things are managed here," a San Francisco street contractor contended. In Chicago, Racine, Rutland, and Philadelphia, the cries at profligacy by the "courthouse clique" carried images of misrule to their extreme. But if one editor considered Chicago's corruption the worst in the nation, the New York *Tribune* thought its own mayor and council "the meanest, most corrupt, stupid and inoperative" in the world. To this, even a Philadelphia newspaper had to concede. Other cities allowed bad men into office, it said. New York positively sought them out. "Our council halls now teem with bribes," the *Evening Post* confessed,[2]

> Our papers blush with diatribes,
> Our court-rooms echo to the jibes
> Of moral insane men!
>
> And votes are offered at the block
> In party marts where sneer and mock
> A shoulder-hitting crew.
>
> Thus, whilst prosperity has shed
> Financial halos sunset-red
> Our morals look so blue!

That was not the whole story of American cities by any means. In most communities, people berated their officials for nothing worse than "old fogyism." Some cities, Boston and Charleston for instance, always kept a high reputation. But other cities were growing all too fast and prospering all too much for the institutions to restrain. Commercial expansion meant a heavier pressure on available land, a greater demand for wharfage and for transportation—all of which meant greater pressure on the city government when the time came to bestow its favors. Famine and revolution were driving millions of Europeans to abandon their homes for the New World; many got no farther than the Eastern ports. There they lived in overcrowded slums downtown or in huts and hovels beyond the last marked streets of the city. Together, commercial prosperity and immigrant poverty had profound results. Administrative agencies found the new burdens beyond their capacity; governments had to embark on construction programs to extend the roads and expand the social services into newly settled areas.

At the same time, the parties discovered in the immigrants a new, reliable source of votes. So much did the newcomers need, so inefficient or unwilling was the city government to provide it that the party organizations became the one recourse. Through them the city-dweller could find jobs on the public payroll, city railroad charters, street-cleaning contracts, or just the attention that seemed so lacking from the mayor and council. Not surprisingly, the "informal constitution" thrived in the cities. With so many voters packed into so close a space, party organizations took on a new sophistication: the Tammany Hall machine in New York City, the Broderick organization in San Francisco, the Miami Tribe in Cincinnati. Nor was it surprising that the costs of running the city went up. Bigger cities needed bigger budgets, and so did political parties based on a generous distribution of the spoils.[3] But middle-class critics grumbled that the tax increases went for graft. They complained that valuable franchises had been sold for a song, that party machines imperiled the Republic.

From the Bowery to the Barbary Coast, the cries rang that men worthiest to rule had been shoved aside and that men both incompetent and dishonest had replaced them. While city government did more than ever before, it also seemed less in control of events: there were too many economic and ethnic groups to satisfy. The cities had never seemed so disorderly as they did by 1850. Newspapers noted the violence and depravity of street gangs in the poorer sections, the "Short Boys" and "Dead Rabbits" of New York, the "Blood Tubs" of New Orleans. The "b'hoys," as such a class of rowdies were generally known, were all the worst examples of what cities did to individual morals. They frequented the rum-holes and bawdy-houses, pimped for prostitutes, and puffed "the most villainous cigars." Worst of all, they were an essential element in politics as vote-hustlers, bullies, and local officeholders.[4]

Thus it seemed that every abuse in the political process was at its worst in the city. What fraud could compare with the Whig primary in 1855, when the election inspectors in New York changed the polling-places just before dawn, so that only their friends would know where to vote? Election violence could not match the riots in Louisville, Cincinnati, or New Orleans, where rival gangs pummeled each other and emptied six-shooters at their foes. Fraud in voting was followed by fraud in counting—hardly surprising when officials in the City of Brotherly Love included the recently-paroled Schuylkill Rangers gang. So notorious was the practice that a Providence newspaper took notice only of "frauds astounding even for New York."[5]

So, too, the spoils system seemed at its most terrible, the appointees among the most unfit in the cities. Bullies who struck home for the organization found their reward in city office. Only such rewards could explain how Henry Monaghan and W. Skelly became messengers to Philadelphia's Board of Health. Skelly had been a professional pickpocket who pleased his party by knocking down opposing voters in the street. Monaghan had been implicated in fraudulent voting for the district attorney. Soon after his appointment he was arrested for passing counterfeit currency. Within months he was haled into court again for an unprovoked attack with a blackjack on an elderly English citizen.[6]

Some were bullies, others were thieves. The major complaint against the city departments was that they had become havens of graft and iniquity. In New Orleans, each recorder kept the fines he collected. New York's Corporation Counsel took fees in proceedings to open and widen city streets. Philadelphia's Commissioner of Markets extorted money from butchers and farmers and when apprehended tried to bribe the witnesses against him.[7] As on the state works, contracts were among the surest means of plunder. Sometimes blame rested on the slipshod way in which party appointees handled their accounting. The Milwaukee Comptroller cited cases in which ward authorities were presented the same bills twice and paid them both times. Many invoices failed to mention where or when the work was done. This, the comptroller suggested, was deliberate: it made oversight more difficult. The Brooklyn Commissioner of Repairs and Supplies certified work as completed that had never been begun, though again he may have done so from laxity rather than cupidity.[8] Feckless bookkeeping could not explain all the contracts so easily. One such arrangement passed the New York City Council in 1852 for removal of offal. Dead animals added to the city's stench in summertime and risked the public health, but they also could provide profit to a resourceful man. So much did the exclusive right to collect such refuse mean to one promoter that he offered the city $11 a day for the privilege, and another promised $50,000 a year. Instead, the city chose W. B. Reynolds for the task, gave him a five-year contract, and paid him $63,000 a year. In return, as a grand jury found, a city inspector received a $500 retainer each month and two aldermen $250 each.[9]

Doing a job for the city could therefore be a "job" indeed. Reynolds was but one example of a common phenomenon. The principle of lowest bidder getting the contract might be law, but city councils awarded as they pleased. In Brooklyn, by contrast, low bidders always were awarded the contracts, but the authorities then would find technicalities to take the privilege away and invest it in their friends. In Milwaukee and San Francisco the Democratic boss decided who got what contracts and at what cost.[10]

Party necessity—as in so much else—explained the allotment of privileges. What Whig in Brooklyn could turn away a bid by a contractor who had herded his employees to the polls for Whiggery? How could Mayor J. B. Cross of Milwaukee ignore the demands of Jackson Hadley, when Hadley's Democrats had provided the margin of victory for city offices, and when Hadley's manipulation of the LaCrosse & Milwaukee had brought the money that Democrats needed for vote-buying? In other cases, department heads decided as their pockets rather than parties required. Joseph E. Ebling, New York Commissioner of Streets and Lamps, had barely come into office before he made a bargain with Smith, Seckel & Co. to get their new street-sweeping machines a contract. He could withdraw any contract on a technicality, and so he did. Soon the firm had four lower wards to sweep, and kept them until each side tried to cheat the other; then Smith, Seckel & Co. took their case to the district attorney.[11]

Usually the sale was done more subtly. City officials would profit by becoming partners in firms they awarded or by giving the work to relatives, as Detroit placemen did when they bypassed the legal restrictions and chose an alderman's son of no experience to build a new workhouse. That a bridge-building job in Chicago went to the firm of Stone, Boomer & Bouton was not surprising when N. S. Bouton was superintendent of public works and could force impossible conditions on lower bidders. So confident had he been of the contract that his company molded all the castings for the bridge before bids were called for.[12]

City privileges could be as misapplied as the contracts. In bestowing the right to run street railways and ferryboats, to open saloons, to raise omnibus fares, to rent municipal piers or buy public lands, the aldermen were bombarded with appeals. They found that one way of choosing whom to favor was by finding out which could grant rewards in return. San Francisco aldermen used dummy partners to buy city lots and cornered municipal fire bonds to please their clients in private practice. In another case, land fronting the Hudson River was offered for sale by New York City. The so-called Fort Gansevoort property was valuable; as much as $300,000 had been bid for it. The aldermen sold it to several dummy bidders including the governor of the Alms House for $160,000. In their defense, the sellers insisted that there had been bids lower still, though these it turned out had been forgeries. Again the connection between sales and personal profit by city officials is easy to trace. San Francisco alderman Rodman M. Price saw to it that the Central Wharf Joint Stock Company obtained a franchise on certain city waterfronts, which was only natural: he and other aldermen were directors of the firm. When his colleagues bought the Market Street Wharf from Samuel Brannan for $100,000, they may have been affected by the fact that Brannan sat on their council.[13]

Where personal involvement did not stir the city fathers, bribery might, and in 1852 newspapers accused New York's aldermen of having turned their deliberations into a shambles in which privileges went to whoever would pay board members the most. Before a grand jury the following spring, witnesses testified that the Williamsburg ferry lease had been awarded only after officials' demand for pay had been met. "It was the damnedest fight that was ever had in the Common Council," an alderman later commented of another ferry lease; "it cost from $20,000 to $25,000." Councilmen also perfected the art of "ringing the bell," which meant the proposal of nuisance ordinances that were meant to bring injured interests running with pay-offs. Alderman Wesley Smith of New York had such a bill when he proposed to reduce coroners' fees. The city coroner paid Smith $250 to kill the resolution in committee.[14]

City officers so ready to provide profit for others could hardly be expected to keep a tight rein on what they spent on themselves, and all through the 1850s critics charged that the placeholders provided themselves with the good life at taxpayers' expense. Bought in bulk, inkstands cost a penny apiece, the New York *Evening Post* protested, yet New York's solons purchased them at $3, $5, even $12. So much might be expected of the rulers in 1852—everyone knew them to be rascals—but this was the "Reform Council" of 1854. For every major steal, reformers glimpsed a dozen minor ones, where too much had been paid for goods or property. "It takes an Alderman from three to eight thousand dollars to be elected," said the New York *Day-Book*, "and it is generally understood that this money is to be got back somehow."[15]

For these reasons as well as others, city expenses soared in the 1850s. In New York City, the "Forty Thieves" Council of 1852–53 increased spending by 70 percent and taxes by 30 percent. Between 1845 and 1855, taxes rose by 250 percent. In one year, Milwaukee's bonded debt increased by nearly $482,000. By 1858 it stood at $700,000, or twenty times its figure in 1851. Out of such incidents reformers fashioned the view of city government as typically corrupt, and of its economic needs as solely explained by official rapacity. Let the common council be kept from borrowing, Horace Greeley pleaded. "They will steal enough without it." The men in power made the same charges, and when accused defended themselves with a ludicrous ineptitude, admitting the bribery attempt but trying to prove themselves coy about having solicited payment.[16]

As a result, aldermen and common councilors, especially in New York, Milwaukee, San Francisco, and Philadelphia, found themselves in constant trouble with the law. For granting privileges in spite of a court injunction, twenty-nine New York officials were cited for contempt in 1853, others were indicted for bribery, and in 1855, three aldermen and three councilmen were arraigned for asking or taking pay-offs. In 1858 nineteen New York officers were charged, including three members of the street commission and the president of a bank in which city funds were deposited.[17]

But could the malefactors be brought to justice? Reformers held out little hope, for the party system and the hunger for profit that had bred civic corruption also skewed the administration of the law. Where a police department existed, politicians saw it as an engine of patronage. In some cities aldermen could choose the patrolmen for their wards. In others, the mayor chose deserving partisans and did not look into their past too closely. In San Francisco, the police were so corrupt and ignorant that they could not write their own names and did their best to avoid their duties, or so it was complained. Philadelphia judges complained that their dockets were overloaded with the trial of police officers, while Chicago patrolmen were indicted for arson and kidnapping. In fact, most police tried to do their duty and were ill-paid for it. Milwaukee did not even create a police department until 1855 and then paid for only a dozen officers, each of whom got $30 a month. Even reformers had to admit that the wages of most officers were too low to live on comfortably, still less when they paid election assessments, as the general practice dictated.[18]

Nor should it have come as a surprise that in many cities the police took money to leave prostitutes and gamblers alone. In Chicago, evidence suggested that one house of ill-fame had been kept by the police department itself, though it had done so modest a trade that the city treasury had to subsidize it. In an investigation of the Tombs and Blackwell's Island, New Yorkers found that the police had a regular arrangement with lawyers. For a share of the fees, police would inform attorneys of each arrest made. Accused parties would be hustled to Blackwell's Island and locked up for a week before charges could be made against them. They might pay the police to bring them back to Manhattan again. In vast sweeps of neighborhoods, police might arrest every woman they saw as a prostitute. To protect her good name, an innocent party would pay to secure a release.[19]

The courts could fight against the corruption on the police force and the abuse of public trust, and many judges did. But because courts, too, were part of the spoils system, other jurists turned a blind eye to corruptionists of their own political faith. Judges were nominated for their services to the party, and they let off defendants whose own services had gone beyond the bounds of the law. William Riley, a ward politician in New York City, fell afoul of the law for having without provocation fired two shots into his victim. He pleaded guilty. Riley was a notorious character, a gambling-house keeper who had been brought to court for assaulting a girl. But Tammany Hall took care of its own. Twenty-one prominent men petitioned the judge to suspend the two-year sentence and pleaded the good behavior of their friend. Let a rowdy elect an alderman, the New York *Tribune* declared, and the prison doors swung open as soon as he committed an offense. One such "b'hoy" came up for arson, and evidence suggested that he had set more fires than one. He escaped his seven-year sentence when men of irreproachable character petitioned to set him free. Thirty days later he was convicted of murder and assault.[20]

Some judges took care of themselves. In San Francisco it was common knowledge that money could induce a court to drop all charges. New York City Judge Sidney A. Stuart was accused of taking a $500 bribe to see that all charges were dropped against a defendant whom he described as a very old man accused of a crime "of no consequence." In fact, the accused was a well-known burglar in the prime of life, one "Buffalo Bill" Cosgrove, and when the district attorney found a new indictment, Stuart sent an officer of the court to Mrs. Cosgrove to have her wire her mate not to return to the state. Apparently the first American judge indicted for bribery, Stuart escaped conviction because the jury was unsure that he had been bribed *in money*, but it urged and got his resignation.[21]

Such conditions in the city were intolerable, but how could they be reformed? Exasperated at the extravagance, editors, merchants, and professionals joined to create reform movements. Well they knew that the two parties were alike responsible. Between Tweed and Weed was but one letter of difference, and a close bond of mutual interest. The "King of the Lobby" was always on speaking terms with William Tweed, the rising star of the Seventh Ward. He did favors for District Attorney A. Oakey Hall, entered traction schemes with Peter B. Sweeny. How, then, could the exchange of Weed's Whigs for Tweed's Democrats make New York a cleaner city? So reformers in Philadelphia, Rutland, Milwaukee, and New York broke party lines and welcomed kindred spirits everywhere under the "People's party" label. All too often, the issues were oversimplified: taxes had gone up, therefore money was being wasted and stolen; honest government meant frugal government; a change of leaders, not a change in laws, could bring reformation.[22]

Honest men seemed the simplest solution to city problems, and reformers usually put their faith in a metropolitan messiah to deliver them from the knaves. Make the People's party nominee mayor, William D. Kelley vowed, and "you will not see a rum-sodden and half-drunk convict pat him on the back in the street, . . . his office blockaded with Carson, the perjurer, and Myers, the skull-cracker, and other ruffians, setting with their feet higher than their head. . . ."[23] It was true that without honest men nothing could be done, but too often the reformers trusted to a change in rulers alone. When the latter failed to purify the system, their backers would turn on them as dupes, noddies, or worse.

Every reform mayor disillusioned his friends. The People's party rejoiced when Philadelphians elected a reform mayor in early 1858. Before summer was a month old, the *Daily News* was apologizing for him as inexperienced, clumsy, and "surrounded by selfish and vindictive men, who abuse his confidence and use his power to promote sinister objects." The worst let-down was Fernando Wood of New York. Elected under the Reform Charter of 1853, Wood at first seemed like a true reformer, and he was never as much a Mephistopheles as his enemies seemed to think. He began by closing the saloons down and working to still public disorder, and though there were later persistent reports of misconduct, no one ever proved that he actually stole funds. Once when a ship-removal contract had proven disadvantageous to the city and went to some of Wood's allies, he offered to pay the city's losses from his own pocket. But at his best, Wood was a spoilsman and permissive enough to let his aides steal from the city and stuff ballot-boxes in his favor. By 1855, critics saw in him a boss in the making. Hampered by his inability to control the other executive departments, the mayor tried to circumvent the charter by creating his own political machine. That took money and spoils, and so Wood assessed city employees and chose a police force loyal to his interests.[24]

There were other reasons that Wood became a demon-figure, and they suggest other reasons that reform did not thrive in the cities. New York's mayor favored expansion of the street railways and a free school system, pushed for sanitary reforms, urged regulations to improve tenement conditions, and after the Panic of 1857 called for government aid to the hungry. Such reforms struck many of his middle-class constituents as demagogic, not to mention expensive; surely only a corrupt, unmitigated scoundrel would so set poor against rich. It was just such narrowness of vision that betrayed the class bias of many outspoken reformers. A taxpayer's movement, for example, at once would set itself apart from the majority of city-dwellers, who owned no taxable house and benefited from city largesse. It was obvious to poorer voters that while some reformers were deeply concerned with misspent money, others were merchants affronted by rising taxes, whatever use they were put to. Indeed, the corruptionists might suspect from some of their critics a selfishness equal to their own. It was not the giving away of lucrative city privileges that roused the wrath of every protestor, but sometimes the inconvenience of paying bribes to get what deference once would have handed over gratis.

Thus, just as with the hue and cry over absconding state treasurers, publicity focused on the bribe-takers, not the bribe-givers, with a conservative effect. The Forty Thieves at City Hall took a daily dose of abuse; the George Laws that paid them did not. Nor did the men of "irreproachable character" who induced the judges to give rowdies with strong political connections a light sentencing. Rich men continued to sit in the high councils of both parties in every city. Tammany Hall, already earning a reputation for low-life with low political methods, in fact continued to be native-run and strongly influenced by the wealthy figures such as the Schell brothers who held high fraternal office in it. Yet already "a businessman's administration" was becoming the reformers' synonym for "an honest administration," and not even the New York *Evening Post* remarked on the irony of the personnel of the reform movement of 1853. When leading bankers and merchants called for an organization against "deep corruption" that year, they included William Aspinwall, Henry Grinnell, and the Brown Brothers, men whose own methods of assuring federal mail-subsidies would not bear close examination.

The cry for good men, then, was a cry into the wind. The whole system of doing public business, the acquisitiveness of respectable men able to pay for what they wanted, the necessities of party success and reward for service given, worked against an upright mayor. Reformers had two alternative solutions, each of them similarly flawed.

First, they proposed a change of laws as well as men. During the 1850s, People's parties pressed for new charters to remove old abuses, only to find that the ways of making a dishonest dollar were infinite. Milwaukeeans changed the city's fundamental laws to limit the council's power, but the administration grew unimaginably worse, and in 1858 new amendments were added to the charter. New York's "Reform Charter" of 1853 corrected many abuses. The mayor got a stronger veto power, all contracts were mandated to the lowest bidders, penalties for bribery were strengthened, and appointment of police was taken away from the aldermen. All the reforms seemed promising, but so decentralized did they leave the executive power that within a year the charter's defenders had given up on it in disgust.[25]

If cities could not be saved from within, reformers were ready to apply force from without, specifically that of the state legislature. Kept from wharfage rights by the city council, New York merchants sought state laws to enrich them. Albany Republicans were only too glad to deprive downstate Democrats of authority by setting up commissions run by

Republicans, most controversially a metropolitan police force chosen by a partisan board, to replace Wood's henchmen on the beat.[26]

Such reforms presumed that the very atmosphere of the city itself was a corrupting force, that in the state legislatures dominated by small towns, virtue could find its true reward. Agrarian thought held the unique degeneracy of city life as a commonplace, but it was delusion. The same forces that drove on the predators and pipe-layers of the city drove them on in the rural counties. Officeholders outside Chicago and Philadelphia may not have been as often bought; that did not make them less susceptible to appeals to self-interest when it was offered. What that meant was that state-based reforms would not cleanse the city. If anything, they assured that the city's corruption would infect the state governments. California lawmakers tried to extend city property beyond the San Francisco shore. The ultimate result was that the bill failed thanks to what one lobbyist described as "a good deal of the 'dust'" distributed to legislators.[27] Thus, Philadelphia corrupted Harrisburg, New York corrupted Albany, Cincinnati corrupted Columbus.

Perhaps the worst corrupter of city assemblymen were the city railroad promoters, and to have permitted them to appeal to state authorities for privileges only begged for trouble. Conceding that more transit lines were inevitable and that the demand would make the franchise-holders wealthy men indeed, businessmen and New York City officials spent eight years debating over where to place the tracks and whom to enrich with the legal rights of ownership. It was a ticklish question. Laying track down major thoroughfares would add to the noise and take away from the property value of many leading householders. Ill-equipped to handle the present commuting needs of Manhattan, established stage lines would be wrecked by competition. Other city railways brooked no new rivals, and those run by George Law had the best friends on the city council that money could buy.

If reports were true, there was plenty of money with which to buy them. Under oath, Thomas Murphy declared that he had helped obtain a franchise for the Third Avenue Railroad by giving the city council some $2100 in bribes. Witnesses declared that one individual was paid $100 to get an opposing alderman too drunk to attend on the night of the vote, though in his defense the accused pleaded that he had badly underestimated how much the member could drink. Other aldermen got $2000 in cash or options on $5000 worth of stock with twenty years to pay.[28] In some cases, the courts overturned the grants. Years of lobbying in the city did most promoters little good. In 1859 they turned to Albany, where rural lawgivers, less responsive to Manhattan pressure, might be swayed to back a "gridiron" of new lines down city streets.

Bills passed that year in the state senate, but died in the house. That fall, more friendly assemblymen were chosen and apparently the schemes enlisted the backing of Tammany Hall sachem Peter B. Sweeny (for many years interested in both the omnibuses and certain railroad projects) and Thurlow Weed. The projectors left nothing to chance. Their worst rival was Law; after he had bought up the senate, the promoters let him buy into their plans. This alliance swept both houses and helped make the legislature the most corrupt in New York's history.[29]

So the corruption of the cities did not just affect their inhabitants, but the parties that relied on the city voters and the states to which townspeople looked for favors. Certainly it offended the sensibilities of silk-stockinged men, but not just them. The city was a testing-ground for political democracy and an example that foreigners might learn from. When foes of free government across the world wanted to make their case, the Hartford *Courant* reported, they used New York City for proof that men were too degraded to rule themselves. Unless New York were cleansed, wrote a Floridian, "this government will become the scoff of the universe."[30]

Not only America's reputation was at stake. Since Jefferson's day, Americans had seen city life as the final step in a civilization's development. It was at this stage, they believed, that corruption became almost inevitable and the values which nourished a republic withered away. As the cities' power grew, the threat they posed to the Republic increased; the corruption of Fernando Wood or "Long John" Wentworth was a warning that the Union's age of innocence had come to an end. Should the cities continue to grow, Senator Andrew Johnson of Tennessee warned, "I fear this government will go as Rome went."[31]

Johnson put his faith in free homesteads as the cure. If all Americans could become independent farmers, the temptations to corruption would vanish. But others took a different, more ominous lesson from city life: that democracy no longer would work. In place of popularly elected officials, the people needed independent agencies, and boards to run them. Free from the contaminating influence of city primaries and spoils politics, a professional bureaucracy might provide good government. Others blamed the masses of foreigners for the poverty and depravity of the cities and the violence on Election Day, and sought to rid politics of their presence.

Wrong though their solutions may have been, the reformers were afraid of something real and tangible: a combination of corruption and chaos, venality and violence, that threatened politics as well as the public order. Their solutions would not be adopted, and the cities would grow no better. Instead, the 1850s saw another solution to the problem of disorder in the rise of the political boss. Combining the power to grant patronage to his lower-class backers with the ability to deliver privileges to the special interests, he would bring some semblance of order to cities. In the decades that followed, metropolitan centers achieved far more than their critics would claim, and the middle-class—even the reformers—would have greater power to make decisions than legend would suggest. Far from being a tyrant, the bosses of the future would serve as brokers and fair dealers between clashing intersets.[32] Yet it would not be a clean government, nor in many cases an honest one. Instead, the evils reformers saw in the 1850s would grow worse. Still, Fernando Wood's New York had prepared the way for the city ruled by Boss Tweed; the political manipulations of "Long John" Wentworth set the tone for the political wolves in the days of "Bathhouse John" Coughlin and "Big Bill" Thompson.

10

Forbidden Fruits of Manifest Destiny

With the end of the Mexican War and the discovery of gold in California in 1848, the Golden Age began. So it seemed at least to Americans in the decade that followed. After the dull years following the Panic of 1837, any prosperity would have been welcome, but this boom surpassed all expectations. Financiers had more money to invest, and they credited "the golden shower" from the Pacific Coast for that. Not only the Wall Street operators but merchants and manufacturers, poets and farmers did well. With the prosperity came a robust optimism. Anything seemed possible, and it seemed that any project, no matter how costly, was being proposed. Real promoters "cannot afford time to think of schemes involving less than six figures," said the New York *Herald*, and it noted how many of these looked to the government for their partner and fund-raiser.[1]

That was why the Age of Gold in business seemed to many the Age of Iron for public ethics. The possibilities of wealth made materialists of all men, and materialists were not fastidious in the methods by which they became rich. With thousands more acres of rich farmland and millions more of desert added to the national domain by treaty, the land speculators took on a new energy. With millions more in revenue pouring into the government coffers, the applicants for a share of the money multiplied. The clamor for land titles, claims, and government favors—these, too, were the effects of the boom that Manifest Destiny had created.

The eagerness for land had been an American trait since the founding of Jamestown. As railroads sped up the westward expansion of population, the speculative fever sharpened. Let a purchaser of a thousand acres choose his site well and do the right job of promotion, and he might see land bought from the government at $1.25 an acre sold to settlers for five times as much. The forests of one year might become the commercial entrepôt of the next. It had happened before, and by the 1850s many Americans were confident that it would happen again on the soil of their choosing. Beloit, Wisconsin, was like many another community. In 1850 a drowsy little crossroads hamlet, by 1858 it boasted a 400 percent increase in population. With the construction of a railroad to Rock River, the town had joined in the boom. It had built a new college and six churches, replaced its wooden business buildings with edifices of stone and brick, and even paved the streets. What town, a promoter asked, could boast "a more exciting moral atmosphere"?[2]

Exciting, perhaps, but the speculative frenzy was not particularly moral. By the summer of 1857 the passion for public lands for immediate resale had thrown real settlers on the defensive. As late as May, the broad Kansas prairies north of the Pottawatomic River lay unclaimed. By the end of June, every inch had been spoken for, hardly any of it by actual farmers. Of 637 parcels sold to supposed inhabitants, the land commissioner commented, 297 were transferred from their first owner to someone else before the latter left the land office. Men hired themselves out to put down stakes on property that speculators wanted cheaply, since no one would bid against a "squatter." In Minnesota that same summer, promoters laid out paper towns, complete with nonexistent railroads and waterways, to lure in immigrants. As any acreage depended on communications for its value, the fever for real estate added to the zeal for railroad construction. That previous winter, the Kansas territorial legislature had granted some fifteen charters to its friends, and its foes no doubt could have done with fifteen more. With reason a newspaperman could declare that the speculative possibilities "turn men's brains."[3]

Hungry as they were for more land at a cheap price, the speculators looked to Congress for satisfaction, and the lawmakers that had seen the nation's holdings increase by a third were ready to oblige. Any settler could buy 160 acres—a quarter-section, as it was known—for $200, with easy terms of payment. Other acts opened new opportunities: reclamation of federal "swamp lands," a quarter-section bounty to every enlisted man in every war, their widows and descendants, military teamsters, wagonmasters, and chaplains.[4]

The only way in which such laws could have prevented the speculators in land from making a profit on the sale of government warrants for quarter-sections would have been to restrict the gift only to the original holders of warrants, which is what the Secretary of Interior tried in 1850. But Congress overrode his interpretation and made the warrants assignable. With that decision, the value to speculators increased, as veterans cashed in their quarter-sections for whatever the market would bear. Before the decade's end some 32 million acres had been conveyed, and an Iowa senator complained that his state had been "literally shingled over with land warrants given to the Wall Street and other speculators, and bounty land warrants. . . ."[5]

Such Congressional prodigality was possible because so many public officials were themselves speculators and interested in the land boom. It would have been more surprising had they not been, for the temptations to invest were nearly irresistible, but their judgment was affected. One Western senator would later charge that the warrants had been made assignable because so many of his colleagues "had their pockets full of land warrants" already purchased. Certainly some had been buying well in advance, including Congressman Bernhart Henn of Iowa, who had made his purchase and sale into a business. Others, including Senator William Seward of New York, were approached with partnership deals. Behind the railroad subsidies of the 1850s lay not just bribe-takers but landholding lawmakers who knew that by their votes they could give their own real estate an enhanced value. In one of the most brazen cases, Senator John Slidell apparently contrived to slip through a measure confirming his own title to the vast Houmas land grant and overturning court decisions to the contrary. As president of the Florida Railroad, Senator David Yulee saw to it that Congress provided it with a land grant.[6]

Nearer to the land rush as they were, territorial governors felt the temptation more keenly. The temptation was worst in Kansas, where the rapid settlement of the mid-1850s ruined the career of Andrew Reeder. He had barely reached the territory before he began to use his official position to buy up land claims and to bargain with the Indians for more real estate. When he visited one tribe, he bought their holdings at $2.50 an acre—which, Indian Commissioner George Manypenny insisted, was robbery: the land was worth twice as much (though Manypenny had bought lands for less in the government's name and his predecessor had paid eighteen cents an acre for Indian land). In all, the government later charged, Reeder had cheated the Indians out of $1500 on each of thirteen claims. Having a political grudge against Reeder, the government may have set an unduly strict standard when it dismissed him for mixing politics with land speculation, but Reeder's behavior was exceptional in one particular. In collusion with the military quartermaster and paymaster departments at Fort Leavenworth, the governor had arranged to speculate in lands owned by the federal government. The commander of Fort Riley shifted military property to the public domain, bought it up in his private capacity, built Pawnee City on it, and Reeder, who held an eighty-acre share, decreed the community the new territorial capital and summoned the legislature to meet there (the legislature, for political reasons of its own, did not oblige him). For these speculations the army court-martialed Fort Riley's commander.[7]

The other way in which an expanding economy and an expanding nation led to a speculative corruption was in the growth of claims against the government. With the end of the Mexican War, the pressure to repay claims intensified, and weaknesses in the system became more apparent than ever. "How many members of this body ever examine into the merits of private claims?" asked a Delaware senator. At best the men on Capitol Hill had time enough to do a cursory job—cursory, inadequate, and time-consuming. Every week, two days were set aside for the private bills and reports, and even then, as one congressman pointed out, not more than half were acted upon. Claims twice defeated could always be pressed again and pushed session after session until they went through. A claimant could always expect support from his congressman, and on some occasions the Senate would refer the request for money to the representative who proposed it for an evaluation of its merits. His report was always favorable. This helped, but few representatives understood what they were voting on, and the arguments used by either side hardly convinced them. Naturally, just claims often went unpaid and unjust ones often passed immediately. A claim might pass easily, and its twin fail overwhelmingly. "'Mighty unsartin,' you see, is Congress," sighed a claims agent.[8]

That was precisely why claims agents were so necessary, to prevent that uncertainty. But to do so they often did more than wheedle and plead. Certainly corruption existed, when congressmen acted as claims agents themselves and claimants found that they must use professional lobbyists' services whether they wanted them or not. Senator James Bayard of Delaware recalled one case that had come before his Claims Committee. The petitioner seemed deserving, but had failed to say how much he wanted. Bayard called him in. Forty thousand dollars would make up for all his costs, said the claimant. Why had he not said so? Because, the man explained, if he had specified, "I should either have had to pay away from one-half to two-thirds of the amount to the claim agents of Washington, or they would have defeated my bill."[9]

Because so much depended on good lobbying rather than good evidence, the claimants advanced cases that withered under scrutiny. Claims for damage done when American troops marched into Spanish Florida in 1812 and 1818 had not yet been settled by the 1850s, and had swollen twenty-five times over in twenty years; they included such items as the cost for crops of cotton at fifty cents a pound that had never been planted because of the disturbance that the invasions had caused. In the states, the same pressure mounted, often for claims just as spurious as those for Florida.[10]

By far the most rapacious agents were those representing Indian tribes. Since the founding of the Republic, the government had tried to buy Indian lands and persuade or force the inhabitants to settle farther west. Officials would soak the chiefs in rum and misrepresent to them the meaning of the treaties they were asked to sign, or would buy certain leaders and let their signatures bind the rest. Most tribesmen had no clear sense of how large an acre was, nor of what precise ground they were giving away. That made them easy marks for the negotiators, but it also made them sure victims of the claims agents, who offered to reopen every bad bargain and give the Indians more, in return for 20 to 50 percent of the take.

Sometimes the claims agents did the Indians a service. No congressman had the time to ferret through archives for the papers that might prove the Indians' rights, but agents did. Yet the lobbyists asked a heavy price, and they found ways of taking out legal expenses before the money could reach the tribes. Indeed, Senator Sam Houston of Texas doubted that a third of the $100 million spent on Indians since the Revolution reached the hands of those for whom it was meant. Incorruptible men might become attorneys, but their scruples vanished where the red man was concerned. "I hardly ever knew a man to lose his position, either in society or in office, for cheating the Indians," said Houston.[11] At the same time, the agents' methods of persuasion in Washington were notorious.

One of the most controversial Indian claims involved Richard W. Thompson and the Menominees of Wisconsin. In 1848, the government had bought a large tract of their land for a pittance and promised them an equal portion of Minnesota lands in the bargain. Because the Indian Commissioner had been vague about how many of their acres he wanted, the Indians complained that they had been cheated and demanded either more money or a smaller cession of land. They sent a delegation to

Washington. Thompson was the Whig commissioner for treating with the Sioux and other tribes, but he offered to act as the Menominees' lawyer and to arrange additional compensation through his superiors. The contract he signed guaranteed him a third of the profits and was approved by Secretary of the Interior Thomas Ewing, who may have been all the more willing because of the close partnership Thompson had with his distant relations, W. G. and G. W. Ewing. The Ewings traded with the tribe and hoped to get half of the expected appropriation themselves.

By the time the Senate got around to voting the supplement for the Menominees, the Democrats were back in power and had heard ugly rumors about Thompson's arrangement. Manypenny, the new Indian Commissioner, sent an agent west to make a new treaty. Keeping Thompson away from the council fires, the emissary got the Menominees to agree to take Wisconsin lands and another $150,000; and to keep Thompson from taking his whole sum off the top, the agreement arranged to pay the Indians in annual installments as soon as the installments on the present payment ran out in 1867. Thompson, who had hoped that the government would award the Indians three times as much, did manage to have the Senate add $92,000 to the award, but what bothered him most was how he and the Ewings were prevented from collecting their fees. Commissioner Manypenny saw to it that the original annuity got to the Indians before Thompson got his hands on it, by paying each brave his own share of the annuity. In doing so, he was simply following the intentions of an 1852 law, which was aimed at preventing just such a prior lien on the funds as Thompson wanted to obtain, but that did not make Thompson any happier. Indeed, he was kept from waylaying the money at one point only by the bayonets of thirteen soldiers, who stood around the paymaster that the government sent out to Indian lands.[12]

Back to Congress Thompson went. In 1854 he induced the chiefs to sign a memorial asking federal officers to give their lawyer his share of the award immediately. Apparently the Indians who signed the memorial did not all know what was in it, some could not read, others were bullied or bribed to sign, and others were told that the money was necessary because Thompson had gone into debt bribing a hostile senator to absent himself on the day that the supplemental appropriation came to a vote. Thompson also let traders and creditors of the tribe know that if they made the chiefs sign the memorial, he would see that their claims, too, were taken out of the supplemental award before the Indians saw any of it. When these revelations came to light, the Indian Commissioner vowed to pay Thompson nothing, memorial or no. Nor did he. In vain Thompson sought a change in the laws to take the decision about payment out of the Commissioner's hands. To have done so would have broken the barrier that the Senate had erected against the Indian agents in 1852, Senator Judah P. Benjamin of Louisiana commented. He continued, "[I]t is easy to see how long it will be before the Indians will not receive one cent out of the annuities that belong to them." The Senate did not oblige Thompson that year. Only with the advent of an Administration of greater ethical laxity would the Treasury doors swing open, and then to repay a political debt.[13]

Many congressmen would have gladly turned the claims settlements over to the Treasury or to independent boards, but neither could be trusted to do its work on a case's merits. By 1850, the Taylor Administration had shown that. Secretary of the Interior Ewing had illustrated the process at its most capricious. In one case, Mississippi politician William Gwin had sponsored a $112,000 claim of the Chickasaws for half the award. One of the signatures on Gwin's power of attorney was clearly invalid, and the new power of attorney that Gwin claimed to have made had vanished by the time Congress asked to see it. Another claim for $77,000 by the Potawatomies was advanced by Thompson's two Indian trade cohorts, the Ewings, in return for a large fee. In the 1840s a Democratic Indian Commissioner had stood in the way of both claims, and Secretary of War William Marcy had vowed that before he saw the Chickasaw claim paid, he would rot in his grave. But when the Whigs came in, Secretary Ewing reopened both cases and paid them. Before the Chickasaws saw any of the settlement, Gwin collected $56,000 for himself and his friends.[14]

Congressional investigators might have grilled Ewing more severely for such generosity to his cousins, had not another scandal broken at the same time, one that added a new word to the lexicon of corruption. In 1772, the Creek and Cherokee Indians had ceded lands to the Crown, in return for which the British promised to pay the Indians' bills to traders. Among the Georgia creditors was George Galphin. Because he supported the Revolution, the Crown chose not to pay him what was owed. In 1793, his heirs sought restitution from the Georgia legislature. While committees regularly reported in the claim's favor, the lawmakers always made the plea that the new state could not afford the expense. Not until the 1830s did the claimants consider tapping the national Treasury.

In 1835, the pledge to pay the Galphin claim appeared in an Indian treaty made by the United States. Before the treaty passed the Senate, the clause was struck off, but from then on Congress was under pressure to make the payment. Georgia politicians were particularly persistent in trying to spare their own taxpayers the burden. So was the lawyer for the Galphins, George Crawford, who stood to collect half of any sum the government provided. At last in 1848 the Congress voted to pay the Galphins; but did the obligation include interest as well as principal? The outgoing Democratic Secretary of the Treasury was not sure. He paid the principal alone. The incoming first comptroller *was* sure. The Galphin claim was no just debt of the United States, he argued. Any payment was a favor to the claimants, and since the law did not specify the payment of interest, no interest should be paid.

Crawford and Joseph Bryan, attorneys and leading Whig politicians, persisted, and the Whigs' new Secretary of the Treasury William Meredith turned to Attorney-General Reverdy Johnson for a second opinion. Johnson thought that the seventy-three years of interest should be paid, though it amounted to nearly five times the size of the principal: $191,352.89 on the $43,518.97 owed. What made this scandalous, besides the size of the payment, was that Crawford happened to be Secretary of War. He had kept his claim after entering the Cabinet, after his friends had persuaded him that the issue would never come before any of his colleagues except the Secretary of the Treasury. The President had been informed, but in such vague terms that he presumed that Crawford's claimholdings were some unspecified ones still pending in Congress.

What a House committee soon discovered did the Administration little good. By five to four, a majority declared the Galphin claim no just debt of the nation and the payment of interest wholly unwarranted. Both the Attorney-General and the Secretary of the Treasury insisted that they had known nothing of Crawford's involvement, which if true showed an unbecoming slackness, since the papers passed on to Johnson included Crawford's power of attorney. Meredith also admitted that he had heard about Crawford's connection with the claim, but that his mind had not absorbed the fact. It also came out that in the Cabinet, Crawford had spoken to both officials several times to hasten them in their decision and may have added that some Georgia friends of his were keenly interested in a favorable settlement. Democrats could uncover no evidence that Crawford had split his winnings with other Cabinet officers, but they were convinced that more such steals remained undisclosed by the investigation. Whig officeholders had a nasty habit of logrolling through such "Gulping claims" to gratify prominent men in their party, said the New York *Herald*. All such takings were compressed into the term "Galphinism," and even Whig newspapers called for a purge of the Cabinet. President Taylor gradually came to the same conclusion. A few days before he died, he confided to Thurlow Weed that he meant to compel his entire Cabinet's resignation.[15]

The alternative was an independent claims commission, but here too the possibilities for fraud were considerable and the worst cases involved Whig officeholders. As part of the peace settlement of 1848, the United States had taken on responsibility for its citizens' claims against Mexico. The Taylor Administration chose a three-man board to judge the merits of each case and dispense the money.

It soon became clear that the process invited improper political influence and outright fraud. The claims commissioners held private sessions, kept secret their opinions on each case's merits, and gave the government no spokesman against the claimants. The board's decisions were final. On their authorization the Treasury would pay what was requested. All three appointees were Whig politicians, and two of them were financially interested in several of the claims that came before them. Congressmen and members of the Administration appeared before them as lawyers for the claimants. All of these factors may explain why among the largest of the 198 claims recognized as valid were several glaring frauds. The claim of John H. Mears, on which $153,000 was realized, for example, proved a tissue of lies. So was that of his partner, George A. Gardiner.

Dr. Gardiner was an amiable young dentist who claimed that when the Mexicans expelled him from San Luis Potosi in October 1846, he had lost several valuable silver mines. His buildings had been burned, his property confiscated, his equipment wrecked—or so he said. The Claims Commission could not give Gardiner the $1.6 million he wanted, but they did allow him $482,000. No doubt the doctor was content to get anything. So bogus were the affidavits in the case that a Treasury clerk brought them to the attention of the police. What investigators found amazed them. Gardiner had no silver mines at all. In fact, no one owned a mine of any sort in the district. His deeds had been forged; their government seal was a counterfeit.

Indicted for perjury, Gardiner could not produce a scrap of evidence in his defense. All efforts to make the doctor locate the mines more specifically failed. The prosecution showed that the ten depositions from Americans in Mexico that Gardiner had produced had all been written in the same handwriting. Each of them swore to a falsity. Indeed, the grand jury suspected that many of the signatories were as fictitious as the mine. The perjury trial ended in a disagreement, though subsequent evidence proved Gardiner's guilt beyond question. The second trial, for forgery, brought in a conviction. Sentenced to ten years at hard labor and unable to bear the shame, Gardiner swallowed strychnine. His funeral was not widely attended. Five years later the government was still trying to wring repayment from his estate.[16]

The case was all the more sensational because of Gardiner's connection with Secretary Meredith's successor, Thomas Corwin of Ohio. Corwin had been a senator when he was hired as attorney before the claims commissioners. So profitable a claim was it that he bought a large share. In part this was because Corwin and his relatives were ardent speculators. The senator also held an interest in the Mears claim and nine others before the Mexican Claims Commission. It was perhaps unfortunate that Corwin should hire himself as advocate and make himself beneficiary before a board on which his cousin and law partner Robert G. Corwin sat. Robert's judgment may already have been affected by his own large financial share in the Gardiner claim. Caleb B. Smith, another commissioner, was one of the sureties for the money the senator borrowed to buy his share. When Corwin entered the Treasury, he rid himself of his claims. The promoter George Law, with an interest in cooperative government officials for his own financial schemes, bought Corwin out for $81,000 in cash. Robert Corwin kept his share, and when the Commission ruled Gardiner's claim legal, made a $20,000 profit on his investment.[17]

None of this was illegal. No statute kept lawmakers or government officials from investing in claims or advocating their merits, though to be sure few had the advantage of a cousin on the Claims Commission. The Secretary pleaded his own ignorance of the holes in Gardiner's case, though Democrats wondered how so experienced a lawyer could have failed to scan the documents that a petty clerk had known at a glance were bogus. A bipartisan House committee examined Corwin's role and found no proof that he had committed any corrupt action. It missed the real issue: that unlike a mere lawyer a senator had a special obligation to serve the public, by showing a special delicacy in the claims he advanced and an exceptional care in making sure that they were not a fraud on the taxpayers. Whigs expressed hopes that Corwin would return his earnings, though they did not insist on it. Their hopes were never realized.[18] Indeed, before he left office, the Secretary arranged one more deal for his clan. Without seeking public bids, he handed out a contract to build lighthouses along the Pacific coast to a group of promoters whose purpose was to sell their rights to a Baltimore firm for $15,000. Among the beneficiaries was Robert G. Corwin.[19]

Scandals like Gardiner's did not just show that any agency could be defrauded of money. Honest men like Manypenny or First Comptroller Elisha Whittlesey were always around to make life harder for the profiteers. When the California Claims Commission recognized claims that relied on frauds nearly as brazen as those of Gardiner and Mears, it found itself overruled seventeen times. A dogged Attorney-General and his relentless agent, Edwin M. Stanton of Pennsylvania, uncovered rascalities enough to bring several federal indictments for forgery and perjury. What the scandals did show was that the claims business was too important to leave to partisans chosen as a reward for office and lobbyists chosen for their effectiveness rather than their ethics. Only slowly did Congress remedy the errors of the past. Because of the Galphin and Gardiner scandals it enacted the first law forbidding bribery in 1853; until then the common law had covered the subject. The same act forbade any department officer from assisting a claimant against the United States either as agent or attorney. Congressmen could press claims before either house only if they took no pay, though they could take a fee to prosecute a claim in the courts. Nor could federal officers share in any claim.[20]

This was a modest beginning, and the next Congress continued the reform by creating a special three-man court to adjudicate claims founded on statute or departmental regulations. Unlike the Mexican Claims Commission—indeed, because of that commission's record—the new court had public sessions. It was required to publish its opinions and was authorized to let the government send counsel to make its case. No congressman could plead before it. Nor would the tribunal have the final decision. Congress must confirm and pay for any claim recommended. Many congressmen hoped that they would be spared the pressure from private claims. Reformers hoped that no new frauds would be passed through the Treasury, and they applauded President Franklin Pierce's choices for judge. All three were men of known probity and high legal standing, and all three were chosen for their reputations as mortal enemies of jobbery.[21]

In fact, the Claims Court did not live up to its promise, honest though its judges and modest though its awards were. The weaknesses built in to prevent a new Gardiner fraud made the tribunal a frustrating alternative to the traditional process. Justly was it called a Claims Court, the Louisville *Daily Democrat* joked, for it only claimed to be a court. It had all the pomp of a bench, but none of the real force. It was "only a kind of breakwater between the committees of Congress and Congress itself," and not a very good breakwater at that. Appellants reluctant to trust to the judges ignored them and ran to Capitol Hill with their appeals. In 1860, the legislative calendar was still covered with claims cases, and the pressure in the closing days of a session were still tremendous. "With general legislation . . . undisposed of," a Kentucky congressman raged, "this floor is farmed out—yes, sir, farmed out—under an agreement. . . . Every gentleman here, with a private bill sticking in his pocket, struggles for the floor, and gets in matters which we cannot investigate; the rules are suspended, and legislation is hurried through without our knowing anything about it."[22] Not until 1863 would Congress give the Claims Court the powers it needed.

Each claim by itself looked disturbing. Yet contemporaries saw a more sinister pattern between them. Each claimant before Congress relied on the rest for his support. No representative with claims of his own state's to advance would vote against those of his colleagues. Congressmen sharing a stake in one land speculation scheme looked to those involved in another project for support. Rumors circulated that all the claimants had banded together to create a mutual corruption fund to work on Congress and the executive departments. Between the Galphin and Gardiner profiteers and the supporters of railroad land grants and steamship subsidies, there was a common strand of self-interest. Some speculators, such as George Law and W. W. Corcoran, had involved themselves in both.[23]

Faced with the prospects of financial advantage, partisan hatreds might dissolve. That may not have been entirely a misfortune. In Kansas, for example, the hostility between proslavery and antislavery settlers had erupted in violence in the mid-1850s. Yet the more the speculative fever swept Kansas, the more the bitter foes in politics made alliances in finance. This was only natural. Any Congressional land grant or railroad aid would need the support of both parties. But it left observers like one newspaper reporter a little dazed to see deadly political enemies "lying down together . . . 'hail fellow well met,' and partners in trade, growing fat in their purses and persons by speculations in town sites; eating roasted turkeys and drinking champaigne with the very money sent here . . . to make Kansas a *slave state*; and refusing to render an account . . . as to how they have disbursed their funds." By 1859, antislavery leader Charles Robinson had tied himself to railroad projects that were backed by the territorial governors with whom he had always been on bad terms and chartered by a proslavery legislature, the validity of which he had refused to recognize. Some men, including one territorial governor, wondered if the greed could be turned to account in settling disputes over slavery. A large land grant to Kansas, the governor thought, might offer spoils enough for both sides to drop their differences.[24]

To be sure, not all differences could have been solved so easily. Men like Charles Robinson or Jim Lane could never have swallowed lands enough to make them gulp down a proslavery state constitution. For all their close business relations as Minnesota land speculators, Senators Stephen A. Douglas and Jesse Bright continued to clash until the death of the former and the expulsion from the Senate of the latter. Still, it was true that claims and land speculations were among the strands that bound officials in all parties to one another. It was equally true that they would look out for each other's financial interests at the Treasury's expense. Out of their investments came a public suspicion that the nation's leaders were a crew of selfish, self-interested men, who used their high positions to further their business careers or used their connections to gouge the governments for claims.

Out of such connections as both parties made grew the suspicion that all the talk about issues and party platforms was mere claptrap, that Whig and Democratic leaders had become not enemies but the most dangerous of friends, and the parties mere engines for the pursuit of plunder. The critics were not quite right, any more than their darkest suspicions in the Galphin scandal had been quite right, but they were right enough. "Galphinism" was the disease of every political organization, and prosperity the bane of public virtue.

III

Prognosis — The Corruption of the Parties

11

Waiting for Caesar

Letters, newspapers, committee reports: all testify to the pervasiveness and variety of corruption in the 1850s. Even after the editorial lies and stump-speech fabrications are sifted out, the facts remaining tell a devastating story of public officials and party hacks who abused their authority to line their pockets or thwart the democratic process. Statesmen in Washington sat next to scoundrels. Some statesmen *were* scoundrels, part-preacher and part-predator. Corruption had grown as the nation grew, and the rapid expansion that began with the Mexican war meant a crowd of crooked claims and land frauds, connived at with government influence. Abuses of the spoils system had grown as the number of officeholders multiplied, and by the 1850s more men sought, enjoyed, and exploited government berths than ever before. Never had both parties been so generous to promoters seeking government aid, and never had the Treasury had so much revenue with which to show that generosity—and how well the lobbyists knew it. Americans should have felt concerned, and so they did.

But should they have felt alarmed? The loss of the nation's virtue was unfortunate, no doubt, but was it not a loss that the Republic could survive? The Republic, after all, had not been founded on the faith that men would lose their foibles, greed, jealousies, nor parochial prejudices. The Founders wrote a constitution that might protect institutions from the consequences of human frailties. Indeed, James Madison trusted to the clash of competing interests to make the government work best. Even a more depraved self-interest had had its defenders. The most notable was Dr. Bernard Mandeville, the humorous Hollander who proposed that a corrupted society might be best, a society in which "Such were the blessings of that State/Their crimes conspired to make 'em great." "Private vices" could bring "public benefits."[1] Yet articulate Americans felt alarmed. We have already seen some of the causes for alarm: corruption added to the violence at election time, cast the political system into disrepute, weakened the power of state parties to resist the national party or state governments to resist the federal authorities, and undermined the newspapers' ability to let the public know the truth. But beyond that abundance of fears was a larger, more general one—fear for the fate of republican government. If this book's first question has been, how much corruption was there? the second must be, why did so many men, apparently rational, advance from their discovery of external corruption to conclusions about the internal decay of American institutions?

When most literate Americans considered the nature of power or republics' fragility, they turned to the views of their forefathers. For Adams and Jefferson, the Mandevillainy of self-interest was out of the question. They knew well that corruption was the inseparable kin of arbitrary power. The fears of the fathers did not translate perfectly into the suspicions of the sons. Much had happened to the republican theory of Jefferson's day before it reached his grandchildren.[2] The classical republican definition of "virtue" encompassed far more than the refusal to cheat and steal that later generations meant by it. Faction and party were no longer seen as fleeting menaces to the ideal republican state, but permanent institutions, perhaps even beneficial ones. By 1850, republican theory had many variations. Still, in several basic respects the philosophy remained unaltered. Republics were fragile things. Subversion from within, not enemies from without, endangered them the most. Corruption and liberty must prove incompatible, for corruption destroyed the public virtue on which any free government must depend.

America was a successful experiment, citizens agreed, but still no more than an experiment. Of course a government of the people was better than any other, and Americans hoped that their society would inspire revolutionaries worldwide in their struggle against monarchy. With its promise of opportunity for the mass of white males, republicanism might dominate the globe.[3] But if it was true that the world could be changed by the contagion of democracy, it was also true that the Republic could be changed by the contamination of the world. This struck Americans as no remote threat. History was littered with the ruins of such experiments as the United States. From the Greek and Roman republics, which had turned to empire, to the Dutch, who bartered away their freedom to princes, to the second French Republic, which had allowed an upstart Napoleon to usurp its liberties, the record had known no exceptions.* "We are not better by nature than other people," Alexander Stephens wrote, "—no better than were the Greeks, the Romans, or the French. The only difference thus far between us and the last named nation has been that our public men have been more thoroughly schooled in sound principles of political morality. In our worst crises of corruption there has been a predominance of public virtue and loyalty to the country in the national councils."[4]

Republics often collapsed in one dramatic incident, such as Bonaparte sending his soldiers into the National Assembly to cast it forth, but that moment was deceptive. Then was the instant at which free government perished, but that government had been dying for some time. Republics were lost by degrees. A sudden usurpation would shock a free people and force it to consider remedies. By contrast, "the gradual, slow, silent, and almost imperceptible" shift from first principles to decay and misgovernment produced the real threat to freedom and always had. First came corruption and the discrediting of a people's right to rule itself. Then came the tyrant. Sometimes he came as a scourge for degeneracy. Sometimes he rose by encouraging profligacy, until the people's virtue had been exhausted. The result was the same in the end.[5]

Could statesmen shape institutions that might forestall a Caesar's plans, before he turned the Republic's sins against itself? A system of constitutional checks and balances seemed the best means of doing so. Each branch would then be jealous of the others and ready to hold them in check, and no one man would find it easy to amass overwhelming power. The hand that held the purse-strings would not hold the sword, nor would the maker of the laws enforce them. The federal structure itself would afford a second protection. By limiting the central government's power and leaving broad authority to the states, the Constitution had made difficult any tyranny arising at the center of national affairs. The states in turn left autonomy to the towns and counties. "There it is, sir, we

*Ironically, Rome remained Americans' symbol for the ideal in purity and the epitome of corruption and decline. Only rarely did public figures challenge the analogy between the Empire and the Republic, though political scientist Francis Lieber did. For most orators, the highest term of praise for honesty was "old Roman," a title bestowed on Jackson and Benton alike. Every evil in republics, similarly, was associated with the fall of Rome: extravagance, vote-buying, party strife, urban growth, personal depravity, violence at the polls, and the rewarding of friends.

must look for the beauty and perfection of our system of government," said a Michigander of the towns, "and hence, from these pure fountains of political power will spring reform; . . . 'look not to your central power for reform.'"[6] Even so, that central power could initiate reform when needed, for the Constitution laid upon it the duty to assure the states a government republican in nature.

Even that was not protection enough, as Americans knew. Bit by bit the institutions would decay, one by one the protections built into the system might be dismantled or discredited. This was natural, because any government but a despotism had instability built into it. "Power is necessary," the political scientist Francis Lieber concluded, "an executive cannot be dispensed with; yet all power has a tendency to increase and to clear away opposition." It was just as natural that those who wielded power would love it too much and seek to expand it. They might not scruple at the means.[7]

It therefore followed that the strongest bulwark of free government was the caution that the people's representatives showed in any innovative use of powers. "We have no fear for our national superiority from abroad," a congressman warned. "The first blow will be struck here in this Hall, and by the exercise of power not delegated to us." Governments were so prone to go wrong, Edmund Ruffin wrote in his diary, that they should even refrain from passing good laws, lest these permit legal encroachments in worse directions. The public must depend as little as possible on government to further their ends, for by depending on the authorities, they put themselves in the market, fit for a would-be tyrant to buy with privileges and favors.[8]

Republics also must rely on the purity of the people. All written guarantees were scraps of paper without public virtue, for would-be Catilines could thrive on appeals to the self-interest of their audiences. All they had to do to overcome the legal safeguards was excite the voters' greeds and fears. "Honesty, industry, sobriety, and virtue forever!" stormed the Jacksonville *Florida Union*. "Believe it, without a preponderance of those elements, our government, in less than one hundred years, would sink into a state of anarchy and confusion to which the condition of Greece and Rome in their decadence offer but a faint parallel."[9] Then not even a righteous President could restore the pristine days of the Founders. It would be too late.

Between the two safeguards, citizens' virtue and officeholders' restraint, Americans in the nineteenth century had added a third: a lively national party system based on issues. In the days of the Founders, Americans had been concerned lest factionalism destroy free government. Some Whigs were not reconciled to parties even in 1850, but most of their contemporaries had come to accept the system in principle. They even appreciated rival organizations as one more check on would-be usurpers and one more proof of the Republic's health. When parties stood for ideals and values that Americans cherished, they became indispensable means of realizing the will of the people. As long as the organizations opposed each other, they would provide the vigilance needed to ferret out peculation and abuses of power in each other. Officeholders might use more caution when the party system allowed an angry people to turn the rascals out and turn good men in.

As long as these three safeguards stood firm, the Republic was safe, but in the 1850s an increasing number of Americans saw all three breaking down. "We are in our swaddling clothes," Senator Andrew Johnson of Tennessee warned, "we have scarcely reached man's estate; yet these spots of decay are visible, and the tendency . . . must be observed by all." So they were, though different groups concentrated on different tokens of decay.[10]

What of the people themselves: had they kept their virtue? Old Jacksonian Democrats thought so, and the cited the results of the 1852 elections to prove it. Even at his most despairing, former President Martin Van Buren felt confident that "the virtue and intelligence" of the masses could remedy all ills. This faith ran deepest among backwoods representatives and the spokesmen for small farmers, though their optimism did not cover the American people in general. Since the days of Jefferson, idealists had seen the ploughman as the true republican, self sustaining and without a hunger for wealth, dependent on no government charity, uncorrupted by the easy vices that city life presented. "I represent a plain, unsophisticated, agricultural people," boasted Congressman A. W. Venable of North Carolina. They asked nothing from government; they harvested their fields to feed themselves and wanted efficient, economical administration more than anything else. Such boasts, however, seemed to suggest the yeoman as a contrast to the average American. "They expect no office," said Johnson of his supporters. "They do not live by politics, but by their labor, and they want the best government, the purest government that they can get."[11] Would other Americans settle for less? Johnson certainly feared so, and he feared it most when he looked at Fernando Wood's New York or the vote-stealers' Baltimore.

Whigs were less sanguine still. Without government action to promote moral behavior, the people were corruptible, perhaps too far corrupted to redeem themselves. Talk though statesmen might about self-reliant yeomen spurning the chance for gain—who really believed it? Men behaved as self-interest dictated, at least in part, and if self-interest dictated that they accept the corruption that brought them profit, could virtue survive? "I agree with the old philosophic doctrine," said one Bostonian, "that man is but a bundle of influences." Some Democrats shared their despair, notably Clement Vallandigham of Ohio. "Thirst for power and place, or pre-eminence—in a word, ambition—is one of the strongest and earliest developed passions in man," he said. That was why no government worked well for long. Ambition manifested itself in intrigues and revolts under a despot, in class warfare under a constitutional monarch, and in strife over place and emolument under democratic governments. The self-interest that made men hunger for office would make them do anything to get it, as John C. Calhoun had warned years before; it would make men without power do everything to gratify those with offices to dispense. In the process, depraved leaders debauched the people.[12]

Even without the spoils system to set the moral tone for Americans, alarmists cried, the debauchery of public values had begun. Every exposure of corruption furthered the decay, by making public virtue seem less and less natural. At first alarmed at grafting, voters would grow bored and accept corruption as the natural state of politics. Then they would nod indulgently as thieves stole from the Treasury and yawn at news of depravity in private dealings. "How soon will it be . . . before they are as bad as their unfaithful stewards?" asked the Newark *Advertiser* of the people. Not long, it would seem, for by the early 1850s the words "corruption" and "bribery" no longer startled, or so the editor lamented. "The public mind is poisoned."[13]

Prosperity dulled Americans' ethical sensibilities as much as scandals did, and this fact did not escape the reformers. Peace and prosperity ever encouraged people to want more money than they had and to sacrifice less for the common good than they would in times of hardship. Avarice was "that sea-worm . . . that will pierce the toughest planks, and bring the stoutest ships to foundering," warned the Reverend Henry Ward Beecher. Then every institution went to the auction-block. "Unlimited wealth and imperial power" destroyed republicanism, only virtue and moderation could preserve it.[14] Yet the 1850s showed a loss of that restraint on which freedom depended, as land speculation and railroad schemes became public manias. From such avarice a host of evils sprang: corrupting lobbyists, bribe-wielding railroad agents, claims and bounty brokers. "Kossuth said of his countrymen that 'they valued freedom more than riches,'" Gideon Welles wrote of the Hungarian patriot. "Ours, I fear, are beginning to value wealth more than freedom. Like the vital air, which sustains us, we regard liberty as necessarily ours, heedless of the many lessons of history of the decay & wreck of republics."[15]

So the way had been paved for a usurper among the masses. What about the government—had that changed, too? So observers in both parties feared, and the changes they saw threw the legislative branch in peril. (No one imagined that the lawmakers would overthrow the other branches of government. For one thing, no one thought much of the average congressman, and for another, as an Indianan remarked, all history showed that the executive was "the serpent of free governments.")[16] The only question was from which direction the threat to the lawmakers might come. Would legislators be corrupted by moneyed powers seeking special treatment, such as mail-subsidies and land grants, or by a President disbursing favors such as jobs and contracts to make both houses dependent on his will? Here the two parties differed. As the champions of a strong executive branch and severe restraints on government's power to grant favors to private interests, the Democrats were more likely to fear the plutocrats. As the defenders of legislative privilege and discretion, Whigs were more likely to fear the executive.

"The power of the Devil himself is not a bit more irrepressible than the money power in a Government like ours," Van Buren wrote. Nor, he might have added, was it more dangerous. The people made all things, did all things, Andrew Johnson complained, but they had no share in legislating: they had no lobby. Speak up for the masses, a Tennessee colleague agreed, and a member would be denounced for demagoguery, but let him restrict his generosity to jobbers and speculators seeking legal privileges, and the hireling press would hail him as a patriot and a true scion of the men of 1776.[17]

Jacksonian Democrats did not just resent the deflection of government from its true responsibilities. They argued that a government that grew used to extravagance would turn dangerously corrupt as well. By doing for the people what the people should do for themselves, Congress would make the citizens into permanent dependents and supplicants. Instead of judging issues by fundamental principles, they would vote their own profit. Encouraged by the liberality of the government, every special interest would, like the Galphins, Laws, and Collinses, rush to Washington to seek its share and buy enough lawmakers to assure friendly treatment. Unprepared to resist, congressmen would fall into the habit of expecting money for their votes. "A rich Government ever has been, and ever will be, a corrupt Government," Congressman Edson Olds of Ohio argued. Small wonder then that many Jacksonians treated "extravagance" and "corruption" as synonymous terms. The two seemed inseparable.[18]

Congressional extravagance had two effects worse still. By helping Americans to see the central government as their prime support, it undermined the states' prestige and took over part of their responsibilities. To pay for its prodigality, the central authority would have to raise more money than before, and the tariffs, taxes, and land sales would not only increase the funds with which a central government could corrupt patriots, but would compel an increase in government employment. Each position would go to reward the executive's friends.[19] Thus, in a sense, the growth of the spoils system, of the "steam beggars," and of executive power came together.

Even wtihout a centralizing effect, the partnership of Congress with the Money Power undermined the legislative branch's effectiveness and credibility. What Francis P. Blair called "Congressional prostitution" would surely destroy public faith in lawmakers and damage the reputation of the democratic process. If Americans concluded that Congress was too dishonest to entrust with public improvement questions, a New Yorker prophesied, their belief would ring "the knell of our liberties." Popular disillusionment would foster demands for a patriot-tyrant, too pure to be purchased, a Caesar to drive out a degenerate Senate. For another thing, because every legislative boon gave the executive new money to spend and new offices to fill, every act enhanced his powers to suborn lawmakers and usurp their functions. Not even the tremendous power of the sword could rival that of the purse, Vallandigham warned his House colleagues. "He who commands that unnumbered host of eager and hungry expectants, whose eyes are fixed upon the Treasury . . . is mightier far than the commander of military legions."[20] Increasing government power in turn made it more certain that the wrong kind of man—thc selfish, ambitious, unprincipled kind—would seek executive power. Each new grant of powers made the job that much more lucrative and temptation more irresistible. To collect and disburse $80 million a year, contemporaries agreed, was a privilege worth every sacrifice.

Any facile description of Presidential seducers and Congressmen of easy virtue would be too simple. The President played an ambiguous role in the melodrama of America's fall that so many politicians and publicists had created in their imaginations. In the final stages, all agreed that a Cromwell would use his executive powers to remove all rivals, but Jacksonian Democrats hoped that until that fatal day the people could choose Presidents that would play the role of "Patriot Kings" above faction, ready to uphold public interest in ways no congressman could.

Faced with a corrupt Congress, idealists longed for a second "Old Hickory" and cherished the belief that his use of power and appeals to the people might redeem a fallen society. Reinforced by a "harmonious cabinet unaddicted to the favoritism of the monied monopolies, or speculating classes," an executive would awaken the people to its danger and rouse them to drive the moneychangers from the Capitol.[21]

For others, especially Whigs and Southerners, the perils from executive power outweighed the benefits. Their assumptions about the selfish nature of man and the corrupting effects of power, and their fear that the party system had put a premium on shiftiness, made them conclude that a chief magistrate would behave badly: appoint relatives to office, as Taylor did, purge worthy officeholders from rival factions, as Fillmore did, and use his influence to give contracts to his cronies, as Buchanan would do. All this had one aim, to augment his authority. "Executive power in all ages has proved the most resistless ravisher of public virtue," Samuel Bayard warned. Already the effects showed in the aggrandizement of the executive office beyond founders' expectations. To hear one Ohio Democrat tell it, the Capitol itself symbolized the change. Built to face eastward, away from the executive mansion, the houses of Congress were meant to stand at the center of the city. To be inaugurated, the President would need to enter Congress by the back door. His home would stand outside the city as planned. By 1852, however, the city had spread westward, and as power shifted to the White House, it was congressmen who directed their attention to the other end of Pennsylvania Avenue.[22]

Patronage had caused the alteration. At his disposal, the President had 150,000 offices, from Cabinet minister to postal clerk, congressmen claimed. Every year the number of favors he had to dispense increased. Each extension of the nation's borders meant more post offices and custom houses to promise to pliant congressmen.[23] Thus, Democrats could declare that a dictator in the White House would arise because of Congressional corruption, but Whigs knew that Congressional corruption would grow and was growing because would-be dictators in the White House were seducing the people's representatives with patronage.

What of that third bulwark, the democratic system and government by party? Here, too, some contemporaries saw those "spots of decay" that Senator Johnson had discerned in the nation as a whole. Conservative Whigs made the broadest indictment, for they had never had much faith in the people's fitness to rule itself, through parties or direct democracy. As they saw matters, demagogues rose to power easily because politics had grown so democratic. When the masses lacked the education or the independent means to make a disinterested judgment, an opportunist could easily appeal to their baser instincts or bribe them with promises, if not something more substantial. Untrained for the full duties of citizenship, a voter became easy prey for the shallow appeals of the subsidized press and the transparent promises of men who would abuse their trust. Something had gone wrong with government by the people, and it may have been that the government had been wrong in concept from the start.

Only a minority of Whigs could reach so bitter a conclusion, and most of those who did concealed their reservations. To lose all faith in popular government would be to lose all faith that the Republic could be saved from its corrupters without a revolution in American institutions. But enemies and dear friends of democracy glimpsed a convenient scapegoat for the people's delusions in the party system. Here, they told themselves, was the real corrupter of popular politics, the real threat to free government. Party for the sake of principle was good, even necessary. Party for its own sake, in which the ideological content had faded and the leaders' primary purpose was to provide offices for their followers, was more dangerous, as it corrupted both the masses and their governors. That party system, idealists protested, had no right to exist. "To belong to a party is a virtual enlistment in a band of public plunderers," said the Cincinnati *Commercial*. "There is no political party in the United States to which an honest man has any right to belong. . . ."[24]

Without the leaven of idealism, every nomination became a mere scramble between ambitious men. In their eagerness to win, they promised all. Running for office became an exercise in demoralization and led the professional partisans into every debauchery: purchasing presses, bribing other office-seekers, vote-buying, influence-peddling. "From it, as from a copious fountain, flow corruption, extravagance, profligacy, and national disgrace," said a Kentucky Democrat of the campaign process. Fights between factions involved no more than cavils over how to divide loaves and fishes. Platforms lost all meaning. No sensible man "any longer puts faith in them," said Daniel D. Barnard, a New York Whig. "The man must be the platform."[25] But what kind of man would such a system bring forth? No friend to liberty or virtue, certainly. Seeking office in such a mêlée, a candidate would find uprightness a handicap.

To say that the Democratic and Whig parties had fallen from their high purposes allots them too much blame. Contemporaries knew party organizations, like republics, were unstable by nature. At first, high principle might separate partisans, but soon the "practical" men took over. Hungry for success, they would compromise the ideals. Panting for office, they would betray the cause. As Calhoun could have told them, parties had been like that since the days of the Gracchi, and then they had so wearied the citizenry with their fight for plunder that a dictator seemed a welcome change. Thus had it been since American politics began. Vallandigham reminded listeners. Every clash was "for the purpose of controlling the powers and honors and the moneys of the central Government." What, then, did it take to keep a party pure and wise? Simply that it never come to power, Horace Binney commented, as he watched his fellow-Whigs wrangle over nominations in 1852. By taking office an organization lost half its virtue and in time became indistinguishable from its basest foes.[26]

Parties also debauched the people. In the most direct way, the parties induced voters to think their suffrage a commodity fit for sale by bribery at the polls. In a larger sense, the loyalty that a party demanded of its members trained them not to think for themselves, but to apologize for every wrong done by its leaders. When devotion to party and a sense of personal interest replaced conscience, a man sacrificed the moral independence on which free government relied. Then he was, as newspapers branded this partisan and that, "the slave of Party, or the tool of Power." Moreover, said Carl Schurz, Wisconsin antislavery orator, the laxity among the rank and file made corruption among its leaders all the more certain, because officeholders knew that their backers would never call them to account. It was a commonplace that government corruption would trickle down to corrupt the people. Schurz offered a theory of "democratic reciprocity," where the party structure let the debauchery spread both ways. A people could force ethics on their representatives, but the voters' laxity had encouraged wrongdoing. An honest man might come to office, but the people "did all they could . . . to make a rascal out of him while he was in power [loud applause], and the virtue of many a man has thus been victimized by his constituency. And when, at last, such a man has become a regular scoundrel, he did in his turn all he could to demoralize all who had made him so."[27]

For these reasons, those concerned for the Republic wondered whether the Jacksonian party system had any right to continue after 1852. If party for its own sake assured abuse, then two parties that had outlived the economic issues of Jackson's day were sure to be sources of corruption in the future. The first party system had lasted no more than a generation; the factions during the Confederation had formed and reformed every few years. By the 1850s it was natural to think that the Jacksonian system would and indeed should end after as brief a life. Reformers argued that no party in a democracy should last more than twenty years, that the ideal lifespan should not exceed twelve. For reasons of political theory, then, as well as the substantial proofs that the party process was debauching voters, newspapers, and officeholders, many Americans expressed a growing disquiet with the party system and a desire for its reconstruction.

That reconstruction must happen soon, and it must be accompanied by steps to cure the government and people of their corruptions. Certainly by the middle of the decade the degenerative process had gone far enough to bring the party system to crisis. "Our present system of party organization is approaching its point of extreme corruption," the Cincinnati *Commercial* warned, "at which it must either come to an end or revolutionize the government." But even if the parties reformed, how long could they remain immune from the influences from below and above? What was most alarming was how quickly decay set in. Corruption had taken a generation to bring earlier parties down from their high ideals. By 1857, said one editor, three-year-old parties had contracted "all the diseases of [their] predecessors." One, he might have added, had died from its malady.[28]

As all of these concerns suggest, Americans distressed by corruption had misgivings about the rapid change over two generations. "Progress" was a shibboleth for Whigs when they supported economic development, and for Democrats when they urged manhood suffrage. Indeed, the doctrine of society's progress and the constant improvement of life was almost universally accepted. But for all that, members of both parties distinguished between transformations in American life that they supported and those that they deplored, and for each many alterations seemed for the worse. Then they invoked the values of the past to justify themselves. Even radical Democrats rooted their arguments in the tradition of the Revolution and pictured a present America gone amiss. Perhaps it was by clinging to tradition in certain things that reformers felt comfortable in bringing change in others.

By the 1850s, change seemed to come so rapidly in so many areas at once that even those who described themselves as liberals had misgivings. Prosperity might be a good thing, but the flush of the 1850s seemed perilously great for the nation if it was to keep its self-restraint. Economic development might make the country more efficient, but if done recklessly it could threaten moral standards, as money became the essential goal in men's lives. Democracy was being realized, but before many Americans had learned the responsibility to vote their opinions. The very way that "progress" had become a term of praise seemed alarming. Things should be supported because they were right; yet many Americans in the 1850s seemed to support change because what would follow it was new. If novelty became grounds for change, how long could institutions survive, or the moral zeal on which a republic must be based?

That was the point of Charles Gayarre's satire, *The School for Politicians.* All his characters spoke for the ideal of progress. "The fact is," Trimsail argues, ". . . it is useless to be squeamish about it. Lately the science of politics has been greatly improved and has progressed with the age. It now consists in buying or being bought—in using tools—or in being used as such." "Political morality is an obsolete idea," Lovedale jeers. "It would be just as out of place now-a-days as the fashion in which our grandfathers used to dress—powdered wigs, knee buckles, and short breeches."[29] Others made the same point, and it was a common method of debate for the foes of corruption to picture themselves as out of date. They stood for tradition, and the new America had no place for them.

If anything stood most distinctly as the antithesis, then, of the enemies of corruption, it would have been the "Young America" movement that made Senator Stephen A. Douglas of Illinois its leader. Those who spoke of "Young America" made "progress" their catchword. The experienced leaders were "old fogies" to them. Instead, they spoke for men of ambition and energy, untrammeled by the traditions of past generations. Such a flippancy about the Republic's heritage was irritating to the keepers of the austere tradition, but the causes the "Young Americans" espoused were alarming. They favored territorial expansion, even the filibustering in Central America, aid to internal improvements, and, in effect, the politics of prosperity, development, profit, and personal advantage. Economic advantage held its supporters together, and the "Young America" movement was particularly popular among steamship contractors angling for government support, backers of railroad land grants, and speculators seeking rapid public land sales and the development of the territories. More than elsewhere, the Democrats in the West embraced "Young America" and its presumption that by an alliance of economic interests the states could be bound together.

This came closer to the ideals of Mandeville than to those of the Founders, and to the foes of corruption, it bespoke every trend most dangerous to freedom. By endorsing a benevolent government, "Young America" threatened states' rights and fostered a partnership between corporations and public servants; it challenged the Whig ideal of politicians above party and accepted the permanence of the present party system; and it endorsed the territorial expansion that added to the spoils system and the growing role of the central government. Most of all, it deemed practicality more important than rigid principle and "progress" more important than traditions. In short, it stood behind processes the critics of corruption believed had inspired depravity at home and could lead to the death of the Republic.[30] Small wonder, then, that for many Democrats and Whigs, young Douglas was an alarming figure, even before his name became associated with the Kansas-Nebraska Act.

Were the Cassandras of corruption unreasonable? Certainly they overstated the peril of a Caesar or a Bonaparte in their own time. All ages had known corruption, and politicians' debauches had not always destroyed free government. England itself should have shown that. One could make a decent case against the doomsayers' claim that "private vices" were a bad thing for a republican government as well. The "informal constitution" of patronage, privilege, and plunder did make a complicated democratic system run more smoothly, and it did not always impair the popular will seriously. Politicians *needed* practical men who could compromise on issues and make deals. Otherwise the system would have been full of clashes and dissensions which might have done as much as corruption did to discredit popular government. Between making a deal and taking a bribe, was there all that much difference?

Practical politicians did not think so, perhaps because the enemies of corruption, in their own fulminations, also occasionally failed to draw a distinction. Political insiders knew what was expected of them—and they could speak the right sort of moral sentiments when pressed—but at times even those who were concerned by corruption felt bafflement, even exasperation with their critics as visionaries. No government could be as clean as idealists demanded, and live. In the midst of his lobbying activities, Francis J. Grund burst out in a rage against the "doctrinaires" who demanded unflinching principle. "The most practical government in [their] hands . . . would be but a boy walking on crutches," he wrote. Those who decried corruptionists failed to see how dependent they themselves were on such men. The high road to principle that a Daniel D. Barnard or a William Cullen Bryant might trudge did not always lead to success. Such men saw their ideals turned into law because of power brokers like Thurlow Weed and S. L. M. Barlow. "I do not dislike Mr. Barnard personally," Weed protested to a friend, "though we differ so widely in political sentiment and sympathies. My difficulty is that he puts *me* so low down in his scale of political morality (rightly enough, perhaps, for we are compelled to do things that will not be a blaze of light to elect to office even as good men as he is) that I do not feel fit for his society."[31]

Nor should we make a simple dichotomy between the corruptionists and the foes of corruption. Newspaper rhetoric might divide politics into idealists and spoilsmen, but the two categories overlapped. Even a righteous editor like Horace Greeley knew how to make moral compromises to obtain public office; even so audacious a scoundrel as Congressman Orsamus B. Matteson, Weed's loyal cohort and railroad lobbyist, had fits of principle where slavery was concerned. In the midst of his land-grant lobbying, Matteson was outraged enough by the Kansas-Nebraska bill to jeopardize all for its defeat. "I told McDougall, if he wanted a road, he & his colleagues, that they must keep their hands off of *this dirty Nebraska business* or we would send their road to Davy Jones," he boasted. "They know where the power lies now." (That was just the sort of logrolling that men like Bryant and Greeley would have labeled corruption, but one wonders if they would have muttered even a mild reproof, had they known that the bill they so detested was being fought by Matteson's means.)[32] We can see public officials best if we imagine a broad spectrum, from those who had their price on any measure, to those who would sell only some principles but not others, to those who would use any means short of outright corruption to get what they wanted, to the idealists who demurred at corrupt methods except as a last resort, to the tiny handful who would neither permit corrupt methods on their own side nor permit the corruptionists in their own ranks to go unexposed, not though the fate of slavery or freedom depended on it. Of these groups, those in the center outnumbered the rest by a vast majority.

Yet it would seem that the critics of mid-century America came nearer the truth and closer to seeing reality than did the men they abused. Something was clearly askew with the morality of men like Matteson, whose solicitations of a bribe brought his ejection from the House in 1857, particularly when he could never understand just what he had done wrong. There was something quite bewilderingly amiss with the moral perspective of the Nebraska legislator accused of offering another member a $250 loan for his support of a bank charter and assuring him an interest-free loan of $5000 as soon as the bank opened its doors. Yes, he had proferred the bribe, he told the assembly; what of it? It was a "*fair* business transaction." No doubt his colleagues were upset because they thought that he would not carry out his promise, he added. Let no man impugn his ethics! The $5000 would be produced when it was called for.[33]

Even if the need to make deals might be conceded as essential to smooth operation of the government, we should not blur the distinction between logrolling and corruption. There *was* a moral difference, and even those who treated the words as synonymous knew that forms of impropriety like bribery and "practicing law in the legislature" were more serious than members leaguing together to pass each others' bills. Then "practical politics" became much less practical. The more cynical a party's maneuvers, the less fastidious it grew about the men it used to achieve its ends, and the more the organization's high ideals were discredited. That gave the opposition a strong argument for driving it out of office. Certainly politics was the art of compromise, but a statesman had to distinguish between what could be given up and what could not. Yet all too often in the pursuit of money the practical politicians seemed ready to compromise principles vital to the Jacksonian party system and to the honest working of the government. Even Weed's closest friends sensed that his judgment had lost its balance because of his search for gain. With that new zeal for "Golden Dollars in the distance," a comrade warned, the King of the Lobby had lost touch with political reality.[34]

There would be no Caesar in the White House, but the corruption had had effects serious enough: plundered treasuries, purchased legislative majorities, fraudulent elections, and discredited Presidencies. As the 1850s progressed, consequences broader and more disturbing began to manifest themselves. Already concern over political depravity had unsettled the Jacksonian party system. By 1852 it had added to the distrust of the established leadership, made election results open to challenge, and the will of the people open to conflicting interpretation. It deflected the course of legislation, robbed Presidents of moral force, aggravated the differences between South and North. By the late 1850s, Mandeville's private vices had turned out to be a public danger.

12

The Politics of Party Decay, 1849–1853

A queer hodgepodge the party system must have seemed to outsiders by 1852. To be sure, both parties saw one another as a shapeless mob of foes. Whigs sneered at the "Locofocos," as if every Democrat was the radical foe of privilege that the name implied. Democrats dubbed their foes "blue-lights" as if every Whig was a Federalist risen from the grave. But party insiders knew better. Some Whigs still cherished their old faith in protective tariffs and moral reform. Democrats might still incline to free trade and states' rights and away from laws regulating personal behavior. But each party was riven with dissensions that at times seemed to make all the old issues trivial. Slavery elicited the worst quarrels of all.

The Compromise of 1850 had drawn the lines of conflict tighter than before. As far as most Americans cared or hoped, that combination of laws had removed sectional disputes from national politics by bringing California in as a free state, strengthening the Fugitive Slave law, and settling other outstanding disputes about the territories won in the Mexican War. The Compromise may well have saved the Union from dissolution; it could not do the same for the two parties. At the political center, Silver-Grey Whigs behind President Millard Fillmore and Secretary of State Daniel Webster, and National Democrats behind James Buchanan and Senators Lewis Cass and Stephen A. Douglas, endorsed the Compromise as good in itself as well as expedient. On either side of the conservatives, other partisans accepted the results of 1850 less happily.

Southern Rights Democrats feared that the Compromise had sold out vital sectional interests. Free-Soil Democrats, (or Barnburners), already angry enough at the Southern influence to have bolted the party ticket in 1848, declared that the Compromise had given the South too much, and many Northern Whigs agreed. By 1852, some of these passions had cooled inside the Democracy. All factions would accept the Compromise, with several crucial conditions and interpretations of its ambiguities. Among Whigs, the frictions had turned into a grudge-match between the Administration on one side and the antislavery wing led by Senator William Seward of New York and his Presidential candidate, General Winfield Scott, on the other.[1] It has been said that the parties lost all their principles by 1852, but this, it would seem, was not quite true. They had principles when the issue of slavery's expansion into the territories arose; they had far too many principles and could not reconcile all of them under the old party labels.

The divisions within the parties over slavery were more rankling because the divisions between the two parties no longer seemed as strong as they had in the early 1840s. Until the system's collapse, there would remain occasional distinctions between Democrat and Whig, but by 1852 a blurriness had set in, as sectional and local advantage began to fray party lines. Many of the old issues such as the high tariff and national bank that Whigs had championed were gone. On other issues the two parties voted more alike than before. "Whigs and Democrats vote for steam lines and the millions which it takes to sustain them," grumbled a North Carolina congressman, "and Whigs and Democrats vote against them. This is also true of French spoliations, and other great and wasteful drafts on the Treasury. Dry-docks, steamers, spoliations, and the whole category of expensive paraphernalia are thrown upon Congress, and Democrats vie with Whigs as to who shall vote the largest sums. I ask, then, where will you draw the party lines?"[2] Where, indeed.

The national party platforms had not changed as much as the views of the rank and file, which went in all directions. In such an age, scruples against alliance with outside parties for a share of the offices would have been difficult to maintain, even if the Democrats had not been under challenge, but they *were* under challenge. After 1848, the political system had begun to transform itself, as minor parties, Free-Soil and Southern Rights, Temperance and People's, all attracted a larger share of the vote. In part, they were a response to the parties' failure to face new issues, in part a protest against the stodginess and cynicism of the old leaders. In either case they could and did deprive both parties of a majority and forced coalitions. At the same time, disaffected Democrats and Whigs seemed readier than before to join with their long-time opponents against their long-time colleagues. In New York, Silver-Grey Whigs courted Democrats to deprive their own party nominee of a Senate seat; in Missouri Democratic and Whig enemies of Senator Thomas Hart Benton joined to drive him from power.[3]

To party regulars, the new coalitions seemed baffling and could only be deduced as an abandonment of principle. Benton's enemies could have nothing in common, thought Francis P. Blair, but "their pursuit of plunder." The combination of antislavery men with Democrats that sent Charles Sumner to the Senate from Massachusetts must have been arranged in a corrupt barter of offices, its enemies exclaimed: the two allies were too discordant to share ideals. Between Democrats and their Free-Soil allies in Rhode Island was no coalition, protested the Providence *Journal.* "When a man goes into the market and buys a horse, he does not form coalition with the horse. . . ."[4] Only in the loosest sense—that any coalition trades advantage for advantage and gratifies mutual ambitions—were any of the coalitions with Free-Soil parties corrupt. But the charges are worth considering. They reflect outdated assumptions that each party had of itself and of the other: the representatives of certain irreconcilable and vital principles. They also suggest the readiness to assume that every action in politics that did not fit those assumptions must stem from corrupt dealings and a greed for office that, polemicists agreed, was the great evil of the age.

Those outside the regular party system agreed in seeing the corruption of the party alignments, but they drew different conclusions from the political shambles. Perhaps, Senator Robert Toombs of Georgia suggested, the parties were open to coalitions because they no longer had anything to offer in their own right except gratification for ambitious men. Perhaps the party organizations were not worth keeping up: "both have degenerated into mere factions, adhering together by the common hope of public plunder. Their success would benefit nobody but themselves, and would be infinitely mischievous to the public weal."[5] Others too saw Whig and Democratic parties as no more than patronage-dispensing machines, though they may not, as Toombs did, depart the Whigs to form a Union party.

If by "corruption" the Jeremiahs of politics had meant no more than "the decay of the old two-party ideology," it would be easier to dismiss their words, but they meant more. For to them, as we have seen, the breakdown of party ties was connected to the growth of opportunities for illegitimate enrichment and for advancement by unethical means, which they saw all around them.

They had every reason for uneasiness. The boom was on, and too many public officials wanted a share in it. "The horrible corruption . . . in our State Legislature and the scarcely less offensive venality discoverable in so many movements of the representatives & offices of the General Government have disgusted me more with the conduct of public affairs & consequently with politics than I ever expected to be," Martin Van Buren admitted in 1851, "so much so that I would be likely to compromise for a candidate of almost any political principles if I could be assured that he was an honest man."[6] Between 1850 and 1854, historians have seen a lull. Contemporaries did not. There was plenty going on, a fever of land and claims speculation, schisms and quarrels in every state, a scramble for contracts and post offices, and these were no trivial matters to observers. They were symptoms of grave ill health in the body politic. It was now that the $9 million canal scandal broke in New York, that Dr. Gardiner became the most notorious dentist in the land, and that Galphinism turned into a household word.

By passing the Compromise of 1850, for example, the Thirty-first Congress gained a reputation for patriotism. Reporters gave it a different fame. In saving the Union, said Free-Soilers and Southern Rights men, lawmakers had made a tidy profit for themselves. House members voted themselves extra funds for books they meant to sell, and listened too willingly to steamship magnates and railroad men hungry for federal aid. "The present Congress furnishes the worst specimens of legislators I have ever seen here," Toombs wrote home. Northern men were the worst, not statesmen but "successful jobbers." Many, he thought, valued their places most for the chance "for a successful foray upon the national treasury."[7]

Most observers considered the Congress of 1852 worse. The steamship lobby got its extra compensation, the public printers their special remuneration, the railroad enough land grants to satisfy their appetites for at least a year more. One Kentucky representative made himself notorious when he wrote a publisher of how well his job as congressman/claims agent/lobbyist served him. "If I could stay here a month," he wrote, "I could make $5,000. As it is, I fear I shall have to hurry off without even completing the business I came on. I saw men in New York, Philadelphia, and here who want my services and are willing to pay for them, and pay well. If I can be reelected, I can make a great deal of money. But this is between ourselves." It did not stay so for long; the newspaperman published the letter.[8]

The most dramatic jockeying came over the indemnity that the Compromise of 1850 had assured Texas. Holders of Texas securities were sure that the money would be used to fund their obligations at par. The lawmakers in Austin had other ideas. When they tried to give certain creditors preference, the neglected ones organized to win federal protection and got it. Lately resigned Attorney-General Reverdy Johnson issued an opinion that all creditors must be treated alike, while Secretary of the Treasury Corwin threatened to release none of the $5 million due the state until Texas had given in. Both men were debtors to W. W. Corcoran, a creditor whose firm was among the most energetic lobbyists against preferential treatment. In return for his "legal advice and services," $1500 of Johnson's debt was canceled, while Corwin was paid $8000 and his assistant secretary $1800.[9]

Corcoran did as well in persuading the Congress. In August 1852, bills were offered to bypass state officers and make federal authorities the paymasters to creditors. Since Texas was resolved to pay a pittance on some of the securities and the federal Treasury was ready to pay full face value, this would have been quite a windfall for those bondholders who had bought Texas paper cheaply. As the measure came to a vote, the lobbyists stepped up efforts to convert congressmen into bondholders. To make purchasing securities easier, Corcoran & Riggs advanced "loans." Senator Jesse Bright of Indiana took a $5000 bribe, Midwestern congressmen accepted funds gladly. Corcoran was a suave lobbyist, though some of his friends were not. Several years later, Congressman Joshua Giddings of Ohio recalled the spectacle that summer. Promoters had scurried through the House making their offer of $100 Texas bonds for $23 with the guarantee of repurchase at $70 as soon as the bill became law. That bribe, Giddings thought, would be worth $47,000 to each member, "for I presume no member was offered less than $100,000 of bonds." Before the House was called to order at noon, "gentlemen of professed honor and respectable standing" waved Texas bonds in their hands and told representatives, "Gentlemen, we would not bribe any one, but we want to employ agents to carry this bill through the House." None of the bills did pass that August, nor the following winter, but reports of the speculative fever dimmed the reputation of Congress and sickened thoughtful men in all parties.[10]

For all this depravity, the lack of moral leadership in the Whig Administration was a scapegoat made to order. Perhaps the Presidencies of Zachary Taylor and Millard Fillmore were not, as one partisan paper declared, "the weakest and most corrupt that ever existed in this land," and even if they were, the record would soon be broken, but observers fretted at the low moral tone in the White House. Perhaps it was the distance between promise and performance, for Democratic administrations had embraced spoilsmanship as the proper policy, while Taylor's backers had promised that he would stand above such sordid considerations in his selections. One appointee had predicted that the Administration would "go very far to root out the heretofore corrupt practices of the Government." It did no such thing. Taylor's crowd was not interested in changing practices—only personnel.[11]

And what personnel they put in! One of Taylor's nephews became postmaster, another was made purser. As soon as New York's naval officer took command, he fired his deputies and replaced them with a son and a nephew. On Fillmore succeeding, like arrangements were made for his family. "Even John Tyler was less infamous in providing for his own Household," Thurlow Weed reported.[12]

The Cabinet won plenty of attention, not all of it favorable. Daniel Webster may have hoped that his statesmanship in backing the Compromise would have given him honor and a better chance at the Whig nomination for President. Instead, it made him the target of scurrilous abuse as a seducer, sot, and purchased politico. In the House, Democrats uttered charges that the "Godlike Webster" was up to the tricks that his other nickname, "Black Dan," would suggest. As Secretary of State, he had legal power to decide which banking firm would serve as government agent in delivering to Mexico the indemnity promised at the war's close. The agency was sure to turn a profit, as the banking houses juggled exchange rates. Each year the issue was reopened, as new financial firms vied for the rights. Webster had been counsel for the Baring Brothers and still held a personal interest in their welfare: over the years, he had lived beyond his means, and they had supplied the extra funds. Webster also owed more than a debt of gratitude to Corcoran & Riggs, the senior partner of which had given him an $8000 gratuity in early 1850. Other businessmen had raised money to help Webster feel secure enough to leave the Senate for the State Department. In his new position, Webster canceled existing arrangements for handling the indemnity and bestowed the privilege on a consortium including Corcoran & Riggs, the Baring Brothers, and some of those contributors. The federal government got less favorable terms under the new arrangement than the old, but the go-betweens did much better. There was even a suspicion that Webster took a share of the profits as payment for having made the new arrangement. As some of the details of the indemnity transaction reached the House, Democrats made a savage, ineffectual attack, and Whigs countered that Webster had known none of the men whose special fund had subsidized him, had shown no preference, and was above all corruptions.[13]

Democrats thought that they might make other charges stick. The Galphin scandal had shown improprieties in Taylor's Cabinet; Fillmore's

Secretary of the Treasury had a compromising entanglement in the Gardiner swindle. Better still, an attack on Whig corruption could bring the enemies of the Administration together and spare them the divisiveness that a political campaign around the slavery issue would be sure to inspire. Why had Congressional spending increased so, Congressman Edson Olds of Ohio asked. "The answer can be obtained in that single word, which, in a sepulchral voice, comes to us from the empty vaults of your national treasury: *Galphinism*!"[14] With the right sort of leader in the White House, Democrats insisted, there would have been no debauch on Capitol Hill.

But where was that sort of leader in either party? On the Whig side, both the President and Webster hoped for the Presidential nomination, but neither could be seen as a symbol of moral leadership. Neither was chosen, though more because of their backing for the Compromise of 1850 than any other ideological reason. Supporters of General Winfield Scott were willing to use corruption as an argument, if no other would do. Webster had been bought for the Compromise and paid to accept the State Department, they cried. Later a railroad promoter would boast that his contribution to the Webster fund "was largely influential in preventing Webster's reaching the presidency by putting him in the position of a candidate subsidized by rich men." To such accusations, Administration supporters suggested that Whigs who profited off New York canal lettings were using their booty to block Fillmore's nomination and that "the Seward gang" would use any method to nominate Scott. When Scott was indeed nominated, Webster Whigs cried that fraud in the convention and forged proxies had helped to defeat their favorite. Southerners damned the nomination as "the corrupt juggling of Seward and Greeley & Co.," though no one had specific proof.[15]

On the Democratic side, the Compromise loomed as less of an issue and the search for a suitable man as more of one. Democrats could not agree on the best nominee, but a startling number had no doubt about the worst—Stephen A. Douglas, the brisk young senator from Illinois. To Congressman Andrew Johnson of Tennessee, the candidate was "a mere hot bed production," backed by "a Set of interested plunderers that would . . . disembowel the Treasury, disgrace the country and damn the party to all eternity that brought them into power." These cormorants included lobbyists for mail contracts and canal repairs, George Law especially, claims agents, and what Gideon Welles called "plunderers of the national domain." Those most hostile to Douglas blamed every Congressional excess on his campaign. To bring the promoters to his side, they shouted, the Illinoisian was pressing their appeals for subsidies, steamship lines, and public works, and was fostering bills to parcel out the public lands among the corporations.[16]

The scenario was more horrifying than true. Every candidate, even William Marcy, the radical Democrats' newfound hero, had "lobby vultures" and steamboat men to advance his cause. Douglas had more of them because he looked like a winner or so some correspondents thought, but the steamship contractors played no favorites. Prosper Wetmore wanted Marcy, Edwin Croswell favored Lewis Cass, and Law financed Douglas. Either they placed personal feelings ahead of profits or they were arranging matters so that whoever won, the ship lines would not lose.[17]

Friends of other candidates saw the local Douglas men in just as bad a light. Senator John Slidell of Louisiana recoiled from the "trading politicians & adventurers" that ran the Douglas movement in his state and vowed that if the Little Giant was nominated, the Republic might well despair. Johnson saw the Illinois senator's allies roistering in the streets and wished all such "poor miserable *Banditti*" in prison. Unfortunately, the scoundrels used money with telling effect, so the losers of city primaries complained. From New York, Marcy heard constant reports that the primaries were being bought with Law and Croswell's money. A Marcy man blamed his own defeat on "ruffians" sent from other wards and on Whig mercenaries. In a Democratic convention in Buffalo, Marcy's foes actually buttonholed two delegates and offered them $100 to desert New York's favorite son.[18]

Douglas had more than villains behind him. Prominent Democrats thought him the fittest candidate, the only one with fresh ideas. Other candidates had men as notorious at their back. Slippery Simon Cameron of Pennsylvania gave Cass's candidacy his aid. Cameron cared little for Cass, but he would have given a great deal to beat his enemy James Buchanan and apparently *did* give a great deal from his Middletown bank. Votes at Dillsburg sold at fifty cents to five dollars apiece. Around Philadelphia, Buchanan supporters reported that "the most unprincipled & mercenary set of delegates that ever assembled in this county" ran the show just as Cameron directed.[19]

After all this infighting, it must have relieved the Democrats when the national convention nominated none of the leading contenders. Instead, Franklin Pierce, governor of New Hampshire, found himself thrust into prominence. Not many delegates knew what he stood for. That was his greatest strength. Delegates knew just who he was *not*, and that was quite enough. Cass and Buchanan men breathed a sigh of relief that Douglas had been checked. Marcy supporters rejoiced that the foremost National Democrats had been routed by a nonentity.

If all factions chorused their benediction for the Granite State's favorite son, it was not just because his views on slavery were too vague to offend anyone. His supporters also imagined that his nomination would rebuke that corrupting ambition that goaded senators to scramble for office by jobbery and barter. The President should never be a toy of "political cliques, fettered by pledges to partizans, which would render him unable conscientiously to discharge his duties," Jefferson Davis reminded Mississippians. None could accuse Pierce of pledging himself or seeking the Presidency at all. Never had he lusted for power, his champions asserted. Nor had he ever been impugned with corruption. He might even end political proscription, thought the New York *Evening Post*, for had he not once made a speech pillorying the Whig spoilsmen as hypocrites? His support for states' rights and rigid economy must make him the true foe of legislation for special interests and classes. Elect Pierce, Samuel J. Tilden promised, and voters "would restore the best days of the republic."[20]

It was that invocation of past virtue that set Pierce off from other Democrats. Indeed, both he and Scott conjured up a pure, bygone America. In some ways, the nomination of two political generals served to rebuke the civilian leaders, most of whom had lapses of ethics to explain away. Scott was not simply a testimonial to the selfless purity of the professional soldier, but a living monument to the age of heroes and unalloyed patriotism: the War of 1812, or, as orators liked to call it, the Second War of American Independence. His irrelevance to the issues of 1852 added to his charm. A symbol of a more upright past, he might be the perfect remedy for a degenerating Republic. The same could be said for Pierce, absent for ten years from the Capitol, associated with neither the promoters clustering around the Congress nor the Compromise dragged through its predecessor. His national record had ended as the Age of Jackson closed, and revived Jackson's memory. Might he not revive Jackson's heritage, the old morality that Democrats were pleased to imagine had once reigned supreme? Over and over his sponsors described him not as an innovator, but as the herald of a restoration. "The times demand such a man," said the *Evening Post*. Could it be because he was not of these times?[21]

For certainly, both parties agreed, the times needed *some* cleansing. The Whigs' nomination of Scott deprived Democrats of the force of their specific charges against a corrupt Administration. Everyone knew that

Scott's selection was a repudiation of the President and his Cabinet, and in the process of Galphinism, Gardinerism, and any other convenient *ism* of plunder. But corruption was too good an issue to drop, and Democrats kept up a running fire on Secretary Corwin and the freebooters in power. This was not the party of Henry Clay, they exclaimed, but of big and little Galphins. "The historian who sits down to chronicle its deeds, need use no instruments finer than a stick, a pot of tar, and a pine board," said one correspondent. "Anything that will make a *blot* will do." He did do Corwin the justice to add that one rumor was false: that the Secretary was in the habit of covering himself with oil from toe to crown "and then making a dive into the Treasury chest, and coming out with the gold pieces sticking all over him. This is false. Tom may have grabbed; he did not dive."[22]

More generally, Democrats described the corruption as a general affliction that demanded the healing appliances of their own standard-bearer. On this at least, Barnburner and fire-eating Southerner could agree, and that agreement was vital if the party was to suppress its quarrelsomeness till election day. There was not an Alabama Democrat who would fail to murmur "amen" when the free-soil New York *Evening Post* warned:

> Corruption has crept from its dens and skulking places, clothed itself in purple and fine linen, and become one of the coordinate branches of the government. It enforces in the halls of legislation, what the President can only recommend; it makes the press speak or be dumb at its command; it sits upon the bench with judges, and beside the prosecuting attorney in the secret deliberations of the Grand Jury; it lifts up its brazen face, unabashed, in the proudest circles, and is not rebuked, even where it is not courted.

Nor would its editor have demurred when Jefferson Davis told his constituents that a Democratic victory would revive the public virtues without which free government must die.[23] Consistently with their views of slavery, both factions could impress audiences with how corruption would strengthen the sectional enemy; for corruption imperiled the checks and balances that protected political minorities in the nation, enlarged central power (either to abolish or expand slavery), and threatened states' rights. Naturally, South and North feared different effects from this corruption and centralization: the domination of slaveholders and their apologists through patronage power on one side, the federal interference with slavery in the states on the other. But both saw the same wrong and prescribed clean government as one remedy.

Whigs fumbled for a proper reply. They could stress that Democrats had taken "constructive mileage." They could blame the Democratic Congress for extravagance and compute its spending at $1.76½ per second. By calling any coalition with Free-Soilers and fire-eaters a corrupt one, they could label Democrats as corruptionists, though not persuasively. It helped them when the House investigators cleared Corwin of conspiracy to defraud the government. Democrats kept up the same cries of "Galphinism" and "Gardinerism" without conceding a point.[24] Corruption was a minor issue. Southern and conservative Whigs accepted Scott's candidacy with loathing or repudiated it; to endorse him was to endorse his friends, who showed slack zeal for the Compromise. Old issues like the tariff lay dormant. Indeed, to judge from some newspapers, the most pressing issue was which party took the least interest in the campaign. Still, what little influence the corruption issue could muster, the Democrats mustered against Whiggery.

As usual, the campaign climaxed in a clamor that the foe would buy votes enough to win the Presidency. New York Democrats had heard of a vast "corruption fund" that would swing the cities. New Jersey Whigs were sure that "Newark Bank bills," "California dust and Virginia gold," all wielded by the Camden & Amboy, would buy the state for Pierce. Later, Whigs would accuse their enemies of having bought the foreign vote, and one Southern Whig had heard that the sale was made by Seward's emissaries—an absurd charge, since Seward could neither have delivered the foreign vote nor would have dreamed of betraying the man he had worked for a year to nominate.[25]

As it turned out, no amount of money could have elected Scott. The Whig general took four states. Many Americans saw Pierce's victory as a rebuke to sectional extremes and an endorsement of the Compromise of 1850, but observers were baffled by the Democratic margin. A few idealists read it as a mandate for honest, old-fashioned administration of the government and a repudiation of Whig ethics. "No intelligent or observing man can for a moment doubt," old Francis Blair wrote the President-elect, "that the controlling sentiment was a settled conviction . . . of the indispensable necessity that the money changers should be driven from the temples, & the foul birds that have defiled our council chambers, exposed & disgraced, to whatever party they may profess to belong." So, too, the *Evening Post* said. "The whig party—the faction of it especially that attempted to navigate . . . with the heavy load of plunder on board, and [has] sunk—will be heard of no more. The bodies even will never be recovered, possibly not be looked for."[26]

Whigs neither expected nor hoped for a cleansing. So large a majority for Pierce would mean just so many more office-seekers and a fracas over the spoils that would discredit this Administration as swiftly as it had its predecessor. Indeed, one Whig joked, the only way Democrats could keep the peace would be to elevate Whigs alone to office, but when this advice was offered, the victorious party failed to appreciate it.[27]

Old Jacksonians wanted a more thorough solution than a change of men. Pierce's first task, they argued, should be to scour out the corruption and put a stop to Congressional looting. A strong-willed magistrate could block the robbers until the public was roused to rescue the legislative branch from its corrupters. Even with a Cabinet free from "favoritism to the monied monopolies, or speculating classes," the fight would take years, Blair conceded, but the conflict must begin at once. On its outcome depended the fate of democracy itself. "Unless a stern stand be taken now against the cohorts of corruption the vitiating principle will become as controlling here . . . as . . . in the decaying states of Europe & Spanish America." Not even secession endangered republican government more. So, too, thought Gideon Welles, Thomas Hart Benton, and Sam Houston. They all gave the incoming President the same advice. Optimistically, William Cullen Bryant foresaw that a new Administration would choose men for merit rather than for political service, cut expenses to the minimum, and give the jobbers the fight of their lives.[28]

Had honest intentions been enough, Pierce might indeed have entered the history books as a second Jackson. Neither the regime before his nor the one that followed could match the integrity that the New Hampshireman brought to Washington. James Guthrie had been an able Kentucky banker and railroad promoter. Now he proved an excellent Secretary of the Treasury. His vigilance against swindles was unceasing. Local collectors had previously reported their accounts yearly. The long delay between reports had made it easier to hide a defalcation until the collector suddenly disappeared. Guthrie demanded monthly reports instead. Secret customs inspectors had used their powers to extort hush-money from shippers. Guthrie abolished the position. He summoned the collectors' books for special audit and set down new rules to tighten revenue collection and slash collectors' fees, forbade clerks time off for political duties, and set up examining boards to test applicants' abilities. No longer could bidders take and then sublet contracts. No longer could a claim be reopened once the government had decided against paying it. With $100 million in auditors' and comptrollers' accounts left unsettled,

Guthrie retrieved three dollars in every four. Beside him were subordinates as determined as he, including two Whigs of stellar reputation. None of these acts made the Secretary popular on Capitol Hill and certainly not with Richard W. Thompson, whose Indian claim finally went through Congress in 1856 but could not penetrate Treasury vaults. Lobbyists railed at "the d––d obstinacy of Guthrie towards every little plan by which our pockets might be quietly and comfortably lined . . . and nobody . . . the wiser for it."[29]

Richard McClelland made almost as clean a record in the Interior Department. A spoilsman who allotted clerkships in proportion to each state's Congressional delegation size, he also demanded solid work from those he chose, steady hours, and an ability to pass written examinations. At first supportive of land grants for railroad companies, he grew disgusted by the mêlée in Congress and blasted the system as corrupting. The Postmaster-General tried to put the mail service on a paying basis and began the policy of refusing carriers more than postage costs.[30]

Pierce himself won a modest reputation for integrity. Tremulous at times, the President did stand by Minnesota's honest territorial governor when the corruptionists lobbied for a more pliable man. He stood firm against the steamship subsidies, much to his Congress's chagrin. Presidents have made a worse spectacle, and some Democrats felt that such conduct showed their leader as the exemplar of the party's best principles. "I especially approve of the *vetoes*, so far as they went," a New Yorker confided, "& am not sure but what I would have applied it even to the appropriation [for maintaining the Navy] rather than have sanctioned the corrupt steam boat plunder of the treasury." "I tell you that Frank Pierce is a great man," a personal friend burst out, "the best President we have had since Jackson, and for the times, the very man we ought to have!"[31]

Hardly. Choosing upright administrators was a good beginning, but a successful President also needs to lead his party, and Pierce was unable to make it treat him seriously. Helpless to guide his followers, with no legislative program to propose and no desire to proscribe any Democrat for his political opinions, Pierce let his obliging nature lead him everywhere and nowhere.

It was not all his fault. Whig heads dropped thick as a hailstorm, but so strong had the lust for offices grown that every replacement bred a dozen resentments. Because Pierce wanted to give something to everybody in the party, no one felt satisfied. Southern Rights men talked as though Pierce had chosen none but abolitionists across the North. National Democrats insisted that Pierce had bought the good will of Southern

Rights men and free-soilers by giving them their every desire. Free-soilers replied that the most extreme of the National Democratic factions, the Hardshell Hunkers, had got the prime spots at the expense of Barnburners and even the more conciliatory Softshell Hunkers. Every time Greene Bronson, the "Hard" collector of the port of New York was asked to choose a good antislavery man, one complained, "he would be seized with a fit of coughing and never could get over it till I went. . . . For several weeks I never went to see the judge, because I thought it aggravated his cough."[32] Perhaps if the President had made a more cynical use of the rewards, there would have been peace in the party; more likely, the quarrelsomeness would have broken out in any case. The desire for material gain and the weakness of unifying issues had gone too far for Democrats to master it easily.

That fall, all across the North, Democrats fell to brawling with each other. We can dismiss those quarrels as fights over spoils, but they were more. Some historians have seen the elections as scant on substance, as though the Jacksonian polity was marking time till new organizations and new concerns could come into being. The returns, to be sure, were full of omens: impressive minor wins for splinter parties devoted to Free-Soil and temperance, Whigs winning by default because they had fewer deserters than did the Democrats.[33] But some races that fall were more than a battle for spoils or a shift to issues unfamiliar to the old parties. Again the cry rose that the Democratic party, this time on the state level, was imperiled by the predators.

As usual, New York Democrats had the wildest donnybrook. By 1853, the conservatives had divided, with the Hards firmly set against any conciliation of the antislavery Barnburners and the Softs welcoming all defectors back as erring brethren. Hards growled when Pierce gave the State Department to William Marcy, a Soft, and were no more happy with Governor Horatio Seymour, who had become less the unbending "Hunker" as he neared office. Both extremes wanted to draw the party line tight. Hards wanted to force out every man who bolted the ranks to vote for the antislavery ticket in 1848, the Barnburners; Barnburners wanted the Softs to help them cast out the Hards as traitors to the party where a frugal policy on the canals was concerned. Neither the Softs nor the Barnburners had forgotten Hards' enthusiasm for the $9 million steal nor Hard Canal Commissioner Mather's role in parceling out the pickings. Now Seymour, Marcy, and the freesoilers sealed their friendship by impeaching the Commissioner. The Senate wrangled for three months and in the end could not muster the two-thirds needed to convict. "But our people are satisfied," a Soft wrote Marcy. "An edition of 50 or 100,000 copies of the arguments will be distributed."[34]

Expensive satisfaction—by September, the quarrel over canals and honest finance had sundered the party. Disputed delegations battled it out at the state convention in Syracuse, where upstaters charged that Hards had imported Whigs to pack county conventions. Both sides declared that the other meant to rule or ruin the ticket. As chairman of the state committee, Minor Story changed the convention site at the last minute and told only the Hards. The Softs marched there, broke down the doors, and chose the temporary officers. During the dinner hour, the Hards reassembled in Commissioner Mather's hotel room. Insisting that the Softs had invited "short boys" from New York City to bully them with pistol and bowie knife, they posted bills beseeching the local gang to protect them. With both factions nominating tickets, the fight began in earnest.[35]

Spoils were part of the issue. The Hards wanted more than they had and used every office they held to strengthen their own faction. Softs called for a purge of every Hard along the canals, where superintendents were forcing their underlings to hustle out the voters. In mid-October, the Softs convened the Canal Board to make "clean work" of "every man who falters" in backing the Administration. Both Bronson and U.S. Attorney Charles O'Conor joined the Hards. As the attacks on Marcy and the governor mounted, Secretary Guthrie entered the fray on the Softs' side with a public letter rebuking Collector Bronson. After a bitter exchange of missives and with the election days away, Pierce dismissed the top custom house officers and chose Softs to replace them. By then the Hards had made themselves into martyrs, resisters of the growing federal power to dictate the results in state contests, enemies of such Presidential "usurpations" as his wielding of patronage permitted him.[36]

The fight went beyond the issue of spoilsmanship. Through the canvass, the Softs saw the issue as higher than mere loyalty to the Administration. The issue was whether the Democracy should be purged of those corrupting influences that had crept in over the years, influences allied with the special interests that craved government funding. The Hards, said the New York *Evening Post*, included "such a corrupt set of rogues" that the party would never poll its full strength as long as such men were members. Not only spoilsmen, but "bank-robbers, steamboat-thieves, canal-contract thimble-riggers, and post-office robbers," they wanted only plunder.[37] Goaded by the wish to share in the pickings that a generous canal program would give them, they had allied to George Law and his jobbers to break the Democratic party two years before and allow the Whigs back into power.

It was a plausible claim, for the Hard leaders were bound together by their financial interest in canal contracts. Among the beneficiaries were Story, N. E. Payne, Stephen Clarke, Benjamin T. Harwood, Oliver Carlick, and of course Croswell of the Albany *Argus*, who had been a longtime partner in the steamship and musket-purchasing schemes of Law and Marshall O. Roberts, schemes that needed government favors and backstairs influence. Law and Roberts supported the Hards too. When Croswell's bank had passed into Whig hands, "Prince John" Van Buren joked, "Croswell passed into the hands of Thurlow Weed," though he was later resold to Law, "and we called it a cheap sale." If all these rascals planned anything, it must be the restoration of Whigs to power in Albany and fat contracts for steamer lines. Who could doubt the canal contracts' importance, when Mather ran for New York Canal Commissioner and the son of the canal's creator headed the Hard ticket?[38]

In such a fight, conciliation was out of the question. Marcy himself welcomed a set-to and urged a Soft ticket of "none but sound materials." Between a corrupt Democratic official and a corrupt Whig, after all, Marcy saw no difference. The fight must go on to the bitter end, wrote J. S. Verplanck, for "the progressive radical men cannot be brought to consent to plunder the State." Faced with certain defeat for both Democratic slates, another regular held out the hope that "we shall purify our party of the rottens," and bring back the honest, deluded defectors. Refusing to extend the olive branch, the governor saw the issue as the first blow in a national fight against "hungry speculators." Let the President beware of the incoming Congress, Seymour warned. The Hard revolt was but one sign of a broader conspiracy. The self-proclaimed National Democrats would soon show that they were national only in their greed for "the *National Treasury* & the *National Domain.*" If Pierce would stand as firmly as Seymour "against plunder," the crisis might yet be weathered.[39]

Disputes over canal policy were more than battles between plunderers and purists, as Seymour should have known, and the governor misread the public will just as badly. Convinced at first that the Hards could not muster a corporal's guard, Seymour soon found that they could nearly outpoll the Soft ticket. The Administration was bewildered. How could such a "causeless defection" have spread so deep, the Secretary of State mused. "There were influences at work which I do not yet fully comprehend."[40]

Nowhere else was the issue of purging the thieves from the party so clearly drawn by Administration men, but across the land the corruption issue stirred controversies. In New Jersey, Whigs combined insurgent Protestantism, nativism, and the fear of corruption, as they accused the Camden & Amboy of debauching the commonwealth's virtue through its Democratic, Irish, and Catholic tools. From Philadelphia, John Campbell wrote exultantly that he had knifed his own party's ticket. "I *struck* [the Democrat] *down* not merely on account of his corruption as a corporate borer but also because the whole strength of the Custom house and post office was brought to his aid to give him the nomination," he explained. Rhode Island Democrats, seeking constitutional reforms to end purchased state elections and the registry tax, quarreled venomously. In Maine, Temperance Democrats feuded with the "Wildcats," a faction deeply hostile to any law restricting the sale of alcohol. Again—not very successfully—the regulars tried to contrast their honest men with the Wildcat thieves. The reason the Democratic governor was so abused, his defenders protested, was because he had chosen an incorruptible land agent to protect the public timber. Wisconsin lawmakers impeached a Democratic supreme court justice for taking money to render favorable decisions, while the Democratic party nominated the avaricious William Barstow for governor. Already the nominee had achieved notoriety when one would-be public printer had urged that money be used on him to get government favors. For a certain sum, the printer wrote, he could buy "Barstow and the balance." A Barstow victory, Free-Soilers warned, would turn the capital into a robber's den. They were right.[41] With Barstow's triumph, the plunderers rushed to Madison.

Outside of Wisconsin, the returns brought no comfort to the Administration: there were defeats in New York, Maine, Rhode Island, and Massachusetts, and victories elsewhere only because the Whigs could not muster the strength to mount a successful challenge. All looked like confusion, and the promise of 1852 had been broken, the promise of a Young Hickory in the White House. The factionalism was not Pierce's fault, but he was blamed for interfering in their local quarrels—and for not interfering soon enough. The party could not find agreement on the slavery issue, or temperance, or other matters—and Pierce was blamed for not having used his spoils to bring about such agreement. In brief, he was damned for having let the party splinter, and for not having given it a platform that would have rallied some of the factions and driven others away. By early 1854, even his allies detested him. "You know my opinion of the President," Seymour wrote Marcy. "I think he is a fool who aspires to be a knave." Far from a leader, Pierce could hardly command his Cabinet. "I don't know what that little fellow Pierce will do," sneered one observer. "I don't think there is enough of him to do much."[42]

Marcy was not the only Democrat who sensed influences at work beyond his understanding. Others sensed a political system sickening and two parties losing all coherence. "Cobb," a friend wrote Georgia's former governor, "what is called the Democratic party is this day in a worse condition than either of us ever saw it in before. Without any recognized head, no bond of Union to bind it together, and no issues with its adversary as formerly, it is blundering along under an administration which does not possess the confidence and cordial good will of a tithe of the party."[43]

What must come? Things could not stay as they were. Of that most observers were sure. Party lines would need some redrawing. Each major organization must find itself a program on which it could stand, and issues that would make parties more than machinery for gratifying appetites. Otherwise, as another Democrat warned, the Republic would be left to "harlots of all stripes, poor in purse & poorer in principle." Then freedom would be devoured by "the burthens & corruptions that would inevitably follow."[44]

13

Nebraskals

No one expected anything good from the Thirty-third Congress. As its members assembled in December 1853, optimists expected it to do nothing at all, pessimists foresaw plunder and a factional fracas. Neither group expected that this Congress would wreck the Jacksonian party system for good and all, but everyone was poised for a struggle over patronage and lobby influence and knew full well that this Administration, under fire from every direction, would be unable to restrain the combatants. A general odor of mild decay hung over Washington.

The first sight most reporters had was of the crowd of lobbyists and office-seekers around the Capitol doors. Former congressmen had returned to work as borers for private jobs. And what jobs! "Gigantic moonshine railroad projects, steam-jobbing contracts, and kindred schemes which require for their successful accomplishment a liberal expenditure of champagne and oysters and large appropriations of the public money," said the correspondent for the Hartford *Times*.[1] Agents had been a common sight for some years, but never had their dickering seemed so visible, so remarked on, or so constantly imputed with rascality.

Before the first session had closed the following summer, members had taken so much time on special committees set up to look into the various swindles that one cynic had suggested a need for a standing committee to examine corruption and fraud. By the time the lame-duck congressmen went home for good in March 1855, the New York *Tribune* could say without dispute that a Congress "so corrupt and profligate—a Congress so prodigal and unfaithful—never before assembled in this country."[2]

What had given it such a reputation? Many things: land-grant bills, the Collins subsidy, French spoliation claims, and Indian claims among them. In May 1854, several former congressmen, among them George Ashmun of Massachusetts and Samuel Vinton of Ohio, were revealed to have sent a circular to railroad companies to induce them to hire the insiders' services. Ashmun and Vinton would pass a measure removing the duty on imported railroad iron, in return for $200 plus 10 percent of the $5 million that the companies would gain. So great was the uproar that the two lobbyists priced themselves out of the market. No representative dared connect himself to such a proposition.[3]

More notoriety hung about Samuel Colt's efforts to renew the 1836 patent on his revolver for seven more years. He hired Ashmun and former Senator Jeremiah Clemens of Alabama to argue his case, and hired others as counsel. Experienced railroad lobbyists E. H. Thompson, Edward N. Dickerson, and George Brega were approached, and Thompson became an active agent. George Harrington, one of the best manipulators in Washington, took a retainer. He invited Thurlow Weed to give him help, though he cautioned that any efforts must be done secretly: if Weed did join in, he must pretend that he had come to press for railroad bills in which both men were deeply interested.[4]

By July the capital hummed with ugly rumors about how the patent extension was being pressed. No moral purist himself, Congressman Matteson termed the patent measure "rotten as hell," and another friend of railroad aid, Congressman T. L. Clingman of North Carolina, rose to charge that colleagues had been bought. The House chose a committee, before which Clingman testified eagerly. A New York editor had told him that Colt had spent at least $60,000 to enact extension, and had cited Colt's brother Christopher as the source for the figures (the editor himself insisted that the precise figure had been mere rumor). Another congressman had joked that the moment he realized that the lobbyists knew him to be married was when they sent his son a pistol (he would later protest that he had never imagined the gift aimed to affect his vote). Other witnesses knew of a dozen or more revolvers that the lobby had disbursed to congressmen. A Washington banker had been enlisted to plead Colt's case. Another lawmaker had been approached and urged to absent himself on the day of the vote. A clerk in one government department urged his friend in the House to support extension, because the clerk stood to make $200 by it. Congressman Jones was told by the editor for the Washington *Union* that his vote for extension would garner him $50,000.

The lobbyists were less obliging. The committee learned that some $15,000 had been spent to improve the bill's chances, and witnesses all insisted that they would be glad to give any information that Congress desired—except what they were paid, what they did with the money Colt gave them, what they paid others, and who the others were. These matters, they argued, were their own "private business," and not for congressmen to trouble themselves over. Samuel Colt insisted that he did not know who his lobbyists were, nor how they used the money. His company accountant professed ignorance of all financial transactions connected with the lobby: these were Mr. Colt's responsibility.[5] Skeptical though the committee was, it did not compel witnesses to elaborate further.

Still, what emerged from the hearings uncovered more than Colt would have liked. His agents had held lavish midnight suppers well supplied with wine and beautiful women. Congressmen's wives received Paris gloves as gifts, and there were enough pistols distributed to arm a dozen House representatives (which was hardly a step forward for public order, since in at least one incident that summer, one House member drew a bead on another). One individual claiming to represent an undecided member was given a loan. Most expensive, blackmailing "strikers" forced the Colt contingent to square the press. As spokesman for purchasable newsmen, Horace H. Day approached Dickerson and for his silence demanded $15,000 as well as other favors. What more cooperative witnesses might have added cannot be known, though the committee and the national press had dark guesses. Having passed the House, the Colt extension was reconsidered and killed by the revelations. The Senate never voted on it.[6]

Thanks to the lack of publicity, perhaps, Congress proved more active in settling the Texas debt. In 1854, Senator Jesse Bright, a leading speculator in Texas securities, proposed a bill that would grant $8.5 million in cash to the creditors. In the House he had help from Congressman John C. Breckinridge, himself financially interested in Texas bonds, and on the outside from leading bankers in Washington and Philadelphia. Bright's bill assured the creditors some $2 million more than the Texas legislature had thought they deserved, once their debts had been scaled to give them a value equivalent to that which the securities had had at the time of purchase. The grant was scaled to $7.75 million in conference committee, but any right by Texas to use any part of the sum as the state legislature saw fit—and many Texans hoped to divert $3 million to build a state railroad system—was denied. The most deserving creditors would get only 78 cents on the dollar. So would creditors who had bought up promissory notes at 12 cents on the dollar and whom the state had arranged to repay at 25 percent of the notes' face value. Texans felt their honor impugned. They resented federal dictation of conditions and with justice they charged that lobbying, even bribery, had been used to win Congressional approval. They did not need to look as far as the Potomac, for as soon as Congress adjourned, the creditors sent lobbyists southwest to plead the bankers' cause.[7]

Though both senators endorsed the congressional settlement and Democrats argued that, after all, if Congress wished to overpay the creditors, that was the federal government's folly and would cost Texans little, the voters did not agree. In a referendum on the national law, they turned out a majority rejecting its provisions. Undaunted, the agents hastened to Austin to bring about reconsideration. "Any action on the part of outsiders, interested in the issue, must be very discreet," one lobbyist wrote. "The proprieties of time, place, and circumstances must be very carefully kept in view at every step." So they were, with a few exceptions. One legislator was sent a forged letter to convince him that his constituents favored the creditors' cause. A leading friend of the measure was charged with having taken $3000 for his services. Foes thundered at the "bribery and corruption" that accompanied the Bright bill in Washington and Austin alike. After the bill passed, the legislature chose an investigating committee, which did a cursory job, pleaded its lack of authority, accused no one, and was denounced as corrupt itself.[8] With that, the Texas debt issue was settled, though for years the problem of payment would linger, as federal officials did their best to fend off creditors.

Projects more fabulous than the Texas debt repayment got greater publicity. Months before the Congress convened, there was talk of a railroad project to the Pacific, one guided by leading Democrats and headed by former Secretary of the Treasury Robert Walker. Not all the talk was favorable. In Clarksville, Tennessee, Cave Johnson had heard alarming rumors, which he reported to James Buchanan:[9]

> Stories are circulating freely in the West that the N. Y. Company, with a capital of one hundred millions, will lobby for the road and distribute stocks among the members of Congress and influential agents, and pass it over a Presidential veto. R. J. W. who is said to have subscribed ten millions is the chief manager in Washington—Law at New York—Foulkes of the Memphis Bank, takes a million, *cum multiis aliis*, of no more means and less character. There is said to be a provision in their agreement that *at*

> *no time is there a call to be made for more than one-fourth of one per cent*—the work is to be accomplished out of the public land and the surplus money—what a stupendous project!! The Yazoo speculation will be thrown into the shade by this magnificent scheme and the frauds perpetrated in it will be molehills beside the mountain when contrasted with the corruption & frauds which that scheme will introduce into our country; but this is not all, several Presidents, vice Presidents, ambassadors, &c. are to be made by it. . . .

Astonishing if true, and many observers thought it all too true. The vision of a transcontinental line had begun with Asa Whitney's arguments in 1844, and by 1853, every state had its own variation on the Pacific project, each of which would end at a different city. Iowans hoped for a north-central line; Whitney himself hoped to run the track from Minnesota to the Oregon coast; cotton state interests insisted that the only just arrangement should cross Texas to San Diego. Naturally, each project entailed a federal land grant, and many hoped for Treasury funds as well.[10]

The New York Atlantic & Pacific was bigger than the rest. Nicknamed the "Moonshine" road, Walker had drawn plans vague enough to please everyone. Albany lawmakers gave it a charter to the Pacific. Walker had visions of connections into Minnesota and Wisconsin, and backed land grants to railroads in both, even as he moved to make his line fit the requirements of a Texas land grant of 12,400 acres per mile. When the A & P could not fulfill the terms set by the state, Walker fashioned a dummy company, the Texas Western, and passed out enough bribes and director's jobs to make the Texas legislature pass a huge land grant over the governor's veto.[11] All this manipulation was very impressive for a railroad with capital as insubstantial as a political promise. Walker took a subscription for $10 million himself, Lieutenant-Governor Sanford Church of New York for $1 million, New York Attorney-General Levi Chatfield for over $39 million—until the board expelled him for distributing the securities among his political friends. Since no one had to put up more than one mill on the dollar, such fantastic subscriptions were for Buncombe only. The company must have a land grant to mean anything; then its members could sell their worthless stock at a tremendous price. A $30 million federal subsidy and a few million acres of public land were what the promoters hoped for. In part to clear the way for the southernmost route, the government bought a strip of desert land, much to Congressman Thomas Hart Benton's fury. He was no friend of a railroad scheme that he suspected would bypass his St. Louis district, and on principle appalled by subsidy legislation, he charged that the Senate had been bribed to make a land cession worthless in itself but of inestimable value to the railroad men.[12]

Walker's project foundered on the shoals of conflicting state ambitions. The farther south the project was located, the less support it had from the North. The nearer it approached the central prairies, the less the South was willing to accept it. Neither South nor North wanted to give its rival so great a commercial advantage—not with taxpayer funds. The most practical political alternative was one which Stephen A. Douglas offered in the Senate: three routes, a northern, a central, and a southern, each of them endowed with a land grant twenty miles wide through the states and forty through the territories, in alternate sections. But if Walker's plan was more than Congress could afford, the Douglas plan was still more so, and the Thirty-third Congress whittled it to a promise of aid for one road. Even that bill failed. Men with lesser schemes had more success than Walker, and with worse methods. "I fear we are in for it," one observer confessed. "From appearances and developments thus far this bids fair to outstrip all former administrations in large appropriations and extravagant expenditures." The passage of the Moonshine bill would be the last straw. Then "a splendid government (based on prodigality and corruption) will be the order of the day."[13]

In such a time, a strong President could have done much, and Jacksonians looked desperately to the White House for guidance. "Unless General Pierce is imbued with a pretty strong infusion of Old Hickory's nerve and vigor," one correspondent warned, "the simple public may expect to see the public treasury bleed pretty freely after next winter." Certainly Pierce tried. He vetoed land grants to relieve the indigent insane and to support river and harbor improvements. When his private secretary Sidney Webster brought in Pierce's veto of the Collins subsidy bill, Benton was standing by the door. Seizing Webster's hand, he gave it a violent shake. "Tell the President he has covered himself with glory," he boomed; "tell him to keep on hand a full supply of blank vetoes for the acts of this d--d corrupt Congress."[14]

Vetoes were one thing, making policy another. The President could not even control his own party. Bitter at last year's slights, the Hards called for reaffirmation of the "national" party line on slavery, a line which, if drawn dexterously, would turn out the former Free-Soilers who now stood on such good terms with the Administration. Southerners concerned with the Administration's dalliance with antislavery Democrats wanted new guarantees and flirted with the malcontents from the North. In its first test of strength, the Administration's choice for Senate printer was beaten and an editor more sympathetic to the South chosen. The upper house also threatened to block federal appointments.[15]

A party adrift—a President unable to provide leadership for a party craving boldness—mounting pressure by the Hards and Southerners for a reaffirmation of the Democracy's repudiation of antislavery men—quickening settlement of the West, spurred by the land grants and railroad promoters—and prairie communities needing territorial government: out of all these problems an adroit politician might make an effective policy. So it may have seemed to Stephen A. Douglas, who was ambitious if not adroit. As chairman of the Senate Committee on Territories, the Illinoisian took up the issue of territorial organization and set up two new polities, Kansas and Nebraska. At first, the Douglas bill said nothing about slavery or freedom. One could infer that the Missouri Compromise, forbidding slavery in both, still applied. But on January 10, 1854, when the bill was reprinted, it had a section hitherto unpublished, which specifically allowed inhabitants to decide the slavery issue for themselves. This, the bill's sponsors explained, was the measure's true meaning: "popular sovereignty" to its friends, "squatter sovereignty" to its foes. Two weeks later, the bill was overhauled, and at a Southern Whig's behest, it explicitly repealed the Missouri Compromise. With that, the political storm that had rumbled across the North for a fortnight broke loose.[16]

Douglas did not expect the tumult to last. He underestimated the breadth and depth of Northerners' distaste for slavery extension and had contempt for those who treated the issue seriously. Like many others, he was convinced that his bill had conceded slavery nothing, as the climate itself must make the West unfit for slavery. To his reading, the Compromise of 1850 had already superseded the Missouri Compromise, which seemed an unfair limit on the people's rights in any case. But perhaps there were additional, less tangible reasons for Douglas's gamble. Deeply interested in land speculation and railroad promotion, he considered these issues of greater moment than ones of race and culture, and to him the alliances between the sections he had helped create for land grants seemed to be stronger than the forces of sectional passion. Finally, Douglas relied on the "informal constitution" of patronage and party loyalty to bring dissident Democrats into line. The bill's passage might provoke one "hell of a storm," as Douglas soon conceded, but there were influences that would still that storm after a time.[17]

He was almost right. Many Americans in both sections saw Douglas's move not simply as belated justice to the South, but as an advance for Jacksonian principles. Now citizens in the territories could shape their own institutions. Others hailed the bill as an excuse to read Free-Soilers out of the Democratic party, especially those around John Van Buren. But "Prince John" was not to be driven from the ranks twice in six years. When the Kansas issue had first been raised in late 1853, he had passed it off with a joke. Now he vowed to stand by his ally, Secretary of State Marcy, on whichever side Marcy chose; both men deplored the bill, and both men held their tongues. Other Democrats regretted the bill but dreaded criticism of it still more. "Don't be so d--d violent," Illinois Democrats begged one dissident editor, ". . . spare Douglas and the Administration,—you will make trouble."[18] True believers, factional manipulators, dutiful followers: the Democracy could count on all three, and the patronage power could swell their numbers.

Douglas and the Administration would need every backer they could get. From the Capitol, the uproar that the Little Giant had stirred was less readily audible. Among Massachusetts Whig congressmen, indeed, a letter circulated to discourage any legislative resolutions at home against the Kansas-Nebraska bill. But Democrats who strayed from the Potomac sent alarming reports back. "The storm is gathering in our State on the Nebrasky bill," a New Yorker warned Marcy, "and depend upon it, it will sweep all down before it." Polling rank and file Democrats, another onlooker found them almost as unanimous in their outrage as were the Whigs. Hundreds, he wrote, who had defended the South in every community, had risen in open war "in all possible battles that can break them down constitutionally."[19] He might better have said "thousands" rather than hundreds.

For the uproar was like none that living politicians could remember. Conservative merchants stood beside Free-Soil ideologues in mass meetings in every Northern city. New Haven citizens met to inveigh one evening and found the time too short to do the subject justice. Exhausted by their fury, they adjourned and reassembled the following night. "Some people affect to think that common people cannot understand a constitutional question," roared John P. Hale to a New York audience. "They think that a man must be as stupid as an overfed Alderman, or corrupt as a member of Congress, before he is fit to appreciate a constitutional question." Whigs rallied at Philadelphia's Chinese Museum to pledge their party against a bill pressed "by venal solicitations and corrupt employment of the patronage." Local Democrats, no less upset, rallied on their own. The Nebraska bill's friends called a rally in Chicago and found it jammed with their foes. Resolutions endorsing the bill were howled down. Five Whig legislatures resolved against the bill; four Democratic legislatures blocked a vote on similar resolutions. In state after state, Democratic conventions erupted with fights over endorsement. "A war now commences, the like of which in point of bitterness and excitement has never been known," one paper concluded.[20]

The reasons were easy to find. To many Northerners, the Missouri Compromise had become a sacred compact. Its first benefits had served the South more than the North. Now, just as the gains were shifting to the free states, the South had applied for an annulment of its provisions. Douglas might insist that the Compromise of 1850, by failing to stretch the 36°30′ line to the Pacific across territories won in the Mexican war, had done away with the Missouri Compromise, but no Northern politician had ever dared suggest that such a repeal had been part of the bargain. Even Northerners who supported popular sovereignty in principle did not want slavery to enter the territories. Many did not want any blacks in the trans-Mississippi West, slave *or* free. The Kansas-Nebraska bill was more than a repeal to them. It was a breach of faith. To many who had till now doubted the existence of a conspiratorial Slave Power, determined to dominate the Union by fair means or foul, the Douglas bill supplied the proof.[21]

Another aspect made the conflict more bitter. The bill would pass only because sectional loyalty broke down in one part of the country, party loyalty in the other. Northern Democrats and Southern Whigs had provided the margin between victory and defeat. Their action was just what was required to merge American fears of corruption with Free-Soiler fears of the Slave Power. It proved a deadly combination.

Northerners had expected much from Southern Whigs at first. "One thing I feel certain of," Alvah Hunt assured Thurlow Weed, "the Nebraska swindle cannot be *bought* through the House, with all the Government patronage—there are yet remaining at the South some few glorious fellows." But how few there were! Some Southern Whigs lauded the territorial bills. Others thought it madness, but said nothing. To have done so would have been political suicide. Southern Whigs knew that Southern Democrats meant the measure as a test of loyalty to sectional interests; Northerners might just as well ask slave-state representatives to hurl themselves from the Capitol roof, as ask a vote in opposition, one member pleaded. Northern Whigs watched their Southern colleagues with bafflement and then rage. "Are they all cravens?" the New York *Tribune* asked. "Do they consent to become participants in this gigantic robbery of the free States, and receivers of stolen goods?" A handful of slave-state Whigs did not so consent, but only a handful. It was the two remaining titans of the Jackson years who led Southern resistance, Sam Houston and Thomas Hart Benton.[22]

So much for the South. But a united North could kill the Kansas-Nebraska bill. Instead, Northern Democratic votes mustered by an Illinois senator and a New Hampshire President pushed the bill through both houses. To enemies of the measure, this was the crowning betrayal, and they probed for the cause. The answer was the one Hale and the Philadelphia Whigs had given: corruption, which made men place personal gain ahead of their constituents' will.

The charges were often grossly unfair. Congressman Theodore Westbrook of New York supported the bill. At once his enemies claimed that his fee had been the right to replace Charles O'Conor as district attorney for New York City. In fact, the Administration gave the position to someone else, and there is no evidence that Westbrook was even interested in the job for himself. When the appointment was announced, however, Westbrook's enemies simply refashioned their argument. The whole business showed Pierce's perfidy, they shouted. He had promised and then broken his word. In the future, the New York *Evening Post* advised Westbrook, when he sold his vote, he should insist on getting the reward in advance.[23]

Even if all the "corruption" surrounding the bill's passage is put beyond dispute as a clear set of quid pro quos, it seems tame stuff indeed: no more than the usual horse-trading. Vacant consulates in Chile, London, and Turin were reputedly dangled over wavering congressmen's heads. The Honorable William Tweed demanded the replacement of a Williamsburgh postmaster before casting his vote, and he got it. "It is surprising to see what small prices govern Members in this market," a reporter commented. "A clerkship in one of the Departments here, for a son, nephew, or brother-in-law, will secure almost any vote of any ordinary Member of Congress, and with a dozen exceptions, they are very ordinary Members." It was said that two senators and four representatives were promised the governorship of the two new territories. Leland Olds declared himself "not such a G–d d–– fool as to be satisfied with a Territorial Governorship," and asked for more. For Whig Senator Badger of North Carolina, there was a lucrative California post for a brother-in-law to fill. Senator George Houston of Alabama obtained offices for two nephews. That was how the spoils system worked, but an excited Northern press now translated these as payments for votes given—which in view of the Southern backing for the bill on its merits, verges on fantasy. Those on whom no reward could be proven to have fallen were charged with expecting one in the future: a consulship in Honolulu for this member's friend, with a split of the fees from the place, the Stockholm mission for that representative, and for a Maine member, the collectorship of Portland's port, though "some old clothes will do." Free-soilers even believed that the Camden & Amboy had promised jobs to two congressmen and that Congressman James Pratt of Connecticut had traded his vote for Administration support for the Colt revolver patent.[24]

False though the specific cases may have been, it was beyond dispute that the Administration used patronage to drive the bill through and that patronage affected votes. Cabinet members promised to cut the bill's foes off from the spoils. Pierce and Douglas both made clear that a proper vote would bring rewards.* Speaking for the executive, the party organ pledged that Northern supporters "shall be sustained by every means within the power of the party, or within the power of the representatives of the people chosen by the party, whether these representatives are to be found in the halls of Congress, or *in the presidential chair.*" That took no interpreting. Anyone who lost his House seat could expect "healing appliances" as long as the offices held out. According to a Chicago congressman, at least a thousand inhabitants in Washington expected to gain office by their representative's vote.[25]

Nor was there any doubt that spoils affected the judgment of Democratic papers across the North. Wherever the loudest apologists for the Kansas-Nebraska bill raised their voices, onlookers spotted editors on the federal payroll. Small wonder that the Milwaukee *News* should endorse the actions of a government which paid it for printing federal mail contracts or that the editors of the Kenosha *Democrat* and Racine *Democrat* should find time to praise the bill put through by an Administration that had made them into postmasters. When Illinois dissidents went to "Long John" Wentworth's newspaper to ask that he publish their arguments, Wentworth refused. "I have too many favors to ask . . . to quarrel with them," he wrote. Patronage alone would certainly not keep a press going, and in such a crisis it would hardly make up for the loss of outraged subscribers in some places, but where it could not encourage support for the bill, it induced silence.[26]

All this was alarming. To Northern Whigs, the use of patronage for sectional advantage reawakened the old fears of executive usurpation. Free-soil Democrats treated it as an unprecedented use of political mus-

*Testimony in a later investigation suggests that alloting a contract to George Steers of New York to build a steam-frigate swung several votes. Between railroad lobbyists and the Kansas-Nebraska bill, however, no clear link exists. Matteson tried to hold certain railway schemes hostage to win votes for free-soil; a Wisconsin railroad lobbyist claimed that he lobbied against the bill; and another insider contended that by meddling in territorial matters, Douglas had delayed any early consideration of railroad aid bills.

cle to form a proslavery party in the North. The worst of it was that the South counted on just such appliances working. The South knew that the North could be bought—it turned sectional venality to its own ends. A Northern party to resist the Kansas-Nebraska Act! The idea made the Charleston *Mercury* mirthful. "If they were not mere hucksters in politics," it joked, where "every man offers himself instead of some other commodity for sale, we should surmise they might do what they threaten. . . . But they will do no such thing. They will bluster . . . and end by knocking themselves under to the highest bidder."[27] Principles were always for sale. If the price was modest, did that matter? A dollar or a petty office alike was a bribe to do the President's will and not that of the Northern people.

So when the bill was passed through the House in May, its foes had taken up one defiant cry: it was passed "by the congenial aid of the spoils peddlers," "with the unscrupulous use of executive patronage," from the application of "cash or cash-offices," by "the midnight robbers of hen-roosts." It must never happen again. A blow must be struck against the "Nebraskals." First and foremost it was to be a blow against slavery extension, but the way in which slavery had made its latest advance also made the battle one to cleanse the North of the corruptions of party and place. "Let me ask you, my friends," Hale cried, ". . . if this is one of those minor questions which you are willing to trade off at the polls for a place in the Custom House? ("No, no," laughter) Are there not some things that are a little higher and holier than to be put in the political shambles for the market, and is not this one of those questions?"[28]

To prevent such sellouts in the future, as it would turn out, took more than a purge within the existing parties, though not all party men came to this moment of truth at once. From the day that Douglas reported his territorial bill, the old parties began to heave and twist to meet the new political question. At each heave, more members were hurled from the organizations and the twisting would go on for years. As early as the summer of 1854, enemies of slavery had founded the Republican party to keep the territories free, but many who voted that ticket in 1860 came late to the cause. For Whigs like Seward and Abraham Lincoln, there was still much in the old Whig organization worth preserving, and it would take more than a year before they gave up trying. For others, the Democratic national convention of 1856 would be the last straw.

The Softshell Democratic convention in New York in 1855 was just one example among many that showed how the power of patronage made self-purification impossible. Already many Democrats had left the ranks, but some free-soil members still hoped that the convention's resolutions would square their views with those of the party. Perhaps three-fourths of them had supported the Free-Soil revolt in 1848, but when the delegates assembled, attitudes had changed. Now some eighty held federal offices, some fifty more sought preferment, and the Administration had sent its drillmasters to cajole the rest. After a night of bargaining and arguing, the delegates drew back from repudiation of the President's Kansas policy. Though "Prince John" backed a resolution decrying the rigged elections that proslavery forces had held in the territory, it was defeated. Instead, the Administration was praised for its fight on speculators, and the opposition was denounced for fostering a "corrupt lobby" in Albany. This was more than one upstate delegate could stand. "I am not here to bow the knee to the Baal of Slavery," he shouted, "or to the Custom-House and Post-Office of New-York." He and others like him joined the Republicans then.[29]

The Whigs, or at least the Northern Whigs, might seem better equipped to adapt to the new issue if they abandoned their Southern allies. That did not prove to be the case. For one thing, any antislavery party would have to make room for disgruntled Democrats, and Democrats, always trained to see Whiggery as the agency of corrupt special interests, would never take on the enemy's name. For another thing, many Whigs had lost faith in their party because of the Southern wing's perfidy. "Shuffling dogs are they all," the New York *Tribune* hooted of the Southerners. The distrust had already sunk deep before the Kansas-Nebraska Act with the trading that surrounded the Compromise of 1850 and the readiness of Northerners such as Webster and Fillmore to concede ground which free-soilers cherished as sacred. It was in that moment, Henry Winter Davis recalled, when congressmen met "to log-roll, to compromise, to divide the plunder and cheat the people," that the soul had fled from the Whig party. All that held it together thereafter were old catchwords, now obsolete.[30]

Therefore, from the first, members of both parties called for an entirely new organization dedicated to Northern interests. "Throw these old fogies overboard," John Whipple challenged his fellow Rhode Island Whigs. "They have been preying upon the State, bribing the people, and quarreling for the spoils long enough. They can't go straight, should some of them . . . make a trial." From a Democrat came the same warning: "the democratic party, and the whig party too, are become so corrupt, that whoever relies upon them . . . will be sadly disappointed. . . ."[31] This was not just because of wicked men, but because of the nature of party itself. When parties put loyalty and rewards ahead of principle, events like the Kansas-Nebraska Act became inevitable. Parties, like republics, decayed as their founding principles faded from view. So Northerners should free themselves from old party names, a form of slavery that made the Slave Power's triumph easier.

But was there not another lesson to be learned from the Kansas-Nebraska Act and the corruption surrounding it? Many Northerners concluded that all compromise was impossible. For compromise to take place, there must be trust on either side and a semblance of honor. Without it, no bargain could survive beyond the moment that one side found profit in breaking it. It was precisely that lack of trust that the Southern Whigs' votes made so clear. "We have tried compromises with Slavery," said the Utica *Herald*; "they have been violated in the basest manner. Hereafter we can have no more of them." The day for a surrender of principle for sectional peace had passed. Many a protestor against repeal of the Missouri Compromise no longer would accept restoration of that arrangement. Thanks to Southern ambitions and Northern avarice, no restoration could be trusted to stand. Nor would it be redress enough. "Now the war must be carried into Carthage," the New Haven *Palladium* declared. "The time to compromise with a system of rank corruption has now gone by forever."[32]

14

"Black Chattels Sell and White Ones Vote Aright"

The Republic was in danger. Free-soilers had no doubt of that. It took them a while, however, before they discerned precisely what form the peril had taken. Gradually, the answer became clear. Freedom, it seemed, was menaced by a corrupt conspiracy of jobbers, spoilsmen, and slaveholders.

We must be cautious in ascribing the myth of Freedom Corrupted to all antislavery men. On the broadest level, corruption's presence did not matter a bit to them. The true issue was slavery's extension. Nor did Republicans doubt the masters' sincerity in seeking to spread the institution into the territories. The means by which the Slave Power won its demands were another matter. Time and again, antislavery men blamed their every setback on corrupt Northern lackeys who did the South's bidding. The "slaveocracy" would have lost their fight had they left decisions to the majority will, but they were determined not to lose. So through deceit and an alliance with the Money Power, the Slave Power advanced. Speculators and spoilsmen made themselves the henchmen of the lords of the lash.

Not all Northerners could express this viewpoint in every detail. Among those Republicans whose views have survived, sharp differences existed in the sophistication of the analysis. When Free-Soilers spoke of the Slave Power conspiracy, some knew only a few specifics. Others cited different ones, still others could fit all the charges into one ornate pattern. So it was, too, with the myth of Freedom Corrupted. Many a Northerner could spout generalities about the link between slavery and stealing, but could not have cited more than a few facts to justify his case. Others could sketch not just the broad outline, but could amass over time the evidence to make a staggering case. Still, in any of its forms the myth had broad appeal because corruption was a political fact; the belief that corruption was pervasive was a political reality.

As Republicans saw it, the Republic was menaced. The Slave Power, the political arm of the slaveholders, represented only a fraction of the Southern people, and the Southern people themselves were outnumbered in the Union. Yet the President, Congress, courts, and party system all were dominated by the Slave Power, which, said Republicans, used its power to take new, dangerous advantages. First, it had brought in Texas; then provoked a war with Mexico for new cotton lands, forcing a compromise on terms unfavorable to the North in 1850; it had enacted a Fugitive Slave law of doubtful constitutionality; and even as it broke the Missouri Compromise in 1854, it pressured the Administration to acquire property in the Caribbean into which more planters could go and from which more spokesmen for the Slave Power could be sent to Congress. In one generation, the South's masters had made tremendous advances toward a Union servile to their will.[1]

How could they have brought off such a coup? Northerners had not been napping since 1830. No revolutionary cell had annulled the Constitution to deprive Northerners of their political power. Yet to some it seemed that the Slave Power had always ruled the government, by purchasing Freedom's representatives. As long as men were corrupt, one Republican wrote, the North would never hold its rightful place.[2]

A few antislavery men explained this choice of tactics on the South's own debauchery. Its congressmen professed themselves opposed to federal aid for internal improvements, but this was a sham, one Northerner declared. Pork for the West violated the Slave Power's sense of the Constitution, but how those scruples vanished when federal money for a rail line across the Southwest was at stake! In 1856, a Washington correspondent reported that among the land grants that railroads desired this year was one for a Mississippi firm, and he broadened this to the charge that the South in general had acquired a positively Northern taste for "public plunder." Had Northerners wanted, they could have cited many examples of Southerners sharing the spoils, from the Georgia politicians tarred by Galphinism to the Virginia editors squabbling over public printing. On occasion, a Republican might paint the Southern Rights men as driven solely by their hunger for Treasury funds and their zeal to

> Batter, shatter and sack the Capitol!
> And like true Gothic thieves,
> From foundation to eaves
> Filch its coffers and archives.

The charge made bad doggerel and worse sense. Republicans had to acknowledge the South's reputation for probity where money was concerned. The South could not be bought for any purpose nor be swayed from its plans, least of all where slavery was concerned. No one seriously suggested that Southern congressmen could be bought to resist the Kansas-Nebraska bill, as Northerners reputedly were. When Southerners believed in something, they stood by it. That was what made them so dangerous.[3]

If the "slaveocrats" were seen as tyros when it came to stealing, they loomed as true professionals when it came to corrupting others. On that score Republicans were convinced. "Why, Mr. Quincy," Josiah Quincy recalled a distinguished Southerner telling him, "we of the South can calculate upon your leaders as we can calculate upon our own negroes."[4] It deepened the irony that Northern money bought Northern men, for, said Republicans, the South used Treasury funds to furnish the bribes.

When Republicans spoke of Northerners being bought, they did not mean merely that money changed hands on the floor of the House. There were many ways to induce a Northerner to trade his principles for personal advantage. To hear free-soil men talk, Southerners encouraged every sort of corruption in the North. The more unprincipled its people, the more chance that the Slave Power could have its way by seducing congressmen. A breeding ground for corruption of one kind proved fertile soil for corruption of a more dangerous sort. Such at least was the reading Northerners might put on the appeal of a leading Southern Rights paper for the free states to elect "the most unscrupulous and corrupt financier, whose veins are burning with the lust for power." Such a Yankee was "emphatically the man for the South," it added. Before the Slave Power assumed dominion in Washington, the New York *Evening Post* declared, any President who tried to offer $200 million for any territory, much less Cuba, would have been impeached. Not till the 1840s did such predators as George Law, Milledge Galphin, and George Gardiner dare to hire Cabinet officers as attorneys; but a corrupted political system served the South's ends best.[5]

Out of this putrefaction had grown an alliance between the Slave Power and the promoters of schemes that needed government aid. In return for the promoters' using their money and influence to drive the true Northern men from politics, the South would help them pass their measures through Congress. When a surrender of Northern rights could be passed, some deal would be worked out with Northern traitors hoping to turn a profit by it. Radical Democrats, those most inclined to back the Free-Soil party in 1848, were loudest in insisting that against them were ranged not just Northern apologists for slavery, but Democrats who had abandoned the issue of limited government. Through them the argument entered the antislavery ideology until even Whigs made it part of their own concept.

Why had the great champion of free-soil Democrats, Governor Silas Wright, been defeated in his 1846 re-election bid? Because, said the *Evening Post*, the Slave Power joined hands with the foes of a restrictive New York constitution that Wright had helped enact. Steamship jobbers and canal promoters saw the document as a barrier between themselves and the treasury, and in Wright they saw the most forthright spokesman of fiscal restraint. Hunkers with their wildcat banking and canal interests saw to it that the ticket was beaten, and they had help from a Tennessee President's placeholders.[6]

Why had Edwin Croswell, editor of the Hunker Democratic Albany *Argus*, helped Whigs push through the Compromise of 1850? Because Croswell had invested in the Canal Bank, and when its operations were wound up he received a generous settlement from Whig authorities. In return, he delivered the margin of victory to the Whig ticket in New York in 1848 and 1849. In his eagerness for mail contracts for the Sloo and Ebony lines, he bought Southern friends by becoming their shill in the North.[7]

How had the Slave Power managed to drive Senator Thomas Hart Benton out of Missouri politics in 1851? By hiring the press to attack him, and by calling in the support and "the wealth of all the corrupt jobbers in the United States." Such men knew that Benton would keep their appropriations from passing through the Senate. He must be removed.[8]

These were slender threads indeed on which to hang the myth of the Slave Power conspiracy. Most Southerners voted against the steamship subsidies, and the strongest Southern Rights advocates were among the most hostile. Polk did not arrange for Wright's defeat and promised to punish the Hunkers for knifing the ticket. Benton had enough enemies in both parties and enough conceit that no jobber was needed to bring about his downfall. In the Texas issue, however, Free-Soilers may have fingered a stronger strand. It was the entry of Texas into the Union that had begun the swift expansion of national domain and of potential slave states. Out of that annexation came the war with Mexico and the conquest of the West, and with it the deal that would settle the status of the new territories for slavery or freedom. Was it statesmanship alone that explained the fateful admission of the Lone Star state in 1845? Not to free-soilers' thinking.

Benton had sensed covert influences from the first, and he had opposed annexation fiercely. Time would not soften his judgment. In closing his memoirs, he hinted that the annexation had begun a dangerous downward swoop in public ethics. Privately, he was more specific. "[A]ll an intrigue for the presidency," he wrote of the Texas treaty, "—land jobbing & stock jobbing—and the dissolution of the Union if the presidential intrigue did not succeed. I have now the proof of what I knew then without proof. . . . Have it from Stuart, now Sec. of the Interior & then a member of congress & who has told me all about and Blair will tell you."[9]

What Blair may well have told former President Van Buren was that the land and securities of Texas had made their owners into friends of annexation and five years later of the Compromise. Established in 1836, the Texas Republic had lasted for nine impecunious years, during which it had sold bonds and notes at a vast discount, sometimes for as little as ten cents on the dollar. By 1845, the republic's outstanding debts had risen to $10 million at par. Texans who held the securities knew that annexation might help their portfolios' value tremendously. So did statesmen in Washington. Many politicians, including Clay, Webster, and former Governor James Hamilton of South Carolina, had dabbled in those certificates. Not surprisingly, many of them also favored annexation. Some securities had been issued with the republic's guarantee that its import duties would go for their repayment. Since the United States alone could set tariff rates for the nation, Texans could assume that after annexation the federal government would take over the guarantee.

Texas bond speculators had never run the show, but they had helped smooth the way for admission into the Union. Jay Cooke, Philadelphia banker and investor, would later declare that all opposition was overcome "through the selfish exertions . . . of the holders of the Texas debt certificates, many of whom were influential Northern men." Among those financially interested were Leslie Combs, campaign manager for

Henry Clay's presidential bid in 1844 and perhaps instrumental in making the candidate soften his stand against annexation during the canvass; Senator Benjamin Tappan of Ohio, who would make $50,000 on his investment; newspapermen Beverly Tucker and Francis J. Grund, who whipped up popular enthusiasm for Texas; John Slidell of Louisiana and S. S. Prentiss of Mississippi. In Texas itself, leading land speculators and bondholders in high office used their powers to advance the cause of annexation on terms that would leave them richer.[10]

That was how Texas came in, said the free-soilers: appeals to greed. Nor should that have been too surprising. A laxity in financial ethics seemed the perfect breeding ground for a lax morality where slavery was concerned. John Quincy Adams, the crotchety Massachusetts congressman and spokesman for political antislavery, had sensed it in the pressure for Texas annexation as early as 1842. "The Texas land and liberty jobbers," he wrote, ". . . spread the contagion of their land-jobbing traffic all over the free states throughout the Union. Land-jobbing, stock-jobbing, slave-jobbing, rights-of-man jobbing were all hand in hand. . . ."[11]

So Texas came in, though it did not bring the promised windfall to speculators. The bonds of the former republic still went unpaid. Another solution must be found. That was where the Compromise settlement of disputes between slave and free states became entangled. New Mexico territory disputed its boundary with Texas, which claimed every acre east of the Rio Grande and coveted the Santa Fe trade. New Mexicans had no intention of ceding everything from Las Vegas to Albuquerque and were prepared to fight the civil officers Texas sent out to rule them. One obvious solution would be to buy Texas off by assuming its public debt. That was part of Henry Clay's original measure. Senator James A. Pearce of Maryland offered a still more generous settlement, which was incorporated into the "Omnibus" of compromises that soon developed. His bill guaranteed payment of the whole $10 million debt in 5-percent bonds. Half the money would be retained until the federal authorities had received waivers from those creditors who claimed Washington responsible for payment of their import-duty certificates.[12]

Philadelphia's stock exchange had been quoting the Texas bonds at 29 cents on the dollar in February 1850. By May the price was 54 cents, by June full face value. Politicians bought in, often at the behest or with the aid of W. W. Corcoran, partner in Corcoran & Riggs banking house and a heavy speculator in Texas paper. Corcoran himself had bought up some $140,000 worth in 1850 and became deeply concerned with the outcome of the Compromise. So was Hamilton of South Carolina

($10,000 worth), who served as agent in Austin for another leading creditor of Texas, the steamship promoter William S. Wetmore. "The payment of the Debt of Texas will enable me I trust to do a partial if not a total & plenary Justice to all my creditors," Hamilton wrote. Not that he would surrender a single principle vital to the South—better his own ruin than that. But, he insisted, not all that persuasively to some Southern leaders, the two interests were akin. By May he had reached the Capitol to act as lobbyist for the Compromise, indemnity included. Clay's Kentucky ally Combs joined him. Gazaway Bugg Lamar of New York and Georgia (close relation by marriage to the Speaker), Thomas Biddle of the Philadelphia banking dynasty, the Drexels of Pennsylvania, and former Senator Tappan all had a financial stake in the Compromise.

They worked hard to make congressmen see their point of view. In the end, they got what they wanted. Down went the "Omnibus," to be sure, but each part was revived separately and passed. The Texas debt issue was the hardest part to resolve. On September 5, the issue came to a vote. Senators Houston and Rusk of Texas moved among House members soliciting help. Claims agents linked to Corcoran's other schemes were visible in the chamber. A favorable ruling by Speaker Howell Cobb allowed the $10 million indemnity to be connected to a bill for organizing the territory of New Mexico. Over it all, Corcoran watched, "occasionally nodding his head to this, buttoning and whispering to that 'leading member.'" "Compromise is the body," a correspondent wrote; "corruption and Texas bonds are the wheel-horses; hungry and unscrupulous whig and democratic politicians . . . are the passengers." Not enough of them were: the new "Omnibus" lost by a margin of 46. A third reading of the indemnity was defeated.

It was not the end. All night the lobbying went on, and the next day the bill, twice-slain, revived again. Fourteen New York Whigs helped provide the margin for victory, 108 to 98. Only half-joking, an Ohio congressman suggested that the lobbyists clustered on the floor could get a better view from the galleries, and the Speaker declared that he would enforce the rules banning them from the floor, though he did no such thing. It was quite a victory. "What is virtue against Texas scrip?" asked the New York *Evening Post* bitterly. "What is the national legislature against Corcoran & Riggs' office? . . ."* As the measure passed, friends of the Compromise greeted the House action with "a deafening shout."[13]

*Corcoran's role in the settlement is suggestive, but obscure. Among his papers are sixty letter-books. The only missing volume is that for 1850. That this one year should have vanished is curious, though it makes definite proof of bribery impossible.

Conservatives might hail the Compromise as a triumph of statesmanship over sectionalism, but Free-Soilers felt differently. The more they knew, the less honest the Compromise looked. A few months after its passage, reports circulated that some Northern support had come from logrolling for tariff protection. Southern congressmen claimed to have won over Pennsylvania lawmakers by promising to repay a vote for Compromise with "adjustments" in the tariff rates. On this understanding, too, the Pennsylvania legislature voted to repeal all laws that handicapped efforts to retrieve fugitive slaves. When the deal became public, the New Orleans *Louisiana Courier* branded it "as plain a proffer of bargain and sale as was ever submitted." It wondered how long such a compromise could last, with Northern support gained in spite of antislavery convictions. Since Southerners were selling their low-tariff convictions, the New York *Evening Post* replied, the arrangement was "equally corrupt" on both sides. Neither section then knew that there were connections between the railroad land grants that Illinois had obtained in 1850 and Illinois votes for the Compromise, nor that Southerners had threatened to block all the cherished internal improvements programs of certain Northern representatives unless they got satisfaction for Southern demands. But if they had known, the freesoilers would not have been surprised.[14]

The greatest victim of the Compromise was Daniel Webster. His apostasy from the antislavery cause was more shocking than any other to freesoil Whigs, and not at all surprising to antislavery Democrats. Other New England men had endorsed the Compromise of 1850 and were criticized, but none so brutally as Webster. None was seen so clearly as an emblem of corruption. There were several reasons for this distinction. First, the senior senator from Massachusetts already had a shady reputation, one which his fondest supporters had denied to themselves, had found explanations to palliate, and yet had been unable to lay at rest. Now the distrust broke out afresh and all the old charges gained new weight. A man of lesser intellect might have been deceived by Southern bluster or the smooth tongue of Henry Clay, but Webster's intellectual prowess was beyond question. It had reached the proportions of a national institution. Greed, ambition, corruption: only these traits could have brought him round. Years later a Republican remembered the anguish of the shock, and through his indignation at Webster's apostasy his grief still showed for the man he had idolized. "His place here was like that of Burke in England. . . . He had said all that was most beautiful of liberty and the Constitution. The language was inimitable—the spirit was glorious. But in 1850 he was deceived, seduced, corrupted, and in the hope of reward he fell." *Deceived*—but deceived by promises to his ambition. Webster was not simply a villain but a victim of the South, which used him, appealed to his desires, and then discarded him.[15]

In every community, said free-soilers, the Southern seducers had done the same and found a thousand Websters to suborn and corrupt to the South's service. Between friends of the Compromise of 1850 and the monied interests seeking subsidies from a Congress that the South and her minions controlled was forged a powerful link. In 1851, the Union Safety Committee organized in New York City to press for a state ticket of men "safe" on the Compromise. What interested the New York *Evening Post* was the personnel of the committee. It included at least ten men with a vested interest in federal steamship mail-subsidies, and there were but twenty committee-members in all. Of course they could afford to spend $100,000 to win tools for the South among New York's electorate, said free-soilers. A friendly Congress would give back ten times as much in subsidies. When it had dug its hands into the Treasury, the organization would disband and save the Union no longer. In this prediction the free-soilers were coincidentally correct.[16]

Wall Street, Broad Street, Beacon Hill—all had used their investors' sense to make a deal at the expense of free-soil, but Whigs led the way in suggesting that a corrupting force of equal menace came from the far end of Pennsylvania Avenue. Ever hungering for power, the executive had always tried to bring the legislative branch to heel through the favors at his disposal. The Slave Power had seen to it that only a man friendly to their interests would be nominated for President by the Democrats and elected by the people, and had made him all the more powerful so that Northern congressmen and state party conventions would be unable to withstand his blandishments.

These blandishments were among the Slave Power's most efficient weapons. A President could buy votes in Congress for slavery with promises of courthouse sites, with increasing funding for certain navy yards, contracts to supply the army or carry federal dispatches. No wonder federal expenses leaped from nearly nothing to $80 million a year, antislavery men exclaimed. This was not just extravagance. It was largesse to win legislators to the Administration's point of view—for it was an easy leap from the claim that the President allowed expenses to rise to the charge that he did so because he held absolute power to decide where and how money was spent. So large a fund could corrupt a saint. In five years' time, said one congressman, there was no doubt that

$20 million had gone "to carry measures and elections; to pay for burying the dead and providing for the wounded; in paying salaries created by party favorites, and for cheating the people generally."[17]

Such inducements had always been around, but their use to pension the appliances of the Slave Power was new, said freesoilers. One innovation was particularly dangerous. Northern congressmen were most likely to bow to slavery when they were freed from fear of their constituents' wrath. The patronage power could end their concern, for if their constituents turned Democrats out of the House, the President would turn them into consuls. This practice "of indemnifying members of Congress for the loss of their political characters and influence in the service of slavery," said the *Evening Post*, began under Polk. By 1854, it was customary.[18] Here was bribery, said Republicans, without the formal promise. Congressmen did not need to be told that they would be rewarded. Each example spoke for itself in tones of thunder. In the process, the representatives broke free of their constituents' will.

That way led the road to tyranny. By such methods the Presidential power thwarted every check upon it. The people's own money was used to buy the Congress to do the President's will. The specter of the Roman Republic was raised anew. For less crimes against liberty than the President had committed, a fellow-Democrat cried, Julius Caesar had been assassinated and Charles I brought to the block; "neither ever perpetrated so many acts of petty tyranny, or did so much to corrupt national morality—a crime, in my judgment, of the highest grade." The swelling of the spoils system also undermined the Northern parties. Executive minions dominated state conventions. Democrats could not call a public meeting or choose an executive committee anyplace, said one editor, without the Administration thrusting its hand into the process. No resolutions could pass unless they had the placemen's approval or were so meaningless that no one could take offense. The central authority threatened states' rights, the government was debauched, and the spoils system wielded by the Slave Power's most potent accomplice was the cause.[19]

With patronage and contracts, the South hardly needed to purchase men for cash, but it had money ready. Ambition might seduce a Douglas or a Webster, but a New York congressman had no hopes of the Presidency. He wanted payment. There was room in the budget for that under "Miscellany." In 1849, Senator Zacharian Chandler of Michigan recalled, "Miscellany" took up only $3.5 million. Was it pure coincidence that the following year, as the Compromise was pushed through, the expenses doubled? In 1854, the figures rose sharply again, but then, that was the year of the Kansas-Nebraska Act. "Where any terrible outrage was to be perpetrated by the slave power," Chandler joked, "Miscellany suffered some. Wherever a 'nigger' showed his head in the fence, Miscellany loomed up, and when the nigger went out, Miscellany loomed down again."[20]

The Freedom Corrupted myth, then, was an inspiring combination of the old Whig and Democratic visions of the Republic's worst nemesis. Democrats had spent a generation inveighing at the corrupting influence of special interest money and the susceptibility of Congress to the Money Power. Now, here was that peril linked to the Slave Power conspiracy. Whigs had raised the alarm over executive usurpation, and here again the Slave Power had merged its fortunes with those of a would-be Caesar to serve their mutual end. There was just enough to appeal both to old Democrats, who admitted that Whig fears of patronage power had been right all along, and to old Whigs, who conceded that the special interests had made as unscrupulous a deal as any Locofoco could have imagined.

From the former Free-Soil party, the Republicans took a third premise for the myth of Freedom Corrupted: the party system itself was too degenerate to be reformed from within. Northern politics had been debauched beyond any chance of redemption within the old Jacksonian parties. Once there had been leaders ready to hazard their fortunes for liberty, but those days were long gone, said Republicans. The present breed of politicians knew no statesmanship, and the Slave Power was to blame. It had purged all great orators and public men and by using the patronage power had fed ambition among the new generation of leaders. Ambition and republican virtue could not live together.[21] In the North, defenders of freedom gave way to "dough-faces."

Only if we sense the nuance to "dough-face" can we assess its true significance and why Northern Democrats so resented being thus labeled. In its original form—that which John Randolph of Roanoke is said to have meant when he invented it—it was "doe-face," and conveyed the timidity of the startled deer. But a face made of dough was quite different. It was a countenance ready to be shaped by any hand, since no force or faith behind it gave the features distinction. If historians define the term as "Northern men of Southern principles," they misstate it. Any free-soiler would have declared that it meant a Northerner of no principles, and therefore one ideally suited to be remade by those kneading hands that had the patronage, power, and pay to make him as they saw fit. In short, a dough-face *had* to be insincere.

Thus it was quite in keeping with Northern understanding that Senator Hale of New Hampshire should vow that the North had "always been in a practical minority here, because you have bought up *dough-faces* enough to control us," and that northern Democrats should thunder at his choice of the term as an insult. Brought to retraction, Hale first pleaded that he had never used the term, for never would he question an enemy's motives, and then, on rereading the account, he admitted that the word occurred and apologized.* Others felt no such remorse, and the term came to be fastened to the image of suborned statesmen, depraved Democrats:[22]

Ye sons of slavedom! seize dominion;
Is not our victory almost grasped?
Lo! Hards and Softs—in our opinion—
Watching for spoils our hands have clasped.
  See how our Atchison the trusty,
  To give us power regards no cost;
  See, too, how Douglas, dough—though crusty—
  For loaves and fish, the Rubicon has crossed.

Ye sons of slavedom, bent on easy profit,
By trade in chattels, whether black or white,
Don't stand for trifles, ne'er mind conscience—scoff it;
Black chattels sell, and white ones vote aright.

To say that the Slave Power used northern Democrats as its tools was not to say that the Democracy was corrupt in every sense—only on this one issue. Still, from the first premise to the second was a modest step, and Whigs had had long practice in taking the broader viewpoint. They had long considered the economic policies of the Age of Jackson as self-serving and probably dishonest finance. Their distrust did not change when Whiggery gave way to Republicanism. Democrats would stop at nothing, the Philadelphia *Daily News* reminded readers, for "fraud is more familiar to them than morality," and many in the ranks would risk the penitentiary for a chance to "swindle and plunder the community." The same presumption that to be a Democrat was by definition to be a

*The *Congressional Globe* carried Hale's speech, but no mention of "dough-faces" at all, and it was nearly a week later before any Northern Democrat rose to protest the offending term. By that time, a pamphlet form of the speech had been circulated, and it seems that here was where the offensive words appeared. It is possible that Hale never actually spoke the words, in spite of his own admission. For one thing, he took pride in never changing a word from any speech delivered before Congress before it was entered in the *Globe*; for another, no newspaper report mentioned his description of Northern Democrats as dough-faces, and several of them gave a thorough coverage to his remarks. Most likely Hale wrote the words in his original speech, sent it off to be printed in pamphlet form, but deleted the controversial passage when he spoke before the Senate.

scoundrel underlay the story one Whig-Republican paper gave of an Iowa Democratic convention, where one contender for state office was being considered. "What sort of man is he?" a delegate asked. "Oh, a first-rate fellow," he was told. "A perfect gentleman, and *an upright honest man.*" "Hold on there," the delegate roared. "I object! I do not want any *new tests* introduced into our party!"[23]

Given the chance, antislavery men could reinforce their argument of the Democrats' susceptibility to Slave Power purchasers by showing that the party loved plunder for its own sake. If the majority of Wisconsin voters chose to be "sheared like so many sheep every year," a free-soil editor snarled, no law could keep Democrats from gratifying that wish, "although it does seem a little hard that those who have the most objections to it are compelled to stand the closest shearing." Michigan Republicans upbraided Democrats for having recognized fraudulent claims, Pennsylvania partisans blamed the dough-faces for pillaging the canals and bestowing contracts on their kin, and New York partisans could cite examples of defaulters during the 1830s.[24]

For all this, Democratic sources produced hearty corroboration. Even among steadfast Democrats, the strains of antebellum politics bred bitter resentments. In quarrels over how little or how much to concede to the South, members were perfectly willing to label each other scoundrels and thieves, especially when some of them were just that. Until 1855, nothing could dislodge the Democratic party from power in Wisconsin, but after the incumbent governor failed to steal the election and investigations showed freebooting at the expense of schools, poorhouses, and asylums, party unity collapsed. By 1857, said the Milwaukee *Patriot* for one wing of the Democracy, the organization was as flat as a pancake made of tar and mud. No one needed to ask why:[25]

> The party . . . has slept with pilfering shavers, scoundrels and knaves and has caught the Barber's itch. It has breathed the pestilential malaria fuming from the lairs of the old, rotten, unprincipled, scurvyheaded, milk-and-water, broken down, cast off, leprous pukes, cancerous thieves, superannuated pickpockets, Treasury-plundering, refuse Abolition office-seeking, whiskey-soaked, double-distilled buffoons and Penitentiary scalawags—who have preyed and gorged upon the party and the people, until the substance of each is exhausted, and they look as lean, lank, thin, savage, and cadaverous as twice-starved hyenas. . . .

New York Democrats described each other less colorfully, but with no less ill will as cheats, dastards, and pirates.

But if some Republicans could contend that the Slave Power dominated the Democrats because of the party's corruption, antislavery men found it more appealing to assume the reverse: the Democrats were corrupt because the Slave Power had made them so where sectional issues were concerned. Decay in one aspect assured a moral collapse in every other. How could it be otherwise, asked Salmon Chase. When statesmen readily bought desert in the Southwest to provide the Slave Power with its own railroad to the Pacific and did so, Chase implied, after bribes had been distributed to senators in secret session, the doughfaces would not balk at enriching their friends from the state treasury. Even the doings of Mayor Wood in New York could be traced to the demoralizing impact that the Slave Power had had on the Democratic party. His outrages were but "a reflex of the Border Ruffianism which has so long prevailed and is still prevailing in Kansas. . . ."[26]

Certainly former Democrats preferred this explanation. It justified their departure from the party to which they had once sworn faith and encouraged them to dream that someday they would return to the old cause in triumph. That, of course, could happen only when the Slave Power had been vanquished and the Democracy restored to its original purity. Not all Republicans thought theirs a permanent departure from the party in which they had been raised. They were true to their first principles; those principles would divide Americans again one day.

That was one reason that Democrats could not assert their free-soil principles under the Whig label, but there was another. The Freedom Corrupted myth insisted that Whigs were no more immune to the Slave Power's appliances than were their opponents. The Kansas-Nebraska Act had shown that. So had the fall of Webster in 1850, and the constant accommodation that the Cotton Whigs of New England had made with Southerners. Once there had been magic in the Whig name, said its survivors. Then the Slave Power fastened its grip. In vain the South demanded that the Whig party surrender its antislavery views, Hugh Ewing recalled: the organization chose to die instead. Less flatteringly, a Maryland Whig charged that the organization *had* given in, and so offensive was the fraud and depravity that followed, that pure men (himself among them) had sought other connections. Whichever interpretation a free-soiler chose, the party was unusable. Too many of its leaders had been seduced, and they controlled the vestiges of the party machinery. Let fools dream of reorganizing the old party, Senator Benjamin Wade told an audience. He had left it and would not return. The party "was not only dead, but stinketh," and it "died the death of a felon." Only the galvanizing shocks of Treasury money could make the Whig carcass twitch, but that was the only semblance of life.[27]

With both parties doing the Slave Power's will, state politics in the North went as Southerners willed it. Certain states struck Republicans as no more than Slave Power satellites. Slaveholders would invade new states to organize the politics and place themselves in charge. So it had been in California, Iowa, and Minnesota, while Jesse Bright's management of Indiana politics was almost as skillful as his management of his Kentucky plantation slaves. Until 1851, in Massachusetts both parties kept every friend of Free-Soil out of office, a correspondent complained—a comment that overlooked John Quincy Adams, among many. Pennsylvania came in for the harshest abuse. "Pennsylvania politicians have generally sold the influence which her position has given her," wrote D. L. Child, "to that section, which has been in the habit and has had . . . the means of buying up men to betray one half of the states, & three quarters of the inhabitants."[28]

The only cure to this miasma of corruption was to fashion a party clear of all connection with the Slave Power. Free from the inducements that Southerners could offer any party that temporized about slavery's extension, the Republican organization would be able to revive America's morality. "We must encourage moral independence in politics," Carl Schurz told Wisconsin listeners. "[W]e must encourage every man to think and to reason for himself, to form his own convictions, and to stand by them; we must entreat them never to accept, unseen and uninvestigated, the principles and opinions of others, even if they be our own." Party discipline had corrupted and blinded Democrats to their administrations' compromise of principle. But Republicans would never humble conscience before "party necessity."[29] As untrammeled politicians, they could wage the fight that neither Whig nor Democrat could, to dismantle the Slave Power and to banish the great corrupting force from politics.

For that to happen, several things must be done. First, the Republican party must awaken the North and show the South that the majority would not go willingly into a "corrupt subserviency to the slave power." What had happened to the political system had happened to the private consciences of too many Northerners. Cotton manufacturers looked South for markets and paid with silence on the slavery issue for the profits their looms amassed. Railroad interests loved their Southern trade too dearly to decry the wrongs of human servitude. The South counted on them all when it committed aggression and presumed that love of prosperity had drained all principle from the North. This must not be. No republic could survive such an acquiescence in wrong. "If you sell your conscience to interest, you traffic with a fiend," Reverend Henry Ward Beecher warned. "The fear of doing right is the grand treason in times of danger."[30] It was also the great corrupter, Republicans would have added. The time had come for the North to show its incorruptibility, though material interests might suffer.

Then much would change, and not only the relationship between North and South. The myth of Freedom Corrupted had provided a pat explanation for all the different forms of depravity that offended Americans: land speculation, steamship lobbies, land-grant logrolling, the hireling press, the packed convention, spoils system abuses, canal contract overruns. So closely intertwined were the problems of corruption and of the Slave Power's growth that one could hardly be solved without solving the other. A few Republicans even began to speak of reform of the civil service and claimed it as right in itself as well as a severe blow against the Slave Power. To be sure, most partisans still cast covetous eyes on the loaves and fishes. Still, there were exceptions: Greeley, Bryant, the New York Republican Convention of 1856, and Senator Henry Wilson of Massachusetts. Whoever held power, Wilson commented, should "get clear of patronage, for patronage is only weakness if you have got any principles to carry." At the same time, the obverse was true. Remove the Slave Power from politics, and much corruption in public life would be cleansed. No longer would the lords of the lash be there to encourage peculation. "The place to begin State Reform, yes, and Municipal Reform," said an editor, "is at the White House in Washington." A Republican President's blows at the Slave Power would have its effect in Manhattan.[31]

Inadequate though the old parties were, would the Republican party be any better, any cleaner? Its members would soon include the wily Simon Cameron, whose ambition and wealth had made him Pennsylvania's least trusted leader; the rapacious Corwin brood in Ohio; crafty professionals such as Thurlow Weed and his cohorts Matteson and Harrington, and a host of lesser opportunists with a skill for framing a legislative steal or for looting a state treasury. Senator John P. Hale excited angry comment when he lobbied for the Collins lines in between terms of office. Senator William Seward, whose fingers never touched graft, was accused of having supported subsidies that were easy to describe as "plunder" of the government for the special interests' benefit. "Not a rogue comes to Washington with a plausible device for spending the money obtained from the people . . . who does not find a friend and champion in Senator

Seward," said the New York *Evening Post*, and so thought the *Tribune*, which racked its past files for a single incident when New York's senior senator had ever denounced "an act of public robbery" or "senatorial stealing."[32]

If reformers muttered their uneasiness in the press, they filled their private letters with darker imprecations still. "Our leaders are mercenary place hunters & nothing can be done till they lose their occupation," wrote radical George W. Julian of the Indiana moderates. "Had we only a *small* party here with *clean hands* (like the old Free Democracy) we could do something, but I am sorry to say that our Republicanism has little to boast over its foe."[33] The corrupting influence of hangers-on who took up party doctrines for advancement was dangerous as well as shameful. It distracted attention from the issue of Freedom Corrupted.

Certainly Democrats were looking for just such an opening, and long before they had any incidents to cite, they did their best to paint the new party as a collection of the same old thieves. After all, they cried, the antislavery party had Whigs in it, and Whigs by nature were corrupt. "Bankruptcy & disgrace" were the "usual fruits of whig rule." That must show that those Democrats who abandoned their old allegiance went simply from disappointed ambitions. Why else would they ally with bandits? "Swiss soldiers," the Indianapolis *Daily Sentinel* sneered at the renegades, men ready to fight for whatever general paid best. Depart the party of their own free will? Nonsense—they had been driven out, and "a purification of [the] party ensued." The trouble was, until early 1857, the Democrats had no proof for the charges. To desert the organization in power for a new, untested party without the chance of winning electoral votes in the South did not strike many people as persuasive proof of a vaulting, avaricious ambition. Opportunists do not usually go out of their way to back losers.[34]

Democrats' other problem was that, for all the unsavory sorts that Republicans would attract by 1860, there really was a strain of virtue, easily visible. The more inclined its members were to hold stern antislavery views or to come out early for a reconstruction of parties, the more strongly they were to express their alarm at the corruption around them. The list of grumblers against depravity in the early 1850s included old Jacksonians like Bryant, Benton, Blair, Welles, Houston, the Van Burens, Marcy, and Horatio Seymour. All of them either toyed with the Free-Soil movement years before the Republican party was formed or actually would leave Democratic ranks after the Kansas-Nebraska bill. "Prince John" Van Buren would stay in the fold, but he did not conceal his resentment that the Kansas issue had obscured what he thought the true question of the age: stealing Negroes was far less important than stealing public funds.[35]

Republicans proclaimed their members as the purest of the pure, and so loudly boasted of the organization's moral tone that it became a trademark. Years would pass before Republicans took on the nickname "the party of moral ideas," but all parties agreed that this was how Republicans saw themselves by 1855. Free-Soilers had always pictured their splendid isolation from major parties' ranks. Many leaders went out of their way to achieve reputations for stainless integrity. Salmon P. Chase was not simply clean, but one of the most dogged foes of every subsidy that came to the Senate. Offered some soap articles by a company angling for a testimonial, Congressman John Quincy Adams took them only after wrestling with his conscience. He was tempted to insist on paying for them, lest even so trivial gift compromise his honor. Years later a story circulated that Thaddeus Stevens, later among the most radical Republicans, had given Southern leaders special terror. As Speaker Howell Cobb heard the Pennsylvanian denounce the Compromise of 1850, he had appreciated good quality. "Our enemy has a general now," the Georgian said privately. "This man is rich, therefore we cannot buy him. He does not want higher office, therefore we cannot allure him. He is not vicious therefore we cannot seduce him."[36]* Fabulous though the story may have been, it was just how slavery's foes liked to see themselves and how many of their enemies saw them. Not corruptionists, but fanatics was what they seemed to Southern slaveholders, and a fanatic, whatever his less appealing qualities, has the virtue of unquenchable sincerity, incorruptible purpose.

Incorruptible they began, incorruptible they must stay, said Republicans. Half their force was moral, and they knew it. Again, it was Schurz who spoke this commitment most heartily, after Wisconsin's Republican governor had been shown up as a bribetaker. "We must not hesitate to denounce every member . . . who prostitutes his trust and power," Schurz shouted, and his audience roared back their approval. A thief was traitor to his party, the orator went on. Only by pillorying such wrongdoers could the demoralization of American life be ended. Other parties

*The story sounds bogus—certainly like nothing Cobb would have said, and it comes from an unusual source: a 1917 study of the Pennsylvania free-school law of 1834. Nor would the words fit Stevens, who wanted higher office badly and had vices enough. In a selective sense, however, the story holds some truth. No Southerner could imagine that *his* side could ever buy "the Great Commoner."

hid their sinners, but Republicans could not. It was their duty to root out "that atrocious, hideous popular notion . . . that a politician who is not knave enough to steal must necessarily be a fool!"[37]

Such a party *could* bring about reform, *could* save the republic but time was running short. By 1856, the Slave Power had grown bolder than before. Now every year saw a new demand put on the North, if the Union was to be kept at peace. "Why, we have to repurchase the Union every year!" protested Judge Oliver Morton in Indiana. "Undoubtedly the Union is dear, very dear to us of the North," but was it really necessary to pay extortion every few months to prevent the South from breaking it up? If the North did not awaken soon, it would be too late, John Murray Forbes wrote. Yankees would "wake to find [themselves] bound through corruption and fraud to the will of the aristocratic minority." Then only a revolution could wrest government from the slaveowning oligarchy.[38]

New incidents in Kansas provided the rouser: damning signs of how desperate the Slave Power had grown. Northern Democrats had insisted that the territory would never fall to the slaveowners. Western settlers wanted no blacks, free or slave, among them. Their territorial legislature would exclude the Southern institution as effectively as any statute from Congress could—that is, if the people's will were respected. But would it be?

Popular sovereignty never had a chance in Kansas. From the first, there had been rumors that antislavery emigrants meant to flood into Kansas and deprive the slave states of their chance of bringing in a new sister. The emigration companies did exist, though they had scant impact. In any case, encouraging people to become permanent settlers in Kansas was hardly against the law. But the stories inflamed the western counties of Missouri, where slavery maintained a precarious existence. Residents there did not like the thought of free territory to their west, and would not stand for it—not as long as they could rig the decison to suit themselves. By October 1854 they had formed a secret society, the "Sons of the South" or "Social Band," with secret grips, signs, and passwords. Its openly avowed aim was to bring Kansas into the Union as a slave state by organizing Missourians and sending them into Kansas long enough to cast a ballot.

The arrangements were tested first in November when Kansans were asked to choose a delegate to Congress. Actual residents cared little about the outcome. Missourians cared a great deal. Over 1700 crossed the border to vote. Brandishing rifles and revolvers, they drove away the election judges, chose officials of their own, and cast their votes for Indian agent John W. Whitfield. Out of 2,871 votes cast, a later investigating committee reported, 1,114 were illegal. In one district, 35 of the 261 voters were residents; of 604 votes cast in another community, only 20 were lawful. Their work complete, the Missourians went home again.[39]

The autumn election excited little comment, perhaps because Whitfield was likely to have won anyhow, but the legislative elections the next March were different. There, the intervention was still more brazen. Governor Andrew Reeder had taken a census in late winter and found 8500 settlers across the territory. They were no match for the 5000 Missouri men, the so-called "Border Ruffians," who crossed the line to choose a proslavery legislature. At Lawrence, a thousand nonresidents arrived the night before the polls opened, trundling two pieces of artillery loaded with musket balls. The election judge took the newcomers' advice that his attendance at the polls might be bad for his health. The Missourians had come well prepared with ballots, which came in handy, as some individuals voted several times, changing coats between trips to the polls. With a vote of over a thousand assured, and 802 of it illegally cast, they went back to Missouri that afternoon.

Free-state residents across the territory, despairing of a fair count and fearing for their lives, stayed home, but the polls were crowded without them. In many areas, antislavery candidates were induced to resign. In others, Missouri residents were elected to the legislature in spite of ineligibility. In the Seventh District, only seventeen of the 252 votes were among the residents noted on the census, and scarcely eight more could have been people that Governor Reeder's emissaries had overlooked. In the Sixteenth District, Missourians armed with pistols and bowie knives dominated the polls, and during the day a steamer puffed upriver to add to the 1400 already present. In the Eighteenth District, former Senator Atchison led the Border Ruffians. His company stopped along the road to the polls at a proslavery convention and voted through a slate they liked more than the one natives had proposed. Eleven hundred citizens of one Missouri county meant to invade Kansas, Atchison had boasted. If that proved too few, he would bring 500 more. Only 831 of the 2,905 legal voters in Kansas showed up at the polls that day, but thanks to the Border Ruffians, six districts polled more votes than the entire territory was supposed to have. Not surprisingly, when the Border Ruffians came home again, their neighbors greeted some of them with a brass band and a round of cheers. They had chosen a strongly proslavery legislature, when a fair count might have registered otherwise. Only one member was an antislavery man.[40]

Had there been time, such an election might have been contested, but the governor had permitted only five days to bring a challenge. That was hardly enough. Before the complaints could be brought, the self-proclaimed winners descended on the governor's home to demand that he sign their certificates of election. His life threatened by armed men, baffled by the claims of either side, Reeder signed the certificates for most of the proslavery claimants. When word of the voting frauds came to him, he set aside the returns in six districts and ordered new elections. Free-state men won all but one of them; the legislature expelled them all and chose the original winners. Reeder looked to the Administration for support. Hastening east to obtain Presidential backing, he found Franklin Pierce friendly. Reeder had done right to challenge unjust returns, the executive insisted, and would be sustained. Once Reeder had left the White House, Pierce lost his nerve and looked for reasons to sustain the territorial legislature against the governor. For its part, the newly assembled body needed no reasons to break. It refused to meet in the town for which Reeder had called it. Instead, it met at Shawnee Mission, near the Missouri border. It also put through the laws of Missouri with hardly a word changed. A ruthless election law made it nearly impossible for free-state men to vote and put control of the polls into the hands of proslavery judges. Freesoil residents dubbed the gathering the "Bogus Legislature," held their own elections, chose a legislature and "Free-State Governor" to challenge the sitting authority, and prepared for war. Whether a revolutionary government created without Congressional sanction was more legal than a legislature elected with the help of election fraud was a ticklish question. Republicans seemed to prefer the former, Democrats apologized for the latter.[41] Whatever the rights and wrongs of the situation, Republicans were furious and not entirely surprised. The fraud was just what they would have expected from the Slave Power.

Such an offense could not be ignored, and with the House report on the Kansas travesty in 1856, the Republican party took on more life. Where a Whig party survived in the Northeast, the news of Border Ruffianism dealt the decisive blow. Forced to choose between the Know-Nothing corruption myth—that the real threat to the Republic was the election fraud and corruption of politicians made possible by the massive influx of foreigners and the surreptitious influence of Rome—and the Republican one, Northerners found in Kansas an excellent reason for believing the latter. Wavering Democrats who pinned their hopes on popular sovereignty fairly administered found their trust mocked. Slavery might well be forced down the throats of the prairie settlers, with Administration appointees and slaveholder ballot-box stuffing to dictate the admission of Kansas. Such a corruption of the suffrage was more than they could bear.[42]

When the Thirty-fourth Congress came into session, the Republicans were in no mood for conciliation. The fight over the Speakership of the House might have seemed wasteful bickering. Though Nathaniel P. Banks in the end managed to muster a coalition of Know-Nothings and Republicans and took the chair, he proved evenhanded and conciliatory to all parties. Still, the symbolism was what mattered. Here, for the first time, Republicans took on the Slave Power and bested it, corrupt appliances and all. Compromises were offered and spurned. Better that no Speaker be chosen than it be dictated by "those *cowboys*, who are running, trading and stealing," a New Englander wrote. Let the conservative press roar at the cost of every day's stalemate, another member shouted: "I am not to be roped in or used as a tool by a corrupt lobby, or by any press in the country." When Banks triumphed, beacons were lit in New York, and with reason; for here, Republicans thought, was a triumph not only over the Administration, but over the temptations and corruptions that the South held out. "For *once* the North has been faithful," Thurlow Weed wrote. "*One* conflict with slavery has been settled without a compromise. . . ."[43]

IV

Corruption and the Death of the Union

15

The Buchaneers

Surveying the Democratic party in May 1856, one Illinois man could not contain his disgust. Between Douglas and Pierce, he commented, "it is enough to give a country the hipochondria. I hope in all mercy we shant, for awhile at least, get another such lummux for a president."[1] His words were unduly harsh on Pierce. Though a weak leader and a poor judge of Northern opinion, the President had shown a personal integrity that the government needed badly.

Four years of James Buchanan's Administration would not have that saving grace. To preserve the nation, Buchanan would buy editors and congressmen, compass election fraud in the territories, and proscribe dissidents in the states. No free-soiler could have helped the Republican party's fortunes as well as this Pennsylvania Democrat. Before he was done, the Democratic party would be shattered and the link between Democracy, corruption, and the Slave Power clear for every doubting Northerner to see.

The last thing Democrats needed in 1856 was a candidate tied directly to the Kansas-Nebraska Act. That worked in Buchanan's favor, for the President had shelved him in an overseas mission. The Pennsylvanian's credentials seemed good. Pierce had lacked broad national experience, but Buchanan had held public office since the War of 1812, and had served in Congress since 1820. Tactful, conscientious, hardworking, devoted to the Union, hostile to the fanaticism he associated with those disapproving of slavery, the "Old Functionary" lacked the strong will to say no to Southern demands, particularly when those Southerners were his personal friends. If he lacked brilliance, perhaps the nation could survive without such acts of inspiration as the repeal of the Missouri Compromise. So Buchanan was nominated, and Democrats praised him not as a new Old Hickory (there were limits even to political hyperbole), but as the best representative of "the only *conservative party* of the country."[2] And perhaps he was—but what was he bent on conserving?

A few old Jacksonians tried to impress the public with the thought that Buchanan would keep the new integrity that Pierce had brought the executive branch. There were reasons to doubt their hopes. Buchanan was supported by his old friend, John Forney, whose aid had helped amend the Minnesota land-grant bill in 1854, and by Daniel Sickles, whose party zeal had permitted him to rob a post office in 1852. Furthermore, had Republicans known it, there was a stronger connection between the speculative frenzies of the decade and the nomination at Cincinnati in the person of the banker Corcoran. As Buchanan's old friend, he rallied his many financial connections from Texas security speculation days to encourage the Pennsylvanian's nomination. Among Buchanan's lieutenants were partners in Corcoran's Minnesota real-estate speculations and in the land-grant bills before Congress that spring. Pierce could not match their influence, though his own patronage power gave him a considerable force on the convention floor: bureau heads, "custom-house officers, postmasters, salaried clerks, packed delegates, straw delegates, political eunuchs, members of Congress, district attorneys, Federal marshals," as Benton declared.[3]

Republicans voiced their uneasiness more loudly that fall when those same officeholders switched their allegiance to Buchanan and paid contributions for the ticket's success. Never had assessments been gathered as professionally and ruthlessly. In the custom houses, every employee was ordered to pay a percentage for the Presidential campaign and another for the state race. The Democratic Executive Committee called on every postmaster to hand over part of his profits, and in the shipyards a dollar was deducted automatically from day laborers' checks. Republicans could not begin to match dollar for dollar, though they did better than the American party. Democrats also did well among the conservative New York businessmen. Senator John Slidell of Louisiana and his friends wanted $50,000 from Wall Street, and New York Democrats called a private conference of merchants to raise the amount. All told, George Plitt, treasurer of the Pennsylvania Democratic committee, had $70,000 to spend, including $10,000 given by a Yankee whaler,

W. C. N. Swift, in return for the promise of government contracts in the new Administration. Other "October states" had heavy financing as well, and for more than the distribution of information.[4]

Certainly that was the case in Pennsylvania, where the state elections in October would be a crucial boost for Democratic morale. As editor of the Philadelphia *Pennsylvanian*, Forney proved an efficient party organizer, but he used means more efficient than ethical. Votes were needed; votes were brought in from other states, bought on the spot, or created by naturalizations. The courts gave citizenship papers to all deserving Democrats; indeed, it was later charged, thousands of those documents were handed out in blank for party followers to fill in their names. When the "extra assessment" list came out a few days before the election, Republicans noted that it had been increased by several thousand names, perhaps as many as 20,000. Later, five hundred of the thousand-vote majority for Democrats in one Philadelphia ward would be proven illegal. A Democratic policeman used two certificates and lent them to fourteen or fifteen "organ-grinders" to use when applying for the vote. When the returns were counted, the Democrats had won and by a vote in Philadelphia 11,000 higher than ever registered in the city before, indeed, 6000 more than any city, even New York, had ever given.[5] In Indiana, too, Republicans blamed the Democratic margin of victory on Irishmen and native-born men brought in from Kentucky. In Illinois, they made the same charges, far less persuasively. Probably, however, the Democrats owed their Indiana win to a less noted but no less unethical arrangement with Richard W. Thompson, head of the state's American party. He prevented any fusion between his followers and Republicans; in return he was guaranteed satisfaction on his Menominee claim and its $80,000 commission. The promise was kept. Corcoran and Senator Jesse Bright lent money to lobby the claim's payment through Congress, and when Pierce's watchdogs left the Treasury the following spring, the claim sailed through.[6]

So the Republicans went to defeat, but they did not go chastened. Fraud had beaten their candidate, they cried. The Northern voters wanted John C. Fremont for President, insisted the New York *Evening Post*, but they had been cheated of their desire by Buchanan, Forney, Slidell, Sickles and their cronies. The Slave Power's crowning corruption had stolen the Presidency. The charges that the American movement had been a purchased concern, surviving only because Democrats had financed it to split the Northern antislavery vote, was the last damning blow at the Know-Nothings' integrity, and they were no more than a name four years later. Not since 1824 had a President entered power with his foes so unwilling to concede his right to lead. "If the Union could in truth only be saved by such means," the New York *Tribune* wondered, "would it be really worth saving?"[7]

Buchanan had his admirers, including Republicans and Know-Nothings inclined to give him the benefit of the doubt. After Pierce, they thought, anyone would be an improvement. They were soon disillusioned. His pronouncements suggested that he might battle against corruption in Washington or find a politic solution to the tumults in Kansas, and his choice of Robert J. Walker and Frederick P. Stanton to govern the territory proved a sound beginning. But quickly it became clear that his appointments lacked the integrity of Pierce's. Across the North, Pierce Democrats lost their offices, and Buchanan loyalists were put in their place. To replace conservative Democrats with other conservative Democrats just because one Administration had succeeded another was an innovation in spoils politics that Southern congressmen begged to be spared. In the Cabinet, Buchanan's choices could hardly compare with Pierce's. John B. Floyd's ethics proved far looser than those Jefferson Davis had brought the War Department, Jacob Thompson kept less of a rein on his subordinates in the Interior than had McClelland, while Howell Cobb, for all his hearty good fellowship, lacked the rigor that made Guthrie a terror to Treasury Department rapscallions. "I had considerable hope of Mr. Buchanan," Benjamin B. French confessed. "I really thought he was a statesman, but I have now come to the settled conclusion that he is just the d——ndest old fool that has ever occupied the Presidential chair." Others described the government as a gang of "Buchaneers."[8]

Presidents can at times lend a moral tone to government service, though even strong Presidents find it hard to make themselves a model that others will follow. Certainly Buchanan's occasional preachings about virtue fell on deaf ears. Indeed, Americans saw public ethics becoming worse in every branch of the government. It was said that in Brazil, a favorite way of introducing a friend was to add, "If he steals anything from you, I am responsible for it." Such manners, thought the New York *Evening Post*, ought to be added to the "Rules of Good Society" in the capital.[9]

The first scandal to break took place in the War Department. Franklin Steele, a Minnesota land speculator with powerful party connections, held huge tracts around Minneapolis and St. Anthony and wanted still more. He set his eyes on the 11,000 acres on which Fort Snelling sat, at which he had been a sutler for twenty years. In 1856, he applied through his ally territorial delegate B. F. Rice to the Secretary of War to buy the land for $75,000. Secretary Davis refused him. The land, as the Quartermaster-General pointed out, was worth more than the price offered, and the fort still served a military need. Nor did the law give the Secretary explicit power to sell useless sites. So in the closing hours of the Thirty-fourth Congress, Rice pushed through an amendment to the statutes to make the sale possible. Newly installed Secretary Floyd obliged Rice further. Without consulting any military officer, he decided to sell the Fort Snelling site.

To this end, he hired a fellow Virginian, Archibald Graham, to visit the property, appraise it, and decide its fitness for sale. Since Graham was a speculator in Minnesota lands, the choice was unfortunate—all the more so because Graham joined a combination to rig the sale. The government sent out a surveyor, who made a careful underestimate of the tract's size. In May 1857, Floyd sent two commissioners to arrange the sale: William King Heiskell, a friend of Graham's, and former Hardshell Canal Commissioner John C. Mather of New York. It was no coincidence that the surveyor was Steele's personal friend or that Mather should have joined Steele and Richard Schell, another leading New York Democrat and campaign contributor in the combination to buy Fort Snelling at private sale.

Such land sales usually were done publicly with everyone allowed to bid. The combination found the requirement inconvenient. The land's value was open to dispute. For farming, it was worth perhaps $55,000. As a town site, however, estimates ran as high as $400,000, and one-twenty-seventh of the land was sold for $6,666. The sale therefore was done secretly. Only Steele bid, and his offer of $90,000 was accepted. The law demanded immediate payment in cash, but Steele was allowed to pay $30,000 at once and the rest over two years. The commissioners also freed him from a need to put up security or pay interest on the deferred portion. This was all the worse because the War Department had on file proposed bids considerably higher than Steele's. In July the President confirmed the sale, and soon thereafter the first payment was given. It was also the last payment. The Panic of 1857 so depressed land prices and caught Steele so short of cash that he could not keep control of the land. During the Civil War, the government would reoccupy Fort Snelling and use it to recruit and outfit soldiers. It remained useful to the century's end. Steele ended up with about half the acreage, much of which the government subsequently bought back from him.

Long before that, the Fort Snelling imbroglio had become common knowledge. One of the senior staff officers, Colonel Lorenzo Thomas, was quick to protest the sale and receive a rebuke, but Floyd's enemies could not be so easily silenced. Could not some Whig be induced to ask for an investigation, a Virginia Democrat wrote the state's senior senator. "There are some *dirty facts* in the chapter, and I can . . . refer you to *persons* and *papers*. He deserves to be exposed naked to the world." In January 1858 the House opened an investigation. The committee reports three months later did Floyd no good. A bipartisan majority concluded that the Secretary had no legal right to sell the land, that he had chosen unfit agents, that the government had been swindled by the conspirators, and that Mather had violated his duty by joining the combination. The Democratic minority cleared everyone involved, and in the end the House passed some frail resolutions clearing Floyd of criminality but denouncing the sale.[10]

The lawmakers were too gentle. An act smuggled through Congress by a possible partner of the interested purchaser, a special deal given to prominent Democratic speculators, a secret arrangement in violation of the law to award a government agent—it was understandable that an Ohio congressman should proclaim that were he to pick any twelve farmers in his state as a jury, he could have brought in a verdict of fraud easily. Republicans marveled that Floyd escaped as lightly as he did. Some saw him not as a dupe but as an accomplice.[11]

Before his tenure was through, it became clear that the Secretary had a penchant for selling military sites to Democratic friends to reward their party services. At Willett's Point, New York, the government decided to build a fort; the Thirty-fourth Congress authorized the purchase of some 130 acres for as much as $150,000. The site had been offered for $20,000 less and rejected as too expensive, but Floyd bought the property for $200,000. By condemnation proceedings, he could have acquired it more cheaply, but his defenders later explained that he had feared lest legal processes cost the government far more. The land speculators, Collector of the Port Augustus Schell and New York Postmaster Isaac Fowler were chosen to evaluate the land and set the final price on it. Schell's brother Richard, fresh from his speculations in Minnesota, advanced the money with which the private party bought the land that only days later he would sell to the government. Again influential Democrats had made a tidy profit. In California, the government arranged for the purchase of land for fortifications at Lime Point for $200,000. Less strategically useful than other possible sites, unfit for defense, the land was worth about $195,000 less than the Administration paid for it.[12]

Each year Floyd fell into worse trouble. The Maynard Arms Company included several leading congressmen, military officers with connections to the War Department, and Corcoran & Riggs among its shareholders.

It produced a carbine which a West Point board of officers concluded was useless. Floyd had the War Department buy the carbines anyway. It took a special provision in an appropriations bill to keep him from breaking the law to give a friend a marble-purchasing contract. When a Virginia doctor with no experience wanted a contract to heat the Capitol, Floyd gave it to him; the doctor sublet it to practical builders and turned an easy profit. William H. DeGroot had been assigned a contract to make and deliver bricks to the government by the original contractors. When Congress stopped work on the public works needing the brick in early 1857, DeGroot found himself with a newly built brickyard and no one to sell to. Original contractors had been indemnified, and in 1860 the Congress decided to pay DeGroot for his losses as well. Rather than pay the value of his construction, Floyd chose to give the luckless contractor all the profit he might have gained had he supplied all the brick that the government intended, which, thought Floyd, came to $119,234.46. This was nearly three times as much as the Attorney-General thought was fair, the Treasury refused to apportion a penny, and when the case was transferred to the Court of Claims, it demanded that DeGroot show proofs justifying any payment at all. DeGroot had none, sought relief from Congress, and after 1876 gave up trying. All of these cases looked like plunder, though they may have been sheer incompetence.[13]

By 1860, even Democrats had wearied of having to explain Floyd's misbehavior. The new appropriations bill curtailed his power of purchase, and every session saw a new investigation proposed of his maladministration. That spring, he clashed with Captain Montgomery Meigs, construction supervisor for the building program that the War Department engineers had been arranging in the district. Since Jefferson Davis's tenure in the War Department, Meigs had overseen construction of an aqueduct for the city, expansion of the Interior and Treasury Department buildings, and completion of the wings and dome planned for the Capitol. Meigs could be exasperatingly honest and short-tempered. Having quarreled with the Capitol's architect so badly that the latter took up all his drawings and refused to show them, the engineer could not tell whether the work met specifications. He therefore refused to pay anything. Both the President and the Secretary of War tried to make Meigs reconsider. When Meigs stood firm, Floyd suspended him and was only prevented by Congressional act from banishing him to build forts in the Dry Tortugas; to prevent Floyd from resigning that summer, Buchanan sent Meigs there anyway and left a less vigilant officer in charge of the Washington aqueduct—in defiance of another law of the recent Congress.[14]

The last straw came in December 1860, as it turned out that Floyd had been the cat's-paw for the Western contracting firm of Russell, Majors & Waddell, suppliers to the army during the Mormon War of 1857. When Congress was slow to appropriate money for the contractors, they became desperate and turned to the War Department for help. The Secretary offered to endorse their bills; then the banks would lend them money on Floyd's acceptances. Once the process began, Floyd seems to have stopped accounting for how much the government owed the contractors. He took every draft they brought him, $6,179,395 unconditionally and $798,000 more on condition that the drafts be paid out of the firm's income. By 1859, Senator Benjamin of Louisiana had heard about it, and when he brought word to the White House, the President was thunderstruck. The War Department was ordered to stop the practice. Floyd paid no attention. So matters went until July 1860, when William H. Russell, one of the contractors, grew desperate. There was no way that his firm could repay all that it had borrowed. Banks now were refusing Floyd's acceptances, and exposure seemed certain unless Russell found funds somewhere else.

That somewhere else turned out to be the Indian trust fund, over $3 million in negotiable bonds of which was locked in a chest in an Interior Department office. Over it one Godard Bailey, a distant relation of Mrs. Floyd, presided. Russell appealed to Bailey's sense of family honor and perhaps to his avarice. If the bonds could be replaced with the drafts Floyd had endorsed and Russell could sell the bonds, all would be well—and the bonds would be replaced in a few weeks. But weeks turned into months, and the number of acceptances under lock and key grew as the supply of bonds dwindled. On New Year's Day, Bailey would have to present the coupons on the bonds in his keeping to collect the interest on them, but with only a fortnight left to go, he was short $870,000 in securities. Unable to cover any longer, he confessed his embezzlement to Secretaries Thompson and Floyd and soon was resting in the district jail alongside Russell. It is possible that Floyd had known of the abuse of Bailey's trust already, just as evidence suggests the possibility that Robert W. Latham, until recently Floyd's business partner, was involved in Russell's schemes. Even then, Buchanan did not dismiss the Secretary of War. He called for his resignation, which Floyd declined to give for the present and finally made when he could make his departure from the Administration seem the result of differences of opinion about treatment of the Southern secessionists.[15]

Secretary of the Navy Isaac Toucey survived to the end of the Administration, though his competence was hardly greater than Floyd's, and his troubles almost as sensational. In 1859, a House committee looked into his purchase of coal for war vessels. It had been the custom to choose an agent for the task who would buy the coal from private contractors, weigh and inspect it, and then dispatch it to the Navy. In May 1858, when the Philadelphia agency became vacant, applicants descended on Washington to fill the place. A few rivals met with House Ways and Means Committee Chairman J. Glancy Jones, a special friend of the President's, and agreed to support the candidacy of Dr. Charles H. Hunter of Reading. In return, Hunter would split the profits with them; one beneficiary was J. Lawrence Getz, a Democratic editor and legislator. Because this was a Pennsylvania position, Toucey deferred to the President's judgment, and Hunter got the post. Having never bought coal before, the physician was worthless as an agent. In fact, he never left his Reading medical practice to visit Philadelphia. He neither knew the coal's market value nor tried to know; but he bought it from Tyler, Stone & Company, a company in which Toucey's nephew had an interest, and falsely signed affidavits certifying that he had inspected specific amounts of coal some seventy miles from his home. Another of Hunter's partners never had anything to do with the coal business either, never saw the coal inspected, weighed, or delivered; he was in the omnibus business. The partnership was simply an arrangement for sharing the fees from a lucrative post. For six months' inactivity, Hunter collected $7500.

Whether the government had been bilked on the price of coal was open to dispute. Several contractors, disappointed in their hopes of government preferment, insisted that the purchase price of $3.85 a ton was fifty cents more than a reasonable profit allowed, though their own prices to private customers were closer to that of Tyler, Stone & Company. Certainly Tyler, Stone & Company sold the coal for fifty cents a ton more than they bought it for. The committee majority admitted that Hunter and his friends were wholly unfit for their jobs, declared the President badly gulled by the misleading recommendations sustaining Hunter, and concluded that no fraud had been committed. This brought the author of the minority report, John Sherman of Ohio, to his feet. "I do not know what the gentleman means by frauds," he replied, "but it seems to me that when an officer of the Government . . . sits by and hears that the emoluments of a sinecure office . . . are to be divided between mere politicians; knows that the coal agent lives . . . where the duties . . . are not to be performed; that none of the parties are fit for the place, or could discharge its duties; and that the whole arrangement was a mere division of public money among partisans; to such transaction, if the word 'fraud' is not to be applied, I do not know to what it is to be applied."[16]

The same House committee uncovered another dubious political payoff in the live-oak contracts awarded to W. C. N. Swift in late 1857. Swift's contributions had helped George Plitt carry Pennsylvania for the Democrats the year before, and true to his vow, Plitt had worked to get a contract for the donor. Since Plitt had arranged to take 10 percent on the gross receipts of any job, he could expect a tidy profit for himself. Live-oak grew only along the Gulf coast and could be cut only during the winter. For these reasons, the government had always permitted two years for contractors to deliver. At Plitt's recommendation, Toucey changed the requirements to force delivery of half the live-oak within thirty days of the contracts' letting at public bidding. There were bidders lower than Swift, but none could meet the deadlines and their contracts were canceled. Toucey then gave $239,960 of work to Swift, whose firm had a great supply of refuse timber. The lumber fit the Navy's standards neither for size nor quality, but it was accepted anyway. Three years later it lay in the navy yards, still unused. The law decreed that if the lowest bidder could not carry out the contract, it should go to the next lowest, but Toucey had violated that provision. To Republicans, the whole deal seemed "a glaring and corrupt collusion . . . between the Secretary and Swift . . . as compensation for partisan services."[17]

Toucey misused his authority in other ways as well. A contract to build a ship's engine for a sloop of war went to Woodruff & Beach at $27,000 more than the lowest bid; Woodruff & Beach had never built an engine, but the junior partner was Toucey's nephew. The Secretary authorized Daniel B. Martin, a member of the Board of Engineers, to report on proposals to make machinery for the Department. Martin had a financial interest in one of the proposals he was deciding between, and decided in its favor. A New York firm was outraged when it bid $97,000 on a steamer-construction contract and was beaten by a Boston company promising to do the job for $7,000 more. "There is corruption within," it complained.[18]

These scandals were mere appetizers; as under Pierce, frauds in Kansas proved the entrée. Under Governor Walker's ministrations, the territory had calmed down. The antislavery free-state party agreed not to make pretensions at governing, and Walker, with the President to back him, promised that Kansas would enter the Union as free state or slave state, whichever the people at a fair election wished. That might have settled the territorial issue; it certainly would have meant a free Kansas, and, Walker hoped, a Kansas dependable for the Democratic party.[19]

Unfortunately, Walker's hopes depended on the reasonableness and fair play of the proslavery lawmakers elected two years before by fraud.

A fair election was the last thing they wanted, and in the spring of 1857 they moved to rig the political system one more time. To vote for delegates to the coming constitutional convention at Lecompton, residents must appear on the territorial census and then on the registration lists that the county officials had set up. The legislature chose proslavery county sheriffs to do the enumeration of all free male citizens over twenty-one years old, and proslavery boards of county commissioners to select the judges of election. No free-state man could take part in the process, challenge returns, or challenge the accuracy of the list; those who arrived in the flood of emigrants that spring had no way of coming on the list in time for the June election for convention delegates, though they might vote in the October election of state legislators. In fact, the process was more skewed than the mere provisions of the law would suggest.

In fifteen of the thirty-eight counties, officials never bothered to register voters at all; in nineteen counties they took no census and made it impossible for them to send delegates to the convention. At least half of the free-staters never had a chance to register. For years a conspicuous citizen of Leavenworth, the mayor was not included on the census form. Nor was the free-state Republican candidate for Congress, Marcus J. Parrott. The town of Lawrence had a thousand eligible voters or more, but no registry books were opened there, no polls set up. Antislavery men refused to have anything to do with the June election, and well they might. Of some 20,000 possible voters, only 9,251 had been registered, and about 2200 voted. Delegates were apportioned so that the eight counties bordering on Missouri had thirty-seven delegates and the other thirty counties, twenty-three.[20]

The October election would be different. Trusting to Walker's guarantees, the antislavery settlers trooped to the polls through the rains, though many expected to be cheated again. They were right. At first, the returns suggested a Republican victory for the Congressional delegate and a proslavery legislature, thanks to a tremendous vote registered from Oxford precinct, a hamlet in southeastern Kansas next to the Missouri border. But the proslavery men had underestimated the resolve of the governor and his aide. The two officers were suspicious of any town with less than one hundred people that could cast 1,628 votes. Climbing into the governor's mule-drawn ambulance, they set out for the precinct. All the way into the county, the land was desolate, and the six-building Oxford belied its election-day promise. Inhabitants declared that the town had never had two hundred dwelling there, much less 1600. The judge of election denied that the returns were his. The governor disallowed the returns as fraudulent on their face. On their way back, Stanton paused at a hotel in Lawrence and unrolled the Oxford returns as a curiosity. Forty-five feet long, the list stretched across the room, and some visitors from Cincinnati began to read it. All at once, they began to shout. They knew the names here, they cried: apparently the people in Williams's Cincinnati Directory for 1855 had voted in Oxford in perfect order, page by page! One of the voters for the Democrats was Governor Salmon Chase, the radical Republican. Soon after, when McGee Precinct brought in another 1200 spurious Democratic votes, Stanton only grinned. "Here comes another directory," he commented. These returns, too, Walker disallowed.[21]

He could not disallow the constitutional convention in Lecompton. Indeed, he dared not attend its sessions for fear of assassination. So unpopular with the proslavery faction was his treatment of the frauds that he ate meals in his private rooms and had a bodyguard beside him wherever he went. The delegates were left to their own devices. A less impressive gathering could hardly have been devised. Some delegates came from counties that had taken no census and registered no voters; a few free-state men applied for the right to represent their counties and were dismissed with contempt. Heading the convention was Surveyor-General John Calhoun of Illinois, a moderate supporter of slavery and an immoderate drinker, but from the first the convention was out of his control. It meant to write a proslavery constitution, and had no intention of following Douglas, Buchanan, and Walker's promise on fair submission of the main issue to the settlers. "Damn the people of Kansas," one delegate cried, "we shall give them such a constitution as suits *us*, and not trouble our heads about what they want." When the delegates' work was done, they had written a foolish, catastrophic fundamental law that protected present slaveholders' property and gave voters the choice between voting for the document with additional slaves forbidden and voting for the document with slavery allowed; if the latter, the people were forbidden to amend the constitution until 1864. Very likely the returns on December 21 would support the latter alternative, for the convention saw to it that Calhoun, as regent, had the power to choose all election officials and count all votes. Quite in violation of Presidential intentions, it encouraged another Border Ruffian invasion by opening the franchise to every adult white male in the territory on that day.[22]

Free-state men would have nothing to do with the constitution. With Walker gone east to enlist the President's support in the fight against the Lecompton swindle, Acting-Governor Stanton called the legislature into session. The Republican majority called an election of its own for January 4, and gave the people the right to vote against the entire document.

On December 21, only 6700 votes were cast, nearly 6000 of them for the constitution; of these, well over three thousand came from three unsettled areas along the Missouri border, including Oxford, Shawnee, and Kickapoo. On January 4, free-staters voted against the constitution by 10,226 to 162. Even on the face of the returns, it would seem that the settlers supported a free Kansas. That made it seem all the stranger in the legislative elections that same January 4 when Regent Calhoun declared the Democrats victors and credited the result to majorities rolled up at Delaware Crossing. How could so tiny a village have such an impact? Lawmakers sent a committee to question Calhoun's clerk. Yes, he had made out the local returns, the clerk admitted, but could not recall just what they were. Might the investigators see the returns? Alas, these had been sent to Calhoun in Washington. That night, however, the clerk pulled out those same returns, hid them in a candle-box, and buried it beneath a woodpile. Roused from slumber with the news, the committee summoned a posse, found the candle-box, and discovered that 43 voters at Delaware Crossing had cast 379 Democratic votes. The proofs laid before him and his clerk arrested, Calhoun temporized, then gave in, and certified a Republican legislature.[23]

The President soon replaced him, but the damage was already done. By early 1858, the Lecompton fiasco had riven the Democratic party. Some Southerners welcomed the new constitution. Kansas, they insisted, belonged to them. Irregularities in getting it should not prevent Congress from ushering a sixteenth slave state into the Union. Northerners of all parties were furious. Never had the Slave Power committed so flagrant a swindle, not even in the Kansas-Nebraska Act. Northern legislatures resolved against Lecompton, instructed Democratic senators to stand fast for true popular sovereignty. Democratic newspapers thundered indignation. Within months of having boasted that Buchanan had settled the Kansas issue forever, partisans vowed that if the government imposed Lecompton on Kansas, they would themselves move to the territory and fight to death beside the antislavery men. "I tell you," an Illinois Republican concluded, "there is nothing that wakes up the people like Lecompton."[24]

They would need that wakefulness. President Buchanan, swallowing his misgivings, decided to support the admission of Kansas as a slave state under the bogus constitution. When Governor Walker called to have past pledges of support redeemed, he found the President courteous but obdurate. Soon Walker would resign in protest, Stanton would be dismissed, and a new governor presumed more friendly to slavery would take charge.

Douglas could not be dismissed as easily. As the news spread east, he was aghast. With his own re-election barely a year away and with hopes of winning the Presidency in 1860, Douglas could not afford to back Lecompton. Letters cascaded in from the Northwest informing him that support for the constitution would kill the Democratic party in every free state. As the champion of a people's right to decide on the slavery issue as they pleased, he could not have supported such a cheat in any case: Lecompton's rigged convention and fraudulent votes made a mockery of popular sovereignty. So Douglas broke with the Administration and led the fight against admission of a slaveholding Kansas. "By God, sir," he raged to one associate, "I made Mr. James Buchanan, and by God, sir, I will unmake him!"[25]

It was not as easily done as that, for Buchanan pressed for the Lecompton constitution with every favor at his command. One might dismiss Pierce's pressure for the Kansas-Nebraska bill as horse-trading, not corruption; it is not so easy to dismiss Buchanan's methods. Never had any President used the patronage power as flagrantly to reward congressmen and penalize the anti-Lecompton Democrats. Across the North, Douglas's friends were informed that they must choose between the senator and their jobs. In Illinois, the Administration fired the state mail agent, the Chicago postmaster, and the federal marshal for northern Illinois and replaced them with Lecomptonites. The new postmaster, Isaac Cook, land speculator and willing politician, had had experience in the post, all of it bad. When he had been dismissed the year before, he left owing the department $18,000. He offered real estate as payment, and the government had refused his settlement; now it accepted it and made him the leader of a faction determined to block Douglas's return to the Senate. Douglas papers lost their government advertising; more dutiful organs received it, and where none existed, officeholders bought out the local Democratic newspaper with government funds or assessed their employees to set up a rival press. "A defaulter was recently summoned here," a correspondent wrote from Washington, "and the alternative was offered him of five years in the penitentiary . . . for taking public money, or an office and a declaration in behalf of Lecompton. He chose the office," but how unpopular the document must be, said the reporter, that it took at least five years in jail to make it worth supporting.[26]

The Senate went for Lecompton, as it had been expected to do, but the House would not be as easily won, and the representatives felt an intense pressure from the White House. Cabinet officers promised patronage rewards to the faithful. The Secretary of the Navy promised contracts for naval construction to firms tied to House members. It was charged, and denied, that one Ohio congressman was brought to the Administration's side by the promise that his son-in-law would be retained as postmaster in Keokuk and that he himself could retire from the House to a marshal's job. The war on the Mormon communities in Utah meant contracts to supply the army. Millions of dollars could be made if the contractors set their own prices, and the Administration's enemies charged that the supply contracts were being awarded on just such a principle to firms in which wavering congressmen held a share. Congressman Garnett Adrain of New Jersey was promised a foreign appointment for a close friend if he would support the Administration. John B. Hickman of Pennsylvania was approached with the same offer. William Montgomery of Pennsylvania was promised whatever he wanted for his vote. All three stood firm, as did an Ohio congressman offered an overseas appointment. "I am not in the market, sir!" he shouted, and stumped off. "If the President were not already as bankrupt as the Treasury," editor Horace Greeley commented, "he would yet win."[27]

Buchanan was not as bankrupt as all that. The printing contracts that Cornelius Wendell enjoyed had been subsidizing Democratic newspapers, notably the Washington *Union*, for some time. Now Wendell was enlisted to push Lecompton. But there were limits beyond which patronage and corruption could not go. Northern congressmen who cared deeply about popular sovereignty or a future career in public life would not be swayed. In April, the Crittenden-Montgomery amendment to force a popular vote on the entire Lecompton constitution passed the House by 120 to 112.[28]

The Administration was beaten, but it rushed to save face by supporting a compromise offered in committee by William English of Indiana that would permit a vote on the constitution. If Kansas rejected the Lecompton document and the land grant that the so-called English bill tied to it, the territory could not enter the Union as a state at all until a census had shown its population to be more than the 90,000 that the average congressional district possessed. Republicans shouted that the bill was a bribe and a threat, that no referendum would be a fair sample of the people's will under those circumstances; anti-Lecompton Democrats were less convinced, and some of them swung behind the English bill.

The Administration gave them every inducement for doing so. Again the Secretaries of Interior and Treasury paced the aisles of the House, distributing promises of favors. Congressman J. A. Ahl of Pennsylvania had been uncertain. Then his brother got an army contract to supply 300 mules at a profit of $55 apiece. Congressman Joseph McKibben of

California was ordered to vote for the measure or see his father removed as Philadelphia naval agent, and his father and brother were earnest in pleading the family's needs. He was also offered a township of land, which he refused. The same offer of a township went to John Haskin of New York, and was rejected. In all, some $30,000 to $40,000 was spent to sway members. F. W. Walker, a lobbyist for the Collins line, was present to distribute money to congressmen; Cornelius Wendell gave him $2500 just before the session's close. Wendell would later testify that he had used $30,000 himself, though the records had been disguised to prevent the tracing of funds. "I took men who I thought would have influence," he explained. When an Ohio editor declared that $10,000 could settle matters, Wendell took him seriously and offered $20,000, to be used to buy Ohio congressmen at $5000 apiece. "A bushel of gold is no object in this matter," Wendell commented. One Ohio representative, Lawrence W. Hall, switched to the English bill after Wendell gave his roommate $5000.[29] With all the pressure, and with even Douglas at first inclined to accept the English bill as a fair settlement, the Administration carried the House by 112 to 103. That August, the Kansas voters voted down the Lecompton constitution by more than five to one, land grant and all.

That fall, the Administration paid the price for its recklessness. Deprived by conventions packed with Administration appointees of renomination, some anti-Lecompton Democrats ran as independents with Republican backing. Others took the party nomination and fought against jerry-rigged Administration candidates. In Illinois, the Buchanan Democrats under Cook, known as the Danites, put their own nominee in the field against Douglas. Francis J. Grund was sent to Chicago to assume command of a German Democratic organ in place of the Douglas man who had founded it. To fund his own voice in Chicago, Cook subscribed $7000 and forced his clerks to supply $100 apiece. To save their places, some officeholders bowed to the Danites. One even worked his way into his superiors' good graces by naming his child after Senator John Slidell, when the latter appeared in Chicago to organize the Buchaneers. Having recently reappointed a Douglas man as postmaster in Quincy, the President removed him. Other postmasters were expected to profit by the example. "Are you *for* or *against* the Administration?" Cook wrote officeholders. "If against it, it is your duty to resign, and if you do not, at an early date you will be invited to do so!" Democrats later charged that Cook's squadron were so determined to beat the Little Giant that they made alliance with the Republicans. In fact, Slidell, Jesse Bright, and J. Glancy Jones sent letters to government workers instructing them to do what they could to defeat legislators committed to Douglas's re-election, even if it meant support of the Republican champion, Abraham Lincoln. Republicans promised to give the Danite organ in Chicago $500, and were accused of having provided the Administration faction with $60,000 in aid. Again, however, the pressure from Washington met its limits. In spite of threats and proffers, 59 of the 69 Democratic newspapers in Illinois stood by Douglas, and the state Democratic convention endorsed him in a shout. That fall the Danites were routed. The new legislature would return the Little Giant to Washington.[30]

Elsewhere, the Administration applied public funds and spoils politics with rare pertinacity. In Pennsylvania, money was needed badly and spent liberally. Commanding the fundraising campaign were Collector of the Philadelphia Port Joseph Baker and his brother George, who edited the Philadelphia *Pennsylvanian* and was paid by the Treasury Department to keep the organ going. George was technically on the custom house payroll, though he never went to the office except on payday, was not on its official list of employees, and discharged no duties except his political ones. To split the opposition, the collector needed an extra $10,000 in funds for subsidizing the American party nominees. That meant renewed assessments. Clerks were ordered to pay a percentage of their salaries; in fact, they were asked to contribute twice, once before and once after the election. The Democratic state committee called on the General Land Office to pay $3000, and the commissioner collected it from his underlings.[31]

When these funds proved insufficient, Cornelius Wendell was called on for more of the proceeds from his printing contracts. Already financing the *Pennsylvanian*, the Philadelphia *Argus*, and the Washington *Union*, the printer was reluctant to subsidize more presses, and he thought $25,000 to $30,000 enough of an annual contribution to Democratic fortunes. What with splitting the profits from post office printing jobs with the *Argus*'s owner, Congressman Thomas Florence, and with the *Pennsylvanian*'s publisher, he had a right to feel overburdened, but he sent the collector $2000 and in Florence's district allotted $3000 more.[32]

Not all the money went for printing costs. Some of it went to permit a brass band and omnibus to tour Florence's district. More may have been spent for colonizing voters. As later testimony showed, the Administration hired 2700 workers for the Brooklyn Navy Yard just before the election and fired them soon after. Since there was no pressing work at hand, Republicans charged that the employment was to raise the Democratic vote. Swollen job-rolls at the Philadelphia Navy Yard helped give Florence his margin of victory. More than 1700 colonists were brought in, old Francis Blair wrote, on condition that they vote Democratic. Along the Delaware River, Republicans declared, the sailors' boarding-houses were filled with eligible voters. In Philadelphia's Fifth Ward, the United States district attorney paid the voters himself to support the Administration. "A King of England would not dare thus to prostitute government patronage," said the Philadelphia *Daily News*, "but we live in a Buchanan era."[33]

Secretary Toucey used his power to give naval contracts to further the party's fortunes as well. With the President's knowledge, possibly with his approval, the machine shop of Merrick & Sons got a sloop contract because they would use the work to increase their labor force and could make the employees vote for the Democratic nominee. So flagrant were these and other political abuses that the lame-duck session of Congress investigated. In each case the Democratic majority cleared Toucey of willful wrongdoing, though it admitted serious abuses. The Thirty-sixth Congress would be less forgiving.[34]

Buchanan's machinations had handed a spectacular issue to Republicans. That fall, they exploited the Lecompton fiasco, Fort Snelling, Willett's Point, the English "bribe," and the Philadelphia colonizers to the fullest. It was the spending for such graft and usurpation, said the New York *Evening Post*, that put the government near bankruptcy and made necessary a Republican governor for New York. From Maine, a Republican credited his success to the issues of assessments, contracts, and Floyd's secret land sales. In Wisconsin, Republicans flayed their own state's band of "Forty Thieves" for peculation in every department. When the Madison *Daily Argus* lamented that the moment Republicans took power was when "corruption open and shameless" became the order of the day, the *Daily State Journal* replied that it had been under Democrats that[35]

> drunken men caroused in the State Treasury . . . money was taken from the public funds, to be used in the gambling saloons of this city . . . State officers were 'in the habit' of going to the Treasury and supplying themselves with money, leaving in its place a mere paper check . . . a State Treasurer proved a defaulter for over $30,000 . . . the school lands were parcelled out among favorites at prices greatly below their value, without the payment of any cash down . . . the midnight fraud of the Lunatic Asylum was consummated . . . there were men employed to procure forged and fraudulent election returns to annul the popular verdict of the ballot-box.

Some Democrats, no less angry at their party leadership, ran independent candidates against the Forty Thieves faction.

It was not simply a matter of money wasted. Republicans insisted that Buchanan's acts had endangered the Republic, thwarted the public will, corrupted the Congress, and turned public contracts into a source of spoils. The boldness of his efforts was as alarming as the methods themselves. They showed that he and the Slave Power would hesitate at nothing. Rousing this fear for American freedom, Republicans and anti-Lecompton Democrats swept to victory across the North. The next Congress would be out of Administration control. In a published letter soon after the last returns were in, the President tried to change the issue from slavery to what he termed a greater peril, the dangers of the "employment of money to carry elections." Such a practice, he warned, would poison "the fountain of free government . . . at its source, and we must end, as history proves, in a military despotism. A Democratic Republic, all agree, cannot long survive unless sustained by public virtue." No Republican could have said it better. The trouble was that employment of money—and that peril of public virtue—seemed to them the Administration's own doing.[36]

None showed more wrath than the anti-Lecompton Democrats. Returned over Administration-backed opposition, Congressman I. N. Morris of Illinois did not accept the President's image as the virtuous steward in a degenerate time. "Singing psalms will not save him now, sir," he cried. "He has already sinned away his day of grace, and all hope for him has become extinct." Let Democrats cut loose from the Administration! "We cannot go into the canvass of 1860 with any hope of success, with its fetid and rotten carcass tied to the party."[37] Armed with that resolve, they joined Republicans in demanding investigations, which produced devastating ammunition against the government.

The culminating investigation was led by "Honest John" Covode of Pennsylvania in 1860. An implacable Republican, personally insulted by the President's suggestion that the opposition had used money to carry the Keystone State in 1858, Covode rose to propose a wide-ranging examination of Administration methods. Anti-Lecompton men were glad to oblige him, though Buchanan himself sent a dignified protest to the House. When it was read, Republicans roared with laughter and assigned it to the Judiciary Committee, headed by John Hickman, another unregenerate Democratic foe of the President. The executive had reason to complain. Covode had no desire to make a fair report. The testimony would furnish a powerful Republican campaign document, and Covode went out of his way to interview anyone who could give evidence. Cornelius Wendell was most eager to talk, for since his testimony the year before, the Administration had cut off the profits he had enjoyed for so long. Friendly House Republicans might give him enough work to keep his printing plant going. Had Wendell been given Administration sustenance, he would have been less talkative. Indeed, he tried to solicit just such support later that spring. Where it was convenient, his memory failed him, and the more the Democratic committeemen cross-examined him, the more his recollection faded about details he had remembered with precision for Republicans just days before.[38]

The Covode committee also skirted around issues that might implicate leading Republicans. Wendell had been open to making a deal with antislavery men in the House in late 1859 in return for contracts, while Pennsylvania Republicans close to Senator Simon Cameron had shared a third of the profits for binding documents in the Thirty-fifth Congress. It also turned out that the printer the present House had chosen had an arrangement with Wendell and other contenders for the Congressional printing. "I said . . . that I was a soldier," Thomas H. Ford testified, "and when I won a battle generally took care of the wounded." Such information Covode had no interest in exploring further, and most of Wendell's links with Administration enemies went undiscussed. Thurlow Weed also had a tale to tell, but was never called. As a friend explained to him, the committee had proof enough for its charges "and do not think it best to open any new question, as it might lead to an issue which it may be as well to avoid. . . ."[39]*

What the Covode committee did uncover was the most devastating proof of government abuse of power since the founding of the Republic. The abuses of printing contracts under two Presidents, the colonization of navy yards in 1858, the naturalization frauds of 1856, the subsidy of party presses from public printing accounts, the bribery and proscription used to pass Lecompton all were on full display. It seemed that in the Thirty-fifth Congress, Wendell had agreed to print the *American State Papers* for $20,000, while the government paid the putative contractors, Gales and Seaton, $50,000. For $75,000, Wendell had bought out the House and Senate printers, but still could make a 33 percent profit on the average from the job. "In my opinion," the federal district attorney in Philadelphia testified, "there has been a general combination among all the federal officers . . . to control the internal party politics of the city."

*By "new question" Spaulding may have meant the reopening of Weed's role in the tariff lobby three years before. But he may also have been referring to Weed's possible involvement with Forney and Wendell in early 1860 in a deal to apportion the printing and elect a Republican Speaker by methods profitable to himself and not above reproach. For related scandals over printing, see Charles Francis Adams Diary, Feb. 4, 8, 13, 15, 24, 1860; Edward L. Pierce to Adams, March 10, 1860, Adams Family Papers.

They could do it because, as Wendell testified, in four years he had passed $100,000 of profits to the Democratic organization in Pennsylvania and several other Northeastern states. Editor John Forney revealed that the President had tried to win his support for Lecompton by offering the foreign missions of Russia and Prussia and the consulate of Liverpool. He could have $80,000 worth of public printing, he was told, for an article as long as his hand. Wendell himself had carried $10,000 in his pocket for weeks in the hopes that Forney would accept it and the Liverpool position. When the Covode report came out in June 1860, Democrats stressed that none of the charges proved an impeachable offense by the President. Buchanan himself sent another protest to the House, declared that the investigation had been aimed to degrade himself and the executive office, added that disappointed officeholders had provided the bulk of the evidence, and insisted that the Covode committee had actually vindicated him by finding no criminal offenses that he had committed.[40]

In that Buchanan was right, but members of both parties were stunned at the depth of corruption that the President had permitted or inspired. Defending the President publicly, most Democrats deplored him in private. "I am inclined to think that this is a little the most corrupt Administration we have ever had," Benjamin French remarked. That June, the House voted to censure the President and his Secretary of the Navy. Among ninety-three Administration Democrats, only sixty-five voted to table the censure motion, and many of them on the technical ground that the House lacked the power to censure. Every one of a series of resolutions of rebuke passed the lower chamber by nearly two to one.[41]

What Republicans glossed over was that the high point of corruption in antebellum America had passed. Investigations of the public printing in the lame-duck session of the Thirty-fifth Congress sent A. G. Seaman, superintendent of the public printing, to prison. In his place was George W. Bowman, who saw to it that printing contracts fell only to the lowest bidders and trimmed printing costs considerably, especially where Wendell was concerned. The Thirty-fifth Congress also ended two of the most serious abuses when it forbade the printers from either House selling their contracts to others and arranged that when House and Senate paid for publication of identical documents, the printers would be paid for setting up the type only once rather than twice. In 1860, Congress ended the printing contracts forever by establishing a Government Printing Office, under a superintendent of public printing. (It would pay $135,000 for Wendell's printworks.) No longer could patent-owners like Chaffee and Colt bombard the Congress for renewals; the Thirty-sixth

Congress decreed that all patent rights would last for seventeen years only.

Thanks to Pierce's Postmaster-General and the officers that followed, the mail-subsidies to steamship lines were also done away with. When the Havre and Bremen contracts expired in 1857, Buchanan's postmaster offered new arrangements based on postage fees alone. Again Collins sent his lobbyists to Washington to renew the line to Liverpool's privileges for ten years; they met a stony resistance, as well as to the effort to change the terminus to Southampton. Not all the reformers were upright men. Commodore Vanderbilt's retainers used their influence to block his foremost Atlantic competitor. After 1858, no postal contract would run longer than two years; no special subsidy would apply to the foreign mails, and in 1861 the same rule was applied to the steamship subsidy to California.[42]

Yet to the public eyes, the investigations of 1859 and 1860 revealed an America more debauched than ever before. Some blamed Buchanan, others blamed Democrats in general, still others blamed the acquisitive spirit of the promoters, and Republicans pointed to the Slave Power. All agreed that the country was in crisis, some dared to suggest the crisis of greater moment than the dispute over slavery's extension. Among the foremost critics was Senator Robert Toombs of Georgia. All through the Buchanan years, he played the role that Benton had played under Fillmore and Buchanan. Assailing the abuse of patronage, revealing thc machinations of the Collins lobby, attacking the printing swindles, the navy yards, and the franking privilege, berating the logrollers, he was quick to charge that Southerners shared equally in the plunder.

Once his indignation nearly outran his hostility to free-soilers. "God knows," he told the Republican side of the Senate, "if you would give us a better Government, if you would give us an Administration that would bring us down to an economical basis, . . . I would be content with a black Republican Administration, for I believe the worst of all curses is corruption."[43] He was quick to add that they were no better than the Democrats with whom he associated, but the quote was revealing.

It also brought up an important question: were the Republicans any more fit to rule? That was a question the Republican rank and file, too, was asking. They had good reason for concern.

16

"We Won't Pay It in Hard Cash to Thurlow Weed"

In a sense, the Republicans would owe their triumph in 1860 to rascals in their own ranks. The irony was all the more piercing because three years before, the new party seemed infected with a fatal decay. Until the Supreme Court decided the Dred Scott case and chased less stupefying blunders from the public mind, most Americans had regaled themselves with the misbehavior of four Republican congressmen. Between the 1856 election and James Buchanan's inauguration, a scandal had added to the unsavory reputation of Capitol Hill.

At first, the friends of land grants and mail-contracts had every reason to expect that the Thirty-fourth Congress's final session would be a fruitful one. Lame-duck sessions usually were, and this Congress had been especially generous to railroads. New projects, particularly those of Minnesota, were clamoring for support. Then every opportunity was blasted by one New York congressman's inexcusable lack of finesse. Francis Edwards had taken a special interest in the Minnesota grant. His brother and he owned thousands of acres along the routes of prospective lines. Just before Christmas, he sat down for a chat with Congressman Robert Paine of North Carolina. Paine's principles revolted at any kind of subsidy, but Edwards thought he knew the way to overcome such scruples. Perhaps Paine did not know that some "friends" in the West were ready to pay for favorable votes, Edwards said. The New Yorker was authorized to promise his colleague $1500. Paine was outraged. Bolting from his chair, he exclaimed that $15 million would not be enough to buy him.[1] Such an incident on the House floor was sure to excite comment, and amid other rumors that bribery had become standard practice in Congress, the House had no choice but to choose an investigating committee.

Insiders knew that the lobby could pass or defeat virtually any measure. Whatever witnesses said, John S. Williams wrote a friend, "there is more behind the scenes than most people dream of." One congressman accused insisted that there were several dozen other members in the plot with him. These "Forty Thieves" demanded money from ever supplicant before they would permit his bill a fair hearing. But could solid evidence be procured? Lobbyists proved shy about detailing their methods, reporters retracted their most sensational charges or made claims that the committee declared contradictory and preposterous. Yet what the witnesses did say was appalling enough. "I had no idea that I was in such a den of damned thieves," a Georgian told Howell Cobb.[2]

The committee found at least four villains, all Republicans or American party men linked to Thurlow Weed and free-soil ideas. Edwards was easily disposed of. He pleaded that he had merely been passing on rumors about what Paine's vote was worth on the market, but just why he passed along such a rumor as part of his argument in favor of the land-grant bill he could not explain. Congressman William Gilbert of New York had voted for the Iowa land grant the previous spring. In return, the lobbyists gave him railroad stock and seven square miles of public land. He also had made a contract with one F. C. C. Triplett. In return for passing a resolution to have the government buy Triplett's book on pension and bounty-land laws, he would receive a share of the appropriation. William Welch of Connecticut had taken another share in the promised book-payment; he had also offered to support a widow's claim in the Committee on Invalid Pensions for $50. All three congressmen were invited to cross-examine the witnesses against them; all three declined.

That the fourth representative snared was Orsamus Matteson seems almost poetic justice. Involved in New York's shady canal contracts in 1851, a lobbyist for the Collins line's subsidy in 1852, deeply involved in Minnesota and Wisconsin land grants and railroad schemes two years later, a ready speculator in Texas securities even as he voted in the House for full payment of creditors such as himself, there was little that Matteson missed among the shoddy dealings of a shabby age, except the Colt revolver patent. Likable though he was, one friend admitted, he had one essential flaw: "he is such an infernal scoundrel." House investigators did not yet know that he had offered a woollens manufacturer his services to buy Congressional support, but they did know that he had invested in Minnesota and Iowa property and had shown special zeal for railroad land grants that would increase his property's value. When John Stryker, director on the Des Moines Navigation & Railroad Company came to Washington to seek financial relief for his firm, the bill was stalled in committee. Nothing seemed to ease the measure's passage, not even the appointment of former Attorney-General Reverdy Johnson as corporation counsel. Then Matteson had approached Johnson. Some twenty or thirty congressmen were pledged not to vote for any law granting lands or money unless paid. For $100,000, he promised to handle these "insiders," and indeed he declared that this was only proper recompense for the $25,000 of stock in his own factory that he had spent to sweeten their tempers: the securities were worth four times their face value.[3]

As the committee report became public, it stirred a real sensation. Southerners were glad that none of their own ranks were implicated, while Republicans insisted that they would brook no such dishonored man. Only seventeen representatives voted in Matteson's defense, and eighty Republicans either voted against him or dodged a roll-call. Three congressmen were permitted to resign; the fourth offered his resignation, it was refused, and he was expelled. Matteson was almost immediately reelected by his district to the incoming Congress, where he sat with little distinction. Two years later, he would be expelled as bank president for misappropriating its funds. The result of the session pleased few. Four down, editors commented—but where were the other thirty-six "Thieves?" No papers apologized for those congressmen apprehended, many thought that the majority had performed the ethical equivalent of cosmetic surgery. A precious few "are pushed forward to bear off the sins of the congregation," sneered the Cincinnati *Commercial*.[4]

It was an uncomfortable winter for the Republicans, the more so because they had made public corruption a vital strand in their myth of Slave Power and Democratic misrule. It made matters no better that the four reprobates were tied to Weed and William Seward, the front-runner for the nomination in 1860. "Nothing has done us such deadly harm as the Matteson & Gilbert expose," wrote one partisan confidentially. "All the scoundrels who are up to their elbows in successful & secret forays on the public crib, have now abundant capital for a protracted bawl, on the note that 'Republicans will steal when they get a chance.'" All their arguments about Southern encroachment might seem a pose to win office.[5] As it turned out, Republicans led a charmed life. Strong proof of the Slave Power conspiracy appeared within days, as the Supreme Court ruled that Congress had no power to keep slavery out of the territories.

Before the year's close, Lecompton and not the Forty Thieves gripped public attention.

Republicans were all the more blessed in having lost Indiana in 1856. Had they won, their own methods of making majorities would have shared the spotlight with Philadelphia naturalization frauds. With two Senate seats at stake in 1857 and the chance to reapportion Congressional districts, Republicans who hoped to deliver the state to their Presidential candidate felt still more keenly the need to win the assembly. That meant sending floaters into districts where they were most needed. For this end, party leaders raised vast sums to colonize doubtful counties. One Republican state senator was said to have boasted that Republicans already had "sufficient MEN AND MEANS to secure the election in Rush and Union counties, and as for Marion and Morgan, they would be adequately supplied from Randolph and Delaware Counties." Residents of Wayne County traveled to Rushville to vote. Some of them later pleaded self-defense before the legislature's investigating committee: Democrats were importing voters too. The rate was $5 per voter colonized, and the secretary of a Republican club recalled paying at least nineteen men.[6]

As the Democratic House studied the frauds, Republicans fled. The treasurer of Henry County suddenly found urgent business in the East to occupy him. Another witness arrested by the sergeant-at-arms violated his parole and fled into Kentucky. A third simply ignored the legislative summons. Other partisans testified frankly, even defiantly. Paying the expenses of three colonists had been within his rights, one declared. Another witness admitted that he had gone into Rushville at the party's behest and only objected to the charge that he had taken pay to do so. Again, Republicans were lucky that Democrats behaved more notoriously still before session's end. In 1855, Democratic senators had blocked a joint legislative session to keep a Republican from becoming senator on joint ballot. Now Republican senators tried the same trick, but Senate Democrats declared their chamber adjourned, went into joint session with House allies, and elected Jesse Bright and Graham Fitch. To take both seats was, as one historian later called it, "plain larceny." For similar irregularities, the Senate had refused to seat an Iowa Republican, but Bright and Fitch sustained Lecompton and harried Douglas so well that Southerners swallowed their scruples and admitted both men on their certificates.[7] If Northerners thought of Indiana frauds thereafter, they brought the joint session and not the Rushville returns to mind.

So Republicans remained in a position to make the most of the corruption issue, and as the Buchanan Administration made itself noxious, the issue became ever more appealing as a means of winning conservatives uninterested in the Slave Power myth. Across the Upper South, old Whigs and Know-Nothings seized the issue to wreck the Democrats. It was all the better because it fitted the traditional Whig hue and cry about executive usurpation. John Bell of Tennessee never spoke more fervently against the spoils system of Jackson's day than he did against that of Buchanan's, when "millions of public treasure" bestowed on the victors promoted "the prevalence of party spirit, that proverbial bane of all free government." North Carolina Whigs made their greatest gains in years by shouting about the spendthrift ways Democrats pursued under "the most wasteful, extravagant, and corrupt" government on the globe. Let Democrats bellow about slavery in danger! "What has Abolitionism . . . to do with Mr. Buchanan's squandering the public moneys upon favorites and politicians?" a Whig asked. The slavery issue was a mere decoy, conservatives insisted.[8] Such a line of argument was not just crafty. Southerners, as we shall see, were deeply concerned by the corruption. Conservative men almost despaired of the Republic, and blamed its woes on low politicians. If the slavery issue were muted, might Republicans find among such men the makings of the party's southern wing?

So, too, the corruption issue seemed a means of bringing the most disaffected anti-Lecompton Democrats into the party. No one had felt the corrupting force of Administration pressure more than the Douglas men, and some of them seemed on the verge of abandoning the Democratic party entirely. Most promising was Senator David Broderick of California, political boss and spoilsman. When the President denied Broderick the federal patronage due him, the rather unsavory politico became an implacable foe. Later, when Douglas considered a compromise with the Administration on the Kansas issue, Broderick exploded. "I shall denounce you, sir," he cried. "You had better go into the streets and blow out your brains!" Back in California, Broderick took the stump against Senator William Gwin and other Administration backers, and he made corruption a prime issue. California Democrats cared little about Kansas, but a great deal about pillage. The money the President sought to buy Cuba with was a "corruption fund," Broderick warned. Lime Point was a swindle engineered by the speculators behind Gwin and former Kansas territorial governor James W. Denver. "Would you have your Senator vote for a measure . . . that would put $200,000 in the hands of speculators?" Broderick thundered, and the crowd roared back its support. It was the senator's last fight. Before the Congress met again, he would be dead, his voice stilled by a duelist's bullet. In death he became not just a martyr but a symbol of the purity in politics against which his foes had only murder as an answer. By 1860, his followers would be trooping over to the Republicans in their leader's name. At the Republican state convention, his name would be invoked as though he had been one of their own in their fight against the Administration thieves.[9]

For conservative men distressed by rising expenditures, Republicans could explain every dollar as a Buchaneer steal. Indeed, when the Administration's enemies spoke of extravagance, they confused profligacy with peculation. As the Panic of 1857 ushered in hard times, Americans felt a keener resentment of the misapplication of tax revenues. It is never as easy to appreciate the good life public officials have given themselves as when one's own rations have been cut. A country with a growing population, rapid westward expansion, and improved government services needed to spend more each year. Additional postal services, customs offices and land-sale bureaus all took increased funds. By shifting from a sailing to a steam-run navy, the authorities found new expenses in buying coal. But how much more convenient it was to blame the budget's rise from $48 million to $80 million in seven years on "profligate, corrupt, and wanton extravagance."[10]

As the recession trimmed government revenues and the Buchanan Administration confronted an empty Treasury, Republicans shouted that rewards to party favorites had done the emptying. Until 1850, Senator Henry Wilson of Massachusetts observed, $2 million would sustain the entire customs service. Now $4 million was asked for the Atlantic coast alone, and Wilson blamed the abuses and corruptions begun under Pierce for the inflated figures. Why had national expenses so risen since 1853? Congressman A. H. Cragin of New Hampshire knew but one reason: "fat jobs and contracts" that littered America with officeholders "like the frogs of Egypt." It was an excellent issue. "Politically it seems to me every thing is working as favorably as possible," wrote James Shepherd Pike from Maine, "& if we can keep the party from raising standing armies & stealing generally, I think its prospects will be good."[11]

Pike may have been speaking in general terms and with good reason, for in the next two years the Republican state treasurers of Maine and Michigan were caught with their hands in the till, a Republican governor was proven to be the purchased tool of a Wisconsin railroad company, and several Republicans were linked to the tariff lobby. More likely he was referring to Senator William Seward, front-runner for the 1860 Presidential nomination and a man whose record on pork-barrel schemes left much to be desired. Certain Republicans could use "a little brushing up on the subject of economy," editor John Bigelow wrote. "Our prominent leaders are not all famous for providence in their expenditures of the public money and a little feeling on the subject among the people may be of service to them." Republicans of Democratic antecedents had been muttering about New York's favorite son for some years, and even more so about his friend Thurlow Weed, "King of the Lobby" and presumed master of New York politics. Still suspicious of the predatory interests that they associated with New York Whiggery, they suspected that a change in party labels had wrought no change in ethics. A Seward Presidency would solidify the power of Whig prodigality in the Republican ranks.[12]

When New York's legislature met in 1860, it confirmed reformers' worst fears. Quickly dubbed the "Gridiron Legislature" because of its support for city railroad charters that would have crisscrossed New York City with trolley tracks, the majority proved a robber encampment. "God grant we may never look on its like again," Weed burst out later. Perhaps four-fifths of its membership was corrupt; the governor claimed that eighty legislators had been bought and paid for. Hungry local interests brought money to bear. Brooklyn councilmen wanted to slash the East River ferry fare to a penny and raised $40,000 to enact a law doing so. The West Washington Market "swindle" legalized certain dubious claims against New York City, enriched several seedy promoters, and banned legal challenges from city officials. To prevent a bill imposing tolls on all railroads competing with the public works, the New York Central Railroad rushed in its lobby and managed to persuade or purchase Republicans enough to stop all action. Worst of all were city railroad franchises, which endowed valuable rights on downstate promoters in return for few conditions and no compensation. At best nonentities, the shareholders in projected lines may well have been dummy members. Some gave false addresses, others were not listed in the city directory at all. As usual, the methods used ranged from the controversial—logrolling and the gift of free passes—to the flagrantly corrupt. Beneficiary companies promised shares of stock to doubtful assemblymen. One hostile observer chargd that virtually every lawmaker had a relative or in-law among the stockholders. Speaker of the House DeWitt C. Littlejohn's brother held $40,000 in shares, his brother-in-law another $40,000. On the day of the final vote, both were lobbying on the House floor for the charters, and both had been admitted on a special pass signed by the Speaker.[13]

Money had been the ultimate incentive. The New York Central was reputed to have spent over $75,000 against the canal tolls bill in the Senate and to have had to bribe several members twice, when the first inducement proved too little. For the city railroad bills, figures varied between $250,000 and $500,000 in cash and common stock, though if, as the New York *Times* claimed, each member was paid $100, it is hard to see how half a million dollars could have been spent in bribes. Nor was there any doubt that the moneyed interests worked in alliance with Thurlow Weed's Republican machine. Doubting party members were told that "the old man" wanted the city railroads to go through for the party's good.[14]

Weed's motives were mixed. In 1859, he had turned down an offer of $25,000 by the railroads' enemies. That year he had been a hearty lobbyist for the Third Avenue line and had received a letter of thanks from the company president. It would later come out that Weed held $60,000 of stock in the road and, indeed, shares in three such lines. Weed insisted that he had bought the stock at fair market value and never lobbied for any measure that he did not believe right. That "right" measures also happened to be lucrative ones for Weed did not strike him as important. A web of mutual favors and fees tied him to the New York Central. That his friends should have rescued the Central that spring seems only natural.

More than personal pelf was involved. The year 1860 was the last, best chance for Seward to get the Republican nomination. A network of financial interests behind Weed would be one more argument in Seward's favor at the coming national convention in Chicago: Republicans could use the money that fall. Common report everywhere spoke of Weed's slush fund raised from needy contractors and corporations. Weed admitted having begun negotiations with transit interests in 1859 for just such a trade-off of legislative votes for campaign funds, but how much they promised to raise was unclear. Editor Bryant put it at $400,000, the New York *Express* at $1 million.[15]

Still, Weed's motives remain a puzzle. How could so gifted a judge of men have blundered so disastrously—for the cost of the corruption fund may well have been the wreckage of Seward's chances at Chicago. One reason may be that Weed, never overly scrupulous where raising funds for party war-chests was concerned, had lost his perspective since the death of the Whig party. He could take fees for lending political influence, but this, he insisted, was not corruption. He could raise a fund by backing promoters' sinister schemes, but this was merely good politics. All during the 1850s, Weed's friends had noticed a change, as the boss became increasingly interested in building his personal fortunes, but they noted another change more serious to his political power. By 1860, he seemed out of touch with the public temper. The "King of the Lobby" was moving one way, while the people were moving another: he grew less circumspect even as the corruption issue took on particular importance.

Weed never quite grasped the Republicans' special sensitivity to "politics as usual," and their latent hostility to well-bossed party organizations baffled him.

Or was there another reason? Is it possible that Weed was no longer able to control the legislature? Certainly Weed's own comments about his failed effort to amend the city railroad bills suggest that explanation. The boss had little time for legislative management in early 1860. Nominating Seward came first, and that would take as much Republican unity as New York could give. To have thrown his influence against the city railroads might well have alienated some of Seward's allies, while leading foes of the "gridiron" included members who under no circumstances would have done Weed's bidding. Weed therefore may have paid the price for cooperation at Chicago in letting special interests and the Republican majority have their own way in Albany.[16]

It was a terrible miscalculation. Certainly former Whigs within Republican ranks protested the "band of brigands" at Albany. D. D. Barnard, Henry Raymond of the New York *Times*, former Senator Hamilton Fish, and Horace Greeley, were all outspoken in their objections. But one-time Democrats far surpassed them in fury. In contrast, the Albany *Evening Journal*, Weed's mouthpiece, never uttered a word of reproof. The New York *Times*, earnestly behind Seward's candidacy, and the *Tribune*, quietly hostile, both restrained their criticism of the franchises in mid-April. Not so the "radical Democracy," as their party comrades still called themselves. The New York *Evening Post* kept a running fire on the legislature. Bradford Wood and David Dudley Field spoke freely and ferociously. All were good Republicans, but given the choice between being Republican and being good, there was real doubt about which they would choose. The railroad bills must be vetoed, William Cullen Bryant warned the Governor, or else many of Seward's best friends would give way to "an 'irrepressible' desire to throw him overboard." Not even Governor Edwin Morgan's vetoes—which were heard contemptuously and quickly overridden—could still the journalistic catcalls closing the session.[17]

Weed's victory was dearly won. Ever distrustful of the master-spirit of Albany, many New York Republicans became actively hostile to his achieving national influence. By April's end, Republican misgivings had spread beyond New York. At least one prominent Seward man, James Dixon of Connecticut, confessed that the events in Albany had converted him to the support of any other candidate instead. Democrats began to link the "Gridiron Legislature" to a pending Seward Administration in Washington. "We put it to you, tax-payers, friends of a righteous administration . . . , honest men of all parties," the New York *Express* warned, "—is it wise, is it safe, to give this Albany Regency an opportunity to transfer their corruptions . . . to the wider field of Washington?" That alone was the issue. "It is a question, simply, of Grand Larceny and Plunder, not a question of 'Freedom,' or 'Slavery,' in the Territories." If slavery extension and free labor were the issues Republicans wanted to make the decisive ones that fall, Seward's nomination would thwart that end. Democrats could use the corruption issue to divert the voters' attention and to make impossible a campaign based on the stark moral choice between slavery and freedom, to say nothing of an exploitation of the issue of Administration plundering.[18]

As the tumult persisted, Seward's foes took heart. "One hundred Thurlow Weeds cannot nominate Seward if he does not happen to suit the fancy of the hour," one Republican wrote Salmon Chase. When the Chicago convention opened, Weed and his friends were there. They had money and the access to money—"oceans of cash," as the Indiana and Pennsylvania delegations were told—for the coming canvass. But those resources could be tapped only through Weed and would not be forthcoming unless Seward were nominated. Many arguments favored Seward, but the most effective was made not by delegates as much as hangers-on, who buttonholed undecided partisans in every bar-room and hotel. With the simple practicality of ward heelers, they asked, "If you don't nominate Seward, where will you get your money?" Less worldly delegates may have seen this as extortion. Not all New Yorkers talked as cynically. But always the less reputable element was visible, and sometimes it may have applied Albany practices. One furious Nebraska delegate wrote that a Weed crony had swayed at least one vote from his state representatives through "Mr. Weed's tactics." It was unavailing: "the moral sentiment of the Republicans . . . repelled the tactics" of the New Yorker "and would have none of his corruptions."[19]

Even as Weed worked to convert Pennsylvania to Seward, Bryant, Greeley, Field, and James Wadsworth—delegates all and, save Greeley, old-line Democrats—did their best to link Albany corruption to the New Yorker's candidacy. Greeley was particularly emphatic in bringing up the corrupt legislature for scrutiny. The debauchery, he declared, would make it hard for Seward to carry his home state that fall, and the editor had corroboratory letters from prominent Republicans to prove it. Other influential Republicans were telling wavering delegates that Seward was personally responsible for the legislative misconduct and warning them that a Seward success meant Weed in the White House, too.[20]

In the end, Republicans chose Abraham Lincoln over Seward. No one reason can explain that victory. Historians make much of Seward's unavailability. His radical antislavery reputation had made him difficult to elect in the West. His recent speeches had made radical Republicans doubt his commitment to their side. His defense of foreigners and Catholics had made him enemies among nativists, whose votes were crucial in key Northern states. He had become too well known for the party's good. All of these reasons stand. The Republicans needed to carry Illinois, Indiana, and Pennsylvania, and Seward could not deliver them as easily as could Lincoln. The Illinoisian's managers could play practical politics with the worst of them. David Davis arranged to issue a thousand counterfeit tickets to pack the galleries with a Lincoln cheering section. Instructed by his leader to make no commitments, Davis snapped, "Lincoln ain't here and don't know what we have to meet!" To bring Indiana around, he promised Caleb B. Smith a Cabinet seat. To win Pennsylvania, he assured a place to favorite son Simon Cameron. In both cases, there is doubt as to whether the commitment was necessary: Indiana had already half-decided that Lincoln would run better than Seward, and Pennsylvania, which had already sold itself several times, could be relied on to join the candidate most likely to succeed. Whatever the reasons, Lincoln became the one candidate most satisfactory to Seward's rivals.[21]

But the corruption factor played its part as well. As Republicans assessed the convention's outcome, this was an issue that many returned to, Seward's friends as well as his enemies. Worthy though Seward might be, one Michigan delegate wrote, his defeat had been for the best, as "he was the candidate of wire-pulling politicians into whose hands the policies of the government had ought not to be placed." Henry B. Stanton had backed Seward, but confessed to Senator Salmon Chase of Ohio that his heart had not been in it. Lincoln's nomination was a relief, for "his surroundings will be free of the Albany taint. . . . New York Republicanism has been made a reproach & a byword by the rascally conduct of our state legislature, under the lobby-lead by Weed."[22]

It was certainly a matter of tactics; Republicans did not want to be thrown on the defensive, but to see corruption in tactical terms alone does the party an injustice. Rank and file members were aghast at the effect of ethical laxity on the party and the nation. The movement to limit slavery was moral, not simply sectional and political. That was why Republicans could be so alarmed over their leaders' ethical lapses. "If you divest the Republican party of its moral element," Bradford Wood commented, "it will crumble like sand." Better to go down to defeat while party goals were noble, said the Binghamton *Standard*, than to win at the price of venality, "faithless weakness and public dishonor." Radicals who linked conservatism with the corrupting effects of commercial wealth had seen the 1860 legislature as one more sign of the fundamental dishonesty in both Seward and Weed. The very moral laxity that could make a Republican power-broker turn a legislature into a robbers' den to raise campaign funds also made a Republican senator tone down his antislavery views to win election. Were such men to be trusted with power? Or would they barter antislavery principles the way they had bartered everything else? Everyone agreed that "the king of the lobby" would add to his influence enormously once his friend sat in the Presidential chair. That must never be. As one Republican put it, "We owe Mr. Seward everything; he founded the party, and built it up to greatness; our debt to him is incalculable; *but we won't pay it in hard cash to Thurlow Weed.*"[23]

In public, of course, most Republicans downplayed the corruption issue in discussing their rejection of Seward. The less they reminded voters of New York's misdeeds, the better they could exploit Democratic stealing. Still, their editorials left little doubt about the implications of the Chicago nomination. The New York *Times*, *Tribune*, and *Evening Post* said it plainly. Others were more subtle. Groping for words to glorify Lincoln in the days after the convention, the first that came to editors' minds were "unstained and untainted," "simple," "honest." "He is no corruptionist," one editor boasted, "no trickster, no time-server, but an honest, brave, straightforward, able man, who will restore the Government to the purity of practice and principle which characterize its early days under the administration of the Revolutionary patriots."[24] He was a throwback to the idealized past of virtuous leadership, unlike other, more contemporary figures. It takes no wild imagination to suspect that in the stress placed on the name "Honest Abe," editors were hinting at who in their own ranks he was more honest *than*.

Round Lincoln the Republicans wrapped a mantle of rustic simplicity and backwoods virtue. Drawing on the images that Whigs had associated with William Henry Harrison and his "Tippecanoe" campaign of 1840, the campaign managers stressed Lincoln's rail-splitting and not his occasionally questionable services as a lawyer for the Illinois Central. They told how "Honest Abe" had served as postmaster of New Salem in Jackson's day. In two years, the government took in about $200. Five years later, when the Postmaster-General got around to collecting the sum, Lincoln turned over the very bills handed him years before. Despite his poverty, his inability to meet his board bills, Republicans boasted, he had refused to dip into the government's money. Such "stern, unbending integrity" could be used in a degenerate age. Making an asset of Lincoln's twelve years out of public office, his friends argued that this relegation to private life made him appreciate the honest toil that no placeman could understand. Raised by his muscle and mind, he was thus "best qualified to raise his vengeful maul to crush out the system of peculation and fraud which has disgraced the country . . . down to the lowest postmaster." Fresh from the people, Lincoln was no politician either, Elihu Washburne declared. He would have no followers to reward, no promises to keep as the price of his nomination. "In these days, when corruption, prodigality, and venality have reached the very vitals of the Government, the people have at last found an *honest man* to administer the affairs of the nation in the spirit in which our institutions were founded."[25]

Against such a man, Republicans depicted all the forces of plunder ranged. John Sherman of Ohio had uncovered the abuses in navy yards in 1859; since then, other committees had detailed printing swindles, tariff lobbying, extortion by House doorkeepers, and the incompetence if not worse of several Cabinet members. When the Covode report came out in June, it became one of the most demanded campaign documents. The Republican national committee franked thousands of them to send into the districts. Senator Preston King of New York was detained well past adjournment keeping up with the requests. As soon as he had won re-election in Pennsylvania, "Honest John" Covode found himself among the best draws the party could offer at a rally. Sherman, too, was asked to appear. Because of his part in the investigations, one Indiana Republican explained, "you must be as well informed on all the corruptions of the administration as any person."[26]

The vision the party conjured was a hideous one, if slightly exaggerated. Why concern oneself with the embezzlement and flight of New York's postmaster, the New York *Tribune* wondered. Under Buchanan, defaulting postmasters were a common sight and grew commoner as the days in which they could steal came to an end. Scores were being fired, a correspondent insisted, from inability to pay what they owed. "As for defaults of small Postmasters, they are as thick as leaves in Vallambrosa." Had he the time, Senator Zachariah Chandler told one crowd, he would tell them of a corruption that would make them shudder. So corrupt was the Democratic party that the only way to purify it would be to destroy it. Did conservatives doubt these claims, Henry Winter Davis asked Marylanders. "Read the Fort Snelling Report. Read the Willett's Point Report. Read the Covode Committee's Report. Read Mr. Sherman's Report. . . . Read of the political brokerages for contracts. Read of the distribution among members of Congress and of the patronage of the navy yard in

Brooklyn. . . . Read of the reckless use of public money in the elections." The rascals must be turned out and men with respect for the duties of the civil service put in their place.[27]

From such cries, one might have assumed that Buchanan ran for a second term. In fact, though Republicans had bruited the prospect that the President would use the spoils to assure himself a second term, the chief executive was probably as sick of the office as the Democrats were of him. Democrats held a convention in Charleston in April, and a bolt by Southern delegations forced another meeting in Baltimore. When Southerners walked out again, the remaining Democrats spurned conciliation. They nominated Douglas, who had a right to complain of Administration abuses if anyone did. Backed by the Administration, the bolters ran Vice President John C. Breckinridge. When the conservatives' Constitutional Union party nominee John Bell was counted, that made a four-way race and all but assured Lincoln's election.

Tying Administration misdeeds to the Breckinridge ticket took no imagination at all. That fall, the assessments and threats to officeholders were used to sustain the Kentucky Democrat. To elect Breckinridge was to continue the same pack of thieves, Republicans warned. Behind the Breckinridge party stood the squalid city politicians of Mozart Hall, and official defaulters eager for a President who might conceal their misdeeds. One transparency at a Republican rally put it more bluntly than would the political speakers. It showed Douglas shaking a sack with $10,000, and warning, "No, you don't, Breck; here's what beats you." "Well, Doug," Breckinridge replied, pointing at the Public Treasury, "the South and this will elect me."[28]

Douglas was more of a problem, but not much. On the one hand, Republicans could hold the Democratic party collectively responsible for four years of corruption, and their nominee to blame for his supporters. Better to give the nation "those men who are gorged already," Senator Chandler exclaimed, "and not those who, having been kept out for four years, would pounce upon the already depleted treasury, and 'leave not a drop of blood' in it." On the other hand, if Douglas could not be tied to the Administration, he could always be tied with state Democratic parties across the North that had put themselves in opposition to the President—for corruption, like the party structure itself, was federal: each state had its own variation. In Wisconsin, Douglas was tied to the "Forty Thieves," Barstow and the balance. In Illinois, former Governor Joel Matteson had cashed in some $230,000 in state canal checks that had been redeemed but not canceled, and credited the sum to his own account. Illinois Republicans declared that Matteson meant to spend $100,000 of his stealings to buy a legislature that would whitewash him. That would take Douglas's influence, and so Matteson must be straining every muscle to make the Little Giant President. Matteson had rented a meeting hall for a Democratic rally in July. He had also freely contributed to other Democratic campaign expenses. In New York, Republicans pointed out that the only legislative backer of the "Gridiron" charters on any ticket acted as a Douglas elector. Dean Richmond of the New York Central Railroad supported Douglas. So did George Law. "If anybody corrupted that Legislature, they did it," said the New York *Tribune*. As Michigan's state treasury collapsed from official misconduct, the incumbents shifted the blame to New York's Artisan's Bank, with its Tammany Democratic ties. When the firm failed that autumn, the Detroit *Daily Advertiser* blamed it on the special deal Douglas had reportedly been given just days before: a $10,000 loan without security for his campaign. With all these charges, Republicans felt justified in claiming that Douglas's administration would make Buchanan's look honest and economical, just as Buchanan's had given Pierce's a comparative respectability.[29]

Not being Democrats, the members of the Constitutional Union party seemed hardest to implicate in frauds. Like Republicans, their leaders had made government corruption a leading issue, though they blamed it on the spirit of party rather than on any one organization. Indeed, in Missouri, the opposition put "corruption and lawlessness" ahead of sectional antagonisms as an issue in its platform. Conservative Whigs throughout the North might think John Bell a better spokesman for their concerns, unless the party's commitment to reform was discredited. Republicans found the means of doing so in efforts to unite Douglas and Breckinridge followers and Union men in the Northeast. How could any party that was sincere about fighting corruption side with the corrupt Administration's anointed candidate? Indeed, fusion must mean that Bell's backers were as insincere as the American party in 1856, which, Republicans had evidence to show, had fielded state tickets to divide the Free-Soil vote—and had been well paid for doing so. Echoing the charge made against Free-Soil coalitions over the years, Republicans roared that fusion was no combination of like-minded men, but a bargain and sale. In New York the "Belleveretts" "sold their effects to Richmond & Co.," and American party members from 1856 were trotted out to Lincoln rallies to renounce all allegiance to "these political traders." Conservative Whigs were summoned to register their disapproval for "the corrupt and selfish men who would sell them to the highest bidder," which since the only other bidder would have been the Republican party, may have been an unfortunate choice of words. But the charge struck home among border-state Whigs. They felt betrayed; more, they were convinced that the deal had killed the party for all future time. In feeling so, a very few of them looked to the Republicans as the only alternative to endorsing the Democratic robbers.[30]

In state races too Republicans manipulated the corruption issue with an unprecedented fervor. In Madison, Wisconsin, they called for voters to throw out "the Court House *regime*" that had robbed taxpayers countywide. In Illinois, Republicans spoke of how Matteson had escaped conviction when Democrats packed the grand jury and when third parties offered a thousand dollars to one juror to clear the former governor. Wisconsin Republicans recalled the LaCrosse & Milwaukee Railroad scandal. Michigan Republicans dredged up decade-old charges to arraign former Democratic officials for prosecuting false claims and giving fraudulent loans to railroads. In Michigan's first Congressional district, Republicans charged, Democrats were trying to buy prominent Republicans to support them. In an adjoining district, they ran a lobbyist for the Vanderbilt steamship lines. When Democrats urged the people, "Vote for Barry. He will reduce taxes, and *stop stealing*," their opponents took this as a confession that Barry had been stealing until then.[31]

The alternative, of course, was a party as pristine as its foremost candidate. Republicans declared that *they* would choose officeholders by their fitness, not just their party affiliation. The Democratic party was too effete and rotten to reform itself, said the New York *Evening Post*. It had taken on the vices once associated only with Whigs (the *Evening Post* had been Democratic). Republicanism still had its youthful vigor and could resist degeneration. "Freemen of Michigan," the Detroit *Tribune* appealed, "if you want to bring back the government to its ancient purity . . . if you are determined to rebuke the extravagance and corruption of Democratic misrule . . . [if] you intend that the reign of the whole tribe of pilferers, blood-suckers, and rogues shall come to an end, THEN VOTE THE REPUBLICAN TICKET!" Certainly the corrupting influence of the Slave Power would be banished forever. That could only improve the political climate. "For the first time in the history of the United States," Seward boasted, "no man in a free state can be bribed to vote for slavery: the government of the United States has not the power to make good a bribe or a seduction by which to make and convert democrats to support slavery."[32]

That the issue did not become more pronounced than it was can be ascribed to two factors. First, Republicans always found the slavery issue more compelling. Their party was intended to scour slavery from the territories and the Slave Power from national politics, and it never concealed that intention. Second, the corruption issue was tricky to use, particularly where state political issues were concerned. Too many Republicans were involved. The New York canvass showed the difficulties with manipulating the issue effectively and why as the campaign progressed the emphasis on plunder faded on all sides. Governor Morgan's vetoes guaranteed him renomination, as politicians scrambled to link arms with so popular a reformer. Weed himself orchestrated the governor's renomination on a platform that repudiated Republican lawmakers in all but name. By then it was evident that if Morgan needed to be right with the "King of the Lobby" to win the delegates, the "King of the Lobby" needed to be right with Morgan to defuse the corruption issue and carry the state.

In the campaign that followed, the scandal remained alive in New York, and not just as a means of blackening the foe. Both parties tried to pin exclusive guilt for Albany's "robber encampment" on their enemies. If Democrats could point to Weed, Republicans could spotlight Tammany Hall and the New York Central Railroad. There was enough blame to go around, as both sides knew. By mid-September, the "Gridiron Legislature" had provoked dissension within Democratic and Republican local organizations. Editors on both sides called for a purge of the brigands in their own ranks. When upstate conventions renominated three of the most influential Republican corruptionists, the New York *Tribune* damned them all and suggested that even a Democratic victory was better than their return to power. That all three were close friends of Weed and supporters of Seward's bid for re-election to the Senate was no coincidence. Faced with such schisms, party leaders shifted to national issues rather than splinter their own ranks.[33]

Indeed, at first glance it might have seemed that Democrats could have made the corruption issue work in their favor. They certainly tried. Republicans in Maine, Michigan, and New York should have been particularly vulnerable. For fraudulent voting, few tricks could compare with the supposed Texas delegation to the Republican national convention. Michigan party leaders had sent them to cast a few more votes for Seward, though several had the good grace to pretend to act in proxy for other Texans, whose names they had concocted. Republicans had bartered and farmed out the House printing on the same appalling principles that every previous majority party had embraced. In Massachusetts, Democrats noted that among the opposition's state senators was a forger, among its assemblymen, a bank embezzler, while its liquor agent watered the stock he sold. A vote for Republicanism in Chicago would be a vote for the political trickery of "Long John" Wentworth, and statewide it would mean new tax giveaways to the Illinois Central, warned the Chicago *Times and Herald.* In doubtful states, the editor predicted, Republicans would import outsiders, buy up "floaters," and win by any method at their disposal.[34]

All these charges blunted the Republican attack; they could not counter it. For one thing, the Administration's record had no equivalent on the opposition's side to explain away. For another, state Democratic parties were so deeply implicated in corruption and so bitterly divided that they could not make a compelling defense. In New York, for example, it was true that more Republican than Democratic legislators had been "corruptionists"—that is, had supported the infamous city railroad charters. But many more of the Republican malefactors had been denied renomination, and by running Morgan for governor, the party had refurbished its reputation at home. Having spent five months citing the executive as a symbol of the honest Republicanism that Weed's crooked schemes had overridden, Democrats found it hard to change direction and treat him as a secret rogue himself. It would also have been impossible to make such charges stick. At the same time, New York Central officers managed the Democratic campaign, contributed heavily, issued free passes to loyal partisans, and ran for Congress. Beneficiaries of city railroad grants sat on Democratic platforms and applauded homilies about Republican steals. The sight of so notorious a corruptionist as Senator Francis B. Spinola shouldering his way, cudgel in hand, onto the party's grandstand to denounce Republican looters was more than even Democrats could stand. No doubt Wisconsin partisans felt the same about the moral pratings of former Governor Barstow.[35]

There and elsewhere, Breckinridge and Douglas Democrats supplied the ammunition for Republican proofs of corruption. New York supporters of Breckinridge blamed the state's corruption on the party's Albany managers, who supported the Little Giant. With some regard for the laws of libel, Administration organs answered that two leading Breckinridge men in Rochester had been seen near the Capitol lobby when the charters were passed. Deriding Douglas men as mere spoilsmen, R. B. Rhett of the Charleston *Mercury* jeered:[36]

> Drum! Drum! Dribbledy, drum!
> See where the paupers and squatters come;
> Some with their Colts, some with hair triggers,
> Cutting their way with the biggest figures,
> Wanting lands, and wanting niggers,
> Wanting office, and sucking thumbs,

Some of them glad of the smallest crumbs,
So they can't get office, let 'em have shows,
They'll thank you for any stray suit of old clothes.

Amidst such abuse, Democrats could hardly spare time to prove themselves more honorable than the Republicans. Certainly they seemed to confess the corruption in their own ranks.

Not even Weed's rumored "corruption fund" produced a winning Democratic issue. For one thing, Western Republicans had their own resources. David Davis had spent months building up a network of contributors across Illinois. Simon Cameron's Pennsylvania allies were also ready to contribute. When Weed's money was needed—and it was sought eagerly for such tasks as colonizing doubtful Illinois counties with Republican voters—Lincoln's political managers had placated the New York politicians with promises of influence in the new Administration. Here, too, Governor Morgan's unchallenged reputation for probity sanctified financial dealings. As unofficial campaign manager in the East, he was the source through whom the funds flowed.[37]

It was not the most honest of elections that followed this campaign for a restoration of virtue. That spring, the elections in Connecticut and Rhode Island had been all too well funded. Rhode Islanders improved on the vote-buying for which they were so well known by paying more per ballot and acting more openly. That October any honest count would have given Pennsylvania to the Republicans, but Philadelphia partisans did not settle for an honest count. In the Fourth Ward, Republicans paid a Democratic election officer to falsify the returns and bring in a Republican congressman. So flagrant was the fraud that a Republican district attorney had arrested and secured the conviction of the officer before the month's end. That November, the Chicago *Times* charged, Lincoln owed his majority to masses of minors, canal boatmen, unnaturalized Swedes, and imported hordes from Kansas. Republicans in turn claimed and may have believed that the South had vowed it would buy a majority in Pennsylvania and that Southern gold was being used to corrupt the voters in upstate New York.[38]

When the returns were counted, however, neither Southern cash nor Weed's "corruption fund" could explain the result. "I am utterly astonished at the extent of our majorities," an Ohioan commented. "Where in the name of God did all the people come from?" The Democratic party had suffered a serious defeat. Lincoln carried most of the North and with it the electoral college. It was a vote to restrict slavery to the South, as everyone knew, but it was more than that. In New York, Morgan ran ahead of the ticket and the handful of corruptionists renominated ran far behind it. Of fifty-five Republicans who had voted to override his veto, only three were returned. When the new legislature opened, the Republican caucus renominated Littlejohn, but also passed resolutions strongly condemning the 1860 Assembly—and Littlejohn himself asked that the resolutions pass unanimously.[39]

John Sherman had no doubt of the reasons for Republican success: attacks on "the narrow sectionalism of Buchanan's administration and the corruptions by which he attempted to sustain his policy." In a letter to the public, the Ohioan committed his party to "purify the administration of the Government from the pernicious influences of jobs, contracts and unreasonable party warfare." Even as greedy expectants were clamoring for places, the Madison *Daily State Journal* declared that victory must mean more than "the loaves and fishes of office." Others credited the Republican victory to the corruption issue, and one cannot read personal correspondence without seeing the impact that the Buchanan Administration's misdeeds had on the public mind.[40]

Wise Republicans, however, knew that the battle was only begun with the victory at the polls. They had given themselves a reputation for honesty not wholly deserved. "Large numbers of men, from all parties, joined our standard because of the corruptions of the national administration," one congressman confided. But if they found their hopes betrayed, they might not remain. If the party fell into corruption, then it would be ruined. Its ability to resist the Slave Power depended on "the confidence that the people shall place in the honesty of its management of the affairs of the nation—and especially its administration of the finances." Without that honesty, the Administration that came in would break down within a year. "It seems to me that the time has come for placing men having a reputation for *honesty* in situations where honest men are required," another partisan wrote. "There is no sense in *talking* honesty, while you allow all the offices to be filled by rogues. . . ."[41]

So the war on corruption had only begun, and it was the same war that had been fought against Ohio canal-contract jobbers in 1857, against the Seward candidacy in 1860. The Augean stables must be cleaned out, a leading Republican wrote, but not every man in the party was fit to wield the broom.[42]

17

"This Accursed Union, Reeking with Corruption"

That November, Republicans hailed the returns as Freedom's decisive triumph over the Slave Power and Honesty's over Depravity. They cheered too soon. As Southern states broke away from the Union, it became clear that the struggle was only begun. Slavery and the rights of the South in the nation sundered the United States. Still, the issue of public ethics appeared once more, to strengthen the secessionists' arguments and thwart any last-minute compromise. What Republicans had not realized was that Southerners had their own Corruption Myth on which to draw for starkly different conclusions.*

*Only after completing the manuscript did I discover Kenneth Greenberg's masterful *Masters and Statesmen: The Political Culture of American Slavery* (Baltimore: Johns Hopkins Univ. Press, 1985), and I was delighted to discover our shared discernment of the tie between fears of corruption and arguments for secession. Our accounts, though, are not parallel but supplementary. While his examines the link between values which slavery imbued and the concern with corruption, I see additional connections not exclusively Southern, but affecting Southerners' viewpoint: the very real scandals of the 1850s, and the national tradition which all major parties nurtured that corruption was both a customary motivation for enemies of liberty and a common explanation of whatever the opposition did. Though the sources Professor Greenberg cites often mean little more by "corruption" than office-seeking and party devotion, he is right not to so limit the definition; Southerners I have cited were disturbed by a much wider array of misdeeds. Their battles on venality were not simply oratorical, but active—Toombs being the most important example; and I lay more stress on the very specific methods which Southern Rights men foresaw as at the disposal of a victorious antislavery President.

The North had no monopoly on political vice. Southern legislators met less frequently, perhaps, than Northern ones, but they knew how to disgrace themselves almost as much. "I was at *the Sink*," one Kentuckian commented after visiting the capitol, ". . . and assure you, I never witness'd so much pillage there before." In North Carolina, lobbyists clustered around the representatives to plead for new grants to railroads, while Arkansas correspondents denounced lawmakers for imbecility and "public theft." Louisiana's assemblage was in a class by itself. How could anyone be surprised to hear that money would pass any bill in Baton Rouge, wondered the New Orleans *True Delta*. Offered a nomination to the lower house, one partisan rejected it with scorn: "there are jackasses enough going to Baton Rouge without [me], whilst many of them . . . ought to go there in irons."[1]

Texas showed the extent of Southern corruption. When state creditors descended on Austin to build a supportive faction, they discovered that the public opposed any settlement partial to speculators. The officeholders were more amenable. Both the state auditor and treasurer solicited a commission in return for their services to the bondholders. A judge proved no less instructive in his chat with one lobbyist. "He says that 'there is a particular way of doing things in the Legislature of Texas,'" the company agent wrote, "and that he and his brother in law . . . the Secretary of State, are willing to attend to the interests of the creditors before the Legislature for a suitable consideration." All across the trans-Mississippi South, indeed, those "particular ways" of men not overly particular about ethics became a serious issue. Arkansas Democrats came to blows over misuse of state funds by the "Family," and in 1860 dissidents overthrew the Johnson dynasty with charges that fraudulent votes had discredited the nominating convention. In 1859, Senator John Slidell's foes tried to wrest Louisiana from him with claims that his rule meant "lying, bullying, trading, outwitting, low, mean, scurvy abasement." Some dissenters sold out for a place on the state ticket that fall. Others like Pierre Soulé and Thomas J. Durant fought to the end, convinced that Slidell had "transformed legislatures and party conventions into open marts where robust and daring votes might be put up at auction."[2]

Like Republicans, Southern Democrats cast a bleak eye on their section's representatives. Once, Alexander Stephens of Georgia reminisced, officials had been more virtuous than the people they served, but no longer. Was there a man left in either chamber who would risk defeat on his convictions? "This is our trouble South as well as North." Senators once scorned to campaign for their own re-election, James Mason of

Virginia grumbled. Now they revisited home just as the crucial vote came and passed appropriations "to distribute alms amongst the people to buy their votes." To be sure, the South had rogues enough in the House, while Senators David Yulee of Florida, John C. Breckinridge of Kentucky, and Rusk of Texas occasionally confused where their public duties began and where their duty to fatten their financial portfolios ended.[3]

Yet most Southerners preferred to see corruption as a Yankee notion, natural in the North, an intruder in the South. As Edmund Ruffin watched the House unmask its bribe-takers in early 1857, he took comfort that no slaveholding congressman was even suspected of complicity with Matteson and his cronies. That all four representatives expelled were Northerners was only right, the Virginia fire-eater commented. "As a body, the majority of northern members of congress are as corrupt & destitute of private integrity, as the majority of southern members are the reverse." A foreign observer echoed this claim: almost every Northerner had paid for his nomination and election and meant to make up the costs. When Northerners echoed the charges, slave-state editors reported the claims triumphantly. "The fact is, our public men are all rogues," New Yorkers told a Charlestonian, "honest men are driven from the polls—the ballot boxes are in the hands of ruffians—the very men who are elected . . . are so many swindlers, stock-jobbers, liars, even forgers and robbers . . . and all honest opinion . . . is awed and confounded, silenced and incapable."[4]

This vision of Northern debauchery was more extreme than any reasonable Yankee would have held, but it was plausible to those most hostile to Northern politics and institutions. Perhaps the fact that most Southern correspondents in the North chose to live in New York skewed their judgment the more, for scandals in Manhattan could hardly be matched in the English-speaking world. "Our aldermen may not be Ciceroes in eloquence and Solons in wisdom," said the New Orleans *Bee*, "*—but they don't steal.*" It was easy to generalize from New York's experience or to assume, as did Senator Andrew Johnson of Tennessee, that all cities were nurseries of corruption. "Legislation seems to be as much a matter of speculation & trade, as our tobacco or cotton," another Tennessean commented, "& much more profitable." Some Southerners assumed that cities dominated the North's politics, and from that could only conclude that the politics of the whole section had been debauched. There were other explanations for the North's moral decline as well: the unchecked power of democracy, the lack of deference for the North's natural leaders, and the untrammeled influence of the parties. Southern political conventions were quiet affairs, Southerners boasted, but in the

North, all was bribery and rowdiness. So far had the spoils system been carried in Northern states, that principle vanished in the campaigns. Or perhaps it was the influx of ignorant foreigners, the Richmond *Enquirer* suggested, dolts ready to sell their votes "for a dollar or a fill of lager beer." The South had fewer immigrants, more restraint on the democratic will, and less of a spoils system. These made it less corrupt.[5]

Worst of all corruptionists, the Southern observers declared, was the Republican party. "It is organized fanaticism led by organized venality," L. M. Keitt wrote. Its governors were swindlers, its legislators embezzlers, its judges suborners, its congressmen extortioners. The "Gridiron Legislature" had no match even in Turkey, the Charleston *Mercury* thought. Louisiana Democrats expressed no surprise when George Law endorsed a Republican for President in 1856: he expected "fat Contracts," they explained. Indeed, the *Louisiana Courier* charged that the British poured $100,000 into the Fremont campaign, since a Republican victory would wreck American agriculture and enhance the value of cotton sold by British colonies. No coalition with antislavery parties was sincere, the Southern press insisted. It was barter and sale. "A bid of one quarter of a dollar more by the other side would have carried the day against them." Yet Southern Rights spokesmen could not single out the Republicans for attack. Northern Democrats and Whigs had bought alliances with the Free-Soilers before the Republican party was formed and so were tainted as well. Indeed, among the most determined supporters of slavery expansion, the Democratic party was damned as corrupt beyond redemption; the Republicans at least had the advantage that in one principle—their hatred of the South and slavery—the rank and file was sincere, implacable, unpurchasable.[6]

It was that final conclusion that bound the fear of Northern corruption to the Southern Rights' appeal for disunion. To the fire-eaters as well as to the Free-Soilers, the 1850s witnessed a crisis not just for slavery but for the Republic itself. The old moral standards seemed to be lost, and so did the principles of states' rights and federal restraint on which the government had been founded. Centralization was the worst peril to state institutions such as slavery, and yet, wrote a North Carolina leader in 1860, everything seemed "to be tending to centralization, corruption and ruin." The Republic was about to collapse, former Congressman Alexander Stephens wrote some months later, and all because the American people had lost their virtue.[7]

That virtue, so lost, was the ability of the average American to stand alone, independent of government aid and unwilling to seek it. On this autonomy the ability of citizens to make a free, fair choice at the polls depended. Without it, government became a dispenser of rewards, and there would never be rewards enough for all. As demands increased, government favors would increase as well, and with them the rulers' ability to dominate the political process. "The days of the Roman Republic, historians say, were numbered when the people consented to receive corn from the granaries," J. L. M. Curry wrote in 1854. "And our doom is sealed when the people are quartered on the Government and accustom themselves habitually to look to it for largesses and favors." In a broad sense, the government was buying the people with bribery, and to Southerners, the process was more than the worst danger to free government. It was the inevitable result of an activist government—precisely the kind that Republicans would inaugurate.[8]

Corruption did not happen simply because new leaders had fewer scruples than old ones; Southern Rights advocates dismissed that belief. A new set of leaders would hardly matter in the long run. Corruption did not come about because of a party conspiracy and certainly not because the Slave Power had induced it. Corruption was inherent in the nature of government, for government would always seek to break down all limitations on its power with whatever tools were at hand, and remove every check that states' rights established. Naturally, the more power a central authority began with, the easier was its ultimate triumph. It had spoils for friends, funds enough to woo jobbers and profiteers to do its bidding for a share of the revenue. In the end, no central government could furnish lasting protection for the rights of the states. "The moment Federal money and Federal office come to be the exclusive objects of political ambition," warned the Richmond *South*, "the poorer pay and cheaper honors of the State governments will be rejected with disdain. . . . Do we not see this effect already? Is not public plunder the cohesive power of the Confederacy? Does not the strongest element of centralization consist in the attractive power of the spoils?"[9]

It was this skepticism about the federal system itself that made Southern Rights men doubt the promise of the Buchanan Administration from the first. Whoever was President, centralization and the corruption of independent judgment would go on. Amid the joyous paeans from Democrats at Buchanan's inauguration, the Charleston *Mercury* had sour words. The national parties were sedating the South, it protested, "with Federal gold . . . and Federal offices." The dismissal of Democratic officeholders across the North to make room for other Democrats disgusted Southern Rights men, who blamed the squabble over spoils for the demoralization of politics across the free states. The scandals only reinforced Southerners' disgust. Within two years, the Democratic press that had so praised the Pennsylvania statesman had begun to rebuke him for harboring corruptionists. A New Orleans newspaper damned him for "the meanest, most worthless, venal and degraded administration" in American history, while to Thomas W. Thomas of Georgia, the President was "that detested old villain who dispenses the patronage of this government."[10]

In the 1850s, then, the theory of republics' decay met the facts that Southern Rights men discerned. If Republicans could conjure up a Slave Power conspiracy, Southerners had a Consolidation conspiracy with which to counter it. As long as the states were strong, slavery would be secure, but it seemed that a plot was underway to weaken the states' powers, not through constitutional amendment, but through the "informal constitution" of rewards and favors. Existing trends were accelerated, as the federal government raised more money and increased the number of favors at its command. By 1860, former Senator Asa Biggs of North Carolina felt alarm at bills introduced for tariff protection, internal improvements, homesteads, and pensions. Their aim, he was sure, was to diffuse "the same corrupting influence that we see . . . operating upon the politicians." Not the insatiable manufacturers but the Northern conspirators for central power were responsible for the high-tariff movement, Southern Rights men cried. The protective duties were meant "to oppress & weaken the South," wrote Edmund Ruffin, "& to foster, enrich & strengthen the northern states." Any subsidy of a transcontinental line might be rife with plunder for contractors, but Governor Henry Wise of Virginia concentrated on how it would hand America "over to the Federal gods of Pacific railroads."[11]

Even popular education could be seen as a corruptionist plot against Southern morals. Because town and state governments in the North educated the people, a Georgia congressman declared, Northerners became convinced of their right "to *live* upon the government." To foster public education in the South would spawn a host of graduates soliciting "a *place* and a *support* from government." As for the advocacy of cheap homesteads in the West, a Southerner viewed each freehold as "a corrupt bribe . . . to vote the Black Republican ticket."[12] That Republicans were the most earnest backers for all such schemes alarmed Southern Rights advocates all the more and confirmed their suspicions that a Northern conspiracy existed to corrupt the Republic.

So, too, the Southern Rights men saw the increasing scramble for spoils in Washington. As the patronage power shifted to Washington, Southern states complained that their control of local politics had been challenged. In the hands of a Buchanan, federal patronage could protect the slaveowner's rights, but what if a Republican held the Presidency? As national offices took on added appointive powers, the danger to the South grew. The danger was all the worse because Southerners saw antislavery politicians as professional spoils-seekers. Indeed, Congressman Clement Vallandigham of Ohio argued, the Republican party had come into being by combining moral fanatics with "the still more enduring, persistent, and prudent passion of ambition, of thirst for power and place, for the honors and emoluments of such a government as ours." For ambitious politicians, then, antislavery was not always a deeply held principle, but a ploy to exploit Northern prejudices against the South. Every coalition with Free-Soilers seemed to prove it, and made Southern Rights advocates insist that any discussion of principles was useless. "When I differ with gentlemen upon principle I can understand them," a congressman exclaimed. ". . . But when it is a perfectly clear and conclusive indication that the difference between us will be about plunder, and not about principle . . . there can be neither cooperation nor confidence."[13]

Still, the Republicans' drive to limit slavery and redefine the proper place of slaveholding states in the Union lay at the heart of the Southerners' Corruption Myth. A few observers might presume that beneath the immediate issue of slavery, fears of centralization and corrupt use of patronage power explained disunion. A Southern sympathizer implied it when he declared that Washington had become "a sink of corruption, and this alone was sufficient cause for secession; which never would have occurred had there been an honest majority of Senators and Representatives. . . ." So too the Charleston *Mercury* would suggest when it blamed all America's travails on an era of corruption, in which Northern politicians, having bought their elections, thought nothing of selling their votes in Congress.[14] The idea was absurd. With or without the sordid tricks of Matteson and Weed, Republicans could not have put through their program without a sectional crisis. But if Republican corruption was not essential to the Southern Rights argument, it was useful. It made the case for secession stronger and added to the reasons for distrusting any promise Northerners might give of restraint in dealing with slavery within the states.

What would Republican victory mean? At the least, it would place a moral stigma on the slaveholding states, but Southern Rights advocates declared that the ban on slavery in the territories would be only the beginning. A Republican President would put his patronage to work at once to break down the South's defenders on either side of the Mason-Dixon line. Antislavery men would take every office at the President's disposal, from customs collector to district attorney. With 94,000 offices and $80 million to dispense, Republicans could create antislavery opinion wherever they pleased. By raising the tariff and promising a share of the revenues to greedy interests, the Administration could make them serve its ultimate goal. In no time, the Republicans would have established a Southern wing among the ambitious, particularly those already "submissionists" at heart. Then supporters of slavery would have to fight on the defensive. With a Republican Army and Navy against them, a Republican Treasury full of revenues to subdue or suborn Southern foes, any resistance was doomed to fail. Then the real Consolidationist revolution would begin. The Administration would repeal the Fugitive Slave law, give several free states two extra senators, ban the transfer of slaves from one state to another, and put a radical like Salmon P. Chase on the Supreme Court to interpret the Constitution in the North's favor.[15]

Southern conservatives might trust to Northern Democrats to protect the slave states; Southern Rights men did not. They had seen Democrats from Illinois and Michigan supporting homestead bills and subsidies for rivers and harbors. Could such men be trusted to oppose centralized power, especially when that power could give Western constituencies a share of the revenue? Spoils politics had degraded the state parties beyond recovery, said the Charleston *Mercury*. Northern Democrats were controlled by "machine politics," said the Philadelphia-based *Southern Monitor*, "the invention of the disgusting loafers and thimble riggers who live upon the organization as camp-followers subsist upon booty rifled from the dead. We have had subsidized presses, we have had packed conventions, we have had Congressional caucuses and Washington combinations. . . ."[16] Could such men be trusted to protect the South, when their future depended on spoils that antislavery voters and officials alone could deliver?

What Republicans had said of Northern Democrats, the Southern Rights faction echoed: they would back the South only as long as Administration patronage made them do so. It was in just such a cynical way that the fire-eaters interpreted Douglas's revolt against Lecompton and the support for his Presidential bid. Northern Democrats could not really believe in popular sovereignty. They must have compromised their true convictions to save themselves at the polls. Even Democrats who stood by the South through the 1860 election could not be trusted. No Northerner cared for the slave states, banker Gazaway Bugg Lamar concluded. It was all a friendship based on spoils, "and as the South can afford no more aid . . . they must seek bread and butter elsewhere." Dough-faces might propose a compromise to keep the South in the

Union, but they could not be relied on to uphold its terms. "Here in the South, the recognition of the rights of the South is a matter of life and death," a secessionist wrote. "In the North it is only a matter of 'spoils.' "[17]

Could Southerners withstand the temptations that Republicans would offer? Southern Rights men did not delude themselves with hopes. Indeed, the sectional crises of the 1850s had proven to them that the slave states had a class of dough-faces, too, and motivated by the same impulses as those in the North. They were susceptible, could be corrupted, *were* corrupted.

If ambition was a corrupter—and disunionists thought it among the worst—then the most prominent Southerners were vulnerable. Many of them aspired to the Presidency. To win Northern votes, they surrendered their section's interests. Such seekers after a national reputation were "bribed by their entirely vain hopes . . . [to] go into the service of our enemies, to buy northern votes," or to remain silent. Others aspired to state office, and hoped to do it through a coalition of Union men in both parties. That was how the Southern Rights men saw the Union parties of the 1850s and their support of the Compromise of 1850. Louisiana Democrats denounced their Senator Solomon Downs as a renegade, and his allies as creatures "spawned in the womb of Congressional corruption—this festering embryo of a new party." Mississippi's coalition was a plot to drive Democrats out and put Whigs in, Ethelbert Barksdale raged, and served none but "corrupt intriguants." Any Democrat who loved his party's principles more than spoils would have nothing to do with "Fraud and Falsehood, and Freesoil, and Foote, and Fillmore," Jefferson Davis told the state Democratic convention in early 1852. By contrast, Davis thought the Southern Rights party the freest of "sordid considerations" of any organization he had ever known. "It was this which sustained me and made mine a labor of love until I sunk exhausted and but narrowly escaped from the jaws of death."[18]

There were more flagrant bargains, as Southern Rights advocates saw it, especially in the passage of the Compromise of 1850, which they insisted had conceded too much to free-soilers. Like the Republicans, they cited the influence of Texas scripholders on the ultimate decision, and heaped abuse on editor Thomas Ritchie of the Washington *Union* for selling out his native South in return for favorable review of his claims. Nine years later the feeling of sell-out still rankled Edmund Ruffin. He had always known Ritchie was bribed, he commented, but the details had not been clear. Now, thanks to a talk with editor Elwood Fisher, he knew just how Ritchie sold out Southern interests for $100,000. Every proprietor of the Richmond *Enquirer* and Washington *Union* since had followed his example, Ruffin added. It was just such mercenary men that kept Southern opinion divided.[19] A Republican President would have no difficulty finding tools for his purposes.

Only disunion could keep the South from being infected with Northern corruption, just as revolution had freed the colonists from the contagion of British practice in 1776. No alliance with "an arrogant, aggressive, mercenary and unprincipled" people would be safe, no matter what concessions were offered the South, said the Charleston *Mercury*. Bargains could only be made with people who could be trusted; but where could one put trust in "a corrupted and foul, rotten, insolent and ruinous confederacy?" To the folk of Charleston, Roger Pryor of Virginia reaffirmed the ideal of secession as a purification. "Gentlemen," he cried, "I thank you, especially that you have at last annihilated this accursed Union, reeking with corruption, and insolent with excess of tyranny. Thank God, it is at last blasted and riven by the lightning wrath of an outraged and indignant people. . . ."[20]

Pryor was mistaken. The Union was broken, not annihilated, and as the cotton states called their conventions and passed ordinances of secession, Northerners shifted from incredulity to indignation, and then to a determination to restore the Union, by force if necessary.

At their most sanguine, Republicans insisted that secession was a bluff. The slave states profited too much by the Union to leave it; for all their cant about states' rights, they would never vote themselves poor. Disunion was a ploy to extract new concessions from dough-faces—nothing more. More indignant Northerners blamed secession on the greed and immorality that slavery instilled in the masters. Wherever disunion ideas raged, former Congressman Horace Binney speculated, Southern "public morality . . . has been turned topsy-turvy, and it is not wonderful that the poison has passed from public bodies to individuals, until we must blush at the baseness of men in every grade of official station."[21] Still others groped for one last sectional compromise that would restore the Union and remove the slavery issue from national politics. One such arrangement, advanced by Senator Crittenden of Kentucky, would have guaranteed enforcement of the Fugitive Slave Law, forced repeal of personal liberty laws, and restored the Missouri Compromise line, with all the territory to the north assured to freedom, all that to the south guaranteed to slavery. Northern Democrats embraced the plan at once, but they had unexpected company on the Republican side, including Thurlow Weed and Senator Simon Cameron. Indeed, when Weed came to Washington to press for the compromise, he came in company of his old friends from the lobby, Edwin Croswell, Erastus Corning of the New York Central, and all-purpose lobbyist George Harrington.

Weed's stand may have been statesmanship, but it was a serious political miscalculation, for Republicans were aghast. Perhaps Weed was simply out of touch, because he had worked behind the scenes and in the lobbies too long. Weed had great faith in officeholding to keep the party together; did he presume that patronage would ease the disgruntlement among the rank and file over the compromise? Making deals with Democrats was nothing new with Weed, where business interests were concerned; compromise was not a tainted word to him, any more than it had been to Douglas in 1854. But like Douglas in 1854, Weed miscalculated the fervor of the antislavery men and the boundaries beyond which compromise was no longer acceptable. Republicans rose in a fury at the prospect that the party that had promised to keep slavery out of the territories would now compromise to let the institution into them. Republicanism was less open to compromise than the Democracy was, more inclined to suspect any compromise as a surrender of principle for immediate advantage. "We believe in what we profess in our heart of hearts," a Maine congressman declared; "we live there, or have no life." Now, it would seem, the new party's values would turn out a sham: Republicans might make the same deals as any other organization, that they might enjoy the offices in peace. The letters poured into Congress. "For God's sake and for that of the people, do what you can to thwart it," an Ohioan pleaded. A compromise would destroy the Republican party forever. Let the Republicans yield one inch, a Wall Street lawyer warned, "and all is lost. Liberty, Constitution, Union—all buried in one grave."[22]

North and south, the compromise became tainted with the stigma of personal financial advantage. That class with the most to lose financially seemed most inclined to reconciliation on Crittenden's terms: merchants, cotton factors, politicians with an eye on Southern patronage. "Artful politicians, rich merchants & speculators, whose god is money, will counsel peace, regardless of principle," wrote a minister to his nephew in the Senate: "see that you yield not to their solicitations." Northern city-dwellers wanted the compromise to fill their pockets with, Reverend Henry Ward Beecher told parishioners. They should be rebuked. Nothing could be worse than "this mercantile cringing in the North." Among Southern Rights spokesmen, compromise had long been derided as the hobby of acquisitive men. "The Compromise," a Southerner had announced in a toast ten years before, "'the best the South can get.' A cowardly banner held out by the *spoilsman* that would sell his country for a mess of pottage." It was the same now. Unionists in the South simply hoped to save "the flesh-pots of their pap-seekers at Washington." Let there be no more deals, advised R. B. Rhett, Jr.:[23]

Fear we tainted honor's breath,
Fear we contumely's brand;
Fear we not the glorious death,
Battling for our rights and land!
Oh, the deep debasing thought!
Cheapened,—bid for—priced and sold!
Sold, and with our own pelf bought—
Willing slaves for chains of gold!
  Raise the standard—shout the cry!
  Fear we shame—but not to die!

So compromise perished, and it was left to the President to lead the way to reunion by a show of force. It was in vain that Northerners looked to James Buchanan for decisive action.

On the faltering Chief Executive fell a torrent of abuse, not all of it deserved. "I have always believed there was nothing too corrupt or bad for Democracy to do," one Republican wrote, but if he was not astonished, he was convinced that more than imbecility explained Buchanan's attitude. Corruption and treason went together. An Administration so shoddy in handling money was sure to be slack in its patriotism as well. In fact, the same weakness that had kept Buchanan from firing Toucey and Floyd for malfeasance also made him keep Southern Cabinet members after they had made clear their intention to support their states in breaking up the Republic, and as the Indian Bureau frauds became public, and Floyd's dismissal inevitable, Republicans were not the only ones to connect the Administration's failure of will and of ethics. In a stormy conference with the President, Edwin M. Stanton, the new Attorney-General, lost his temper. "No Administration has ever suffered the loss of public confidence and support as this has done," he cried. "Only the other day it was announced that a million of dollars had been stolen from Mr. Thompson's department. . . . Now it is proposed to give up Sumter. All I have to say is that no Administration, much less this one, can afford to lose a million of money and a fort in the same week." As the scandal broke, radicals called for impeachment of both the President and his Secretary of War, and observed that if the executive dared to appear in New York, "he would be hung so quick that Satan would not know where to look for his traitorous soul."[24]

It would take more than a show of force to draw Union men behind the national government; it would take a Cabinet of men in whose integrity the public had confidence. So it seemed to one conservative when he blamed disunion on Washington's lack of "high-toned statesmen." So Republicans believed. If a conflict must come, with the Southern insurrectionists on one side and the central government on the other, the latter must retrieve the respect due to it. Only then would Americans consider it worth saving. If corruption and demagogery had made the government contemptible and secession popular, then the choice of better men might restore the government's honor.[25]

It was this need that gave Lincoln's Cabinet selections a special importance, and in particular the choice of Salmon Chase, Simon Cameron, and William Seward. From the first, radicals hoped to place Chase among Lincoln's councilors, and not for his militance on the slavery issue alone. His backers also knew him for a senator with a long reputation of opposition to subsidies and steals, a watchdog on the public revenue. With so high a reputation for integrity, the Ohioan seemed indispensable to the old Jacksonian wing of the party. Hardly had the returns been counted before Charles A. Dana was penning an appeal to Chase to take the premiership of the new Administration. Now the Republicans faced their worst crisis, he wrote, and it was not the slavery question, but "the plunder question." But, he continued, "With you at the head of the Cabinet, we shall be safe on that side, for I am confident that no man will be made Secretary of the Treasury . . . who has any stealing either in his antecedents or his possibilities. But without you, I do not see how we can [begin] to resist the vast power and unknown genius of the thieves." Already others had urged the Treasury on Chase, while Cassius M. Clay had pressed him to take the State Department, not as a radical but as a reformer. Only then could the Administration keep out "any combination of plunderers such as infest the Democratic ranks," and prevent the party's disgrace and permanent destruction.[26]

The same concern added to certain Republicans' uneasiness at the choice of Seward for Secretary of State. It was not just that Seward was suspected of favoring a sectional compromise; it was the moral tone he would give the Lincoln Administration. No less than in May, Seward was seen as a man of lax ethics and dubious friends. Seward in the Cabinet meant Weed in the capital. In New York, Greeley, Bryant, and the old Jacksonians fretted that Seward's appointment would undo their yearlong fight against the "Gridiron legislature's" corruption. As soon as the returns were in, they mounted a campaign to drive the few surviving scoundrels from power, including House Speaker DeWitt Littlejohn. With Seward dispensing federal jobs, that crusade would be hopeless. He would reward his friends, and his friends were Weed's. Unless Weed's power were checked, the next legislature might grow as degenerate as the last. Lincoln himself was aware of the reformers' complaints, and as one condition of Seward's appointment he had the New Yorker give his agreement to the rule of "Justice for All" in dispensing jobs. "Mr. Seward understands that he will not allow the democratic or anticorruption republicans of New York to be deprived of their full share," the reformers learned. In fact, their worst fears were realized. Seward's enemies were given nothing in New York, while Littlejohn, "the head of that corrupt set which degraded our set," got the coveted Liverpool consulate.[27]

An unpromising beginning, and the continuation was worse still. Early in 1861, Cameron returned to Pennsylvania waving around the President-elect's offer of a portfolio. Radicals were horrified, and not only because he seemed too willing to conciliate the South. If Seward had been thought too indulgent with corruptionists, Cameron was notorious as a corruptionist in the flesh. Popular report accused him of having bought his election to the Senate in 1857, after having tried to buy it two years before. When it became clear that Lincoln had offered him the Treasury, reformers were all the more aghast. They suspected an alliance between him and Seward, as well they might, since Cameron had been one of Seward's earliest backers for a Cabinet place, while Seward and Weed had worked hard to persuade Lincoln to give Cameron the prominent position that had been promised the previous May. Between two alarming trends, toward corruption of ethics and toward a corrosion of Republican principles, the link seemed obvious: statesmen willing to compromise their principles for cash would not shrink from bartering their party's ideals.[28]

The outcry rose across the North. Pennsylvania Republicans from the anti-Cameron faction rushed to Springfield to make Lincoln withdraw his offer. As with Seward, they stressed the importance of wavering men, who looked to the Republicans for a reform of public ethics. To such observers, the Cabinet post would be a test. With Cameron able to turn any department into "a den of thieves," Thaddeus Stevens predicted, the Republicans would never last beyond the next election. In the end, Lincoln reneged on his commitment to Cameron, though he later placed him in the War Department. There, the Secretary nearly outdid Floyd in incapacity, and within a year he had been shunted overseas to the mission at St. Petersburg.[29]

The choice of Cameron and Seward made Chase's appointment all the more imperative. With Seward in the Cabinet, Charles A. Dana wrote, "we must have a firm hand, an immovable will, and an unyielding power of refusing in the Treasury, or we are lost." Only by "the superior blaze of honesty" could the "brand of corruption" be extinguished, James S. Pike of Maine argued. If it were not extinguished, the Republicans' goals were done for. Not just radicals but members of all factions united in advising Chase to lend his integrity to the new Administration. If he refused, more disreputable sorts would take power. There was talk that lobbyist and former Congressman George Ashmun would have a Cabinet post, wrote one Republican. Rather than him, Cameron would be one hundred times better; but only Chase could keep such men from enjoying the confidence of the President-elect. Most clear of all was John P. Hale's appeal. "Your being in the Cabinet would go far to dissipate an anticipation which has involuntarily been forcing itself upon my mind," he wrote, "that the only ultimate result we have obtained at the recent Presidential election, is to turn one set of public robbers out of the Treasury to let another in." So radicals welcomed Chase's appointment as Secretary of the Treasury, not only for what it said about party principles but what it said about party ethics.[30]

Upright men might increase the respect due the central government; they could not maintain the Union without coercion. By the time Lincoln called his first Cabinet meeting, the prospect of Southern reconciliation was long gone. Before April was out, the new Southern Confederacy would open fire on Fort Sumter, and war would begin, a more terrible war than Americans had experienced or dreamed possible. It was democracy's most bitter test, the worst failure of the republican experiment to settle the differences between different groups by lawful methods. And the struggle was welcomed by many on both sides sick of half-way compromises, sordid political deals, and the moral lapses they thought had kept the peace for so long.

After all the jockeying and bickering, there was something clean and attractive in the use of violence. Antislavery men did not dread the consequences; some of them considered war a cleansing agent. That was what old John Quincy Adams had said fifteen years before, when a member of the peace movement called upon him. War might be brutal, the Massachusetts congressman admitted, but he believed that "war was not a corrupter, but rather a purifer, of the moral character of man; that peace was the period of corruption to the human race." The same faith in force inspired Lincoln's law partner, W. H. Herndon, when he heard that fistfights had broken out on the House floor. "For one I almost begin to think that all the *fuss*, and *fire*, and *anger*, & *war* are one of the phases of human progress and man's development, and if this is so, we are prepared, the sooner the issue comes the better."[31] To such men, compromise, whatever its terms, only extended a demoralizing issue.

We must not make too much of this. Those Americans who bespoke a purifying conflict did not think that it would take much of a bloodletting for purification: a quick thrust into enemy territory, a decisive victory, and terms of peace before the year's end. That would be time enough for patriotism to surge through every heart and banish sordid gain, but not so long that war-weariness and a hunger for war contracts would corrupt the idealism. But a small, controlled conflict—a crisis soon resolved—was an attractive notion to those whose ideals outdistanced their common sense. But would they have welcomed the cleansing besom of war, had there not been so much moral depravity to cleanse? Not just slavery and secessionism would be eradicated, Reverend Henry Ward Beecher promised his flock. "We are to be tested and tried; but if we are in earnest, and if we stand, as martyrs and confessors before us have stood, . . . we shall have given back to us this whole land, healed, restored to its right mind, and sitting at the feet of Jesus." Revolutions only went forward, an antislavery Ohioan wrote, and this one would lead to a purer land. "Yes, sir, reformed, reconstructed, regenerated and consolidated from one end of the country to the other."[32]

EPILOGUE

The Plundering Generation

The Civil War did not cleanse America of corruption, though ministers prayed and reformers hoped that it would. War contractors became rich selling shoddy materials to the government; Thurlow Weed did a thriving business arranging contracts for a 5 percent share in them; Orsamus Matteson took advantage of the low point in the Union's fortunes to speculate in government bonds and even tried to induce Seward to join his consortium. Cotton speculators made a profit by paying Treasury officials to notice nothing. With the war's close, the energies that had been turned to saving the Union were shifted to moneymaking, and the postwar era was known for its depravity. The Credit Mobilier scandal damaged the reputations of prominent Republican congressmen who had taken stock in a railroad construction company that was bilking the government. All the debauchery of Fernando Wood's mayoralty could hardly compare with the stealing that the Tweed Ring did from New York City, though Tweed owed his rise to the growing power and dexterity of Tammany Hall during the 1850s and to the alliances that the street railway bills had brought about.

Under President Ulysses Grant, the national corruption matched that of Buchanan's day. His personal secretary took kickbacks to help whiskey distillers evade their taxes; his Secretary of War was forced to resign after having sold Indian trading posts to keep his wife in fine clothing; his Secretary of the Interior, long before a speculator in Mexican war claims, was by the 1870s on good terms with sutlers who pillaged the Indians; his ambassadors defrauded the Brazilian government and peddled phony silver mine stock. North and south, state politics were rocked with scandals. In New York, Governor Samuel Tilden made a national reputation for himself battling the canal contractors—different men, perhaps, from those he had fought in 1851, but with the same principles. In Kansas, a senator was expelled for trying to bribe his way to re-election. In Louisiana, as the governor pleaded, corruption remained the fashion.

Had nothing changed? Had nothing been learned? In fact, there were some striking differences from the antebellum years. First, the issue of corruption had been cut loose from fears for the fragility of the Republic. By 1875, most Americans believed that the institutions that a Revolutionary generation had established would last. The outcome of the Civil War (for Northerners) and of Reconstruction (for white Southern conservatives) underlay this confidence. So did the world situation. Until 1860, one could believe that democracy was both fragile and fleeting. The lessons thereafter changed. Had observers cited Napoleon III as a living example of the man in jackboots kicking over corrupted republics? In 1870 the Emperor fell and the French restored their republic. New men on horseback arose, uproarious scandals toppled presidents, but the republic endured. In Britain even the Conservatives expanded democratic rights. In Italy and central Europe, autocrats gave way to parliaments. Was democracy, then, so weak, so vulnerable?

It did not seem so to postwar Americans. With a few exceptions—and brief periods of hysteria—they no longer overestimated the would-be Caesars—it took profound depths of intuition to see conspiratorial cunning in such dim citizen-soldiers as Grant, Sherman, or Thomas. When a powerful figure came to power, a few alarmists might express their fears of Grant as Caesar, Theodore Roosevelt as Kaiser, but they did not associate the peril with internal corruption as much as with his presumed usurpation of other's powers. An usurper might also be corrupt, but corruption would neither open the way for him nor help him to seize control. In Grant's case, it was far easier for reformers to see him as the tool of designing men and his third-term ambitions as his friends' way of keeping in control of the best offices. There was no dictator in the wings, at least not one waiting to corrupt the people to make himself emperor. America was not Rome.

It was not Rome, because it could regenerate itself. That lesson, too, Americans now believed. If the perils to free government were weaker than they had thought, the safeguards were stronger. Thus, when historian James Parton examined the lobby at Washington in 1869, he distanced himself from the reformers before the war in separating shadow from substance. Corruption was nothing new, he wrote; it went back to Hamilton's day and had been used for good purposes as well as bad. There was less now than in the era of the Revolutionary fathers, less in this country than in any other. Corruption did not destroy freedom, and at its worst could still be eradicated and the ancient virtue restored: England's history taught both lessons. Let no American despair, Parton cautioned, even the pessimist who mistakenly thought most lobbyists corrupt, most Congressmen venal, and most bills "jobs." "Every age has its difficulty. This is ours, and we shall overcome it." To the same sunny conclusions came elder statesman Horatio Seymour in 1876. Undistressed by the breaking scandals all about him, New York's former governor forecast a more virtuous second century for the Republic. There was not more corruption than before, he insisted. People simply noticed more, because their own sensibilities, had grown refined.[1]

Second, the reformers had no demon-figure comparable to the Slave Power to wave before the people. The closest they could come was a vision of the Boss, a local phenomenon, or the Robber Baron. In dealing with either, however, the Gilded Age reformers showed an inflexibility that augured ill for their efforts. The Robber Baron must be defeated—but the liberals were reluctant to challenge the doctrine of laissez-faire, by now a shibboleth with more academic backing than before the war. Government action was part of the problem, they insisted; special privilege was the great corrupting temptation that made businessmen willing to buy congressmen to have their way. In fact, the free market no longer entirely existed, and those privileges that liberals wanted to uproot were too deeply embedded. Perhaps only other violations of the doctrine of laissez-faire in the consumers' interest could have succeeded. So, too, to fight the Boss, reformers turned to restrictions on foreigners and limited the right to vote to what they called "the best men." There had always been pessimists about the possibilities of popular government, and even among liberal reformers there would always be dissidents who put their faith in the people, but never before the war had the skeptics so controlled the reform movement. Never before had they been so convinced that a large portion of the American people were unfit to govern themselves.

The third change was the most disconcerting. In the 1850s, most Americans had accepted the party system as the best means of expressing the national will, but they had not accepted the idea that any party should be permanent. That was why Republicans could abandon the Whig party as corrupt and begin a new organization. That was why Democrats who left the party's ranks hoped to see parties re-formed on new principles after the war. Once in a generation, scholarly observers presumed, the parties would die and new ones take their place. But after the war, not only the party system but the two reigning parties became associated with the fortunes of the Republic. Liberals might leave the Republican fold in 1872, but their hopes of a new party were dashed; they either had to join the Democrats or return to the Republicans. As a generation grew up under the Democratic and Republican ascendancy, they became too committed to the organizations to care for change, even when corruption in their own ranks would have given them excuse. Historians focus on the Mugwumps who left the Republicans in 1884 because they could not abide the candidate; but how many reformers remained loyal behind a candidate whose honesty they doubted! In this way, Americans came to revile corruption—and yet, in the name of party regularity, to accept it, apologize for it, and assume it the inevitable effect of "politics." Reformers before the war would never have admitted corruption ineradicable. To have done so would have been to challenge the validity of republican institutions.

The generations that followed the Civil War misunderstood the lessons that the antebellum decade had taught. As the corruption of the Reconstruction years became public knowledge, most Americans forgot that the years before the war had been corrupt at all.

Were there indeed lessons to be learned?

In a recent study of comparative political systems, James C. Scott suggested a few rules for the right climate for an "informal constitution" to flourish. Corruption, he argued, thrives most when the formal political system is unable to cope with the scale or nature of the demands imposed upon it. If the political institutions are unable to bear the burdens that rapid change and urban growth impose, then officials will find ways of getting around the institutions to do what needs to be done. As economic power shifts into one set of hands and political power into another, a conflict can break out, but it need not. "When economic wealth and political authority are in different hands within a system, corruption may firmly bind them together. In this fashion, corruption may serve as a stabilizing or conservative force that provides access to influence for a wealthy elite that might otherwise finance opposition parties or even assist in violent attempts to overthrow the existing regime."[2]

Between the newly independent African states that Scott studied and the antebellum republic lies less of a gap than we might think. American institutions were not as unstable as their critics thought, but they were unstable enough. It was the failure of the poitical system that brought on secession and the Civil War. Perhaps no institutions could have held in the disparate demands of North and South, but those which the Founders had built certainly could not. The demands on the institutions were certainly heavy. With millions of new citizens to absorb, with cities growing too quickly for the facilities to keep up, with rapid expansion of population and government agencies across a continent, and with an expansion in public wealth which the promoters lacked the moral stamina to handle, institutions that the Constitution did not recognize played a greater role in solving problems: the parties, the spoils system, and the political machine. Corruption replaced the formal political process in some circumstances and supplemented it in others. As economic interests found that their designs took more money than they could amass, they sought privileges from the government. As the number of interests multiplied, they found that backstairs influence must supplement their public appeals if the government was to favor their plans. Corruption *did* serve as a stabilizing, conservative force, though not for the wealthy elite as much as for the political leadership.

In 1904, Henry Jones Ford suggested that corruption may also serve to bring political stability in an unwieldy system, where too many different branches of government share the task of policy-making. To overcome the impediments that the constitutional separation of powers provides, Ford argued, people look to a boss or are ready to use bribery to make different agencies work as one. This, too, is a tempting thesis. Presidents Fillmore, Pierce, and Buchanan certainly used the patronage power to make Administration views match those of Congress, though later observers would not treat all such uses as lapses of ethics. Certainly this standardizing, conformist use of influence was one of the evils that Southern States' Rights men and Northern Free-Soilers alike dreaded: a power to grant favors or offices centered in Washington that would make puppets of the sovereign state legislatures and craven lackeys of the state party organizations.

But the corruption had several other effects, and these are equally essential to see. Disreputable means stabilized the legislative process only when one interest alone had the influence of corruption on its side. When the same weapons—bribery, colonization, vote-buying, spoilsmanship—were available to both sides in a conflict, it added to the chaos of political life. To Scott's assumption, we must add another essential corollary: corruption stabilizes only when its use is generally acceptable to ruler and ruled alike. Without that public tolerance, insidious methods became the foster-parents of radicalism, both north and south. When corruption became public, it made issues far more bitter and differences between either side far less reconcilable. Instead of solving difficult problems of policy, as the battle over Kansas showed, corruption became one of the reasons that those issues could not be settled. Instead of bringing state parties to heel, the cries of "Federal pap" gave dissident factions new cause for complaint and Southern Rights advocates new grounds for concern. Use of money to push through Lecompton did not make the House Democrats more likely to walk in step with the Administration, except perhaps the unnamed few who took money; for the dozens of others who refused bribes or heard of bribes being offered, the corruption drove the two branches of government farther apart. The very suspicion of corrupt dealings was enough to put into question the results of an election, a Congressional session, or a political compromise.

It is well to stress the word "suspicion," for even in a scaled-down form, the critics' view of the decadence of public morals did not approach the truth. Corruption always had its limits. People noticed the one thief in office and passed by the thousand honest men. Justly they awarded a high reputation for probity to the Guthries, Toombses, and Sumners, but many other public officials stayed honest without fame—or was slandered as a rogue and purchased dough-face. Even the political brokers set strict limits on negotiable merchandise. Orsamus Matteson and Robert Walker might have taken or given bribes to put through railroad schemes, but neither would have dreamed of changing his views on the Kansas issue for a bushel of gold. For James Buchanan's sake, editor Forney might help along election fraud in Pennsylvania, for a corporation's sake he might rewrite a House-passed bill in a back room, and for his own sake he might try to bribe through his election to the Senate. But Buchanan could offer him no price sufficient to swing him behind the Lecompton fraud. Weed might modify his high-tariff views when the fee to lobby for a lower woollens duty was good enough, but no price could have made him sell out Seward or his beloved Whig party. Even slippery Simon Cameron, with the most blighted reputation of his generation, was above taking bribes to become a free-trade man. That was one reason that corruptionists so often failed of their purposes. Not all the White House influence could force Northern Democrats to accept Lecompton, nor the settlers of Kansas to accept a vicious constitution.

Indeed, one is tempted to imagine that corruption bred its own cure. The shady tactics of the LaCrosse & Milwaukee Railroad ruined the company and its political tools. Dr. Gardiner's greed brought him to a suicide's grave and prompted the creation of the Claims Court. The "Nine-Million-Dollar Steal" was exposed, its legal basis overturned in court, its friends expelled from politics. From this set of circumstances, it seems a small leap of faith to conclude that corruption made no difference at all in how the 1850s turned out. Without distributing favors to assure a majority, the "steam beggars" would have had many friends and in some cases might have passed their measures. Without bribery, the railroads still might have got their land grants, and *possibly* they would be the same railroads that ended up benefiting. Even with all the scoundrels excluded, enough honest aspirants clamored for places to make every new Administration a battleground over spoils.

And yet, this leap of faith is a deceptive one. Corruption did not fail as often as it did because it was ineffectual. It *was* effective. Sometimes the wrongdoers got away with their gains, as Gibson and Breslin could testify; at other times their failure to profit by their methods was a mere element of chance or act of God, as Collins found when the seas swallowed his finest liners. Would Elder Peck's defalcations have come to public attention if he had invested more fortunately, or the legislative committee have been able to prove fraud in Kansas in 1858 if the offending clerk had not risen in the night to hide the returns in a candlebox under a wood-pile? What made corruption fail so often was its importance to contemporaries and the willingness of men to do anything to expose and rebuke the wrongdoing. Had corruption been less significant as a moral issue, it would have played a more significant role in making policy. Even when the corrupters lost, matters did not rest at the end as they would have done had no corruption been used. The shoddy dealings around Lecompton turned a difficult situation into a crisis that rent the Democratic party, discredited the Buchanan Administration, revitalized the opposition parties in the Upper South, and gave Republicans a new issue for 1860.

Reformers before the war had declared that corruption put the Republic in danger. It is easy to laugh at their fantasies of Bonapartes and Tiberiuses. Yet in a larger sense they were right. The corruption *did* endanger the Republic. The revelations of railroad and pistol-patent lobbyists damaged the good name of Congress and made its resolution of the sectional conflict less trustworthy. The naturalization frauds of 1856 helped rob the Buchanan Administration of its legitimacy, the frauds in Kansas helped undermine the proslavery position. Republican institutions are based on the trust of the people in their fairness. Corrupt use of those institutions makes them less worthy of faith. By the 1850s, many Americans were not only worried by slavery, but wondering whether democracy itself had failed, whether the price of it—demagogues, bribetakers, ballot-box stuffers—was too high to bear. The shift to laissez-faire thought was not simply a statement of faith in the business world, but a declaration of a loss of faith in republican institutions to handle business matters fairly or honestly.

Historians have blamed the war on a "blundering generation." But the Civil War was also made more likely by the "plundering generation" that so many Americans thought had betrayed the spirit of the Founders. There were many roads to Fort Sumter and the collapse of the Union, and many were more direct than those that began in the assembly halls of Albany and Madison, the treasury vaults of Columbus and Augusta, the hotel suites of Austin and Washington; but the roads ran there in the end. It was a Union sickening unto death that perished on that April morning, and the sickness had been growing upon it for a dozen years.

NOTES

Introduction

1. Daniel D. Barnard to Hamilton Fish, Jan. 30, 1855, Fish mss., LC.

2. Morton Keller, *Affairs of State: Public Life in Late Nineteenth-Century America* (Cambridge: Harvard Univ. Press, 1977), 241–45; Matthew Josephson, *The Politicos, 1865–1896* (New York: Harcourt, Brace, 1938), 52–56, 94–127.

3. John Patrick Diggins, *The Lost Soul of American Politics: Virtue, Self-Interest and the Foundations of Liberalism* (New York: Basic Books, 1984), 58–60, 110–18, 305–12.

Prologue: The Republic Degenerate

1. New Orleans *Crescent*, Nov. 6, 1851.

2. John Cannon, *Parliamentary Reform, 1640–1832* (Cambridge: Cambridge Univ. Press, 1973), 23–39; Lewis Namier, *England in the Age of the American Revolution* (New York: St. Martin's, 1966), 224–28.

3. Bernard Bailyn, *The Origins of American Politics* (New York: Knopf, 1970), 66–68; Jack P. Greene, *The Quest for Power: The Lower Houses of Assembly in the Southern Royal Colonies* (Chapel Hill: Univ. of North Carolina, 1963), 223–50, 297–302.

4. Caroline Robbins, *The Eighteenth-Century Commonwealthman* (New York: Atheneum, 1968), 115–24, 278; Edmund S. Morgan, "The Puritan Ethic and the Coming of the American Revolution," reprinted in Jack P. Greene, ed., *The Reinterpretation of the American Revolution, 1763–1789* (New York: Harper & Row, 1968), 247–51; Bernard Bailyn, *The Ideological Origins of the American Revolution* (Cambridge: Harvard Univ. Press, 1967), 134–36; Stephen E. Lucas, *Portents of Rebellion: Rhetoric and Revolution in Philadelphia, 1765–76* (Philadelphia: Temple Univ. Press, 1976), 108, 115, 140.

5. Morgan, "Puritan Ethic," 250–51; Gordon S. Wood, *The Creation of the American Republic* (New York: Norton, 1972), 107–24; Lucas, *Portents of Rebellion*, 141–42.

6. Lance Banning, *The Jeffersonian Persuasion: Evolution of a Party Ideology* (Ithaca: Cornell Univ. Press, 1978), 204–7, 270, 274.

7. Robert Remini, *Andrew Jackson and the Course of American Freedom* (New York: Harper and Row, 1981), 116–17, 130, 147; Marvin Meyers, *The Jacksonian Persuasion: Politics and Belief* (Stanford: Stanford Univ. Press, 1957), 14–17, 20–21.

8. William Marcy to Prosper M. Wetmore, Feb. 15, 1851, C. Stebbins to Marcy, Oct. 14, 1852, Marcy mss., LC; Philadelphia *Pennsylvanian*, Jan. 2, 4, 11, 1854; Charles Buxton Going, *David Wilmot, Free Soiler: A Biography of the Great Advocate of the Wilmot Proviso* (New York: Appleton, 1924), 434; see also Buffalo *Commercial Advertiser*, April 1, 1851; Lancaster *Independent Whig*, Feb. 20, 1855; Jonathan M. Kirkpatrick to Simon Cameron, Aug. 24, 1857, Cameron mss., LC; "A gentleman of Philadelphia" to William Bigler, March 26, 1852, Bigler mss., HSP.

9. Buchanan to John Nelson, Feb. 3, 1852, Buchanan to Franklin Pierce, June 21, 1852; see also William R. King to Buchanan, March 6, 1852, Cave Johnson to Buchanan, June 8, 1852, Buchanan mss., LC.

10. Azariah Flagg to Martin Van Buren, Jan. 26, 1852, Gideon Welles to Van Buren, July 23, 1852, Blair to Van Buren, Van Buren mss., LC; Van Buren to Welles, July 31, 1851; F. L. Burr to Welles, Jan. 15, 1854, Welles mss., LC.

11. Charles C. Binney, *Life of Horace Binney* (Philadelphia: Lippincott, 1903), 264; Washington Hunt to Fish, Feb. 8, 1852, Weed to Fish, Aug. 16, 1852, Fish mss., LC.

12. New Orleans *Crescent*, July 12, 1851; Houston (Miss.) *Southern Argus*, June 1, 8, 1853; Ohio Constitutional Convention, *Reports of the Debates and Proceedings of the Convention for the Revision of the Constitution of the State of Ohio* (Columbus: S. Medary, 1850), 979.

13. House Report 243, 34th Cong. 2d sess., 66.

14. *Congressional Globe* (hereafter cited as CG), 35th Cong., 1st sess. (May 13, 1858), 358; New York *Evening Post*, May 5, 1860.

15. Glyndon Van Deusen, *Thurlow Weed: Wizard of the Lobby* (Boston: Little, Brown), 66–67, 77, 107; John Upton Terrell, *Furs by Astor* (New York: Morrow, 1963), 308; Remini, *Jackson and the Course of American Freedom*, 16–17.

16. Weed to Hamilton Fish, Aug. 16, 1852, Fish mss.; Van Buren to Welles, July 31, 1851, Welles mss., LC.

17. David Loth, *Public Plunder: A History of Graft in America* (New York: Carrick and Evans, 1938), 48–72; Gustavus Myers, *History of the Great American Fortunes* (New York: Modern Library, 1936), 43; Alfred Young, *The Democratic-Republicans of New York: The Origins* (Chapel Hill: Univ. of North Carolina, 1967), 9, 64, 300; Forrest McDonald, *The Presidency of George Washington* (Lawrence: Univ. Press of Kansas, 1974), 57–58; Nathan Schachner, *The Founding Fathers* (New York: Putnam, 1954), 97.

18. Remini, *Jackson and the Course of American Freedom*, 13–25; Gustavus Myers, *The History of Tammany Hall*, 2d ed., rev. and enl. (New York: Boni and Liveright, 1917), 70–71, 96–99; *The Works of John C. Calhoun*, Richard K.

Cralle, ed. (New York: Appleton, 1853), 2: 551–53, 568–69. For use of the misquotation, see F. L. Burr to Gideon Welles, Jan. 15, 1854, Welles mss., LC; Buffalo *Commercial Advertiser*, Dec. 6, 1851; Cleveland *Plain Dealer*, July 8, 1852. Though a misquote, the recollected phrase certainly was in keeping with the point that Calhoun was trying to make.

19. Myers, *Great American Fortunes*, 78, 124–26, 144; Myers, *Tammany Hall*, 119–23, 133; Remini, *Jackson and the Course of American Freedom*, 198–99.

20. Myers, *Great American Fortunes*, 124–26; William H. Masterson, *William Blount* (New York: Greenwood, 1969), 171–76, 277–81, 298–99; C. Peter Magrath, *Yazoo: Law and Politics in the New Republic: The Case of Fletcher* v. *Peck* (Providence: Brown Univ. Press, 1966), 3–7.

21. T. A. Osborn to William Marcy, Nov. 5, 1852, Marcy mss.; Indianapolis *Daily State Sentinel*, April 7, 1857; Hartford *Courant*, Feb. 19, 1851; see also John Charles Nerone, "The Press and Popular Culture in the Early Republic: Cincinnati, 1793–1848," unpublished Ph.D. dissertation, Univ. of Notre Dame, 1982, 161.

22. House Report 243, 34th Cong., 2d sess., 154–61.

23. Philadelphia *Daily News*, July 21, 1858; New York *Evening Post*, July 31, Aug. 27, Sept. 9, 1852, June 9, 1860; New York *Daily Tribune*, July 30, 1852. In justice to the *Tribune*, it published a retraction of its false report and blamed "the stupid blundering of a reporter," on Aug. 7.

24. Bridgeport *Republican Farmer*, Nov. 16, 1860; Chicago *Daily Times*, Feb. 25, 1858; Boston *Commonwealth*, Sept. 21, 1852; New Orleans *Louisiana Courier*, Dec. 17, 1853; Portland *Eastern Argus*, March 22, 29, April 2, 1860; New Orleans *Daily Crescent*, March 27, 1854.

25. Gordon S. Wood, "Conspiracy and the Paranoid Style: Causality and Deceit in the Eighteenth Century," *William and Mary Quarterly*, 3d series, XXXIX (1982), 401–41; Ira D. Gruber, "The American Revolution as a Conspiracy: The British View," *ibid.*, 3d series, XXVI (1969), 360–72; David Brion Davis, *The Slave Power Conspiracy and the Paranoid Style* (Baton Rouge: Louisiana State Univ., 1969), 3–5, 11–15; Richard Hofstadter, *The Paranoid Style in American Politics and Other Essays* (New York: Knopf, 1965), 3–40; Wood, *Creation of the American Republic*, 28–43.

26. New York *Evening Post*, July 11, 12, 1851; Chicago *Daily Times*, June 30, 1858; Cincinnati *Daily Commercial*, Feb. 17, 1857; Detroit *Free Press*, March 23, 1860.

27. New York *Evening Post*, March 9, 1855; for examples, see Nashua *Gazette*, Jan. 13, 1853; House Report 414, 35th Cong., 1st sess., 84. A prime example would be the investigation of railroad lobbyists in the New Hampshire legislature. The legislator accused admitted that he had been offered money for his vote, and accepted it—but insisted that he did so merely to keep from hurting an old friend's feelings. The bribegiver admitted offering payment and expressing a desire for a vote in return; conceded that he had declared that to pass the bill, money would be no object; confessed that he also bought stock at a premium

from the lawmaker's friend to sway the former's vote. But all these acts, he insisted, were not corruption, nor were they meant to buy friends: the whole thing was a terrible misunderstanding.

28. New York *Semi-Weekly Tribune*, Oct. 2, 1855.

29. Providence *Journal*, April 14, 1854.

30. New Orleans *Louisiana Courier*, Nov. 3, Dec. 17, 1853; Detroit *Free Press*, April 6, 1860; *The People v. John McKinney*, Michigan Reports, 10 Michigan 54; *Horace Ferris v. Victor Adams*, Vermont Reports, 23 Vermont 136–42.

31. House Report 648, 36th Cong., 1st sess., 181.

32. George W. Patterson to Thurlow Weed, May 8, 1854, Weed mss., Rochester.

33. Bernard A. Weisberger, *The American Newspaperman* (Chicago: Univ. of Chicago Press, 1961), 117; Glyndon Van Deusen, *Horace Greeley, 19th Century Crusader* (Philadelphia: Univ. of Pennsylvania Press, 1953), 130–32.

34. *CG*, 35th Cong., 1st sess. (June 1, 1858), 2605; Charleston *Mercury*, April 4, 1857; *Isaac Cook v. Elias Shipman*, 24 Illinois Reports 616; Henry Ward Beecher, *Patriotic Addresses in America and England, from 1850 to 1885, on Slavery, the Civil War, and the Development of Civil Liberty in the United States* (Boston: Pilgrim, 1887), 252; George E. Allen and others to Charles Francis Adams, March 2, 1860, Adams Family mss.

35. New York *Times*, April 19, 1860.

1. Spoilsmanship

1. Hartford *Courant*, March 9, 1853.

2. Benjamin B. French to Henry F. French, Oct. 21, 1861, French mss., LC; Allan Nevins, *Ordeal of the Union*, I (New York: Scribner's, 1947), 160; see also G. Robertson to Thomas Ewing, April 5, 1849, Ewing family mss., LC; Charles Francis Adams Diary, Nov. 21, 1860, April 14, 15, 16, 1861, Adams Family mss.

3. Thurlow Weed to J. Nathan, Nov. 1, 1858, D. D. Barnard to Hamilton Fish, Jan. 22, 1859, Fish mss., LC; W. D. Blocher, *Arkansas Finances* (Little Rock: *Evening Star*, 1876), 38–41; Providence *Journal*, July 10, 1854; Samuel P. Thurmond to Howell Cobb, Nov. 21, 1853, M. M. Johnson to Cobb, Dec. 11, 1853, Jonathan Lumpkin to Cobb, Dec. 28, 1853, Cobb mss., Univ. of Georgia.

4. William Derlingers to William Bigler, Dec. 3, 1856, Bigler mss., HSP; Charles Machin to Thurlow Weed, Feb. 12, 1857, Weed mss.; A. B. Anderson to Simon Cameron, Sept. 29, 1857, Cameron mss., LC.

5. Roger W. Lotchin, *San Francisco, 1846–1856: From Hamlet to City* (New York: Oxford Univ. Press, 1974), 224; Benjamin B. French to Henry F. French, Nov. 23, 1852, French mss.; Horatio Seymour to Marcy, Oct. 24, 1853, Marcy mss.; Providence *Journal*, March 28, 1854; George N. Sanders to John J. Crittenden, April 7, 1854, Crittenden mss., LC.

6. French to Henry F. French, Oct. 31, 1861, French mss.; for "drippings" phrase, see New York *Evening Post*, March 11, 1853.

7. A. Boyd Hamilton to William Bigler, June 26, 1850, Bigler mss.

8. John Bradley to Thurlow Weed, July 10, 1854, William Brown to Weed, Aug. 16, 1855, Weed mss.; Philadelphia *Daily News*, April 28, 1858; see also Hugh White to Horace Greeley, July 26, 1860, Greeley mss., LC.

9. Philadelphia *Daily News*, July 19, 24, 1858; New York *Evening Post*, March 29, 1860.

10. A. D. McClure to William Bigler, Feb. 22, 1850, Bigler mss.; C. H. Holden to Thurlow Weed, Dec. 8, 1860, D. M. Arnold to Weed, Nov. 23, 1860; George W. Patterson to Weed, Dec. 11, 1860, Weed mss.; Hartford *Courant*, March 19, 1853; Gary van Sacket to William Seward, Jan. 15, 1857, Seward mss., Rochester.

11. Hamilton Fish to Zachary Taylor, June 18, 1849, Fish mss.; Lancaster *Independent Whig*, Dec. 30, 1851.

12. Stephen E. Maizlish, *The Triumph of Sectionalism: the Transformation of Ohio Politics, 1844–1856* (Kent, Ohio: Kent State Univ. Press, 1983), 80–83; Benjamin Perley Poore, *Perley's Reminiscences of Sixty Years in the National Metropolis* (Philadelphia: Hubbard Brothers, 1886), 1:355; Nicholas Dean to Thomas Ewing, April 4, 1849, Ewing to Joseph Signe, June 13, 1849, Ewing family mss.; W. L. Marcy, "Washington Revisited, 1850–51," in Marcy mss.

13. Leonard D. White, *The Jacksonians: A Study in Administrative History, 1829–1861* (New York: Macmillan, 1954), 313–14.

14. New York *Semi-Weekly Tribune*, March 17, 1854; John M. Daniel to Stephen A. Douglas, June 10, 1854, Douglas mss., Univ. of Chicago.

15. New York *Evening Post*, June 15, 1855; Cincinnati *Daily Commercial*, July 19, 1854. It should be added, however, that one man's sinecure was another's essential post, that most government departments were understaffed, and that a customs collector's services cannot be judged simply on whether he brought in more revenue than the collectorship cost the government.

16. Little Rock *Arkansas True Democrat*, June 30, July 7, 28, 1860; John Eddins Simpson, *Howell Cobb: the Politics of Ambition* (Chicago: Adams Press, 1973), 90–91; Franklin Pierce to Stephen A. Douglas, July 20, 1855, Horatio King mss., LC; Poore, *Reminiscences*, 1:356; Hamilton Fish to Richard Morris, Dec. 24, 1849, Thurlow Weed to Fish, Aug. 16, 1852, Fish mss.

17. Chicago *Daily Times*, March 17, 1855; New York *Evening Post*, Jan. 9, March 28, 1855; O. P. Carford to John Sherman, Jan. 17, 1861, Sherman mss., LC; Peter Straub to Weed, Dec. 26, 1860, Weed mss.

18. John T. Wood to C. H. Loomis, Nov. 7, 1853, Marcy mss.

19. A. Oakey Hall to Weed, Dec. 26, 1860, C. D. Marsh to Weed, Dec. 19, 1860, Weed mss.

20. Springfield *Illinois Daily State Journal*, Jan. 5, 1851; Pittsburgh *Daily Morning Post*, April 18, 1853; New York *Evening Post*, June 16, 1858; Chicago *Times and Herald*, Aug. 15, 28, 1860; Cincinnati *Daily Commercial*, Aug. 11, 1854.

21. Roy F. Nichols, *The Disruption of American Democracy* (New York: Macmillan, 1948), 313; New York *Semi-Weekly Tribune*, May 18, 1860; House

Reports, Executive Document 91, 36th Cong., 1st sess.; Nahum Capen to Horatio King, May 26, 1860, King mss.

22. Charles W. Carrigan to Horatio King, March 2, 1860, King mss.; Hamilton Fish to W. J. Cornwell, Dec. 24, 1855, Fish mss.; William H. Ludlow to William Marcy, Sept. 16, 1853, Marcy mss.; J. E. Sargent to John H. George, Jan. 27, 1854, George mss., NHHS; Harry C. Victor to John Sherman, March 21, 1859, M. S. Clark to Sherman, Jan. 12, 1859, Sherman mss., LC; New York *Semi-Weekly Tribune*, Sept. 8, 1854.

23. New York *Evening Post*, July 28, 1854, Sept. 9, 1859; Philadelphia *Daily News*, Feb. 4, 1858; *CG*, appendix, 34th Cong., 1st sess., 600.

24. Springfield *Weekly Republican*, Oct. 13, 1860; Gideon J. Tucker to Edmund Burke, March 16, 1859, Burke mss., LC. In 1854, the Springfield *Republican* charged that five Democratic postmasters came together to choose the ticket in one county. False, Democrats cried: there had been twelve delegates, and only three had been postmasters. Springfield *Daily Republican*, Oct. 16, 26, 1854.

25. Michael Holt, *The Political Crisis of the 1850s* (New York: Wiley and Sons, 1978), 107; James A. Hamilton to Hamilton Fish, Dec. 15, 1859, Fish mss.; New York *Weekly Tribune*, July 12, 1851; New York *Evening Post*, June 9, 1858; M. W. Tappan to John P. Hale, June 19, 1854, A. P. Stinson to Hale, March 22, 1854, George G. Fogg to Hale, April 21, 1854, Hale mss., NHHS; Clement Vallandigham, *Speeches, Arguments, Addresses and Letters of Clement Vallandigham* (New York: J. Walter, 1864), 272–74.

26. *CG*, 35th Cong., 2d sess., 1449.

27. John W. Forney to Howell Cobb, Jan. 15, 1854, Cobb mss.; J. W. Merriam to John H. George, Dec. 20, 1857, W. C. Sterroc to George, Jan. 30, 1854, A. D. Speed to George, Oct. 27, 1856, George mss.; Hamilton Fish to J. Phillips Phoenix, May 25, 1850, Fish mss.

28. Brooklyn *Daily Eagle*, Nov. 12, 1851.

29. Philadelphia *Daily News*, Feb. 10, 1854; Simeon Draper to Thurlow Weed, Jan. 5, 1851, Elias W. Leavenworth to Weed, Aug. 28, 1859, Weed mss.

30. *CG*, 35th Cong., 2d sess., 1419; Charles Gayarre, *The School for Politics* (New York: Appleton, 1854), 87.

31. Holt, *Political Crisis*, 136–37; New Orleans *Crescent*, Oct. 18, 1855: Lancaster *Independent Whig*, Oct. 17, 1854.

32. Jacksonville *Florida Republican*, Oct. 1, 1856.

33. John M. Bradford to Hamilton Fish, Nov. 8, 1855, Fish mss.: New York *Evening Post*, Nov. 15, 1854.

2. The Hireling Press

1. New York *Evening Post*, April 29, 1852; for other suspicions of the Brooks brothers, see James S. Pike to William Pitt Fessenden, Sept. 28, 1859, Pike mss., LC.

2. Weisberger, *The American Newspaperman*, 111–14; Alfred L. McClung, *The Daily Newspaper in America: the Evolution of a Social Instrument* (New York: Macmillan, 1937), 166, 197; Nerone, "The Press and Popular Culture," 80–94; see also Isaac Diller to Stephen A. Douglas, Sept. 16, 1850, J. W. Sheahan to Douglas, Sept. 29, 1854, Douglas mss.

3. C. H. Ray to Elihu Washburne, Jan. 12, 1855, Washburne mss., LC.

4. G. Plitt to James Buchanan, Jan. 24, 1854, Buchanan mss., LC; Moses Bates to Caleb Cushing, Nov. 11, 1852, Cushing mss., LC; William W. Green to William Marcy, July 8, 1850, Marcy mss.; J. F. Dewey to John Sherman, May 4, 1858, Sherman mss.

5. S. M. Major to John C. Breckinridge, Jan. 25, 1854, Breckinridge mss., LC; William Hawley to Stephen A. Douglas, Dec. 15, 1857, Douglas mss.

6. W. F. Alston to William A. Graham, July 30, 1850, in *Papers of William Graham*, J. G. de Roulhac Hamilton, ed. (Raleigh: State Dept. of Archives, 1960), 3:339; Ezra Horton to William Marcy, Nov. 18, 1853, Marcy mss.

7. Charles G. Greene to Marcy, Feb. 1, 1854, Marcy mss.

8. J. M. Allen to Marcy, Oct. 20, 1853, Levi Hubbell to Marcy, Feb. 24, 1855, Marcy mss.; R. Brinkerhoff to John Sherman, March 3, 1858, Sherman mss.; H. E. Baldwin to John H. George, Feb. 2, 1854, H. C. Simpson to George, Nov. 17, 1856, George mss.

9. August Belmont to James Buchanan, Dec. 6, 1851, Buchanan mss., LC; Buchanan to Cave Johnson, Dec. 22, 1851, in *The Works of James Buchanan*, John Bassett Moore, ed. (New York: Antiquarian Press, 1960), 8:429; Horatio Seymour to William Marcy, Nov. 13, 1853, Marcy mss.; *The Papers of Andrew Johnson*, Leroy Graf and Ralph W. Haskins, eds. (Knoxville: Univ. of Tennessee Press, 1972), 3:581; Philadelphia *Daily News*, Sept. 4, 1858; E. H. Rauch to Simon Cameron, Aug. 18, 1857, Cameron mss., LC.

10. Henry R. Bass to Elihu Washburne, Feb. 13, 1860, Washburne mss.; New York *Evening Post*, Oct. 12, 1855; Charles G. Greene to William Marcy, Feb. 1, 1854, Marcy mss.

11. New York *Evening Post*, March 13, 1852; Racine *Advocate*, July 13, 1853; Culver H. Smith, *The Press, Politics, and Patronage: the American Government's Use of Newspapers, 1789–1875* (Athens: Univ. of Georgia Press, 1977), 171–73, 190; Buffalo *Commercial Advertiser*, March 13, 1851: John A. Dix to Horatio King, June 8, 1860, King mss.

12. Lotchin, *San Francisco*, 222; New York *Tribune*, Oct. 25, 27, 1860; *CG*, 35th Cong., 1st sess., appendix, 358.

13. Ohio Constitutional Convention *Debates* (1850), 1207–10; Michigan Constitutional Convention *Debates* (1850), 152–53, 438; Indianapolis *Daily State Sentinel*, June 29, 1857; Richmond *Enquirer*, Dec. 18, 1857; Lancaster *Independent Whig*, March 29, 1853, Jan. 23, 1855.

14. White, *The Jacksonians*, 290–93; Buffalo *Commercial Advertiser*, March 13, 1851.

15. *CG*, 32d Cong., 1st sess., appendix, 124; *ibid.*, 2d sess., 514–15; Buffalo *Commercial Advertiser*, Dec. 24, 1851.

16. New York *Evening Post*, Sept. 30, Oct. 26, 28, 1850; *CG*, 31st Cong., 2d sess., 514–19; Smith, *Press, Politics, and Patronage*, 212.

17. *CG*, 31st Cong., 2d sess., 232–33.

18. Roy Nichols, *The Democratic Machine, 1850–54* (New York: Columbia Univ. Press, 1923), 32–34; New York *Evening Post*, Sept. 18, 19, 27, 30, Oct. 24, 1850, Feb. 18, March 3, 1851; Jonathan S. Williams to Gideon Welles, June 30, 1850, Welles mss.; Benjamin B. French to Henry F. French, Jan. 22, 1851, French mss.; Thomas Ritchie to W. W. Corcoran, March 8, 11, 1851, W. W. Corcoran mss., LC.

19. Nichols, *Democratic Machine*, 32–35; F. P. Blair to Van Buren, April 30, 1851, VB mss.; Edward Everett, Diary, Feb. 6, 1854, Everett mss., LC; New York *Evening Post*, Jan. 14, 27, 28, March 26, April 22, 1852.

20. *CG*, 32d Cong., 1st sess., appendix, 120–22; Nichols, *Democratic Machine*, 151–52.

21. John W. Forney to William Bigler, Jan. 2, 17, 1856, Bigler mss.; Nichols, *Disruption of American Democracy*, 59, 92; Smith, *Press, Politics, and Patronage*, 215–18.

22. White, *The Jacksonians*, 293–94; John S. Williams to Gideon Welles, Jan. 3, 1856, Jan. 18, 1857, Welles mss., NYPL; John J. Perry to Nathaniel P. Banks, Feb. 7, 1856, Banks mss., LC; John A. Dix to Horatio King, June 8, 1860, King mss., LC; House Report 249, 36th Cong., 1st sess., 429–30; Charles Francis Adams diary, Feb. 8, 1860, Adams Family mss.

23. New York *Evening Post*, Feb. 26, 1852, March 2, 1859; House Report 189, 35th Cong., 2d sess.

24. Cincinnati *Daily Commercial*, April 15, 17, 19, 1854; J. W. Gray to Horatio King, June 13, 1859, King mss.

25. Van Deusen, *Thurlow Weed*, 226; Kenneth W. Duckett, *Frontiersman of Fortune: Moses M. Strong of Mineral Point* (Madison: State Historical Society, 1955), 134; Madison *Daily State Journal*, Sept. 1, 1858.

26. J. Cazneau to William Marcy, Oct. 1852, Marcy mss.; David Wilmot to Simon Cameron, Oct. 8, 1857, Cameron mss., LC.

27. J. Cazneau to William Marcy, Oct. 1852, Horatio Seymour to Marcy, Nov. 5, 1853, Marcy mss. For the impact of the independent press, see Nerone, "Press and Popular Culture," 85–94.

28. Robert W. Johannsen, *Stephen A. Douglas* (New York: Oxford Univ. Press, 1973), 448–49; C. J. Whitney to Douglas, March 21, 1855, Douglas mss.; New York *Semi-Weekly Tribune*, July 11, Aug. 11, 1854; Chicago *Times*, July 30, 1858.

29. James S. Pike to William Pitt Fessenden, Sept. 28, 1859, Pike mss.; Boston *Post*, Jan. 22, 1855; on Grund's career, see Holman Hamilton and James L. Crouthamel, "A Man for Both Parties: Francis J. Grund as Political Chameleon," *Pennsylvania Magazine of History and Biography* XCVII (Oct. 1973), 465–84.

30. *The Papers of Thomas Ruffin*, J. G. de Roulhac Hamilton, ed. (Raleigh: State Dept. of Archives, 1918), 2:609.

31. *CG*, 32d Cong., 1st sess., appendix 457.

32. Frank L. Burr to Gideon Welles, March 30, 1854, Welles mss., LC; Philadelphia *North American*, May 18, 1854; New York *Evening Post*, March 1, 1858; Sol. Parsons to Stephen A. Douglas, Dec. 15, 1857, Douglas mss.

33. New York *Evening Post*, Jan. 2, 1852, Aug. 20, 1856.

34. *CG*, 32d Cong., 1st sess., appendix, 457.

35. Ohio Constitutional Convention *Debates* (1850), 1207; Michigan Constitution (1850), Art. IV, sec. 22; New York *Semi-Weekly Tribune*, Feb. 3, 1854; *Walker v. Dunham*, 17 Indiana Reports 438–85; Summit *Beacon*, Feb. 20, 1850; Charles Francis Adams diary, Feb. 14, 1860, Adams Family mss.

36. Martin van Buren to Francis P. Blair, May 6, 1860, Blair family mss., LC.

3. "My God, We Have Voted Like Hell!"

1. James Shepherd Pike to ——, Aug. 31, Sept. 7, 18, 1858, Pike mss., LC.

2. Bangor *Whig and Courier*, March 9, 1859.

3. *Ibid.*, March 9, 10, 11, 1859.

4. Newark *Advertiser*, Jan. 14, 30, 1857.

5. Maryland Constitutional Convention *Debates* (1851), 27: Detroit *Free Press*, March 7, 1860. For discussion of vote fraud, see William Gienapp, Thomas B. Alexander, Michael F. Holt, Stephen E. Maizlish, and Joel H. Silbey, *Essays on American Antebellum Politics, 1840–1860* (College Station, Tex.: Texas A. & M Univ. Press, 1982), 25–32; Howard W. Allen and Kay Warren Allen, "Vote Fraud and Data Validity," in Jerome M. Clubb, William H. Flanigan, and Nancy H. Zingale, eds., *Analyzing Electoral History: A Guide to the Study of American Voting Behavior* (Beverly Hills: Sage Publications, 1981), 154–83; John Reynolds, "'The Silent Dollar': Vote Buying in New Jersey," *New Jersey History* XCVIII (Fall-Winter 1980), 191–211; Peter H. Argersinger, "New Perspectives on Election Fraud in the Gilded Age," *Political Science Quarterly* C (Winter 1985–86), 669–87.

6. New Orleans *Bee*, Nov. 10, 1853; see also Marius M. Carriere, "The Know Nothing Movement in Louisiana," unpublished Ph.D. diss., Louisiana State Univ. and Agricultural and Mechanical College, 1977, 57–59.

7. New York *Evening Post*, Nov. 3, 1859, April 6, 1860; Maryland Constitutional Convention *Debates* (1851), 25–26, 92; Detroit *Free Press*, March 7, 1860.

8. House Reports 3, 65, 34th Cong., 1st sess.; House Report 446, 36th Cong, 1st sess.; House Report 435, 35th Cong, 1st sess.; Chicago *Tribune*, Jan. 5, 10, 14, 23, March 2, 28, 1856.

9. Detroit *Free Press*, April 7, 1860; Chicago *Times and Herald*, Nov. 16, 1860; Ellis Roberts to Orsamus Matteson, June 28, 1854, Weed mss.; E. L. Conner to John H. George, March 7, 1854, George mss.

10. Cleveland *Leader*, Oct. 8, 1858; J. Rodgers to Orsamus Matteson, June 20, 1851, Weed mss.; L. P. Rankin to John C. Breckinridge, Feb. 13, 1855,

Breckinridge mss.; Providence *Journal*, April 14, 1854; New Orleans *Crescent*, Nov. 1, 3, 1851; Indianapolis *Daily State Sentinel*, Nov. 10, 1857.

11. Kentucky Constitutional Convention *Debates* (1849–50), 201, 226; New York *Evening Post,* March 25, 1851; Clement Eaton, *The Freedom of Thought Struggle in the Old South*, rev. and enl. (New York: Harper and Row, 1964), 223–24, 265.

12. Chicago *Daily Times*, March 25, 1858.

13. A. D. Speed to John H. George, Oct. 27, 1856, William Yeaton to George, Oct. 30, 1856, George mss.; Cincinnati *Enquirer*, April 8, 1860; Providence *Daily Journal*, April 14, 1852; Lansing *State Republican*, April 10, 1860; New York *Weekly Tribune*, Sept. 25, 1852; New York *Morning Express*, Nov. 5, Dec. 12, 1852; New York *Evening Mirror*, Aug. 19, 1852; House Report 563, 36th Cong., 1st sess., 4; House Report 87, 36th Cong., 1st sess., 19; Providence *Journal*, Feb. 8, 1854.

14. Van Deusen, *Thurlow Weed*, 101; Ferenc A. Pulszky, *White, Red and Black: Sketches of American Society in the United States During the Visit of Their Guests* (New York: Redfield, 1853), 188; Brooklyn *Daily Eagle*, Nov. 1, 1851; Iowa Constitutional Convention *Debates* (1857), 862; New Orleans *Crescent*, Nov. 1, 1855; Indiana Constitutional Convention *Debates* (1850), 1295.

15. New Orleans *Commercial Bulletin*, Nov. 1, 1851; Philadelphia *Daily News*, Oct. 11, 1858; Chicago *Democratic Press*, Sept. 11, 1854; Chicago *Times and Herald*, Nov. 9, 1860; Louisville *Journal*, Aug. 9, 1859.

16. Lotchin, *San Francisco*, 226; Francis P. Blair, Jr., to Francis P. Blair, Sr., Sept. 22, 1858, Blair Family mss., LC; New York *Morning Express*, Nov. 1, 1852; Indianapolis *Daily State Sentinel*, Nov. 19, 1857; Philadelphia *Daily News*, Nov. 1, 8, 1855, Feb. 4, 1858.

17. Philadelphia *Pennsylvanian*, Oct. 2, 4, 1851; New Orleans *Louisiana Courier*, Nov. 11, 1853; New Orleans *Bee*, Nov. 1, 1852.

18. Samuel A. Pleasants, *Fernando Wood of New York* (New York: Columbia Univ. Press, 1948), 88; Maryland Constitutional Convention *Debates* (1851), 26; New Orleans *Crescent*, Oct. 30, 1855; Providence *Daily Journal*, March 22, 1852; Cincinnati *Daily Commercial*, Oct. 10, 1854.

19. Lafayette *Daily Journal*, May 5, 1857; New Albany *Daily Ledger*, Oct. 23, 1854; Maryland Constitutional Convention *Debates* (1851), 27; Benjamin Graves to John C. Breckinridge, Jan. 10, 1854, Breckinridge family mss.; Cleveland *Plain Dealer*, Oct. 11, 1852.

20. *Digest of Arkansas Statutes* (1858), Josiah Gould, ed., 29; Maryland Constitutional Convention *Debates* (1851), 52; Iowa Constitutional Convention *Debates* (1857), 865; Indiana Constitutional Convention *Debates* (1850), 1293–94; Michigan Constitutional Convention *Debates* (1850), Art. 7, sec. 6; James W. Harry, *Maryland Constitution of 1851* (Baltimore: Johns Hopkins Univ. Press, 1902), 73; Bangor *Whig and Courier*, March 10, 1859; Shelbyville *Republican Banner*, Feb. 24, 1859.

21. Newport *Advertiser*, April 5, July 13, 1853; for similar practices, see Louisville *Journal*, March 16, 18, 1859; on the taxpaying qualification, see Chilton

Williamson, *American Suffrage from Property to Democracy, 1760–1860* (Princeton: Princeton Univ. Press, 1960), 267–70.

22. House Report 563, 36th Cong., 1st sess., 4; *Papers of William A. Graham*, 3: 253–55; Chicago *Times and Herald*, Oct. 15, 19, 22, Nov. 16, 1860; New Orleans *Crescent*, March 25, 1854; New Orleans *Bee*, Oct. 16, 1855; Indianapolis *Daily State Sentinel*, Feb. 16, July 7, 1857; Philadelphia *Daily News*, Feb. 4, Oct. 18, 1858; Indiana Constitutional Convention *Debates* (1850), 1306–7.

23. Lotchin, *San Francisco*, 225; New York *Evening Post*, Oct. 28, 1854, Aug. 20, 1856; Chicago *Times and Herald*, Nov. 13, 16, 1860.

24. Lancaster *Independent Whig*, Aug. 30, Sept. 27, 1853; Hamilton Fish diary, Oct. 14, 1851, Fish mss.; see also New York *Evening Post*, Aug. 27, Sept. 29, 1852, Nov. 7, 1859.

25. H. H. Coots to William Marcy, Oct. 19, 1853, Marcy mss.; New York *Evening Post*, May 14, 1852, Sept. 14, 16, Oct. 4, 15, 1859; New York *Evening Mirror*, Aug. 19, 1852.

26. New York *Evening Post*, Oct. 28, 1854; for similar concerns, see House Report 538, 36th Cong., 1st sess., 2–5.

27. James S. Pike to —, Aug. 31, 1858, Sept. 18, 1858, Pike mss.; J. Turrell to William Marcy, Aug. 14, 1853, Marcy mss.; Henry B. Stanton to John Bigelow, Nov. 9, 1849, Bigelow mss., NYPL: Rowland, *Jefferson Davis*, 2:212; Gayarre, *School for Politics*, 119; Sidney Webster to John H. George, Feb. 9, 1856, George mss.

28. Samuel Dickson to Thurlow Weed, Oct. 11, 1854, Weed mss.; Nathan Lapham to Edwin D. Morgan, Oct. 2, 1858, Morgan mss., New York State Archives; B. F. Whidden to John H. George, Aug. 16, 1852, Dyer H. Sanborn to George, Aug. 16, 1852, George mss.

29. A. S. Wait to John H. George, Oct. 28, 1852, J. V. Fowler to George, Feb. 29, 1856, George mss.; Lancaster *Independent Whig*, June 22, 1852; New York *Evening Post*, May 14, 1852, Jan. 6, 1858, March 22, 1859; Hamilton Fish to Millard Fillmore, Nov. 1, 1851, Fish mss.

30. Iowa Constitutional Convention *Debates* (1857), 863–64; Maryland Constitutional Convention *Debates* (1851), 52; William S. King to Thurlow Weed, Nov. 27, 1858, Weed mss.

31. Harry, *Maryland Constitution*, 73; Maryland Constitutional Convention *Debates* (1851), 102–3; *Digest of Arkansas Statutes* (1858), Art. 4, sec. 12; *Laws of Connecticut* (1850), 32, (1854) 138, (1855) 137, (1958) 36–37, (1860) 36–40; Indianapolis *Daily State Sentinel*, Feb. 18, 1857; Detroit *Free Press*, March 6, 24, 1860; Indiana Constitutional Convention *Debates* (1850), 1293, 1303–6; Iowa Constitutional Convention *Debates* (1857), 863; Minnesota Constitutional Convention *Debates* (Republican, 1857), 380.

32. William S. King to Thurlow Weed, Nov. 27, 1858, Charles Gilpin to Weed, Oct. 7, 1856, Weed mss.; Philadelphia *Daily News*, Oct. 12, 1856; Cleveland *Leader*, Oct. 9, 1855.

33. New York *Evening Post*, Oct. 10, 1851, April 20, 1852; House Report 538, 35th Cong., 1st sess., 18–20; New York *Herald*, Nov. 23, 28, 1855.

34. Minneapolis *Northwestern Democrat*, Sept. 9, 1854; Little Rock *Arkansas True Democrat*, July 21, 1860; Marcellus Eells to Hamilton Fish, Aug. 16, 1856; William J. Cornwell to Fish, Feb. 9, 1856, Fish mss.; Cincinnati *Daily Commercial*, Aug. 4, 12, 1854.

35. Providence *Journal*, Feb. 8, 1854; *Nichols v. Mudgett*, 32 Vermont Reports, 549.

36. Holt, *Political Crisis of the 1850s*, 159–69; Cincinnati *Daily Commercial*, Aug. 15, 1854; New Orleans *Bee*, Sept. 29, Oct. 18, 1855; New Orleans *Daily Creole*, July 12, 1856; Troy (Ohio) *Times*, Oct. 5, 1854; Baton Rouge *Advocate*, Aug. 23, 27, 1855; New Orleans *Daily Crescent*, March 23, 28, 29, 30, 31, 1854.

37. Joel H. Silbey, *The Partisan Imperative: the Dynamics of American Politics before the Civil War* (New York: Oxford Univ. Press, 1985), 141–53; Jeremiah Black to James Buchanan, Feb. 17, 1855, Buchanan mss., LC: Philadelphia *Public Ledger*, Feb. 24, 1855; Philadelphia *Daily News*, Feb. 19, 20, 1855; Carlisle *Herald*, Feb. 28, 1855.

4. Offices of Profit and Broken Trust

1. J. C. Hamilton to Hamilton Fish, March 1, 1849, Fish mss.

2. New York *Evening Post*, July 18, 1854; Harrisburg *Patriot and Union*, Oct. 8, 1857; Lancaster *Independent Whig*, Feb. 20, 1855; Buffalo *Commercial Advertiser*, July 11, 1851; Indianapolis *Daily State Sentinel*, March 10, 1857; New Orleans *True Delta*, Feb. 16, 22, 1859; A. Tarrant to John C. Breckinridge, Jan. 9, 1854, Breckinridge mss.

3. New York *Weekly Tribune*, April 26, Oct. 11, 25, 1851; Rowland, *Jefferson Davis*, 4:231; *CG*, 32d Cong., 1st sess., 2045–46; Hartford *Courant*, Oct. 27, Dec. 6, 1851.

4. House Report 412, 35th Cong., 1st sess., 2–3, 38, 62; *CG*, 32d Cong., 1st sess., 2137–39, appendix, 125; New York *Evening Post*, Aug. 20, 30, 1850; Cincinnati *Daily Enquirer*, Aug. 13, 1852.

5. Little Rock *Arkansas True Democrat*, March 9, 1859; Racine *Advocate*, July 13, 1853; Pittsburgh *Morning Post*, April 27, 30, 1853; Detroit *Free Press*, Jan. 14, 1860; Massachusetts Constitutional Convention *Debates* (1853), 3:126–28.

6. Detroit *Free Press*, Feb. 8, 18, 22, 1860; Joint Special Committee in Relation to the State Insane Asylum, Evidence, &c., *California Legislative Documents* (James Allen, 1857), 7; J. Watson Webb to Hamilton Fish, Jan. 21, 1849, Fish mss.; New York *Semi-Weekly Tribune*, March 16, 1855; Cincinnati *Daily Gazette*, March 11, 27, April 3, 1856; Chicago *Daily Tribune*, March 17, April 5, 1856.

7. San Francisco *Alta California*, Jan. 8, 20, 21–30, 1857; Report of the Committee on Accounts and Expenditures, *California Legislative Documents* (1857); *Collier v. Frierson*, 24 Alabama Reports, 100–111; Indianapolis *Daily*

State Sentinel, April 22, 1857, Grand *Rapids Eagle*, Jan. 21, 1860; Lafayette *Daily Journal*, Dec. 20, 1857; L. D. Campbell to Thomas Ewing, Jan. 2, 1851, Ewing mss.; Chicago *Daily Tribune*, Feb. 12, 1856.

8. Montpelier *Vermont Patriot*, Nov. 10, 1860; Rutland *Herald*, Nov. 8, 15, 1860.

9. Portland *Eastern Argus*, Jan. 5, March 14, 1860; Bangor *Whig and Courier*, March 10, 1860.

10. Lansing *State Republican*, March 6, 1861; Detroit *Free Press*, Jan. 31, March 3, April 4, 1860.

11. Detroit *Free Press*, Jan. 13, 22, 25, May 29, 30, 31, June 1, 12, 1860; Kalamazoo *Gazette*, Feb. 3, 10, 1860; Lansing *State Republican*, March 6, 1861.

12. Lansing *State Republican*, March 6, 1860, Jan. 16, Feb. 13, March 6, 1861; Kalamazoo *Gazette*, Feb. 22, 1861.

13. Cincinnati *Daily Commercial*, June 15, 17, 1857; William H. Gibson to Salmon Chase, June 27, 1857, Chase mss., LC.

14. Ohio Treasury Investigation *Report* (1859), 7–20.

15. *Ibid*., 30–48, 77–78; W. H. Gibson to Samuel Galloway, April 23, 1855, Galloway mss., OHS; Cleveland *Plain Dealer*, March 16, 1859.

16. H. C. Westervelt to Hamilton Fish, March 31, 1856, Fish mss., LC; Lafayette *Daily Journal*, Dec. 20, 1857.

17. Albany *Atlas*, Jan. 4, 1850; Grand Rapids *Eagle*, Jan. 4, 1850.

18. Ohio Treasury Investigation *Report*, 103; Carlisle *Herald*, Jan. 31, 1855.

19. Chicago *Daily Times*, Sept. 28, 1858; New York *Evening Post*, May 5, 1859.

20. Benjamin B. French to Henry F. French, July 3, 1853, French mss.

21. Ohio Treasury Investigation *Report*, 32–33; Bangor *Whig and Courier*, March 10, 1860.

22. Cleveland *Plain Dealer*, July 6, Sept. 2, 11, 1857; Bucyrus *Journal*, Aug. 27, 1857; Portland *Eastern Argus*, March 14, 1860; Bangor *Whig and Courier*, March 10, 1860.

23. Ohio Treasury Investigation *Report*, 32–37; Painesville *Telegraph*, Sept. 3, 1857; Montpelier *Vermont Patriot*, Dec. 1, 1860; Portland *Eastern Argus*, Jan 6, 19, 1860.

24. Cincinnati *Daily Commercial*, June 30, 1857; Bangor *Whig and Courier*, Jan. 4, 6, 17, March 10, 1860; Detroit *Free Press*, Feb. 24, 1860.

25. James S. Pike to ——, Jan. 6, 1860, Pike mss.; Montpelier *Vermont Patriot*, Nov. 10, Dec. 1, 1860; James M. Ashley to Salmon Chase, June 16, 1857, Chase mss., LC.

26. Portland *Eastern Argus*, March 10, 1860; Cleveland *Plain Dealer*, March 17, 1859.

27. Ravenna *Portage County Democrat*, Sept. 2, 1857; Cleveland *Plain Dealer*, March 10, 11, 1859; Cincinnati *Daily Commercial*, July 8, 1857; Rutland *Herald*, Nov. 22, 1860.

28. Michigan Constitution (1850), Arts. 4, sec. 30, 9, sec. 1; Kentucky Constitution (1849), Art. 2, sec. 28; Indiana Constitution (1850), Art. 2, sec. 10; Iowa

Constitution (1857), Art. 3, sec. 31; Maryland Constitutional Convention *Debates* (1851), 533; *Digest of Arkansas Statutes* (1858), Art. 4, sec. 11; Cleveland *Plain Dealer*, Jan. 5, 1860; *Bartolett v. Achey*, 38 Pennsylvania 273.

5. Suckers, Strikers, Borers, and Bribes

1. Benjamin B. French to Henry F. French, Feb. 18, 1859, French mss.; Hartford *Daily Times*, Dec. 24, 1853.

2. Benjamin Benson to John Sherman, March 10, 1858, Sherman mss.; M. S. Barnes to Elihu Washburne, Sept. 2, 1858, Washburne mss.; New York *Evening Post*, Jan. 11, Feb. 28, 1855; Philadelphia *Pennsylvanian*, Jan. 2, 1854; Brooklyn *Eagle*, April 22, 1857; Robert Struble, Jr., "House Turnover and the Principle of Rotation," *Political Science Quarterly*, XCIV (Winter 1979–80), 654–666.

3. *Alexander J. Marshall v. Baltimore & Ohio Railroad Co.*, 57 U.S. Supreme Court Reports (6 Howard), 317.

4. Albany Atlas, May 9, 1851; J. L. M. Curry to Edmund Burke, Jan. 24, 1854, Burke mss., LC; Buffalo *Commercial Advertiser*, Nov. 22, 1851; J. V. L. Pruyn diary, March 25, 1854, Pruyn mss., NYSDAH.

5. George Law to Thurlow Weed, March 29, April 9, 1855, Aug. 12, 1856, Feb. 3, 1857, Robert Minturn to Weed, April 17, 1858, Feb. 7, April 14, 1859, Moses Grinnell to Weed, April 2, 1855, Erastus Corning to Weed, Dec. 2, 1856, Weed mss.; Albany *Atlas*, May 9, 1851; Newark *Advertiser*, March 21, 1855; Hartford *Courant*, June 18, 1853; Brooklyn *Eagle*, April 15, 1857; New Orleans *Louisiana Courier*, Nov. 26, 1853.

6. Springfield *Daily Republican*, Feb. 25, 1860; *Alexander J. Marshall v. Baltimore & Ohio Railroad Co.*, 318; House Report 243, 34th Cong., 2d sess., 131; New York *Evening Post*, March 3, 1860.

7. *Alexander J. Marshall v. Baltimore & Ohio Railroad Co.*, 318.

8. *Ibid.*, 317.

9. French to Henry F. French, Jan. 22, 1851, April 17, 1853, April 1, Dec. 23, 1855, July 24, 1856, Sept. 11, 1858, March 14, 1851; Henry F. French to Benjamin B. French, May 25, 1856; Benjamin B. French diary, March 9, 1851, French mss.

10. New York *Semi-Weekly Tribune*, Aug. 29, 1854; New York *Evening Post*, Feb. 8, 1859.

11. New York *Herald*, April 4, 5, 1851; New York *Evening Post*, April 5, 1853, Sept. 6, 1859; George W. Bull to Thurlow Weed, April 19, 1857, Weed mss.; *Devlin v. Brady*, 32 Barbour (New York) 518; House Report 353, 33d Cong., 1st sess., 49–50.

12. C. M. Saxton to Thurlow Weed, March 10, 1857, A. S. Diven to Weed, April 15, 1857, John O'Brian to Weed, March 29, 1860, Weed mss.; Benjamin B. French to Henry F. French, Dec. 19, 1858, French mss.; New York *Evening Post*, May 1, 1860; New York *Semi-Weekly Tribune*, Aug. 29, 1854.

13. House Report 353, 33d Cong., 1st sess., 28–30; James S. Pike to William Pitt Fessenden, Sept. 28, 1859, Pike mss.; Benjamin B. French diary, Nov. 23, 1850, French mss.; New York *Tribune*, Sept. 16, 1861; *Rose v. Truax*, 21 Barbour (New York) 361.

14. House Report 353, 33d Cong., 1st sess., 20, 25; Philadelphia *Pennsylvanian*, May 23, 1854; New York *Evening Post*, Dec. 26, 1853, Sept. 6, 1859; Cincinnati *Daily Gazette*, July 26, 1856.

15. J. V. L. Pruyn diary, March 26, 1860, Pruyn mss.; New York *Evening Post*, Dec. 13, 1853; Rochester *Union and Advertiser*, Sept. 14, 1860; House Report 243, 34th Cong., 2d sess., 32.

16. Nichols, *Disruption of American Democracy*, 138; Buffalo *Commercial Advertiser*, Nov. 22, 1851; Newark *Advertiser*, March 1, 23, 1855; New York *Evening Post*, Aug. 30, 1850; House Report 353, 33d Cong., 1st sess., 32. Examination of the way New York representatives voted in 1850 disproves the antislavery charge, it must be added.

17. J. Watson Webb to William Seward, Nov. 27, 1849, James Buchanan to W. W. Corcoran, Nov. 29, 1849, Cave Johnson to Corcoran, Feb. 14, 1849, Corcoran to John McClernland, Feb. 7, 1849, Reverdy Johnson to Corcoran, Sept. 16, 1850, J. Ross Browne to Corcoran & Riggs, Aug. 9, 1852, Thomas Bayly to Corcoran & Riggs, Aug. 10, 1852, A. J. Glossbrenner to Corcoran & Riggs, Sept. 27, 1850, Corcoran mss. See also, for fuller and disturbing detail, Henry Cohen, *Business and Politics* (Westport, Conn.: Greenwood Press, 1971).

18. Robert Murray to Thurlow Weed, Oct. 1, 1858, David Mallory to Weed, April 21, 1856, Newark *Advertiser*, March 21, 1855.

19. Indianapolis *Daily State Sentinel*, May 14, 1855; New York *Tribune*, Sept. 16, 1861; see also Poore, *Perley's Reminiscences*, 1:443.

20. Nevins, *Ordeal of the Union*, 1:168; *Harper's Weekly*, Dec. 4, 1858; New York *Tribune*, Nov. 5, 15, 16, 1858.

21. French to Henry F. French, Jan. 21, 1856, French mss.

22. New York *Evening Post*, Feb. 16, 1860; New Orleans *Crescent*, May 24, 1854.

23. *Sedgwick v. Stanton*, 14 New York Reports (4 Kernan) 289; *Alexander J. Marshall v. Baltimore & Ohio Railroad Co.*, 314–37; Philadelphia *Pennsylvanian*, May 12, 1854; Lafayette *Daily Journal*, May 22, 1857; Providence *Journal*, Feb. 22, 1854.

24. New York *Evening Post*, May 3, 1852; Brooklyn *Eagle*, April 15, 1857; New Orleans *Louisiana Courier*, Nov. 26, 1853; Duckett, *Frontiersman of Fortune*, 132.

25. Duckett, *Frontiersman of Fortune*, 114; Newark *Advertiser*, March 3, 14, 1855.

26. House Report 243, 34th Cong., 2d sess., 131; New York *Evening Post*, May 3, 1852.

27. House Report 353, 33d Cong., 1st sess., 14; Brooklyn *Eagle*, April 24, 1860; New York *Times*, April 4, 1860; Chicago *Times*, May 15, 1858.

28. Mobile *Daily Advertiser*, Jan. 26, 1854.

29. Cincinnati *Daily Commercial*, June 17, 1857; New York *Tribune*, July 2, 1855; New York *Evening Post*, July 6, 1855; Albany *Evening Journal*, Aug. 27, 1860; House Report 243, 34th Cong., 2d sess., 66; George Harrington to Thurlow Weed, June 25, 1854, Weed mss.

30. *Powers v. Skinner*, Vermont Reports, Feb. term 1861, 280–81; *Rose v. Truax*, 21 Barbour (New York) 373–74; *Bryan v. Reynolds*, 5 Wisconsin 200; House Report 353, 33d Cong., 1st sess., 2.

31. *Alexander J. Marshall v. Baltimore & Ohio Railroad Co.*, 335.

6. Public Self-Improvements, Steam Beggars, and Railroad Robbers

1. Philadelphia *Public Ledger*, Feb. 24, 1855.

2. New York *Evening Post*, Feb. 28, 1855; Philadelphia *Pennsylvanian*, Jan. 2, 1854.

3. Michigan Constitutional Convention *Debates* (1850), 696; Canton *American Citizen*, March 6, 1852; Massachusetts Constitutional Convention *Debates* (1853), 3:23, 66.

4. John W. Cadman, *The Corporation in New Jersey: Business and Politics 1791–1875* (Cambridge: Harvard Univ. Press, 1949), 112–20; Ronald E. Seavoy, *The Origins of the American Business Corporation, 1784–1855: Broadening the Concept of Public Service During Industrialization* (Westport, Conn.: Greenwood Press, 1982); "A gentleman of Philadelphia" to William S. Bigler, March 26, 1852, Bigler mss.; George J. Kuenhl, *The Wisconsin Business Corporation* (Madison: Univ. of Wisconsin Press, 1959), 143–45.

5. Houston (Miss.) *Southern Argus*, Feb. 15, 22, 1854; Monticello *Southern Journal*, Nov. 5, 1853; Mobile *Daily Advertiser*, Jan. 13, 1854; Austin *Texas State Gazette*, Feb. 14, 1854.

6. Massachusetts Constitutional Convention *Debates* (1853), 23; Mobile *Daily Advertiser*, Feb. 3, 1854; New York *Weekly Tribune*, May 31, 1851; Charles T. Dupont to John M. Clayton, Feb. 15, 1855, Clayton mss., LC.

7. Newport *Advertiser*, May 9, 1855; Austin *Texas State Gazette*, Sept. 13, 1856; Indianapolis *Daily State Sentinel*, Jan. 24, 1857; Cincinnati *Daily Commercial*, March 31, 1857.

8. New York *Times*, Sept. 8, 1854.

9. *Charles Perrin Smith: New Jersey Political Reminiscences, 1828–1882*, Hermann K. Platt, ed. (New Brunswick: Rutgers Univ. Press, 1965), 10–13, 92; New York *Semi-Weekly Tribune*, Feb. 17, Aug. 18, Sept. 1, 1854; Newark *Daily Advertiser*, March 24, 1857; New York *Evening Post*, Feb. 11, 15, 18, March 9, 1860.

10. New York *Semi-Weekly Tribune*, Jan. 24, Feb. 14, 17, 24, March 3, 14, 1854; Newark *Daily Advertiser*, Nov. 5, 1853, Jan. 27, Feb. 8, 9, 25, March 1, 10, 15, 1854.

11. House Report 414, 35th Cong., 1st sess., 2–80; E. D. Morgan to Thurlow Weed, May 7, 1858, Weed to Morgan, May 8, 12, 1858, Ezra Lincoln to Weed,

May 11, 1858, William Seward to Weed, May 7, 1858, Weed mss.; Henry Terry to John Sherman, May 29, 1860, Terry to O. S. Ferry, May 29, 1860, Sherman mss.

12. David B. Tyler, *Steam Conquers the Atlantic* (New York: Appleton-Century, 1939), 141–50, 215; John G. B. Hutchins, *The American Maritime Industries and Public Policy, 1789–1914* (Cambridge: Harvard Univ. Press, 1941), 359–62; New York *Semi-Weekly Tribune*, Sept. 25, 1852; New York *Evening Post*, Sept. 23, 24, 1850, Feb. 28, 1851, Sept. 22, 1852.

13. New York *Evening Post*, Aug. 5, 22, Sept. 19, 21, 23, 25, 27, 1850, March 3, 1851, Nov. 15, 1853; Prosper M. Wetmore to William Marcy, Nov. 28, 1851, Marcy mss.; John L. Schoolcraft to Thurlow Weed, Dec. 1851, Weed mss.; Benjamin B. French diary, March 9, 1851, French mss.

14. Cohen, *Business and Politics,*, 109–10; Tyler, *Steam Conquers the Atlantic*, 146–47; *CG*, 32d Cong., 1st sess., 1720, 1730.

15. New York *Evening Mirror*, Feb. 4, March 1, 1852; *CG*, 32d Cong., 1st sess., 1714–34, 1746, appendix, 785, 824; Cohen, *Business and Politics*, 112; Tyler, *Steam Conquers the Atlantic*, 200–209.

16. New York *Herald*, July 15, 1852; *CG*, 32d Cong., 1st sess., 1718.

17. Cohen, *Business and Politics*, 111, 296–97; French to Henry F. French, Sept. 5, 1852, French mss.; Lancaster *Independent Whig*, July 20, 1852; John Bigelow, *Retrospections of an Active Life* (New York: Baker and Taylor, 1905), 2:125; Brown Brothers to Corcoran & Riggs (hereafter cited as C & R), April 22, 24, 1852, William Grandin to C & R, July 21, 1852, H. S. Wetmore to Elisha Riggs, April 12, 1852, William S. Wetmore to Riggs, Jan. 27, 1852, Erastus Corning to C & R, March 13, 1852, William S. Cayce to C & R, March 1, 1852, Riggs mss., LC; *CG*, 32d Cong., 1st sess., 785.

18. New York *Semi-Weekly Tribune*, Feb. 23, March 6, 9, 1855; New York *Evening Post*, March 5, July 16, 1855; Benjamin B. French to Henry F. French, April 1, 1855, Jan. 17, May 29, 1856, Henry F. French to Benjamin B. French, Feb. 10, 1856, French mss.

19. New York *Evening Post*, Sept. 10, 1850; Edmund Burke to C & R, Aug. 16, 1852, Riggs mss.

20. Myers, *Great American Fortunes*, 282–83.

21. Cohen, *Business and Politics*, 173–78; Carter Goodrich, *Government Promotion of American Canals and Railroads, 1800–1890* (New York: Columbia Univ. Press, 1960), 170–71; *CG*, 32d Cong., 1st sess., appendix, 130, 428, 431, 452.

22. Alvah Hunt to Weed, March 12, July 7, 21, 1854, Weed mss.; New York *Semi-Weekly Tribune*, March 14, 1854.

23. New York *Semi-Weekly Tribune*, Aug. 29, 1854; Alvah Hunt to Weed, July 7, 21, 1854, Weed mss.

24. Cohen, *Business and Politics*, 160–66; Orsamus B. Matteson to Thurlow Weed, March 26, April 30, July 2, 4, 1854, Elihu Washburne to Weed, March 12, 1854, Weed mss.; House Report 353, 33d Cong., 1st sess., 74.

25. Orsamus Matteson to Thurlow Weed, June 30, July 2, 1854, Matteson to Simeon Draper, July 6, 1854, Simeon Draper to Weed, July 8, 1854, Weed mss.; Chicago *Daily Democratic Press*, Aug. 26, 1854.

26. New York *Herald*, July 25, 1854; H. H. Foley to Elihu Washburne, Aug. 24, 1854, Washburne mss.; Cohen *Business and Politics*, 183–85; for the subsequent career of the railroad, see H. H. Sibley to Washburne, Feb. 10, 1855, J. B. H. Mitchell to Washburne, Feb. 19, 1855; Boston *Post*, Feb. 3, 1855; Minneapolis *North-Western Democrat*, Feb. 3, 17, March 9, 1855, Feb. 23, 1856.

27. Benjamin B. French to Henry F. French, May 10, 29, July 24, 1856, Dec. 19, 1858, French mss.; George Ashmun to Thurlow Weed, April 19, 1857, Calvin Chaffee to Weed, April 20, 1857, Orsamus B. Matteson to Weed, April 28, 1857, Weed mss.; Cohen, *Business and Politics*, 194–95; John B. Rae, *Development of Railway Land Subsidy Policy in the United States* (Ann Arbor: Edwards Brothers, 1938), 30–31; Philadelphia *Daily News*, Nov. 30, 1858.

28. Duckett, *Frontiersman of Fortune*, 110–15, 127–29; Madison *Daily State Journal*, Sept. 30 to Oct. 6, 1856, Feb. 2, 1858; Madison *Argus Democrat*, Oct. 2, 3, 1856.

29. Duckett, *Frontiersman of Fortune*, 132–33.

30. *Ibid.*, 130–35; Richard N. Current, *A History of Wisconsin, Volume 2: The Civil War Era, 1848–1873* (Madison: State Historical Society, 1976), 245, 267–68; Madison *Daily State Journal*, Feb. 16, 23, June 1, 2, 1858.

31. Madison *Daily State Journal*, July 31, 1858.

32. *Ibid.*, June 7–10, 1858.

33. *Ibid.*, Feb. 16, Aug. 2, 1858; Clarkson F. Crosby to Thurlow Weed, May 29, 1854, Weed mss.

34. Orsamus B. Matteson to Thurlow Weed, Sept. 13, 1853, Allen Munroe to Weed, Dec. 10, 1860, Weed mss.

35. Erastus Corning to Weed, Feb. 4, Aug. 5, 1856, March 13, 20, 1858, Orville Clark to Weed, March 18, 1854, A. S. Diven to Weed, April 15, 1857, D. P. Barhydt to Weed, March 29, 1860, Weed mss.; Samuel Blatchford to William Seward, Nov. 30, 1855, Seward mss.

36. John S. Coe to Thurlow Weed, Oct. 30, 1860, N. Darling to Weed, April 12, 1854, Sept. 2, 1855, Chauncy Vibbard to Weed, Dec. 12, 1860, Allen Munroe to Weed, Dec. 10, 1860, John A. Cooke to Weed, March 29, 1860, Weed mss.; Lewis Benedict to William Seward, Oct. 20, 1854, Seward mss.

37. New York *Tribune*, Oct. 10, 29, 1860; New York *Evening Post*, Sept. 17, 1860; Brooklyn *Eagle*, Sept. 20, 1860.

38. Nevins, *Ordeal of the Union*, 1:139.

39. Edwin Croswell to Thurlow Weed, April 12, 1854, Weed mss.; Gideon Welles to Edmund Burke, Nov. 3, 1851, Burke mss., LC; New York *Evening Post*, Sept. 10, 24, 1850.

40. *Papers of Andrew Johnson*, 3:234.

7. How Public Works Worked the Public

1. Lancaster *Independent Whig*, July 25, 1854, Jan. 9, 16, 1855; Henry Fitzhugh to Thurlow Weed, April 9, 1854, Weed mss.; Cincinnati *Daily Commercial*, July 26, 1854.

2. Lancaster *Independent Whig*, Feb. 6, 1855; *State of Ohio v. Executor of Joel Buttles*, 3 Ohio Reports, 309–25.

3. Lancaster *Independent Whig*, Sept. 7, Oct. 5, 1852; Philadelphia *Daily News*, Feb. 9, 1854; Lewis Coryell to William Bigler, April 6, 1852, Bigler mss.

4. Ohio Public Works Investigation *Report* (1857), 47–48.

5. New York *Evening Post*, Oct. 28, 1852; Detroit *Free Press*, Feb. 10, March 24, 1860.

6. New York *Evening Post*, Feb. 2, April 15, 18, 20, May 27, June 1, 20, 23, 1853.

7. Ohio Public Works Investigation *Report* (1857), 48; Albany *Atlas*, May 9, 1851; New York *Herald*, April 6, 1851; New York Assembly Document 89 (1852) 154; Rochester *Daily Advertiser*, Oct. 23, 1851.

8. Lancaster *Independent Whig*, March 16, May 25, Oct. 9, 16, 1852; Cleveland *Plain Dealer*, Aug. 21, 1857; Cincinnati *Daily Commercial*, Jan. 12, 1857.

9. J. Rodgers to Orsamus B. Matteson, Jan. 20, 1851, Weed mss.; E. S. Hamlin to Salmon Chase, Feb. 18, 1858, Chase mss., HSP; Lansing *State Republican*, March 6, 1861; Detroit *Free Press*, Jan. 15, 1857; Cincinnati *Daily Commercial*, April 6, 1857.

10. Cincinnati *Daily Commercial*, Feb. 21, 1857; Ohio Public Works Investigation *Report* (1857), 134–35; Rochester *Daily Advertiser*, Nov. 1, 1851; Samuel P. Allen to Thurlow Weed, March 10, 1855, Weed mss.; New York *Evening Post*, March 20, 23, April 2, 16, 1852; Carlisle *Herald*, March 14, May 16, 1855; Buffalo *Commercial Advertiser*, Nov. 7, Dec. 26, 1851.

11. Ravenna *Portage County Democrat*, April 1, 1857; Cincinnati *Daily Commercial*, Aug. 4, 12, 1854; Harrisburg *Patriot and Union*, Aug. 26, 1857; Lancaster *Independent Whig*, Sept. 7, 1852; Ohio Public Works Investigation *Report* (1857), 135; James Ashley to Salmon Chase, June 16, 1857, Chase mss., LC.

12. W. J. Bascom to Benjamin Wade, Feb. 16, 1857, William Dennison to Wade, Feb. 16, 1857, Wade mss., LC: O. P. Brown to Salmon Chase, July 24, 1857, Chase mss., LC; Cincinnati *Daily Commercial*, Feb. 16, 23, March 10, 18, April 3, 8, 21, 1857.

13. Jackson *Mississippian and State Gazette*, March 4, Aug. 19, Nov. 4, 1853; Ted R. Worley, "The Control of the Real Estate Bank of the State of Arkansas, 1836–1855," *Journal of American History*, XXXVII (1950–51), 403–26; Little Rock *Arkansas True Democrat*, Sept. 21, 1859; Arkansas Real Estate Bank Report (1856), 37–41.

14. Indianapolis *Daily State Sentinel*, March 10, May 6, 13, June 1, Nov. 17, 1857; Hugh McCulloch, *Men and Measures of Half a Century: Sketches and Comments* (New York: Scribner's, 1889), 127–28.

15. Indianapolis *Daily State Sentinel*, Feb. 27, 28, March 4, 6, 10, May 6, June 1, 11, July 18, 1857; Princeton *Clarion*, Jan. 13, 1856.

16. Cincinnati *Daily Commercial*, Jan. 15, 23, 1857; Ravenna *Portage County Democrat*, May 27, 1857.

17. Lancaster *Independent Whig*, Oct. 31, 1854; Alexander K. McClure, *Old-Time Notes of Pennsylvania* (Philadelphia: J. C. Winston, 1905), 1:225.

18. Philadelphia *Daily News*, Feb. 10, 1854; Cincinnati *Daily Commercial*, Feb. 7, 1857.

19. Harrisburg *Patriot and Union*, April 7, 1855, April 22, 1857; Philadelphia *North American*, April 6, 8, 14, 20, 1854: McClure, *Old-Time Notes*, 224–25, 478–81; Philadelphia *Daily News*, April 26, 1854, June 15, 21, 23, 1855.

20. Cincinnati *Enquirer*, March 17, 20, 21, 27, April 1, 14, 18, 20, 1860; Harry N. Scheiber, *Ohio Canal Era: A Case Study of Government and the Economy, 1820–1861* (Athens: Ohio Univ. Press, 1969), 304–5.

8. The Nine-Million-Dollar Steal

1. New York *Evening Post*, Jan. 1852.

2. Ronald E. Shaw, *Erie Water West: A History of the Erie Canal* (Lexington: Univ. of Kentucky Press, 1966), 331–33.

3. Shaw, *Erie Water West*, 355–56; Albany *Atlas*, March 11, April 11, 15, 1851.

4. Shaw, *Erie Water West*, 362–65; Albany *Atlas*, Feb. 5, 17, March 26, 1851.

5. New York *Herald*, April 4, 1851; Buffalo *Commercial Advertiser*, March 1, April 15, 30, 1851.

6. Albany *Atlas*, March 25, April 4, 15, 25, 29, May 2, 6, 1851.

7. Rochester *Daily Advertiser*, April 29, 1851; Albany *Atlas*, March 17, 18, April 15, 1851.

8. Buffalo *Commercial Advertiser*, May 6, 1851.

9. William Cullen Bryant to Salmon P. Chase, May 12, 1851, Chase mss., HSP; Albany *Atlas*, April 19, 1851; New York *Herald*, April 21, 1851; Henry Fitzhugh to Thurlow Weed, May 13, 1851, Weed mss.

10. Brooklyn *Daily Eagle*, April 8, 1851; New York *Journal of Commerce*, April 23, 1851; New York *Evening Post*, April 4, 7, 21, 26, 1851.

11. Ansel Bascom to Weed, May 30, 1851, Ambrose W. Clark to J. L. Schoolcraft, May 16, 1851, Hamilton Fish to Weed, May 5, 1851, H. C. Goodwin to Weed, May 14, 1851, Seth Hawley to Weed, May 30, 1851, Theodore B. Hamilton to Weed, May 16, 1851, Weed mss.; S. B. Jewett to William Marcy, June 4, July 15, 1851, Marcy mss.; Buffalo *Commercial Advertiser*, June 4, 5, 1851.

12. Orsamus B. Matteson to Thurlow Weed, June 16, 29, 1851, William Crandal to Weed, June 7, 1851, Weed mss.; New York *Evening Post*, June 23, 26, July 8, 12, 1851.

13. Rochester *Daily Advertiser*, Aug. 15, 1851; Brooklyn *Daily Eagle*, Oct. 27, Nov. 12, 15, 1851.

14. Buffalo *Commercial Advertiser*, Nov. 3, 17, 20, 1851; New York *Evening Mirror*, Oct. 28, 1851.

15. New York Assembly Document 89 (1852), 13, 27.

16. Buffalo *Commercial Advertiser*, Nov. 25, Dec. 26, 1851; John E. Devlin to Thurlow Weed, Nov. 10, 1851, Weed mss.; New York *Evening Post*, March 13, 1852; New York Assembly Document 89 (1852), Min. Rept., 39–40.

17. James C. Forsyth to Thurlow Weed, Dec. 23, 1851, Alvah Hunt to Weed, Jan. 11, 1852, Weed mss.; New York Assembly Document 89 (1852), Testimony, 57 (hereafter referred to as NYAD *Testimony*).

18. NYAD *Testimony*, 23, 46, 56, 128; David H. Abell to Thurlow Weed, Jan. 1, 1852, Weed mss.

19. Abell to Weed, Jan. 1, 1852, James C. Forsyth to Weed, Dec. 23, 1851, Weed mss.; Alvah Hunt to Hamilton Fish, Dec. 24, 1851, Fish mss.; NYAD *Testimony*, 86, 88, 89, 127–34.

20. NYAD *Testimony*, 94, 120; New York *Evening Post*, Jan. 6, 9, 21, 1852.

21. William Marcy to Prosper M. Wetmore, Dec. 23, 1851, N. E. Paine to Marcy, Dec. 7, 1851, P. G. Buchan to Marcy, Dec. 22, 1851, Marcy mss.; Alvah Hunt to Hamilton Fish, Dec. 24, 1851, Fish mss.; David Hamilton to Thurlow Weed, Jan. 23, 1852, Weed mss.; Seth Hawley to William Seward, Jan. 4, 1852, Seward mss.

22. New York *Evening Post*, Jan. 6, 7, 15, 1852.

23. NYAD, *Majority Report*, 6–7, 14, *Testimony*, 37, 102.

24. NYAD, *Minority Report*, 48.

25. New York *Evening Post*, Jan. 28, March 26, April 8, 1852; NYAD *Minority Report*, 54, 55, 59.

26. New York *Evening Post*, Feb. 3, 17, March 13, 1852.

27. NYAD *Testimony*, 47, 93, 94, 114–116.

28. David H. Abell to Thurlow Weed, Jan. 1, 1852, Weed mss.; NYAD *Minority Report*, 49, *Testimony*, 21–22, 35–47.

29. NYAD *Testimony*, 47, 56–58, 114, *Minority Report*, 39–40; New York *Evening Post*, Jan. 6, 7, March 13, 1852; David H. Abell to Weed, Jan. 1, 1852, George Dawson to Weed, Jan. 8, 1852, Weed mss.

30. NYAD *Testimony*, 27–31, 92–93; George H. Boughton to Thurlow Weed, March 26, 1852, Lewis Benedict to Weed, Feb. 1852, Weed mss.; New York *Evening Post*, Jan. 15, March 12, 13, 17, 1852.

31. Lewis Benedict to Thurlow Weed, Feb. 1852, Weed mss.; New York *Morning Express*, Jan. 15, 29, 1852; New York *Evening Post*, Feb. 13, March 17, 1852.

32. NYAD *Testimony*, 56.

33. NYAD *Majority Report*, 4–6, 15–17.

34. NYAD *Minority Report*, 38, 45, 61–63; New York *Evening Post*, March 17, 1852.

35. New York *Evening Post*, Jan. 28, March 17, 25, 30, April 3, 15, 1852; W. A. Sackett to Thurlow Weed, Jan. 30, 1852, Weed mss.

36. New York *Herald*, May 12, 13, 1852; New York *Evening Post*, Feb. 17, March 9, 11, 20, 22, 1852.

37. Seth Hawley to William Seward, Jan. 4, 1852, Seward mss.; Horace Greeley to Seward, April 20, 1852, Greeley mss., LC; R. W. Bradford to Hamilton Fish, Jan. 16, 1852, Fish mss.; William Marcy to Thomas A. Osborne, Aug. 27, 1852, C. Stebbins to Marcy, Oct. 14, 1852, Marcy to A. Campbell, Sept. 8, 1852, L. B. Jewell to Marcy, Sept. 15, 1852, James S. Wadsworth to Marcy, Sept. 14, 1852, Marcy mss.

38. New York *Evening Post*, Oct. 28, Nov. 5, 1852; New York *Morning Express*, Sept. 24, Nov. 5, 1852.

39. Washington Hunt to Thurlow Weed, Sept. 18, 1853, Weed mss.; Alvah Hunt to Hamilton Fish, May 30, 1853, Fish mss.; New York *Semi-Weekly Tribune*, March 28, June 23, Sept. 8, 1854.

40. Herman J. Redfield to William Marcy, May 31, 1853, George R. Davis to Marcy, June 25, 1853, Horatio Seymour to Marcy, June 12, July 2, 1853, H. H. Coots to Marcy, Aug. 21, 1853, G. W. Newell to Marcy, July 26, Sept. 16, 1853, Marcy mss.

9. "Frauds Astounding Even for New York"

1. New York *Evening Post*, Nov. 16, 1854.

2. Rutland *Herald*, Nov. 15, 1860; Cincinnati *Daily Gazette*, April 2, 1856; Lotchin, *San Francisco*, 226; Chicago *Daily Times*, June 27, 1858; Racine *Advocate*, March 28, 1851; Philadelphia *Daily News*, May 3, July 3, 1858; New York *Evening Post*, Jan. 21, 1858; New York *Semi-Weekly Tribune*, Nov. 8, 1853.

3. New Orleans *Daily Crescent*, May 6, 1854; Edward K. Spann, *The New Metropolis: New York City, 1840–1857* (New York: Columbia Univ. Press, 1981), 284–95.

4. New York *Evening Post*, Oct. 6, 1852, Oct. 29, Dec. 6, 1859; New York *Weekly Tribune*, Oct. 11, 1851; Chicago *Tribune*, March 5, 1856.

5. Louisville *Daily Democrat*, April 3, 1859; Philadelphia *Daily News*, Feb. 3, 4, March 31, April 1, 2, May 3, 1858; Lotchin, *San Francisco*, 225–26; New York *Evening Post*, Sept. 26, Oct. 28, 1854, Aug. 21, Oct. 3, Nov. 15, 16, 1855; Nevins, *Ordeal of the Union*, 1:186.

6. Philadelphia *Daily News*, March 26, April 28, 1858; J. Addison Thomas to William Marcy, Jan. 9, 1852, Marcy mss.

7. New Orleans *Daily Crescent*, March 25, 1854; New York *Evening Post*, March 25, 1853; Philadelphia *Daily News*, Sept. 25, 1858.

8. Bayrd Still, *Milwaukee: The History of a City* (Madison: Wisconsin Historical Society, 1948), 146; New York *Evening Post*, Sept. 6, 1855, May 15, 22, 1860.

9. New York *Evening Post*, May 27, 30, June 14, 1853, Oct. 22, 1855.

10. Brooklyn *Daily Eagle*, July 1, 1851; Still, *Milwaukee*, 145; Lotchin, *San Francisco*, 218; Portland *Eastern Argus*, March 28, 1860.

11. New York *Evening Post*, Oct. 22, 1855.

12. Chicago *Daily Times*, June 5, 1858; Detroit *Free Press*, May 22, 1860; Still, *Milwaukee*, 146; Chicago *Daily Tribune*, March 20, 1857.

13. Lotchin, *San Francisco*, 218, 226–27; Pleasants, *Fernando Wood*, 92; Denis Tilden Lynch, *Boss Tweed: The Story of a Grim Generation* (New York: Boni and Liveright, 1927), 209; New York *Times*, March 2, 1853; New York *Evening Post*, June 6, 1853.

14. New York *Evening Post*, May 31, June 16, Nov. 2, 1853; Pleasants, *Fernando Wood*, 40; Spann, *New Metropolis*, 301–4, 322.

15. New York *Evening Post*, Oct. 25, 1854; Spann, *New Metropolis*, 329; see also Chicago *Tribune*, Jan. 29, 1856; New Orleans *True Delta*, Sept. 28, 1859.

16. Spann, *New Metropolis*, 322, 366; Still, *Milwaukee*, 145; Chicago *Times and Herald*, Oct. 3, 1860; Horace Greeley to Henry Raymond, Nov. 21, 1851, Raymond mss., NYPL; Charles R. Adrian and Ernest S. Griffith, *A History of American City Government: The Formation of Traditions, 1775–1870* (New York: Praeger, 1976), 315–18; New York *Times*, March 3, 1860; New York *Evening Post*, March 19, 24, 1853, Feb. 28, March 1, 1860.

17. Spann, *New Metropolis*, 299–304; New York *Times*, March 2, 10, 14, 15, 1853, Oct. 22, 24, 1855, Oct. 27, 1858.

18. Spann, *New Metropolis*, 317–19; New Orleans *Commercial Bulletin*, Oct. 27, 1851, Oct. 28, 1853; Philadelphia *Daily News*, March 26, April 29, May 1–3, 1858; Brooklyn *Daily Eagle*, July 12, 1851; Chicago *Times*, June 20, July 29, 1858; Still, *Milwaukee*, 232; New York *Semi-Weekly Tribune*, Sept. 25, 1855; Lynch, *Boss Tweed*, 152.

19. New York *Evening Post*, Dec. 7–11, 1855; Chicago *Times*, June 15, 17, 18, 1858, Chicago *Times and Herald*, Aug. 7, 1860.

20. Charleston *Mercury*, Sept. 10, 1860; New York *Weekly Tribune*, Oct. 11, 1851; Philadelphia *North American*, April 6, 7, 1858; Chicago *Times*, Aug. 3, 7, 1858; New York *Evening Post*, Jan. 12, 1858, June 11, 1860.

21. Reuben Withers to William Marcy, June 12, 1850, Marcy mss.; New York *Times*, Nov. 13–21, Dec. 21, 1855.

22. Van Deusen, *Thurlow Weed*, 228; Rutland *Herald*, Nov. 15, 1860; Chicago *Tribune*, Feb. 23, 1857; Cincinnati *Daily Enquirer*, Sept. 11, 15, 1850; New York *Evening Post*, March 3, 1853; New York *Times*, March 7, 1853; Amy Bridges, *A City in the Republic. Antebellum New York and the Origins of Machine Politics* (New York: Cambridge Univ. Press, 1984), 127–38.

23. Philadelphia *Daily News*, May 3, 1858.

24. Philadelphia *Daily News*, July 19, 1858; Spann, *New Metropolis*, 368–88; Pleasants, *Fernando Wood*, 56–57; Bridges, *A City in the Republic* 139–40; Jerome Mushkat, *Tammany: The Evolution of a Political Machine, 1789–1865* (Syracuse: Syracuse Univ. Press, 1971), 288–89, 296–308.

25. Still, *Milwaukee*, 142–48; New York *Times*, March 19, 31, 1853; New York *Evening Post*, June 9, 1854; Chicago *Daily Tribune*, Jan. 24, 1857.

26. Isaac Newton to Thurlow Weed, Jan. 27, 1857, Robert B. Minturn to Weed, April 7, 19, 1854, Chandler Starr to Weed, Feb. 4, 1853, Weed mss.; Brooklyn *Daily Eagle*, April 18, 20, 1857; Leon Cyprian Soule, *The Know-Nothing Party in New Orleans* (Baton Rouge: Louisiana Historical Association, 1962), 86–90.

27. Philadelphia *Daily News*, May 1, June 1, 1858; New York *Evening Post*, May 1, 1860; Lotchin, *San Francisco*, 246.

28. Spann, *New Metropolis*, 289–90, 297–304; Pleasants, *Fernando Wood*, 39–44; Lynch, *Boss Tweed*, 69–76.

29. New York *Evening Post*, March 10, 15, 16, April 17, 18, 1860; New York *Tribune*, April 18, 19, 1860, Sept. 16, 1861; for further details on this maneuvering, see Mark W. Summers, "'A Band of Brigands': Albany Lawmakers and Republican National Politics, 1860," *Civil War History* XXX (June 1984), 102–9.

30. Hartford *Courant*, March 2, 1853; Jacksonville *Florida News*, Nov. 3, 1855; Providence *Journal*, Dec. 16, 1854.

31. *Papers of Andrew Johnson*, 3:539; see also Philadelphia *North American*, April 27, 1858.

32. Bridges, *A City in the Republic*, 149–54; Seymour J. Mandelbaum, *Boss Tweed's New York* (New York: Wiley and Sons, 1965), 59–75; Jon C. Teaford, *The Unheralded Triumph: City Government in America, 1870–1900* (Baltimore: Johns Hopkins Univ. Press, 1984), 174–87.

10. Forbidden Fruits of Manifest Destiny

1. Spann, *New Metropolis*, 281–85; New York *Herald*, Feb. 5, 1853.

2. Madison *Daily State Journal*, Dec. 29, 1858; see also David G. Taylor, "Boom Town Leavenworth: the Failure of the Dream," *Kansas Historical Quarterly* XXXVIII (Winter, 1972), 389–96.

3. Nichols, *Disruption of American Democracy*, 104; New York *Tribune*, July 9, 1857; Boston *Daily Advertiser*, Aug. 21, 1857.

4. Vernon R. Carstensen, *The Public Lands: Studies in the History of the Public Domain* (Madison: Univ. of Wisconsin Press, 1963), 113; New York *Herald*, March 1, 4, 5, 11, 1855; *CG*, 35th Cong., 2d sess., appendix, 33.

5. Benjamin B. French to Henry F. French, March 17, April 25, 1851, Oct. 10, 1852, June 10, 1855, French mss.; George M. Stephenson, *The Political History of the Public Lands from 1840 to 1862: From Preemption to Homestead* (New York: Russell and Russell, 1967), 120.

6. Cohen, *Business and Politics*, 146, 154–55; D. H. Abell to Thurlow Weed, Sept. 8, 1855, Weed mss.; L. B. Fleak to William H. Seward, Jan. 2, 1852, Seward mss.; Madison Kelley to Caleb Cushing, May 20, 1853, Cushing mss.; Carstensen, *Public Lands*, 115; Louis Martin Sears, *John Slidell* (Durham: Duke Univ. Press, 1925), 166; *CG*, 36th Cong., 1st sess., 2423–31, 2653–75.

7. New York *Evening Post*, Feb. 13, May 2, Aug. 3, Dec. 20, 1855; Nevins, *Ordeal of the Union*, 2:388–89.

8. *CG*, 33d Cong., 2d sess., 70, 36th Cong., 1st sess., 1124, 1127; Benjamin B. French to Henry F. French, Dec. 23, 1855, French mss.; Samuel G. Howe to Charles F. Adams, Feb. 14, 1860, Charles Francis Adams Diary, Jan. 19, 1861, Adams Family mss.

9. *CG*, 36th Cong., 1st sess., 983, 1127.

10. New York *Herald*, Feb. 16, 1855; *CG*, 33d Cong., 2d sess., 739–41; for states, see Detroit *Free Press*, Feb. 12, 1860; Detroit *Daily Advertiser*, Oct. 5, 15, 1860; New York *Herald*, Feb. 16, 21, March 8, 1855.

11. *CG*, 33d Cong., 2d sess., 699–700, 726, 728.

12. *Ibid.*, 700, 721.

13. George W. Manypenny to Samuel Galloway, March 21, 1855, Galloway mss.; *CG*, 33d Cong., 2d sess., 699–706, 721–26; Benjamin B. French to Henry F. French, April 1, 1855, French mss.

14. Cohen, *Business and Politics*, 119–122; New York *Herald*, April 23, 25, May 22, 1855; for the Speaker's involvement in connected Indian claims and his role in assuring Ewing a friendly committee, see New York *Evening Post*, Oct. 12, 1850; Mary A. Harden to Howell Cobb, Feb. 2, 1854, Cobb mss.

15. John J. Crittenden to Orlando Brown, April 13, 1850, Crittenden mss.; Holman Hamilton, *Zachary Taylor: Soldier in the White House* (Indianapolis: Bobbs-Merrill, 1951), 345–48; Gideon Welles to ——, April 20, 1850, Welles mss., NYPL; Jonathan Williams to Welles, June 30, 1850, Welles mss., LC; New York *Herald*, April 4, 10, May 18, 22, 1850; William P. Brandon, "The Galphin Claim," *Georgia Historical Quarterly* XV (June 1931), 113–30.

16. Cohen, *Business and Politics*, 125; Springfield *Illinois State Journal*, March 10, 1854; *CG*, 32d Cong., 2d sess., 217–18; New York *Semi-Weekly Tribune*, March 7, 14, 1854; Louisville *Daily Democrat*, March 25, 1859; New York *Evening Post*, Oct. 9, 1852.

17. *CG*, 32d Cong., 2d sess., appendix, 289–94; W. W. Corcoran to John Parrott, July 24, 1851, Thomas Corwin to Corcoran, Oct. 5, 1849, Corcoran mss.; the correspondence also makes clear the Corwins' heavy involvement in Indian claims and suggests that the Secretary of Treasury may have used his influence to shove several claims through the Indian Affairs office and the Senate. See J. W. Allen to Corwin, March 27, 1852, John Probasco to Corwin, March 31, 1852, Corwin mss., LC.

18. Cleveland *Plain Dealer*, Oct. 6, 14, 25, 1852; *CG*, 32d Cong., 1st sess., appendix, 266, 1st sess., 2305.

19. New York *Evening Post*, Oct. 23, 1852; in 1856, both W. W. Corcoran and Thurlow Weed would try to buy Corwin for their respective parties with well-timed loans. See Cohen, *Business and Politics*, 356; Alexander H. Greene to Weed, Oct. 5, 1856, Weed mss.

20. William N. Brigance, *Jeremiah Black: A Defender of the Constitution and the Ten Commandments* (Philadelphia: Univ. of Pennsylvania Press, 1934), 50–54; New York *Herald*, Feb. 28, 1853, Feb. 14, 1855; B. F. Walcott to John H. George, Jan. 9, 1854, George mss.

21. *CG*, 33d Cong., 2d sess., 70; New York *Semi-Weekly Tribune*, March 9, 1855; New York *Evening Post*, June 4, 1855; Sidney Webster to J. J. Gilchrist, March 5, 1855, Gilchrist to William L. Foster, June 5, 1855, George mss.

22. Association of the Bar of the City of New York, *Conflict of Interest and the Federal Service* (Cambridge: Harvard Univ. Press, 1960), 31–32, 36–37; Louisville *Daily Democrat*, Jan. 15, 1859; *CG*, 36th Cong., 1st sess., 984, 1123–24; Charleston *Mercury*, Jan. 11, 1860.

23. Francis P. Blair to Martin Van Buren, June 5, 1851, Van Buren mss., LC; W. W. Corcoran to Robert W. Corwin, May 12, 1851, Corcoran to Elisha Whit-

tlesey, May 13, 1851, Corcoran Letter-Books, LC; Myers, *Great American Fortunes*, 458.

24. Paul W. Gates, *Fifty Million Acres: Conflict over Kansas Land Policy, 1854–1890* (Ithaca: Cornell Univ. press, 1954), 107–9; A. Phillips to John Sherman, Jan. 13, 1859, Sherman mss.; Nichols, *Disruption of American Democracy*, 108–11.

11. Waiting for Caesar

1. Bernard Mandeville, *The Fable of the Bees*, Philip Harth, ed. (Suffolk, U.K.: Penguin Books, 1970), 13–14.

2. See Diggins, *Lost Soul of American Politics*, 18–32, 60–68; for classical republicanism, see J. G. A. Pocock, *The Machiavellian Moment: Florentine Political Thought and the Atlantic Republican Tradition* (Princeton: Princeton Univ. Press, 1975).

3. Paul C. Nagel, *One Nation Indivisible: The Union in American Thought, 1776–1861* (New York: Oxford Univ. Press, 1964), 147–76; New York *Evening Post*, Nov. 3, 1854.

4. "Correspondence of Robert Toombs, A. H. Stephens, and Howell Cobb," Ulrich B. Phillips, ed., *American Historical Association Annual Report* (1911), 2:493 (hereafter referred to as Toombs-Stephens-Cobb Letters); Gideon Welles to Franklin Pierce, Dec. 16, 1852, Welles mss., LC.

5. New Orleans *Bee*, Aug. 24, 1855; Cincinnati *Daily Gazette*, July 22, 1856; New York *Evening Post*, May 12, 1860; Jacksonville *Florida Union*, Dec. 15, 1855; New York *Herald*, Feb. 28, 1853; *CG*, 32d Cong., 1st sess., appendix, 430.

6. Michigan Constitutional Convention *Debates* (1850), 606.

7. Francis Lieber, *On Civil Liberty and Self-Government* (Philadelphia: J. B. Lippincott, 1853, enlarged ed., 1859), 365.

8. *CG*, 32d Cong., 1st sess., 1719; Edmund Ruffin, Diary, Feb. 23, 1859; Rowland, *Jefferson Davis*, 4:259.

9. Jacksonville *Florida Union*, Dec. 15, 1855; Hartford *Courant*, July 19, 1851.

10. *Papers of Andrew Johnson*, 3:539; Hartford *Courant*, Sept. 19, 1853; Perry M. Goldman, "Political Virtue in the Age of Jackson," *Political Science Quarterly* LXXXVII (March 1972), 46–62.

11. Martin Van Buren to Gideon Welles, July 31, 1851, Welles mss., LC; *CG*, 32d Cong., 1st sess., 141; *Papers of Andrew Johnson*, 3:539.

12. Massachusetts Constitutional Convention *Debates* (1853) 3:22; Vallandigham, *Speeches, Addresses*, 267–68; William W. Freehling, "Spoilsmen and Interests in the Thought and Career of John C. Calhoun," *Journal of American History* LII (June 1965), 25–28.

13. Newark *Advertiser*, March 8, 1853, March 13, 1855; Beecher, *Patriotic Addresses*, 250–51.

14. Beecher, *Patriotic Addresses*, 252; see also New York *Evening Post*, June 17, 1854.

15. Gideon Welles to Franklin Pierce, Dec. 16, 1852, Welles mss., LC; F. Byrdsall to James Buchanan, Dec. 1, 1851, Buchanan mss., LC.

16. Indiana Constitutional Convention *Debates* (1850), 1325; see also Memphis *Daily Appeal*, Sept. 22, 1852; Cincinnati *Daily Gazette*, Feb. 21, 1856.

17. Van Buren to Francis P. Blair, Jan. 26, 1852, Blair mss., LC; *CG*, 35th Cong., 1st sess., 2273; *CG*, 32d Cong., 1st sess., appendix, 189.

18. Moore, *Works of James Buchanan*, 8:434; *CG*, 32d Cong., 1st sess., appendix, 265, 430, 825; Gideon Welles to Edmund Burke, Nov. 3, 1851, Burke mss.

19. *Works of James Buchanan*, 8:435; J. L. M. Curry to Edmund Burke, Jan. 12, 1860, Burke mss.; J. Mills Thornton, *Politics and Power in a Slave Society: Alabama, 1800–1860* (Baton Rouge: Louisiana State Univ. Press, 1978), 335.

20. Francis P. Blair to Franklin Pierce, Nov. 25, 1852, Blair mss., LC; *CG*, 32d Cong., 1st sess., 1872; Vallandigham, *Speeches, Addresses*, 276.

21. Francis P. Blair to Franklin Pierce, Nov. 25, 1852, Blair mss., LC; D. D. Barnard to Hamilton Fish, Jan. 13, 1852, Fish mss.; *CG*, 34th Cong., 1st sess., appendix, 600.

22. New York *Evening Post*, June 17, 1854; Vallandigham, *Speeches, Addresses*, 273–75.

23. Alexandria *Red River Republican*, Aug. 20, 1853; Francis A. March to John J. Crittenden, Dec. 31, 1860, Crittenden mss.; James A. Hamilton to Hamilton Fish, Dec. 15, 1859, Fish mss.; Vallandigham, *Speeches, Addresses*, 272–76.

24. Maizlish, *Triumph of Sectionalism*, 17–20; Gayarre, *The School for Politics*, 120; Richard Hofstadter, *The Idea of a Party System: The Rise of a Legitimate Opposition in the United States, 1780–1840* (Berkeley: Univ. of California Press, 1969), Ronald Formisano, "Political Character, AntiPartyism and the Second Party System," *American Quarterly* XXI (1969), 683–709; Francis Lieber, *Manual of Political Ethics* (Philadelphia: Lippincott, 1838), 252–61; Cincinnati *Daily Commercial*, March 2, 1857; Cincinnati *Daily Gazette*, June 30, July 8, 1856.

25. Grant Thorburn to Horatio King, March 1855, King mss.; *CG*, 32d Cong. 1st sess., appendix, 301; D. D. Barnard to Hamilton Fish, Jan. 22, 1859, Fish mss.

26. Freehling, "Spoilsmen and Interests," 32; Vallandigham, Speeches, Addresses, 278; C. C. Binney, *Life of Horace Binney*, 263–64.

27. Madison *Daily State Journal*, Nov. 22, 1858; New York *Times*, Oct. 16, 1858.

28. Cincinnati *Daily Commercial*, March 2, April 9, 1857; C. C. Binney, *Life of Horace Binney*, 263–64; New York *Semi-Weekly Tribune*, Aug. 17, 1855.

29. Gayarre, *The School for Politics*, 79, 121.

30. For positive expressions of "Young America," see Cleveland *Plain Dealer*, Aug. 6, 16, 1852; William Grandin to Stephen A. Douglas, Feb. 7, 1852, D. M.

Armstrong to Douglas, Jan. 12, 1853, B. H. Cheever to Douglas, April 29, 1856, H. J. Harris to Douglas, May 3, 1856, Douglas mss.

31. Francis J. Grund to Caleb Cushing, Jan. 1, 1853, Cushing mss.; Thurlow Weed to Hamilton Fish, Nov. 13, 1853, Fish mss.; "An old friend" to William H. Seward, Jan. 10, 1861, Seward mss.

32. Matteson to Thurlow Weed, March 30, 1854, Weed mss.

33. Madison *Daily State Journal*, Nov. 17, 1858; Matteson to Thurlow Weed, April 28, 1857, Weed mss.

34. M. Schoonmaker to Hamilton Fish, July 3, 1856, Fish mss.; Simeon Draper to Thurlow Weed, Jan. 5, 1851, J. L. Schoolcraft to Weed, Feb. 3, 1853, Weed mss.

12. The Politics of Party Decay, 1849–1853

1. A good overview can be found in Michael Holt, *The Political Crisis of the 1850s*, 96–138. See also New York *Evening Post*, April 7, 21, 1852.

2. New Orleans *Commercial Bulletin*, Sept. 11, 16, 20, 28, 1852; Kalamazoo Gazette, Sept. 8, 1854; *CG*, 32d Cong., 1st sess., appendix, 456; see also Joel H. Silbey, *The Shrine of Party: Congressional Voting Behavior, 1841–1852* (Pittsburgh: Univ. of Pittsburgh Press, 1967), 126–36.

3. Hartford *Courant*, Feb. 20, 26, Aug. 2, Nov. 20, 1851; Buffalo *Commercial Advertiser*, Nov. 21, 1851; Frederick J. Blue, *The Free Soilers: Third Party Politics, 1848–54* (Urbana: Univ. of Illinois Press, 1973), 162–87, 207–27; Hamilton Fish to George W. Baldwin, Oct. 31, 1851, Fish mss.

4. Francis P. Blair to Montgomery Blair, April 20, 1851, Blair mss.; Going, *David Wilmot*, 435; Hartford *Courant*, April 12, Nov. 26, Dec. 4, 1851; *CG*, 32d Cong., 1st sess., 250.

5. Toombs-Stephens-Cobb Letters, 229; *Papers of Thomas Ruffin*, 2:304; Racine *Advocate*, Aug. 4, 1852.

6. Van Buren to Francis P. Blair, July 15, 1851, Blair mss.

7. Toombs-Stephens-Cobb Letters, 188; see also New York *Evening Post*, Sept. 23, 27, 1850.

8. Nevins, *Ordeal of the Union*, 1:168; see also Gideon Welles to Edmund Burke, Nov. 3, 1851, Burke mss.

9. Cohen, *Business and Politics*, 133.

10. *Ibid.*, 134–37; Austin *Texas State Gazette*, March 3, 1855.

11. Baltimore *Republican and Argus*, March 8, 1854; Robert Paine to William A. Graham, June 14, 1849, in *Papers of William A. Graham*, 3:305; Hamilton, *Zachary Taylor*, 203–9.

12. Hamilton, *Zachary Taylor*, 140, 164, 207; White, *The Jacksonians*, 398–99; Weed to Hamilton Fish, July 27, Aug. 16, 22, 1852, Fish mss.

13. Cohen, *Business and Politics*, 63–91; Nevins, *Ordeal of the Union*, 1:336; Cleveland *Plain Dealer*, Sept. 23, 1852.

14. *CG*, 32d Cong., 1st sess, appendix, 266; 32d Cong., 1st sess., 2301, 2306; Francis Blair to Montgomery Blair, April 20, 1851, Blair mss.

15. John Murray Forbes, *Letters and Recollections of* . . . Sarah F. Hughes, ed. (New York: Houghton-Mifflin, 1899), 118; C. C. Binney, *Life of Horace Binney*, 264; New York *Evening Post*, March 4, May 15, July 21, 1852; Boston *Commonwealth*, July 15, 1852; Joseph Minton to W. A. Graham, June 23, 1852, in *Papers of William A. Graham*, 4:321; Marcellus Eells to Hamilton Fish, Aug. 16, 1856, Fish mss.

16. Nevins, *Ordeal of the Union*, 2:8–11; William R. King to James Buchanan, March 6, 1852, August Belmont to Buchanan, Dec. 6, 1851, Buchanan mss., LC; Gideon Welles to William S. Romney, Jan. 27, 1852, Welles mss., LC.

17. Caleb Lyon to Marcy, Feb. 6, 1852, Marcy mss.; Azariah Flagg to Martin Van Buren, Jan. 26, 1852, Van Buren mss.

18. John Slidell to James Buchanan, Feb. 26, 1852, Buchanan mss. LC; Andrew Johnson to David T. Patterson, April 4, 1852, in Andrew Johnson mss; William Marcy to Prosper Wetmore, Nov. 26, 1851, L. B. Shepard to Marcy, Dec. 15, 29, 31, 1851, H. K. Smith to Marcy, Jan. 25, 1852, J. Addison Thomas to Marcy, Jan. 9, 1852, Thomas N. Carr to Marcy, Feb. 3, 1852, Marcy to A. Campbell, Feb. 8, 1852, Marcy mss.

19. Henry Walsh to James Buchanan, Dec. 5, 1851, Jan. 3, 5, 1852, John G. Brenner to Buchanan, Feb. 5, 1852, Buchanan mss., LC.

20. New York *Evening Post*, June 11, 12, Oct. 26, 1852; Rowland, *Jefferson Davis*, 4:270–71.

21. New York *Evening Post*, June 7, 1852; Rowland, *Jefferson Davis*, 4:263; Cincinnati *Daily Enquirer*, July 4, 1852; Memphis *Daily Appeal*, Oct. 8, 1852.

22. Cleveland *Plain Dealer*, July 12, 1852; Cincinnati *Daily Enquirer*, Aug. 20, 22, Sept. 22, 26, 1852; Memphis *Daily Appeal*, July 30, Oct. 8, 14, 1852.

23. New York *Evening Post*, Feb. 4, May 11, 1852; Rowland, *Jefferson Davis*, 4:259, 263, 270.

24. New Orleans *Commercial Bulletin*, Sept. 20, 28, 1852; Lancaster *Independent Whig*, June 22, July 6, 1852; A. F. Perry to Thomas Corwin, Oct. 10, 1852, Corwin mss.; Cleveland *Plain Dealer*, Sept. 22, 24, 1852.

25. J. Addison Thomas to William Marcy, Oct. 28, 1852, Marcy mss.; Newark *Advertiser*, Oct. 27, 1852; New Orleans *Bee*, Oct. 25, 1855; J. H. Clay Mudd to Thomas Corwin, Nov. 13, 1852, Corwin mss.

26. Blair to Pierce, Nov. 25, 1852, Blair mss.; John Lorimer Graham to Charles A. Wickliffe, Nov. 6, 1852, Joseph Holt mss., LC; New York *Evening Post*, Nov. 5, 1852; Preston King to Jonathan Niles, Nov. 19, 1852, Gideon Welles mss., LC.

27. Robert Toombs to John J. Crittenden, Dec. 15, 1852, Crittenden mss.; Schuyler Colfax to Thomas Corwin, Nov. 18, 1852, Corwin mss.; Thomas M. Blount to William A. Graham, *Papers of William A. Graham*, 4:433–34.

28. Francis P. Blair to Pierce, Nov. 25, 1852, Blair mss., LC; New York *Evening Post,* Feb. 15, March 4, 1853.

29. White, *The Jacksonians*, 183–85; Hartford *Daily Times*, Dec. 14, 24, 1853; Pittsburgh *Daily Morning Post*, April 15, 1853; New York *Tribune*, March 10, 16, 1857; Lafayette *Daily Journal*, Jan. 6, 1857; B. F. Walcott to John H. George, Jan. 9, 1854, George mss.

30. White, *The Jacksonians*, 398, 403; Roy Nichols, *Franklin Pierce: Young Hickory of the Granite Hills* (Philadelphia: Univ. of Pennsylvania Press, 1931), 273–74.

31. H. V. Willson to John C. Breckinridge, Jan. 18, 1855, James Guthrie to Breckinridge, March 30, 1855, Breckinridge mss.; Benjamin B. French to Henry F. French, July 10, 1853, French mss.

32. Nevins, *Ordeal of the Union*, 2:70; Nichols, *Democratic Machine*, 199; Isaac Nelson to John H. George, Jan. 20, 1854. George mss.; Samuel Treat to Caleb Cushing, Nov. 3, 1853, Cushing mss.; New York *Evening Post*, Oct. 31, 1853.

33. Nevins, *Ordeal of the Union*, 2:70–77; Richard H. Sewell, *Ballots for Freedom: Antislavery Politics in the United States, 1837–1860* (New York: Oxford Univ. Press, 1976), 249–53; Holt, *Political Crisis of the 1850s*, 130–38.

34. New York *Evening Post*, Feb. 15, 17, 22, March 10, April 5, 6, 14, May 28, June 9, 13, 16, 18, 1853; G. W. Newell to William Marcy, Sept. 16, 26, 1853, Horatio Seymour to Marcy, June 12, 1853, Marcy mss.

35. H. H. Coots to William Marcy, Oct. 19, 1853, J. Addison Thomas to Marcy, Sept. 13, 1853, S. McArthur to Marcy, Sept. 10, 1853, John Cochrane to Marcy, Sept. 17, 1853, Anson H. Allen to Marcy, Sept. 20, 1853, W. C. Beardsley to Marcy, Sept. 10, 1853, Marcy mss.

36. Nichols, *Franklin Pierce*, 287–92; J. Addison Thomas to William Marcy, Sept. 26, 1853, Henry S. Randall to Marcy, Sept. 24, 1853, Jonathan C. Wright to Marcy, Oct. 11, 1853, John Van Buren to Marcy, Oct. 17, 1853, Charles A. Purdy to Marcy, Oct. 17, 1853, Herman J. Redfield to Marcy, Nov. 5, 1853, William S. Bergen to Marcy, Nov. 8, 1853, Marcy mss.

37. New York *Evening Post*, Sept. 15, 1853.

38. *Ibid.*, Oct. 14, 15, 31, 1853; Hartford *Daily Times*, Oct. 21, 1853.

39. Marcy to Dean Richmond, Aug. 29, 1853, J. S. Verplanck to Marcy, Oct. 15, 1853, George R. Davis to Marcy, Oct. 28, 1853, Horatio Seymour to Marcy, Oct. 17, Nov. 5, 1853, Marcy mss.

40. Seymour to Marcy, Nov. 11, 13, 15, 1853, Marcy to Herman J. Redfield, Nov. 14, 1853, Marcy mss.

41. Newark *Advertiser*, Oct. 13, 19, 1853; John Campbell to Caleb Cushing, Oct. 20, 1853, J. Nayson to Cushing, Oct. 18, Nov. 3, 1853, Cushing mss.; Lancaster *Independent Whig*, Oct. 4, 11, 1853; New York *Evening Post*, Nov. 2, 8, 1853; New York *Semi-Weekly Tribune*, Jan. 25, 1854; Racine *Advocate*, Aug. 16, Nov. 1, 8, 1853.

42. Seymour to Marcy, Sept. 9, 1854, Marcy mss.; N. C. Read to Thomas Ewing, Nov. 15, 1853, Ewing family mss.

43. G. W. Jones to Howell Cobb, Feb. 16, 1854, Cobb mss.; F. L. Burr to Gideon Welles, Jan. 15, 1854, Welles mss., LC.

44. Howell Cobb to John ——, Dec. 4, 1853, Cobb mss.; Samuel Treat to Stephen A. Douglas, Dec. 18, 1853, Douglas mss.

13. Nebraskals

1. New York *Evening Post*, Dec. 26, 1853.

2. Providence *Journal*, July 27, 1854; New York *Semi-Weekly Tribune*, March 6, 1855; see also T. A. Osborne to William Marcy, April 4, 1855, Marcy mss.

3. Philadelphia *Pennsylvanian*, May 23, 1854; New York *Evening Post*, Feb. 24, 1855.

4. House Report 353, 33d Cong., 1st sess., 20–25, 40, 71–73; Harrington to Weed, June 25, 1854, Weed mss.

5. Chicago *Democratic Press*, July 13, 1854; House Report 353, 33d Cong., 1st sess., 14–15, 19, 30–32, 44–46, 80–82.

6. House Report 353, 33d Cong., 1st sess., 20–32, 39, 49–50, 66, 74, 83–84; New York *Herald*, Feb. 11, 14, 16, 1855.

7. Cohen, *Business and Politics*, 138–40; Austin *Texas State Gazette*, Aug. 26, 1854, March 3, 10, 17, 24, May 19, June 23, 1855; Gazaway B. Lamar to Howell Cobb, Dec. 6, 1854, Cobb mss.

8. Austin *Texas State Gazette*, June 30, 1855, Sept. 6, Oct. 4, 1856; Anthony Hyde to Elisha Riggs, Sept. 11, 1855, Hyde to W. D. Miller, Sept. 11, 25, 1855, Hyde to W. W. Corcoran, Oct. 1, 8, 15, 1855, Riggs mss.

9. Cave Johnson to Buchanan, Nov. 20, 1854, Buchanan mss., LC; see also B. Balch to Caleb Cushing, Aug. 11, 1853, Cushing mss.

10. Nevins, *Ordeal of the Union*, 2:82–83; S. Pellet to Thurlow Weed, Dec. 7, 1856, Weed mss.; Austin *Texas State Gazette*, Feb. 14, 1854.

11. Robert Walker to John C. Breckinridge, Feb. 6, 1854, Breckinridge mss.; S. M. Harrington to John M. Clayton, Feb. 15, 1855, Clayton mss.; New York *Semi-Weekly Tribune*, Jan. 6, June 30, Aug. 25, Nov. 10, 24, 1854; Austin *Texas State Gazette*, Jan. 20, 1855, Sept. 6, Oct. 4, 1856.

12. New York *Semi-Weekly Tribune*, Nov. 8, 1853, June 16, 1854; Boston *Post*, Jan. 15, 1855; Jackson *Flag of the Union*, Nov. 25, 1853; New York *Evening Post*, July 7, 1854.

13. Nevins, *Ordeal of the Union*, 2:83–86; Boston *Pilot*, May 19, 1855; Boston *Post*, Jan. 16, 1855; Edward Everett diary, Jan. 19, 1854; G. W. Jones to Howell Cobb, Feb. 16, 1854, Cobb mss.; House Report 353, 33d Cong., 1st sess., 18; Orsamus B. Matteson to Thurlow Weed, June 30, July 2, 1854, Matteson to Simeon Draper, July 6, 1854, Weed mss.

14. New York *Evening Post*, July 21, 1853; New York *Tribune*, March 3, 6, 1855.

15. Hartford *Daily Times*, Dec. 22, 24, 1853; C. A. Clinton to Hamilton Fish, Dec. 29, 1853, Fish mss.; Samuel Treat to Caleb Cushing, Aug. 26, Sept. 12,

1853, Cushing mss.; Cave Johnson to James Buchanan, Nov. 20, 1853, Buchanan mss.

16. Nevins, *Ordeal of the Union*, 2:93–100.

17. *Ibid.*, 102–9; Johannsen, *Stephen A. Douglas*, 389–95.

18. John Cochrane to William Marcy, Feb. 9, 1854, Marcy mss.; Joseph Robinson to John H. George, Jan. 31, 1854, George mss.; Herman J. Redfield to Stephen A. Douglas, Feb. 27, 1854, M. McConnell to Douglas, Jan.. 28, 1854, Horatio Seymour to Douglas, April 14, 1854, Samuel S. Cox to Douglas, March 24, 1854, J. C. Van Dyke to Douglas, March 10, 1854, Douglas mss.; C. H. Ray to Elihu Washburne, Feb. 14, 1854, Washburne mss.; James Pratt to Gideon Welles, Jan. 26, 1854, Welles mss., LC; New York *Semi-Weekly Tribune*, Nov. 4, 1853; see also John Van Buren to Marcy, Feb. 12, 1854, Marcy mss.

19. Edward Everett Diary, Jan. 27, 1854; J. P. Jones to Marcy, March 21, 1854, George R. Davis to Marcy, Feb. 21, 1854, Marcy mss.; B. D. Silliman to Hamilton Fish, March 4, 1854, Fish mss.; Charles W. March to Caleb Cushing, March 10, 1854, Cushing mss.

20. New York *Evening Post*, Feb. 21, March 31, 1854; Philadelphia *Daily News,* June 5, 1854; Nevins, *Ordeal of the Union*, 2:127, 146–47; Hartford *Daily Times*, March 17, 1854; New York *Semi-Weekly Tribune*, May 30, 1854; J. Washington Smith to Hamilton Fish, Feb. 26, 1854, Washington Hunt to Fish, March 4, 1854, Fish mss.

21. Nevins, *Ordeal of the Union*, 2:122–23.

22. Hunt to Weed, March 12, 1854, Weed mss.; John W. Forney to Howell Cobb, Feb. 16, 1854, Cobb mss.; Nevins, *Ordeal of the Union*, 2:132–35; New York *Semi-Weekly Tribune*, Feb. 10, 17, 1854; Holt, *Political Crisis of the 1850s*, 148–49.

23. New York *Evening Post*, July 8, 11, 1854; Horatio Seymour to William Marcy, July 6, 1854, C. F. Purdy to Marcy, July 6, 1854, L. B. Shepard to Marcy, July 6, 1854, Marcy mss.

24. New York *Semi-Weekly Tribune*, April 4, May 30, June 13, 1854; New York *Evening Post*, Aug. 15, 1854; Providence *Journal*, June 22, 1854; Scioto *Gazette*, May 27, 31, 1854; Chicago *Tribune*, Sept. 27, 1854; Thomas Shankland to Gideon Welles, Dec. 3, 1854, Welles mss., LC; House Report 353, 33d Cong., 1st sess., 82.

25. Philadelphia *Daily News*, May 29, June 2, 1854; Going, *David Wilmot*, 450, 459–61; Providence *Journal*, May 15, 1854; Sidney Webster to John H. George, June 5, 1854, George mss.; Frank L. Burr to Gideon Welles, March 30, 1854, Welles mss.; New York *Evening Post*, May 23, 25, 1854; New York *Semi-Weekly Tribune*, June 6, 1854; New Orleans *Daily Crescent*, May 15, 1854; Chicago *Tribune*, Sept. 27, 1854; New York *Independent*, June 1, 8, 1854.

26. J. P. Jones to William Marcy, Feb. 17, 1854, Marcy mss.; Racine *Advocate*, Feb. 20, 1854; New York *Semi-Weekly Tribune*, May 30, June 30, July 4, 1854; Scioto *Gazette*, May 31, 1854.

27. New York *Evening Post*, Oct. 30, 1854.

28. New York *Evening Post*, Feb. 21, May 30, 1854; Providence *Journal*,

May 30, June 17, 1854; Lancaster *Independent Whig*, May 30, 1854; Chicago *Daily Tribune*, Jan. 22, 1856, Feb. 16, 1857; Washington Hunt to Thurlow Weed, May 25, 1854, Weed mss.

29. New York *Semi-Weekly Tribune*, Aug. 31, Sept. 11, 1855; Eric Foner, *Free Soil, Free Labor, Free Men: the Ideology of the Republican Party before the Civil War* (New York: Oxford Univ. Press, 1970), 158–63; Holt, *Political Crisis of the 1850s*, 149–58, 195–99.

30. New York *Semi-Weekly Tribune*, March 17, 1854; Baltimore *American and Commercial Advertiser*, Nov. 1, 1855; Edgar Ketchum to Hamilton Fish, Oct. 27, 1855, Fish mss.

31. Providence *Journal*, Feb. 8, 1854; New York *Evening Post*, June 8, 1854.

32. New York *Semi-Weekly Tribune*, Feb. 27, May 30, 1854; Cincinnati *Daily Gazette*, July 17, 1856; Daniel Lord to Hamilton Fish, Feb. 27, 1854, Fish mss.

14. "Black Chattels Sell and White Ones Vote Aright"

1. Foner, *Free Soil, Free Labor, Free Men*, 87–102; Providence *Journal*, March 22, 1854; *CG*, 36th Cong., 1st sess., appendix, 355; Chicago *Tribune*, Jan. 7, 1856; Charles Adams to Stephen A. Douglas, Dec. 12, 1857, Jacob Corl to Douglas, Dec. 15, 1857, Douglas mss.

2. *CG*, 36th Cong., 1st sess., appendix, 355; Chicago *Tribune*, Jan. 12, 1856; Miles Benham to William H. Seward, April 16, 1860, Seward mss.; Thomas Shankland to Gideon Welles, Jan. 1, 1855, Welles mss., LC.

3. New York *Evening Post*, Aug. 7, Oct. 10, 1856; John Forney to James Buchanan, Feb. 23, 1855, Buchanan mss., LC; Charles E. Clarke to Stephen A. Douglas, Dec. 15, 1857, Douglas mss.; Chicago *Tribune*, Feb. 20, 1856.

4. Providence *Journal*, March 22, 1854.

5. Boston *Commonwealth*, June 18, 1852; Cincinnati *Daily Gazette*, July 17, 1856; New York *Evening Post*, Oct. 9, 1855.

6. New York *Evening Post*, Nov. 9, 1853, Oct. 9, 1855.

7. *Ibid.*, Sept. 10, 24, 1850, Aug. 11, 1851.

8. Francis P. Blair, Jr., to Francis P. Blair, Sr., Dec. 18, 1851, Blair-Lee mss.

9. Thomas Hart Benson to Martin Van Buren, July 14, 1851, Van Buren mss.

10. Cohen, *Business and Politics*, 128–29; Elgin Williams, *The Animating Pursuits of Speculation: Land Traffic in the Annexation of Texas* (New York: Columbia Univ. Press, 1949); Kinley J. Brauer, *Cotton versus Conscience: Massachusetts Politics and Southwestern Expansion, 1843–1848* (Lexington: Univ. of Kentucky Press, 1967), 45–46.

11. Adrienne Koch and William Peden, *Selected Writings of John and John Quincy Adams* (New York: Knopf, 1946), 391.

12. Cohen, *Business and Politics*, 130–31.

13. Holman Hamilton, *Prologue to Conflict: the Crisis and Compromise of 1850* (Lexington Univ. of Kentucky Press, 1964), 126–31; Hamilton, "Texas Bonds and Northern Profits," *MVHR*, XLIII (1957), 579–84; Albany *Atlas*,

Sept. 10, 1850; New York *Evening Post*, Aug. 30, Sept. 6, 7, 1850; Cleveland *Plain Dealer*, Sept. 10, 1850.

14. New York *Evening Post*, Feb. 21, 1851; Hamilton, *Prologue to Conflict*, 120–21.

15. Edgar Ketchum to Hamilton Fish, Oct. 27, 1855, Fish mss.

16. New York *Evening Post*, Sept. 20, 24, 1852.

17. *CG*, 35th Cong., 2d sess., appendix, 176.

18. New York *Evening Post*, Oct. 9, 1855.

19. *CG*, 35th Cong., 2d sess., appendix, 171; New York *Evening Post*, Aug. 15, 1855, June 9, 1858; Going, *David Wilmot*, 481–83; Cincinnati *Daily Gazette*, June 26, 1856; P. C. Bulkley to John P. Hale, March 3, 1856, Hale mss., NHHS.

20. Springfield *Illinois State Journal*, Aug. 25, 1860.

21. New York *Evening Post*, April 30, 1856; James Butler to Hamilton Fish, Aug. 12, 1856, Fish mss.

22. *CG*, 34th Cong., 1st sess., 592; see also appendix, 117–18; New York *Evening Post*, July 7, 1856; Chicago *Tribune*, Jan. 22, 1856; Cincinnati *Daily Gazette*, July 18, 1856; O. Freeman to Thomas Ewing, May 1, 1854, Ewing family mss.; James Anderson to Stephen A. Douglas, Dec. 25, 1857, Douglas mss.

23. Philadelphia *Daily News*, Oct. 7, 1858; Albany *Evening Journal*, Oct. 12, 1854; J. N. Snyder to John Sherman, Dec. 20, 1857, Sherman mss.

24. Francis A. Freeman to John P. Hale, Sept. 18, 1855, M. W. Tappan to Hale, March 25, 1854, Hale mss.; New York *Evening Post*, Oct. 9, 1855; Racine *Advocate*, Nov. 15, 1853; Cincinnati *Daily Gazette*, Oct. 8, 1856.

25. Madison *Daily State Journal*, July 27, 1857.

26. New York *Evening Post*, Aug. 9, 22, 1855; Ravenna *Portage County Democrat*, Dec. 2, 1857.

27. Hugh Ewing to Charles Ewing, June 23, 1860, Ewing family mss.; Baltimore *American and Commercial Advertiser*, Oct. 1, 1855; Indianapolis *Daily State Sentinel*, Jan. 28, 1857; New York *Evening Post*, Aug. 16, 1855.

28. Cohen, *Business and Politics*, 190; New York *Evening Post*, Aug. 20, 1856; Thomas H. Genin to Thomas Ewing, Jan. 19, 1851, Ewing family mss.; D. L. Child to Nathaniel P. Banks, Jan. 3, 1856, Banks mss.

29. Madison *Daily State Journal*, Nov. 22, 1858.

30. William B. Dodge to Elihu Washburne, Jan. 2, 1855, Washburne mss.; Cincinnati *Daily Gazette*, June 25, 30, 1856; Going, *David Wilmot*, 451; Beecher, *Patriotic Addresses*, 230.

31. New York *Evening Post*, Aug. 15, Oct. 9, 1855, Sept. 19, 1856; *CG*, 35th Cong., 2d sess., 1460; Cincinnati *Daily Gazette*, July 17, 1855; Charles Francis Adams diary, Feb. 10, 1860, Adams Family mss.

32. New York *Evening Post*, May 11, 1855; New York *Semi-Weekly Tribune*, Feb. 9, 1855.

33. Julian to Salmon Chase, March 29, 1857, Chase mss., HSP.

34. T. A. Osborne to William Marcy, April 4, 1855, Marcy mss.; Indianapolis

Daily State Sentinel, Oct. 26, 1855; Newport *Advertiser*, April 25, 1855; Sidney Webster to John H. George, March 8, 1855, George mss.; New York *Semi-Weekly Tribune*, Aug. 24, 31, 1855.

35. New York *Evening Post*, Feb. 15, 1853; John Van Buren to William Marcy, Feb. 12, 1854, Marcy mss.; Gideon Welles to Franklin Pierce, Dec. 16, 1852, Welles mss., LC.

36. Montpelier *Vermont Patriot and State Gazette*, Jan. 5, 1854; Racine *Advocate*, Nov. 8, 1853; Portland *Eastern Argus*, March 22, 1860; New York *Daily Tribune*, May 3, 1851; *Memoirs of John Quincy Adams: Comprising Portions of His Diary from 1795 to 1848*, Charles Francis Adams, ed. (Philadelphia: Lippincott, 1874–77), 12:267; Albert B. Hart, *Salmon P. Chase* (Boston: Houghton-Mifflin, 1899), 118–19; Fawn Brodie, *Thaddeus Stevens: Scourge of the South* (New York: W. W. Norton, 1959), 110; Martin B. Duberman, *Charles Francis Adams* (Boston: Houghton-Mifflin, 1961), 218; Mary Adams to Henry Adams, Feb. 26, 1860, Adams Family Papers; Benjamin F. Wade to Oran Follett, Feb. 21, 1860, Follett mss., Cincinnati Historical Society.

37. Madison *Daily State Journal*, Nov. 22, 1858.

38. New York *Evening Post*, July 16, 1855; Cincinnati *Daily Gazette*, July 18, 1856; Forbes, *Letters and Recollections*, 1:144.

39. Nevins, *Ordeal of the Union*, 2:313–14; *CG*, 34th Cong., 1st sess., appendix, 90–91; House Report 200, 34th Cong., 1st sess., majority report, 3–8.

40. House Report 200, 34th Cong., 1st sess., majority report, 9–39.

41. Chicago *Tribune*, Jan. 5, 1856; Cincinnati *Daily Gazette*, July 8, 1856; Nevins, *Ordeal of the Union*, 2:384–87; G. J. Park to John J. Crittenden, Dec. 20, 1855, May 20, 1856, Crittenden mss.

42. New York *Evening Post*, July 16, 1855; G. J. Park to Crittenden, May 20, 1856, Crittenden mss.

43. D. L. Child to Nathaniel P. Banks, Jan. 3, 1856, John J. Perry to Banks, Feb. 7, 1856, Thurlow Weed to Banks, Feb. 3, 1856, L. M. Barker to Banks, Feb. 7, 1856, Banks mss.; *CG*, 34th Cong., 1st sess., 28; New York *Evening Post*, Dec. 13, 1855.

15. The Buchaneers

1. W. Richardson to Nathaniel P. Banks, May 3, 1856, Banks mss.

2. New York *Evening Post*, July 30, 1856.

3. *Ibid.*, Sept. 12, 1856; New Orleans *Daily Creole*, Aug. 30, 1856; Cohen, *Business and Politics*, 202–4; James Buchanan to W. W. Corcoran, May 29, 1856, Corcoran mss.; John Cochrane to Sidney Webster, March 1, 1856, George mss.

4. Nichols, *Disruption of American Democracy*, 45–47; House Report 249, 36th Cong., 1st sess., 22, 552–54; Horace Greeley to Elihu Washburne, Sept. 26, 1856, Washburne mss.; New York *Evening Post*, Sept. 20, Oct. 21, 1856; New Orleans *Daily Creole*, July 24, 1856.

5. New York *Evening Post*, Oct. 8, 17, Nov. 1, 1856; Philadelphia *Daily News*, April 28, 1858; Truman Smith to Francis P. Blair, Oct. 31, 1856, Weed mss.; House Report 249, 36th Cong., 1st sess., 554–56; Chicago *Daily Tribune*, Feb. 24, 1857.

6. Shelbyville *Republican Banner*, July 31, 1856; Cohen, *Business and Politics*, 205, Cincinnati *Daily Commercial*, April 16, 1857; New York *Evening Post*, Oct. 24, 1856; for election fraud in New Hampshire, see James W. Green to John H. George, Oct. 23, 1856, George mss.

7. New York *Tribune*, Sept. 19, 1860; New York *Evening Post*, Oct. 22, Nov. 25, 1856; Ravenna *Portage County Democrat*, Nov. 12, 19, 1856.

8. New York *Herald*, March 5, 1857; Benjamin B. French to Henry F. French, Dec. 17, 1857, French mss.; see also Preston King to Salmon Chase, Jan. 29, 1858, Chase mss., HSP; J. N. Snyder to John Sherman, Dec. 30, 1857, Sherman mss.; Louisville *Journal*, July 28, 1859.

9. New York *Evening Post*, May 18, 1858.

10. W. W. Folwell, "The Sale of Fort Snelling, 1857," *Minnesota Historical Society Collections* XV, 398–406; Richard Cralle to R. M. T. Hunter, Oct. 24, 1857, in "Correspondence of R. M. T. Hunter," *American Historical Association Annual Report* (1916), 2:244; Peoria *Daily Democratic Union*, Nov. 9, 1858; H. M. Rice to John C. Breckinridge, April 28, 1857, Breckinridge family mss.

11. *CG*, 35th Cong., 1st sess., 2616; Horace Greeley to Elihu Washburne, May 2, 24, 1858, Washburne mss.; Cohen, *Business and Politics*, 113.

12. Senate Report 389, 35th Cong., 2d sess.; Nichols, *Disruption of American Democracy*, 190; George Barns, *Denver, the Man: The Life, Letters, and Public Papers of the Lawyer, Soldier, and Statesman* (Wilmington, Ohio: n.p., 1949).

13. Cohen, *Business and Politics*, 113–14; Nichols, *Disruption of American Democracy*, 258, 329–30, 553–54.

14. Nichols, *Disruption of American Democracy*, 329–30.

15. *Ibid.*, 423–25; Detroit *Free Press*, Dec. 27, 28, 29, 1860.

16. *CG*, 35th Cong., 2d sess., 1371–73; House Report 184, 35th Cong., 2d sess., 19–20, 57–58; New York *Evening Post*, Feb. 23, 25, 1859.

17. *CG*, 36th Cong., 1st sess., 2938–44, 2948; also H. H. to John Sherman, Feb. 14, 1859, Sherman mss.

18. New York *Evening Post*, Jan. 29, 1859; *CG*, 36th Cong., 1st sess., 2949; D. B. Allen to John Sherman, Jan. 12, 1859, John Winslow to Sherman, Jan. 22, 1859, M. S. Clark to Sherman, Jan. 12, 1859, E. B. Sadler to Sherman, Jan. 21, 1859, Harry C. Victor to Sherman, March 21, 1859, Sherman mss.

19. Nichols, *Disruption of American Democracy*, 102–12; Nevins, *Emergence of Lincoln*, 1:148–50; George Crawford to Horatio King, July 13, 1857, King mss.

20. New York *Tribune*, Sept. 22, 1857; Springfield *Daily Republican*, Oct. 6, 1857; George Crawford to Horatio King, Oct. 12, 1857, King mss.

21. Springfield *Daily Republican*, Oct. 27, Nov. 5, 1857; Boston *Daily Advertiser*, Dec. 12, 1857.

22. New York *Tribune*, Sept. 15, 19, 22, Nov. 18, 19, Dec. 7, 1857; Boston *Daily Advertiser*, Nov. 19, 20, 1857; Springfield *Daily Republican*, Sept. 26,

Dec. 30, 1857; David E. Meerse, "Presidential Leadership, Suffrage Qualifications, and Kansas: 1857," *Civil War History* XXIV (Dec. 1978), 293–313.

23. W. B. Roberts to John Sherman, Jan. 23, 1858, Sherman mss.; Thomas Ewing, Jr., to Thomas Ewing, Sr., Feb. 3, 1858, Ewing family mss.

24. Springfield *Daily Republican*, Nov. 19, 1857; B. J. Bartlett to John Sherman, March 5, 1858, Daniel S. Pond to Sherman, Feb. 2, 1858, John McKee to Sherman, March 13, 1858, Sherman mss.; C. G. Cotting to Elihu Washburne, April 9, 1858, Washburne mss.; Dwight Jarvis to Thomas Ewing, Jan. 7, 1858, T. C. Jones to Ewing, Sept. 28, 1858, Ewing family mss.; Simon Cameron to George Bergner, March 28, 1858, Cameron mss., LC; S. B. Benson to Stephen A. Douglas, Dec. 12, 1857, John Pearson to Douglas, Dec. 15, 1857, R. B. Collier to Douglas, Dec. 25, 1857, Jacob Kightlinger to Douglas, March 12, 1858, Douglas mss.; Robert P. Letcher to John J. Crittenden, Dec. 26, 1857, Leslie Combs to Crittenden, March 10, 1858, Henry Pirtle to Crittenden, March 24, 1858, A. Beatty to Crittenden, April 3, 1858, Crittenden mss.

25. New York *Tribune*, Nov. 30, Dec. 2–7, 1857; John Bigelow to William Cullen Bryant, Dec. 28, 1857, NYPL; J. H. Cook to Stephen A. Douglas, Dec. 15, 1857, H. F. Waite to Douglas, Dec. 25, 1857, Nathaniel Harris to Douglas, March 28, 1858.

26. Chicago *Times*, March 17, 18, 21, 24, 1858; James Millson to Stephen A. Douglas, Dec. 22, 1857, Samuel Spinney to Douglas, Dec. 22, 1857, Caleb Pink to Douglas, March 22, 1858, R. J. Lloyd to Douglas, March 22, 1858, William Broderick to Douglas, March 23, 1858, Philip A. Hayne to Douglas, March 27, 1858, Douglas mss.

27. New York *Evening Post*, Feb. 12, 13, March 31, 1858, Dec. 14, 1859; Horace Greeley to Elihu Washburne, Feb. 10, 1858, Washburne mss.; A. P. Sharp to John P. Hale, Feb. 15, 1858, Hale mss.; Indianapolis *Daily Journal*, Feb. 17, 1858.

28. Nevins, *Emergence of Lincoln*, 1:293–96; Nichols, *Disruption of American Democracy*, 165–68; H. Marshall to John Sherman, Aug. 7, 1858, Sherman mss.

29. House Report 249, 36th Cong., 1st sess., 120–28, 178, 185–86; Philadelphia *Daily News*, July 23, 1858; David A. Williams, *David C. Broderick: A Political Portrait* (San Marino, Cal.: Huntington Library, 1969), 177; Nichols, *Disruption of American Democracy*, 170–75.

30. Chicago *Times*, May 27, June 20, 24, July 23, Aug. 1, 1858; Johannsen, *Stephen A. Douglas*, 648–50; see also *CG*, 35th Cong., 2d sess., appendix, 171; *Isaac Cook v. Elias Shipman*, 24 Illinois Reports (14 Peck), 614–18.

31. House Report 249, 36th Cong., 1st sess., 11, 560; Madison *Daily State Journal*, Oct. 18, 1858; Nichols, *Disruption of American Democracy*, 205.

32. Nichols, *Disruption of American Democracy*, 205–7; House Report 249, 36th Cong., 1st sess., 460–65.

33. Philadelphia *Daily News*, Oct. 8, 9, 11, 14, 16, 1858; Francis P. Blair to Simon Cameron, Oct. 20, 1858, Cameron mss., LC; see also New York *Evening Post*, Jan. 29, 1859.

34. *CG*, 36th Cong., 1st sess., 2944–49; New York *Evening Post*, Jan. 19, 20,

Feb. 25, 1859; Springfield *Illinois State Journal*, Jan. 9, 1859; M. S. Clark to John Sherman, Jan. 12, 1859, Sherman mss.; Louisville *Journal*, March 15, 1859.

35. New York *Evening Post*, Nov. 1, 1858; F. A. Morse to William Pitt Fessenden, Oct. 8, 1858, Fessenden mss.; Philadelphia *Daily News*, Sept. 17, Oct. 8, 1858; Madison *Daily State Journal*, Oct. 15, 1858.

36. Nichols, *Disruption of American Democracy*, 221.

37. *CG*, 35th Cong., 2d sess., appendix, 174; see also John Bigelow, *Retrospections of an Active Life* (New York: Baker and Taylor, 1909–13), 224; New Orleans *True Delta*, Feb. 20, 1859.

38. Springfield *Weekly Republican*, March 10, 1860; Erwin S. Bradley, *The Triumph of Militant Republicanism: A Study of Pennsylvania and Presidential Politics, 1860–1872* (Philadelphia: Univ. of Pennsylvania Press, 1964), 52; New York *Evening Post*, March 30, 31, April 2, 4, 1860; J. D. Andrews to John Sherman, Nov. 30, 1859, Sherman mss.; House Report 249, 36th Cong., 1st sess., 184–90; Charles Francis Adams diary, March 29, June 8, 1860, Adams Family mss.

39. Portland *Eastern Argus*, March 15, 1860; Detroit *Free Press*, April 6, 1860; George M. Weston to Simon Cameron, Dec. 23, 1857, Cameron mss., LC; J. D. Andrews to John Sherman, Nov. 15, 18, 1859, Sherman mss.; Elbridge G. Spaulding to Thurlow Weed, March 26, 1860, Weed mss.

40. House Report 249, 36th Cong., 1st sess., 10, 332–33, 423–25, 459–63; White, *The Jacksonians*, 294–95; New York *Evening Post*, March 15, 22, 27, May 5, 26, June 13, 14, 1860; Nichols, *Disruption of American Democracy*, 205–6, 285–86, 331.

41. Benjamin B. French to Henry F. French, March 3, 1859, French mss.; A. K. Earl to John Sherman, Oct. 17, 1860, Sherman mss.; William Watson Wick to R. M. T. Hunter, April 27, 1860, in "Correspondence of R. M. T. Hunter," 322; Samuel Birdsall to William Seward, July 9, 1860, Seward mss.; *Papers of Andrew Johnson*, 3:620–21; *Diary of Edmund Ruffin*. William K. Scarborough, ed. (Baton Rouge: Louisiana State Univ. Press, 1972), 1:433; New York *Evening Post*, June 14, 15, 20, 1860.

42. Nichols, *Disruption of American Democracy*, 244–46, 258, 476; White, *The Jacksonians*, 293; *CG*, 35th Cong., 2d sess., 1425; appendix, 25; *CG*, 35th Cong., 1st sess., 2825–29, 3029; Myers, *Great American Fortunes*, 283–84; Tyler, *Steam Conquers the Atlantic*, 241–42; John Dix to Andrew Froment, Oct. 15, 1860, King mss.; Charles Francis Adams diary, Feb. 26, March 2, 1860, Adams Family mss.

43. Louisville *Journal*, Aug. 5, 1859; *CG*, 35th Cong., 2d sess., 1449.

16. "We Won't Pay It in Hard Cash to Thurlow Weed"

1. House Report 243, 34th Cong., 2d sess., 15–16; John S. Williams to Gideon Welles, Jan. 18, 1857, Welles mss., NYPL; S. L. M. Barlow to Thurlow Weed, Dec. 29, 1856, Weed mss.

2. John S. Williams to Gideon Welles, Jan. 18, 1857, Welles mss., NYPL; Nichols, *Disruption of American Democracy*, 69; Poore, *Perley's Reminiscences*, 1:492.

3. House Report 2433, 34th Cong., 2d sess., 3, 9, 12–17, 22–25, 56–57, 132–33.

4. Nichols, *Disruption of American Democracy*, 189; Nathaniel P. Banks to Thurlow Weed, Dec. 12, 1856, Orsamus Matteson to Weed, April 28, 1857, Weed mss.; Cincinnati *Daily Commercial*, March 2, 1857; New York *Herald*, March 2, 4, 1857.

5. Edward Stansbury to Salmon Chase, Aug. 19, 1857, Chase mss., HSP.

6. Indianapolis *Daily State Sentinel*, Jan. 21, 24, 26, 28–31, Feb. 4, 7, 23, March 2, 7, 1857; Rockville *True Republican*, Oct. 30, 1856; Jesse Bright to W. W. Corcoran, Oct. 25, 1856, Corcoran mss.; Calvin Fletcher diary, Sept. 24, 25, 28, Oct. 16, 1856, Indiana Historical Society.

7. Indianapolis *Daily State Sentinel*, March 2, 1857; Nichols, *Disruption of American Democracy*, 176; Lyman Trumbull to Salmon Chase, Feb. 7, 1859, Chase mss., HSP.

8. *CG*, 35th Cong., 1st sess., appendix, 531; Louisville *Journal*, March 5, 7, 11, July 28, 30, 1859; *Papers of Jonathan Worth*, J. G. de Roulhac Hamilton, ed. (Raleigh: North Carolina Dept. of Archives and History, 1909), 1:116.

9. Nevins, *Emergence of Lincoln*, 1:300; Williams, *Broderick*, 179–81, 198, 200, 216, 219, 245–46; *Proceedings of the Republican Convention, Held at Sacramento, June 20, 1860.*

10. Madison *Daily State Journal*, Oct. 23, 1858; Nichols, *Disruption of American Democracy*, 177–87.

11. *CG*, 35th Cong., 1st sess., 2897; New York *Evening Post*, June 16, 1858; James S. Pike to Salmon P. Chase, Feb. 27, 1858, Chase mss., HSP.

12. John Bigelow to Francis P. Blair, 1858, Blair-Lee mss.; New York *Evening Post*, May 16, 1855; George Thomas to John Sherman, May 1860, Sherman mss; even Seward's friends conceded the point: see Charles Francis Adams Diary, May 11, 1860.

13. Van Deusen, *Thurlow Weed*, 221: New York *Tribune*, Sept. 16, 20, 1861; New York *Evening Post*, March 6, 8, 10, 15, 16, April 17, 1860; Brooklyn *Eagle*, April 9, 10, 12, 17, 18, 24, 1860; William Cullen Bryant to Edwin Morgan, April 11, 1860, Greene Bronson to Morgan, April 4, 1860, Morgan mss.; D. D. Barnard to Hamilton Fish, April 16, 1860, Fish mss; much of what follows is taken from my article, "'A Band of Brigands': Albany Lawmakers and Republican National Politics, 1860," in *Civil War History* XXX (June 1984), 101–19.

14. New York *Tribune*, Sept. 16, 1861; New York *Times*, April 4, 1860; Brooklyn *Eagle*, April 24, 1860; Albany *Atlas* and *Argus*, Sept. 21, 1860; New York *Evening Post*, March 10, Sept. 16, 1860.

15. Van Deusen, *Thurlow Weed*, 221, 225, 229, 247, 297; H. R. Rusen to Weed, Feb. 10, 1860, John A. Cook to Weed, March 29, 1860, J. A. Haddock to Weed, April 19, 1860, Weed mss.; New York *Express*, April 18, 1860; Brooklyn *Eagle*, April 19, 1860.

16. George D. Morgan to Edwin Morgan, Jan. 89, 17, April 5, 1860, Morgan mss.; New York *Times*, May 25, 1860.

17. James A. Rawley, *Edwin D. Morgan, 1811–1883: Merchant in Politics* (New York: Columbia Univ. Press, 1956), 100; Arphaxad Loomis to Morgan, April 17, 1860, Bryant to Morgan, April 11, 1860, Gideon Welles to Morgan, April 26, 1860, Arphaxad Loomis to Morgan, April 17, 1860, George D. Morgan to Morgan, Jan. 18, March 29, April 3, 9, 1860, Morgan mss.; New York *Evening Post*, April 17, 18, May 23, 1860; New York Assembly *Journal*, 1860, 1363–66; Bigelow, *Retrospections*, 253; George W. Blunt to John Sherman, April 20, 1860, Sherman mss.

18. New York *Express*, April 29, May 7, 1860; Detroit *Free Press*, May 18, 1860; James Dixon to Gideon Welles, April 26, 1860, Welles mss., LC; Bradford Wood to Salmon Chase, April 21, 1860, Edward L. Pierce to Chase, April 13, 1860, Chase mss., LC; Will Cambuck to Samuel Galloway, Jan. 25, 1860, Galloway mss.

19. Edward L. Pierce to Salmon Chase, May 13, 1860, J. R. Meredith to Chase, July 14, 1860, Chase mss., LC; Van Deusen, *Thurlow Weed*, 250; Joshua Giddings to George W. Julian, May 25, 1860, Giddings mss., LC; William B. Hesseltine, ed., *Three against Lincoln: Murat Halstead Reports the Caucuses of 1860* (Baton Rouge: Louisiana State Univ. Press, 1960), 160, 162, 174; New York *Semi-Weekly Tribune*, May 22, 1860.

20. New York *Times*, May 25, 1860; New York *Semi-Weekly Tribune*, May 25, 29, 1860; Rawley, *Edwin D. Morgan*, 108; Bradford Wood to Salmon Chase, June 28, 1860, Chase mss., LC.

21. Nevins, *Emergence of Lincoln*, 2:255–58; Bradley, *Triumph of Militant Republicanism*, 66; James B. Baxter to John Sherman, April 26, 1860, James A. Riggs to Sherman, May 5, 1860, Sherman mss.; Carl R. Curry, "Pennsylvania and the Republican Convention of 1860: A Critique of McClure's Thesis," *Pennsylvania Magazine of History and Biography* XCVII (April 1973), 183–198.

22. James Dixon to Gideon Welles, May 1, 1860, Welles mss., LC: J. H. Maze to Salmon Chase, June 18, 1860, Henry B. Stanton to Chase, July 10, 1860, Chase mss., LC; New York *Times*, May 25, 1860; *Harper's Weekly*, June 2, 1860; P. W. Glen to Samuel Galloway, July 16, 1860, Galloway mss.

23. Forbes, *Letters and Recollections*, 1:184; Horace Greeley, *Recollections of a Busy Life* (New York: J. B. Ford, 1868), 312; Hart, *Salmon P. Chase*, 184–85; James S. Pike to William P. Fessenden, April 9, 1858, Pike mss.; New York *Times*, May 21, 1860; Detroit *Free Press*, June 13, 1860; Lucy Lowden, "'The Only Fit and Proper Nomination. . . .': New Hampshire at Chicago, 1860," *Historical New Hampshire* XXIX (Spring 1974), 31.

24. New York *Times*, May 21, 1860; New York *Semi-Weekly Tribune*, May 22, 1860; James Dixon to Gideon Welles, May 25, 1860, Welles mss., LC.

25. New York *Tribune*, Sept. 3, 1860; Detroit *Weekly Tribune*, Oct. 23, 1860; *CG*, 36th Cong., 1st sess., appendix, 380; Jonathan F. Dewey to John Sherman, June 22, 1860, Sherman mss.; but see G. S. Boritt, "Was Lincoln a Vulnerable Candidate in 1860?" *Civil War History* XXVII (March 1981), 37–42.

26. Frank Sawyer to John Sherman, Feb. 27, 1859, J. Webster to Sherman, May 28, 1860, A. Stiver to Sherman, June 23, 1860, Edwin A. Kennedy to Sherman, June 22, 1860, B. J. Smith to Sherman, June 6, 1860, James N. Chamberlain to Sherman, July 10, 1860, Preston King to Sherman, Oct. 22, 1860, Sherman mss.; J. D. Murphy to Elihu Washburne, June 16, 1860, Washburne mss.; Preston King to William Seward, July 16, 1860, Seward mss.; David A. Meerse, "Buchanan, Corruption, and the Election of 1860," *Civil War History* XII (1966) 116–31; Edward W. Chester, "The Impact of the Covode Congressional Investigation," *Western Pennsylvania History Magazine* XLII (1959), 343–50.

27. New York *Tribune*, Sept. 5, 6, Oct. 23, 24, 1860; Detroit *Free Press,* May 4, 1860; Springfield *Illinois State Journal*, Aug. 25, 1860; Detroit *Daily Advertiser*, Oct. 26, 1860; Bangor *Whig and Courier*, July 25, 1860; Henry Winter Davis, *Speeches and Addresses Delivered in the Congress of the United States, and on Several Public Occasions* (New York: Harper Brothers, 1867), 150.

28. New York *Tribune*, Sept. 11, 1860; Springfield *Weekly Republican*, Sept. 29, 1860; Albany *Evening Journal*, Aug. 24, 1860.

29. Springfield *Illinois State Journal*, July 24, 28, Aug. 25, Sept. 22, 24, 1860; New York *Tribune*, Oct. 1, 2, 4, 1860; Henry S. Gilbert to Thurlow Weed, Oct. 13, 1860, Weed mss.; Detroit *Daily Advertiser*, Sept. 27, Oct. 6, 1860; Bangor *Whig and Courier*, Sept. 20, 1860.

30. Washington *Daily National Intelligencer*, March 6, 10, 1860; "A Slaveholder" to John Sherman, Dec. 10, 1859, Jonathan S. Carlisle to Sherman, Jan. 13, 1860, J. Webster, Jr., to Sherman, May 28, 1860, Sherman mss.; New York *Tribune*, Sept. 14, 20, Oct. 6, 1860; Davis, *Speeches*, 180–82; Emerson Etheridge to Horace Greeley, Sept. 13, 1860, Greeley mass., LC.

31. Madison *Daily State Journal*, Sept. 22, 1860; Detroit *Weekly Tribune*, Oct. 23, Nov. 6, 1860; Detroit *Daily Advertiser*, Sept. 22, 28, Oct. 10, 16, 26, 30, 1860; New York *Times*, May 25, Aug. 18, 1860; Springfield *Illinois State Journal*, Aug. 24, 1860.

32. New York *Evening Post*, May 12, 1860; Charleston *Mercury*, Oct. 8, 1860; Detroit *Weekly Tribune*, Oct. 23, 1860; Albany *Evening Journal*, Aug. 23, 1860.

33. Allen Munroe to Thurlow Weed, Nov. 3, 1860, E. Hawk to Weed, Oct. 11, 1860, De Witt C. Littlejohn to Weed, Sept. 14, Oct. 9, 1860, Weed mss.; New York *Times*, Aug. 18, 22, 24, 1860.

34. Chicago *Times and Herald*, Aug. 27, Oct. 13, 27, 1860; Charleston *Mercury*, March 15, 26, 1860; Jonesboro *Gazette*, June 23, 1860; Detroit *Weekly Tribune*, Nov. 26, 1860; Detroit *Free Press*, May 30, 31, July 19, Aug. 17, 26, 1860; Bridgeport *Republican Farmer*, June 22, Oct. 19, 1860; Brooklyn *Eagle*, Sept. 24, Oct. 26, 1860; Edward L. Pierce to Charles F. Adams, March 10, 1960, Adams Family mss.

35. Boston *Post*, July 20, Aug. 17, 1860; Brooklyn *Eagle*, April 19, Oct. 1, 11, 1860; Albany *Atlas and Argus*, Sept. 11, 1860; Columbus *National Democrat*, Sept. 24, 1860; New York *Semi-Weekly Tribune*, Nov. 9, 1860.

36. Charleston *Mercury*, May 9, 1860.

37. John Stanton Gould to Thurlow Weed, Nov. 7, 1860, Simeon Draper to Weed, Oct. 20, 1860, Weed to Abraham Lincoln, Nov. 3, 1860, Weed mss.; James S. Pike to ——, Aug. 26, 1860, Pike to William Pitt Fessenden, Sept. 8, 1860, Pike mss.; McClure, *Old-Time Notes*, 1:421–23.

38. Thomas Webster to John Sherman, Oct. 12, 15, 1860, Sherman mss.; David Davis to Edwin D. Morgan, Sept. 22, 28, 1860, Morgan mss.; Portland *Eastern Argus*, March 27, 1860; Detroit *Free Press*, April 7, 1860; Chicago *Times and Herald*, Oct. 17, 18, 26, Nov. 3, 5, 8, 9, 1860; McClure, *Old-Time Notes*, 432–33; John B. Brown to William Seward, Nov. 7, 1860, Seward mss.

39. Sam E. Brome to John Sherman, Nov. 8, 1860, Sherman mss.; New York *Evening Post*, Nov. 8, 9, 1860; New York *Tribune*, Sept. 20, 1861; De Witt C. Littlejohn to Thurlow Weed, Dec. 17, 1860, Alonzo Hawley to Weed, Dec. 28, 1860, Weed mss.

40. John and William T. Sherman, *The Sherman Letters: Correspondence between General and Senator Sherman from 1837 to 1891*, Rachel Sherman Thorndike, ed. (New York: Scribner's Sons, 1894), 85–86; Madison *Daily State Journal*, Dec. 13, 1860; Horace B. Sargent to William Seward, Nov. 7, 1860, Seward mss.; Edward A. Stansbury to Salmon Chase, Oct. 1, 1860, Chase mss., HSP; Z. Phillips to John Sherman, April 3, 1860, William Bacon to Sherman, May 8, 1860, John Young to Sherman, May 20, 1860, Sherman mss.; C. H. Shapley to Elihu Washburne, Jan. 12, 1860, Edward S. Hayden to Washburne, Feb. 11, 1860, Washburne mss; David M. Potter, *Lincoln and His Party in the Secession Crisis* (New Haven: Yale Univ. Press, 1942), 190–91.

41. B. Brockway to Horace Greeley, Nov. 8, 1860, Greeley mss., LC; F. E. Spinner to Salmon Chase, Jan. 22, 1861, Chase mss., LC; Preston King to Hamilton Fish, July 13, 1860, Fish mss.

42. Bradford R. Wood to Salmon Chase, June 28, 1860, Chase mss.

17. "This Accursed Union, Reeking with Corruption"

1. A. Tarrant to John C. Breckinridge, Jan. 9, 1854, Breckinridge family mss.; Asa Biggs to Thomas Ruffin, Jan. 8, 1855, Ruffin mss.; W. W. Holden to John W. Ellis, Jan. 19, 1857, Ellis mss.; Little Rock *Arkansas True Democrat*, March 9, 1859; New Orleans *True Delta*, Feb. 16, 1859; St. Louis *Missouri Republican*, Feb. 3, 1858; Lexington *Kentucky Statesman*, Feb. 28, March 3, 10, 1854.

2. William M. Gouge to Corcoran & Riggs, April 26, May 7, 1852, W. D. Miller to Corcoran & Riggs, June 14, 1852, Riggs mss.; Little Rock *Arkansas True Democrat*, July 7, 28, 1860; New Orleans *True Delta*, April 5, May 29, 31, Nov. 6, 12, 1859.

3. Toombs-Stephens-Cobb Letters, 493; *CG*, 36th Cong., 1st sess., 2884; Weldon N. Edwards to Thomas Ruffin, Sept. 4, 1858, in Hamilton, *Papers of Thomas Ruffin*, 2:610; Edmund Ruffin *Diary*, 1:66.

4. Ruffin, *Diary*, 1:38; Thomas L. Nichols, *Forty Years of American Life* (London: Longmans, Green, 1874), 283; Charleston *Mercury*, Sept. 3, 1860; Richmond *Enquirer*, Feb. 20, 1857; Tallahassee *Floridian and Journal*, Jan. 10, 1857; for Northern agreement with the presumption of Southerners' superior virtue, see Philadelphia *North American*, April 27, 1858.

5. Betty L. Mitchell, *Edmund Ruffin, a Biography* (Bloomington: Indiana Univ. Press, 1981), 83; New Orleans *Bee*, Oct. 3, 1855; Cave Johnson to James Buchanan, April 4, 1852, Buchanan mss., LC; Richmond *Enquirer*, Feb. 20, 1857; Charleston *Mercury*, Sept. 10, 19, 27, 1860; Opelousas *Courier*, Aug. 16, 1857; Madison *Daily State Journal*, Oct. 21, 1856.

6. Baton Rouge *Advocate*, Aug. 19, 1856; New Orleans *Louisiana Courier*, Oct. 12, 1856; Opelousas *Courier*, June 26, 1858; *CG*, 32d Cong., 1st sess., 140; Charleston *Mercury*, Sept. 10, 1860.

7. "Correspondence of R. M. T. Hunter," 308–9; Toombs-Stephens-Cobb Letters, 493, 496.

8. Thornton, *Politics and Power*, 216, 334; Charleston *Mercury*, Aug. 31, 1860.

9. Charleston *Mercury*, April 14, 1857.

10. *Ibid.*, March 27, 1857; Edmund Ruffin, *Diary*, 1:229; Toombs-Stephens-Cobb Letters, 429; New Orleans *True Delta*, Aug. 24, 1859; Lewis Harvie to R. M. T. Hunter, March 11, 1857 in "Correspondence of R. M. T. Hunter," 205; Louisville *Journal*, Aug. 5, 1859.

11. "Correspondence of R. M. T. Hunter," 308; Ruffin, *Diary*, 1:446; New York *Evening Post*, April 25, 1859.

12. Nichols, *Disruption of American Democracy*, 324; Philadelphia *Southern Monitor*, March 17, 1860; New Orleans *True Delta*, Aug. 27, 1859.

13. Vallandigham, *Speeches, Addresses*, 283; *CG*, 32d Cong., 1st sess., 141.

14. Nichols, *Forty Years*, 283, 329; Charleston *Mercury*, Feb. 25, 1857, Dec. 26, 1860.

15. Charleston *Mercury*, Jan. 10, April 18, 21, May 9, 16, 19, 31, Sept. 5, 8, Oct. 11, 1860; Opelousas *Courier*, April 24, 1860; Charleston *Daily Courier*, Aug. 10, 1860.

16. Charleston *Mercury*, April 4, 1857, Jan. 9, 1860; Philadelphia *Southern Monitor*, May 12, 1860.

17. Sears, *John Slidell*, 172; Ruffin, *Diary*, 1:430, 432–33, 436; Cleveland *Plain Dealer*, Sept. 29, 1859; New York *Day-Book*, April 11, 25, 30, May 1, 2, 8, 1860; Toombs-Stephens-Cobb Letters, 551; Charleston *Mercury*, Dec. 14, 1860.

18. Ruffin, *Diary*, 1:399; "Correspondence of R. M. T. Hunter," 308; Toombs-Stephens-Cobb Letters, 360; New Orleans *Crescent*, Oct. 4, 1851; Rowland, *Jefferson Davis*, 2:122; *Papers of Jefferson Davis*, 4:234–35, 295.

19. "Correspondence of R. M. T. Hunter," 124; Toombs-Stephens-Cobb Letters, 217; Ruffin, *Diary*, 1:267; Opelousas *Courier*, April 24, 1860; John Barnwell, ed. "'In the Hands of the Compromisers': Letters of Robert W. Barnwell to James M. Hammond," *Civil War History* XXIX (June 1983), 162–66.

20. Charleston *Mercury*, Dec. 12, 1860; Brodie, *Thaddeus Stevens*, 137; Michael P. Johnson, *Toward a Patriarchal Republic: The Secession of Georgia* (Baton Rouge: Louisiana State Univ. Press, 1977), 6.

21. Detroit *Weekly Tribune*, Nov. 6, 1860; Binney, *Life of Horace Binney*, 317; John Beach to John Sherman, March 22, 1858, Sherman mss.; Hugh Ewing to Thomas Ewing, Jr., Jan. 2, 1861, Ewing family mss.; Robert Carter to John P. Hale, Dec. 6, 1860, Hale mss.; Lansing *State Gazette*, April 24, 1861; Horace B. Sargent to William Seward, Jan. 9, 1861, "A Friend" to Seward, Jan. 10, 1861, Seward mss.

22. Nevins, *Emergence of Lincoln*, 390–410; Edwin Croswell to Thurlow Weed, Dec. 30, 1860, James W. Beekman to Weed, Dec. 14, 1860, Samuel L. M. Barlow to Weed, Nov. 30, 1860, Weed mss.; L. S. Abbott to John Sherman, Feb. 8, 1861, Dexter A. Hawkins to Sherman, Jan. 16, 1861, Sherman mss.; *CG*, 36th Cong., 1st sess., appendix, 355.

23. J. P. Fessenden to William P. Fessenden, Jan. 10, 1861, Fessenden mss.; Beecher, *Patriotic Addresses*, 243; Thomas Hart Benton, *Thirty Years' View, or, A History of the Working of the American Government for Thirty Years from 1820 to 1850* (New York: Appleton, 1859–60), 2:784; Charleston *Mercury*, Dec. 12, 29, 1860.

24. Nevins, *Emergence of Lincoln*, 2:372–74; Alfred Minuse to John Sherman, Jan. 26, 1861, Sherman mss.; Joshua C. Oliver to Stephen A. Douglas, Dec. 21, 1860, Douglas mss.; Lansing *State Republican*, March 6, 1861; William Balch to William H. Seward, Jan. 9, 1861, Seward mss.

25. Hugh Ewing to Thomas Ewing, Sr., Jan. 12, 1861, John W. Andrews to Ewing, March 2, 1861, Ewing family mss.

26. Charles A. Dana to Salmon Chase, Nov. 7, 1860, Edward A. Stansbury to Chase, Oct. 1, 1860, Chase mss., HSP; Cassius Clay to Chase, May 26, 1860, Chase mss., LC.

27. Hart, *Salmon P. Chase*, 186; B. Brockway to Horace Greeley, Nov. 8, 1860, Greeley mss., LC; H. B. Stanton to Salmon Chase, July 10, 1860, Chase mss., LC; H. B. Stanton to Chase, Dec. 7, 1860, William Cullen Bryant to Chase, March 28, 1861, Chase mss., HSP; Abraham Lincoln to William Seward, Dec. 8, 1860, Seward to Lincoln, Dec. 13, 1860, Weed mss.; Hiram Barney to William Cullen Bryant, Jan. 17, 1861, Bryant mss., NYPL; George Fogg to Lincoln, Feb. 2, 1861, Fogg mss., New Hampshire Historical Society.

28. Erwin Stanley Bradley, *Simon Cameron: Lincoln's Secretary of War* (Philadelphia: Univ. of Pennsylvania Press, 1966), 164–69; Simon Cameron to Thurlow Weed, Nov. 13, 1860, Weed mss.; H. B. Stanton to Salmon Chase, Jan. 7, 1861, in Salmon Chase, "Diary and Papers" (New York: Da Capo Press, 1971; reprint of *American Historical Association Annual Report*, 1903); William Holfentine to Simon Cameron, Jan. 22, 1861, H. Taylor to Cameron, Jan. 12, 1861, Cameron mss., LC; John Covode to Samuel Galloway, Jan. 3, 1861, Galloway mss.

29. Brodie, *Thaddeus Stevens*, 147; Jonathan Webster to John Sherman, Jan 7, 1861, Sherman mss.; Hiram Barney to William Cullen Bryant, Jan. 17,

1861, Bryant mss.; General Larimer to Simon Cameron, Feb. 6, 1861, James Peacock to Abraham Lincoln, Feb. 25, 1861, Joseph Geiger to Cameron, Feb. 7, 1861, Lincoln to Cameron, Jan. 3, 1861, David Taggart to Cameron, Jan. 12, 1861, Cameron mss., LC.

30. J. D. Baldwin to Salmon Chase, Jan. 14, 1861, James Walker to Chase, Jan. 12, 1861, Elihu Washburne to Chase, Jan. 18, 1861, Chase mss., LC; Nathaniel P. Banks to Chase, Jan. 23, 1861, Edward A. Stansbury to Chase, March 5, 1861, John P. Hale to Chase, Jan. 11, 1861, Chase mss., HSP; Jonathan Briggs to John Sherman, Jan. 16, 1861, Sherman mss.; Martin Crawford, ed., "Politicians in Crisis: The Washington Letters of William S. Thayer, Dec. 1860–March 1861," *Civil War History* XXVII (Sept. 1981), 237.

31. William Balch to William H. Seward, Jan. 9, 1861, Seward mss.; *Memoirs of John Quincy Adams*, 12:255; W. H. Herndon to Elihu Washburne, Feb. 10, 1858, Washburne mss.

32. Beecher, *Patriotic Addresses*, 266, 277; G. W. Gant to John Sherman, Jan. 23, 1861, Sherman mss.

Epilogue: The Plundering Generation

1. *Atlantic Monthly* XXIV (Aug. 1869), 217–18; (Sept. 1869), 361–76; New York *Herald*, April 26, 1876. For postwar corruption and responses to it, see Clifton K. Yearley, *The Money Machines: The Breakdown and Reform of Governmental and Party Finance in the North, 1860–1920* (Albany: State Univ. of New York Press, 1971), 97–134; Morton Keller, *Affairs of State: Public Life in Late Nineteenth Century America* (Cambridge: Belknap Press, 1977), 242–49; Richard Jensen, *The Winning of the Midwest: Social and Political Conflict, 1888–1896* (Chicago: Univ. of Chicago Press, 1971), 34–57; New York *Herald*, Nov. 2, 3, 6, 7, 1882; Jan. 15, 1883; Oct. 22, Nov. 2, 1888; New York *Tribune*, April 1, 4, 5, 6, 16, Oct. 6, 8, 17, 1889; *Nation*, Nov. 18, Dec. 9, 16, 1880.

2. James C. Scott, *Comparative Political Corruption* (New York: Prentice-Hall, 1972), 26, 35. See also West Georgia College Studies in the Social Sciences, *Political Morality, Responsiveness, and Reform in America* XIV (Carrollton, Ga.: 1975), 5; Arnold J. Heidenheimer, ed., *Political Corruption: Readings in Comparative Analysis* (New York: Holt, Reinhart and Wilson, 1970), 300–304; but for arguments to show the intensely destabilizing effects of corruption, see Herbert H. Werlin, "The Consequences of Corruption: The Ghanaian Experience," *Political Science Quarterly* LXXXVIII (March 1973), 71–85.

SOURCES

Manuscripts

Adams Family papers, microfilm copy, Massachusetts Historical Society
Nathaniel P. Banks manuscripts, Library of Congress
D. D. Barnard manuscripts, New York State Library
Thomas M. Beer manuscripts, Ohio Historical Society
John Bigelow manuscripts, New York Public Library
William Bigler manuscripts, Historical Society of Pennsylvania
Jeremiah Black manuscripts, Library of Congress
Blair Family manuscripts, Library of Congress
Blair-Lee manuscripts, Princeton University
John C. Breckinridge manuscripts, Library of Congress
Joseph E. Brown manuscripts, University of Georgia
William Cullen Bryant and Parke Godwin manuscripts, New York Public Library
James Buchanan manuscripts, Library of Congress
Simon Cameron manuscripts, Library of Congress
Lewis Campbell manuscripts, Ohio Historical Society
William Carter manuscripts, Ohio Historical Society
Salmon P. Chase manuscripts, Library of Congress
Salmon P. Chase manuscripts, Historical Society of Pennsylvania
Zachariah Chandler manuscripts, Library of Congress
C. H. Cleaveland manuscripts, Ohio Historical Society
W. W. Corcoran manuscripts, Library of Congress
Thomas Corwin manuscripts, Library of Congress
Thomas Corwin manuscripts, Ohio Historical Society
Howell Cobb manuscripts, University of Georgia
John Covode manuscripts, Library of Congress
S. S. Cox manuscripts, Ohio Historical Society
John M. Clayton manuscripts, Library of Congress
John J. Crittenden manuscripts, Library of Congress
J. L. M. Curry manuscripts, Library of Congress
Caleb Cushing manuscripts, Library of Congress
Henry Dawes manuscripts, Library of Congress

Stephen A. Douglas manuscripts, University of Chicago
Ewing Family manuscripts, Library of Congress
Thomas Ewing manuscripts, Ohio Historical Society
William P. Fessenden manuscripts, Library of Congress
Millard Fillmore manuscripts, Library of Congress
Hamilton Fish manuscripts, Library of Congress
Seabury Ford manuscripts, Ohio Historical Society
Benjamin B. French manuscripts, Library of Congress
Samuel Galloway manuscripts, Ohio Historical Society
John H. George manuscripts, New Hampshire Historical Society
Horace Greeley manuscripts, Library of Congress
Horace Greeley–Schuyler Colfax manuscripts, New York Public Library
John P. Hale manuscripts, New Hampshire Historical Society
Joseph Holt manuscripts, Library of Congress
Washington Hunt manuscripts, New York State Library
Illinois Central archives, Newberry Library
John Pendleton Kennedy manuscripts, Peabody Institute
Horatio King manuscripts, Library of Congress
Abraham Lincoln manuscripts, Library of Congress
John McLean manuscripts, Ohio Historical Society
William Marcy manuscripts, Library of Congress
Samuel Medary manuscripts, Ohio Historical Society
William Medill manuscripts, Ohio Historical Society
Edwin D. Morgan manuscripts, New York State Library
William B. Ogden manuscripts, Chicago Historical Society
Uriah Painter manuscripts, Historical Society of Pennsylvania
Franklin Pierce manuscripts, Library of Congress
James Shepherd Pike manuscripts, Library of Congress
Henry J. Raymond manuscripts, New York Public Library
Elisha Riggs manuscripts, Library of Congress
William H. Seward manuscripts, University of Rochester
Horatio Seymour manuscripts, New York Public Library
John Sherman manuscripts, Library of Congress
William T. Sherman manuscripts, Ohio Historical Society
Edwin M. Stanton manuscripts, Library of Congress
Alexander Stephens manuscripts, Library of Congress
Thaddeus Stevens manuscripts, Library of Congress
Zachary Taylor manuscripts, Library of Congress
Benjamin Tappan manuscripts, Ohio Historical Society
John A. Trimble manuscripts, Ohio Historical Society
Lyman Trumbull manuscripts, Library of Congress
Daniel Ullman manuscripts, New York Historical Society
Martin Van Buren manuscripts, Library of Congress
John Van Pruyn manuscripts, New York State Library
Benjamin F. Wade manuscripts, Library of Congress

Elihu Washburne manuscripts, Library of Congress
Thurlow Weed manuscripts, University of Rochester
Gideon Welles manuscripts, Library of Congress
Gideon Welles manuscripts, New York Public Library
Reuben Wood manuscripts, Ohio Historical Society

Newspapers

Albany *Argus*
Albany *Atlas*
Albany *Evening Journal*
Alexandria *Red River Republican*
Austin *Texas State Gazette*
Bangor *Whig and Courier*
Baton Rouge *Advocate*
Binghamton *Standard*
Boston *Commonwealth*
Boston *Daily Advertiser*
Boston *Pilot*
Boston *Post*
Bridgeport *Republican Farmer*
Brooklyn *Eagle*
Buffalo *Commercial Advertiser*
Canton (Miss.) *American Citizen*
Charleston *Courier*
Charleston *Mercury*
Chicago *Daily Democratic Press*
Chicago *Tribune*
Chicago *Times*
Cincinnati *Commercial*
Cincinnati *Enquirer*
Cincinnati *Daily Gazette*
Cleveland *Leader*
Cleveland *Plain Dealer*
Detroit *Daily Advertiser*
Detroit *Free Press*
Detroit *Republican*
Grand Rapids *Daily Enquirer*
Grand Rapids *Eagle*
Harrisburg *Patriot and Union*
Hartford *Daily Times*
Hartford *Courant*
Hocking *Sentinel*
Houston (Miss.) *Southern Argus*
Indianapolis *Daily Sentinel*
Jackson *Flag of the Union*
Jackson *Mississippian*
Jacksonville *Florida Republican*
Jacksonville *Florida News*
Jacksonville *Florida Union*
Kalamazoo *Gazette*
Lafayette *Daily Journal*
Lansing *State Republican*
Lexington *Statesman*
Louisville *Courier*
Louisville *Daily Democrat*
Louisville *Journal*
Lancaster *Independent Whig*
Little Rock *Arkansas Gazette*
Little Rock *Arkansas True Democrat*
Madison *Argus Democrat*
Madison *Daily State Journal*
Memphis *Daily Appeal*
Minneapolis *North-Western Democrat*
Mobile *Daily Advertiser*
Monticello (Miss.) *Southern Journal*
Montpelier *Vermont Patriot and State Gazette*
Newark *Advertiser*
Newport *Advertiser*
Nashua *Gazette*
New Orleans *Bee*
New Orleans *Commercial Bulletin*
New Orleans *Crescent*
New Orleans *Daily Creole*
New Orleans *Louisiana Courier*
New Orleans *Picayune*

New Orleans *True Delta*
New Albany *Daily Ledger*
New York *Day-Book*
New York *Evening Mirror*
New York *Evening Post*
(New York) *Harper's Weekly*
New York *Herald*
(New York) *Independent*
New York *Morning Express*
New York *Times*
New York *Tribune*
New York *Journal of Commerce*
Opelousas *Courier*
Peoria *Daily Democratic Union*
Philadelphia *Daily News*
Philadelphia *North American*
Philadelphia *Pennsylvanian*
Philadelphia *Public Ledger*
Pittsburgh *Daily Morning Post*
Portland *Eastern Argus*
Princeton (Ind.) *Clarion*
Providence *Daily Journal*
Racine *Advocate*
Ravenna *Portage County Democrat*
Richmond *Whig*
Richmond *Enquirer*
Rochester *Daily Advertiser*
Rochester *Daily Democrat*
Rutland *Herald*
San Francisco *Alta California*
Scioto *Gazette*
Shelbyville *Republican Banner*
Springfield *Illinois State Journal*
Springfield *Illinois State Register*
Springfield *Republican*
Summit *Beacon*
Tallahassee *Floridian and Journal*
Vicksburg *Weekly Sentinel*
(Washington, D.C.) *National Intelligencer*
Washington, (D.C.) *Union*

INDEX